Emotion, Social Relationships, and Health

Series in Affective Science

Series Editors
Richard J. Davidson
Paul Ekman
Klaus R. Scherer

Emotion, Social Relationships, and Health

Edited by Carol D. Ryff &
Burton H. Singer

OXFORD

UNIVERSITY PRESS

2001

OXFORD
UNIVERSITY PRESS

Oxford   New York

Athens   Auckland   Bangkok   Bogotá   Buenos Aires   Calcutta
Cape Town   Chennai   Dar es Salaam   Delhi   Florence   Hong Kong   Istanbul
Karachi   Kuala Lumpur   Madrid   Melbourne   Mexico City   Mumbai
Nairobi   Paris   São Paulo   Shanghai   Singapore   Taipei   Toyko   Toronto   Warsaw

and associated companies in
Berlin   Ibadan

Published by Oxford University Press, Inc.
198 Madison Avenue, New York, New York 10016

Oxford is a registered trademark of Oxford University Press

Library of Congress Cataloging-in-Publication Data

Emotion, social relationships, and health /
edited by Carol D. Ryff and Burton H. Singer.
p.   cm—(Series in affective science)
Includes bibliographical references and index.
ISBN 0-19-513973-9; ISBN 0-19-514541-0 (pbk.)
1. Emotions—Social aspects.   2. Interpersonal relations.
3. Health—Psychological aspects.   4. Mind and body.
I. Ryff, Carol D.   II. Singer, Burton   III. Series.
BF531.E496   2000
152.4—dc21   00-035628

1 3 5 7 9 8 6 4 2

Printed in the United States of America
on acid-free paper

Contents

Contributors

Vicki Aken
Agricultural and Life Sciences
University of Wisconsin
Madison, WI 53706

Kathryn E. Angell
Department of Psychology
University of Wisconsin
Madison, WI 53706

Angela Cloninger
Department of Psychology
University of Wisconsin
Madison, WI 53706

Christopher Coe
Department of Psychology
University of Wisconsin
Madison, WI 53706

Sheldon Cohen
Department of Psychology
Carnegie Mellon University
Pittsburgh, PA 15213-3990

John Gottman
Department of Psychology
University of Washington
Seattle, WA 98195

Rachel Kimerling
Department of Psychiatry
Stanford University School
   of Medicine
Stanford, CA 94305-5544

Christine Kwan
Department of Psychology
University of Wisconsin
Madison, WI 53706

Gabriele R. Lubach
Department of Psychology
University of Wisconsin
Madison, WI 53706

Harry Reis
Department of Clinical
   and Social Sciences
   in Psychology
University of Rochester
Rochester, NY 14627

Teresa M. Reyes
Salk Institute for Biological
   Studies
La Jolla, CA 92037

Ted Robles
Department of Psychology
University of Wisconsin
Madison, WI 53706

Carol Ryff
Department of Psychology
University of Wisconsin
Madison, WI 53706

Teresa Seeman
Division of Geriatrics
UCLA School of Medicine
Los Angeles, CA 90095-1687

Burton Singer
Office of Population Research
Princeton University
Princeton, NJ 08544-2091

David Spiegel
Department of Psychiatry
Stanford University
School of Medicine
Stanford, CA 94305-5544

Victoria von Sadovszky
School of Nursing
University of Wisconsin
Madison, WI 53706

Meg Wise
School of Education
University of Wisconsin
Madison, WI 53706

Emotion, Social Relationships, and Health

1

Introduction

Integrating Emotion into the
Study of Social Relationships and Health

Carol D. Ryff & Burton H. Singer

his volume emerged from the Third Annual Wisconsin Symposium on Emotion, which was held in Madison in 1997. The purpose of this symposium on "Emotion, Social Relationships, and Health" was to build bridges between the ever-expanding field of emotion research and the large body of literature that documents linkages between social relationships and health. Epidemiological studies have shown connections between social isolation or lack of social support and increased risk of various disease outcomes and reduced length of life (Berkman & Breslow, 1983; House, Landis, & Umberson, 1988; Seeman, 1996; Seeman, Berkman, Blazer, & Rowe, 1994; Uchino, Cacioppo, & Kiecolt-Glaser, 1996). While emotion is sometimes part of such inquiries (for example, the inclusion of limited questions about whether individuals feel they have someone to talk to in time of need), most studies have focused on the amount (that is, number of individuals, frequency of contact) of those in the social network, not on the day-to day emotional experience ensuing from ties to significant others. This is the starting point for the present volume: we aim to dig more deeply into the nature of emotional interaction with significant others and its role in illuminating the established ties between social relationships and health.

To examine how emotion may play a key role in the social relations–health nexus requires multiple forms of expertise, and it demands the synthesis of multiple avenues of prior inquiry, each of which has evolved as a largely separate scientific agenda. The goal here is to weave these strands together. First, we must incorporate insights and recent advances from the growing field of emotion research, giving particular emphasis to those who probe the emotional texture of social relationships (e.g., Berscheid & Reis, 1998; Carstensen, Gottman, & Levenson, 1995; Carstensen, Graff, Levenson, & Gottman, 1996; Cassidy & Shaver, 1999;

Fitness, 1996; Fitness & Fletcher, 1993; Hazan & Shaver, 1994; Reis & Patrick, 1996; Spiegel, 1990) and their role in understanding human flourishing (Ryff & Singer, 1996, 1998a, 2000). Second, we must draw on the advances of those who map the biological processes that underlie social relational and/or emotional experience (e.g., Carter, 1998; Coe, 1993; Cohen & Herbert, 1996; Kiecolt-Glaser et al., 1997; Kiecolt-Glaser, Malarkey, Cacioppo, & Glaser, 1994; Kiecolt-Glaser, et al., 1996; Knox & Uvnäs-Moberg, 1998; Lubach, Coe, & Ershler, 1995; Panksepp, 1998; Seeman, 1996; Seeman, Berkman, Blazer, & Rowe, 1994; Seeman & McEwen, 1996; Spiegel, 1996, 1998; Uchino, Cacioppo, & Kiecolt-Glaser, 1996; Uvnäs-Moberg, 1998). This is the task of explicating mechanisms at multiple physiological levels (cardiovascular, neuroendocrine, immunological). Third, the larger agenda requires bringing to the table those who build bridges between the interpersonal life and actual health outcomes, such as indicators of disease susceptibility or severity as well as length of life (e.g., Berkman, 1995; Berkman & Breslow, 1983; Berkman, Leo-Summers, & Horwitz, 1992; Berkman & Syme, 1979; Coe, 1993; Cohen, Doyle, Skoner, Rabin, & Gwaltney, 1997; House, Landis, & Umberson, 1988; Lubach et al., 1995; Seeman, 1996; Seeman et al., 1993; Seeman & Syme, 1987; Spiegel, 1993, 1998; Uchino et al., 1996).

The contributors to this volume represent leading investigators from each of these above avenues of inquiry. Notably, most have traversed the territory *across* these different strands. Our aim is to build on the prior research, theirs' and others', and importantly, to push to the forefront the intersections among these diverse agendas. This is the larger tapestry of emotion, social relationships, and health, which is the fundamental purpose of this volume.

John Gottman brings to the integrative task a prior program of clinical and empirical research that addresses emotion in primary social relationships: parents and children, husbands and wives (e.g., Buehlman, Gottman, & Katz, 1992; Carstensen, Gottman, & Levensen, 1995; Gottman, Katz, & Hooven, 1995, 1996; Gottman & Levensen, 1992). A prominent theme in this work is how feelings, especially negative emotions, are experienced and expressed in key social relationships. Such questions have been linked to consequential outcomes, such as marital stability or instability and optimal or compromised child development. Gottman and colleagues emphasize "meta-emotion," or feelings *about* feelings, as a way of understanding how individuals deal with their own and others' communication about emotion.

In chapter 2, Gottman elaborates on "emotion-coaching" versus "emotion-dismissing" parents and characterizes the different emotional styles they bring to the task of rearing children. The fundamental question is how these parental meta-emotions nurture or impede the development and well-being of children, particularly their understanding and regulation of their own emotions. A major difference between the two parenting types is their distinctive modes of responding to children's experience of negative emotions, such as anger, sadness, or fear. Gottman argues that emotion-coaching parents help children understand and label their own negative affect, which in turn, contributes to the child's developing sense of control and optimism or, more generally, to effective emotion regulation. Emotion-dismissing parents, in contrast, equate such emotions with selfishness, loss of control, passivity, cowardice, or failure. From the health angle, Gottman further suggests that children with emotion-coaching parents have higher vagal tone, which he argues conveys a greater capacity for self-calming after emotional upset. Interestingly, such children are also found to have fewer infectious illnesses compared to children with emotion-dismissing parents.

Harry Reis brings to the larger inquiry a microanalytic perspective on day-to-day social interaction. He studies everyday, naturally occurring social exchanges and argues that they provide a richer—and possibly more accurate—understanding of social life than global, retrospective reports. Conceptually, Reis formulates these naturally occurring social interactions within the frameworks of attachment theory and intimacy theory (Berscheid & Reis, 1998; Reis & Patrick, 1996; Reis & Shaver, 1988). Methodologically, the day-to-day interactions are monitored via daily diary studies (Sheldon, Ryan, & Reis, 1996; Tidwell, Reis, & Shaver, 1996). The guiding assumption is that emotional well-being follows from the nourishment one obtains from daily social contact with others. In chapter 3, Reis emphasizes the importance of "affirmative social interactions," which contribute to the satisfaction of core needs for autonomy, competence, and relatedness. Satisfaction of these needs, in his view, is what mediates the connection between social interaction and emotional well-being (defined as low negative and high positive affect).

Reis's event-sampling method thus situates the study of social relationships in the details of daily life. As such, his chapter brings a richly textured understanding to assessment of social interactions in situ and their consequences for well-being. With this approach, Reis is able to characterize what sorts of social activities contribute to feeling close and connected to others. He finds that it is feeling understood and appreciated by others that strongly predicts a sense of closeness and connection. Everyday social interactions that foster these feelings are shown to enhance emotional well-being more generally. Although physical symptoms have sometimes been assessed (e.g., Reis & Franks, 1994; Sheldon, Ryan, & Reis, 1996), linkages among day-to-day social interactions and health have not been a central feature of his research. Nonetheless, the formulation offers important new directions for assessing social relational experience at the microanalytic level, which may in itself comprise a worthwhile addition to understanding the underlying biological mechanisms that follow from social relationships and that contribute to health outcomes.

The research program of David Spiegel (1990, 1993, 1996, 1998; Spiegel, Bloom, & Yalom, 1981) brings to the emotion, social relationships, and health agenda a specific health challenge (cancer) and a targeted social intervention (support group). Reviewing the literature on group psychotherapy with cancer patients, *David Spiegel and Rachel Kimerling* emphasize the importance of such interventions in promoting social support and emotional expression, dealing with death and dying, reordering life priorities, increasing family support, and facilitating communication with physicians. Across these, drawing on a wide body of research, they document significant health effects. Particularly pertinent to this volume is the therapeutic emphasis on accessing, expressing, and working through emotional reactions to the stressors of cancer. They summarize the health benefits of emotional expression, particularly surrounding traumatic events, in cancer studies and beyond. Such expression, they emphasize, is facilitated by close relationships.

Health outcomes of psychotherapies for cancer patients include reductions in anxiety and depression as well as increased survival time and lower rates of recurrence. Common to all studies with demonstrated survival effects is facilitation of interpersonal support and emotional expression. The authors suggest that these psychosocial interventions may affect survival via promotion of improved health behaviors and medical decision making, increased adherence to treatment regimens, and specific biological pathways. Multiple possible mechanisms within the endocrine (e.g., endogenous corticosteroids) and immune (e.g., natural killer cell activity) systems are considered. Spiegel's overall research program, while focused on cancer patients, may well offer insight for dealing with other life stresses. The strong emphasis on social support and emotional expression and their links to adjustment, physiology, and, indeed, survival has import for health promotion more generally.

The chapter by *Carol Ryff, Burton Singer, Edgar Wing, and Gayle Dienberg Love* probes the phenomenology of social relational experience, that is, how individuals evaluate the nature and quality of their social ties with significant others. This work emerges, in part, from prior studies of psychological well-being, one dimension of which is positive relationships with others (Ryff & Singer, 1996, 1998b). Using data from a recent national survey, the authors underscore the theme of gender differences and show that men report notably lower levels of interpersonal well-being than do women, a finding that has been replicated across multiple studies. Linking specific social relationships to health in the same survey, they also show that those of both genders who report more positive emotions (e.g., feeling understood and appreciated) in ties to their spouse, other family members, and friends also report fewer health symptoms, fewer chronic conditions, and better subjective health. Alternatively, those who report more negative emotions (e.g., feeling criticized having more arguments) in ties to key others show more negative health profiles (more symptoms, more chronic conditions, poorer overall health).

Moving to a life history approach and a longitudinal study (Singer, Ryff, Carr, & Magee, 1998), the authors of chapter 5 emphasize the cumulative aspects of social relationships via assessments of emotional ties to mother and father during childhood as well as via ratings of multiple aspects of intimacy (emotional, sexual, intellectual, recreational) with spouse in adulthood. Probing the physiological substrates of such cumulative relational experience (Ryff & Singer, 1998a), they link the cumulative emotion profiles to "allostatic load" (Seeman, Singer, Rowe, Horwitz and McEwen, 1997), which is an array of biological markers of wear and tear on multiple physiological systems. These analyses reveal that those on a positive relationship pathway from childhood to adult life have signficantly lower allostatic load than those on a negative relationship pathway. Addressing implications for health, Ryff, Singer, Wing, and Dienberg Love summarize prior findings that document linkages among allostatic load and various indicators of morbidity (e.g., incident cardiovascular disease, cognitive impairment, functional decline) as well as mortality.

Teresa Seeman brings to this volume an epidemiological perspective (1996; Seeman, Berkman, Blazer, & Rowe, 1994; Seeman & McEwen, 1996; Seeman & Syme, 1987). She summarizes a large body of research from the 1980s and 1990s, which shows consistent associations between social integration and longevity in community-based prospective samples. The question Seeman poses is: how do social ties influence intermediate health outcomes, such as coronary heart disease and stroke? Diverse findings on the link between social support and social networks to both incidence and severity of these health problems as well as to recovery following myocardial infarction or stroke are reviewed. Results are generally supportive with the strongest effects occurring between social integration and prognosis following disease onset. Evidence on the nexus between social relationships and mental health is also presented.

The latter half of Seeman's chapter focuses on the biological pathways through which social relationships get "under the skin." She examines findings on both human and nonhuman primates, some involving experimentally induced social stress. Monkeys in such groups were found to develop greater atherosclerosis. Alternatively, among free-ranging baboons in Kenya, those of dominant social status in stable social environments were found to have multiple physiological benefits (e.g., lower basal cortisol, higher HDL cholesterol, better immune function). Emphasizing positive social connections, males with high affiliative interactions (e.g., grooming and being groomed) exhibited lower basal cortisol and less cortisol reactivity under stress.

The community-based population studies of humans that are summarized by Seeman offer further evidence of associations between higher reported levels of support and better physiological profiles (lower heart rate, lower systolic blood pressure, lower serum cholesterol, lower urinary epinephrine). Multivariate models—that controlled for various health conditions, age, health behaviors—also show strong associations between neuroendocrine markers and high emotional support, especially for men. Seeman suggests that the weaker patterns for women may reflect different combinations of emotional support, demand, and conflict in their key social relationships. Experimental studies in humans, which vary social support conditions, also show effects on cardiovascular reactivity (blood pressure) and autonomic activation. Broadly speaking, the research described by Seeman underscores both the ameliorative and deleterious effects, at the physiological level, that ensue from social relationships.

Sheldon Cohen focuses specifically on the role of social relationships in the body's ability to resist infection (Cohen, Doyle, Skoner, Rabin, & Gwaltney, 1997). He brings to this question a large prior program of research which has conceptualized and measured how social support and health are linked (1988; Cohen & Herbert, 1996; Cohen & Wills, 1985). Chapter 7 builds on an array of prior studies that have connected both positive and negative aspects of social relationships to a host of outcomes (e.g., cellular components of immune function, upper respiratory infection, mortality). Cohen asks: how does social conflict or social participation influence susceptibility to upper respiratory infection? He follows an experimental paradigm in which healthy volunteers are exposed to a virus that causes the common cold. The central issue is whether an individual's social environment prior to exposure predicts infection. Following exposure, volunteers are quarantined over the course of the study (five days).

Conceptually, the disease susceptibility process formulated by Cohen gives central place to cognitive and emotional states, which are seen as negative in the context of social conflict and as positive with regard to social participation. Such socially based thoughts and feelings are hypothesized to influence health behaviors and practices as well as to activate (or dampen) endocrine responses, with subsequent consequences for immune function and, therefore, disease. Cohen persuasively elucidates the nature of research designs that are required to disentangle social conflict or participation from social interaction that simply increases exposure to infectious agents when accounting for differences in the ability of the immune system to fight off infection.

Controlling for numerous pre-exposure factors (e.g., body mass, season, demographics, antibody response to experimental virus) and employing multiple outcome measures (e.g., presence of infection, objective and subjective signs of illness), Cohen found that rates of colds decreased as social network diversity (not just size) increased. Those with more acute stressful events prior to exposure were more likely to develop colds, as were those reporting work or interpersonal difficulties. Thus, those with more types of social relationships and with fewer interpersonal difficulties had less disease susceptibility. Social network or conflict measures were, however, not linked to hormone or immune measures. Cohen points to the need for refined assessments of the latter in future studies.

Chapter 8, by *Christopher Coe and Gabriele Lubach,* furthers the emphasis on the nexus between social ties, particularly in early life, and immunity (Coe, 1993; Lubach, Coe, & Ershler, 1995). They review several studies that show the effects of different rearing events on immune competence in young monkeys. This work builds on the growing field of psychoneuroimmunology (PNI), which in nonhuman primates has shown that stressful events can compromise immune responses in the young, some of which show lasting effects into adulthood. The physiological mechanisms believed to link psychosocial factors to immune alterations typically include brain-mediated change in endocrine activity (especially adrenal hormones) or the autonomic nervous system (especially the sympathetic nervous system, SNS) as intervening steps. However, proving the mediating role of substances released by the SNS or endocrine system continues to challenge PNI investigators. How alterations in immunity, short- or long-lasting, actually result in disease is a further challenge because, as emphasized by Coe and Lubach, most psychologically induced immune alterations do not cause disease directly, rather, they create a window of opportunity for a pathogen to initiate a disease process.

Most immune responses and disease prevalence rates vary with age. The authors' research and studies by others show that psychosocial events, particularly those in early life, can influence the immunologic trajectory, and thereby establish a bias for health or disease as development unfolds. For example, separating young monkeys from their mothers decreases the number of lymphocytes in the bloodstream, which in turn, is linked to decreases in the T-helper–to–T-suppressor ratio. Such cellular alterations are of significance for disease susceptibility as they compromise the ability to mount an antibody response. Studies

spanning rodent to monkey to human models show a period of immune dysregulation following stressful social events, which increases risk for disease in the
event of exposure to a pathogen. Importantly, cognitive and emotional responses
determining the magnitude and duration of the initial immune sequelae after social stress are important in facilitating recovery.

Coe's program of studies examines social stresses in multiple paradigms: disruption of the mother-infant relationship, abnormal rearing conditions, and gestational stress. Of particular interest is whether the consequences described above
have more lasting effects if they occur at younger ages (many cellular immune responses are immature at birth). A major strength of his research is that the effects
span a number of important cellular functions and reflect different aspects of immunity (lymphocyte proliferation and cytotoxicity, antibody production, alterations in cell subsets in circulation). As such, the chapter richly elaborates immune system changes following social stress and underscores the importance of
bringing a developmental perspective to the task of linking emotion, social relationships, and health.

The contributors to this volume all bring vital expertise to the larger task at
hand. Some probe the depths of emotional experience in key social relationships
or in response to social stressors. Others focus on mapping the links among the
social realm and health outcomes, both in epidemiological and experimental
studies. Still others are pushing the frontiers of understanding the mechanisms
that connect social emotional experience to disease, illness, or death. Each chapter represents a much larger literature on which the contributors draw, and the
fundamental point is that all of the angles are needed to meet the challenge
posed. It is at the intersections among these separate agendas where key advances
lie. Despite their distinctive territories, there are recurrent themes across the various chapters. The following describes how these contribute to a larger synthesis
across chapters.

Cross-Cutting Themes

Running through the chapters that follow are a number of themes that pertain to
the larger goals of linking emotion in social relationships to health. Five such
themes are examined, each of which is viewed vis-à-vis input from the various
contributors. These themes demonstrate complementarities across the chapters
and point to important directions for future studies.

Role of Positive and Negative Emotion

At first glance, it appears that optimal health would be nurtured by an abundance
of positive emotional experiences with others and a dearth of negative ones. This
volume challenges such thinking and calls into question the simple models that
tie negative emotion to poor health outcomes and positive to good (see commentary by Wise; Ryff & Singer, 2000). Gottman, for example, argues that negative
emotions are a fundamental part of healthy social relationships. The emotion-

coaching parent, as opposed to the emotion-dismissing parent, sees negative affect as sometimes legitimate and even valuable, because it provides an opportunity for intimacy and/or teaching. Anger, sadness, and fear are thus viewed as appropriate feelings, which convey important information about a situation. Thus, the magical moment in parent-child interaction is when the child is emotional. On this occasion, the parent can play a vital role in helping the child explore, label, and respond to these feelings. In so doing, the bond between parent and child is strengthened, and the child gains a greater sense of control and optimism in managing personal feelings. Gottman argues that such children are better able to calm themselves and focus their attention, and they perform better in school. Interestingly, he also finds that such children also have fewer infectious illnesses. In short, Gottman's framework construes negative feelings as important routes to emotion self-regulation, strong parent-child bonds, and even better health.

Reis, using daily experience methods, probes what kinds of relational interactions promote (or hinder) secure attachments, adult intimacy, and a sense of emotional well-being. He argues that intimacy interactions are those in which self-disclosure occurs *and* in which there is partner responsiveness to such disclosure. This can be, and frequently is, in the context of difficult, negative, painful topics, including relational conflict. The strongest predictor of affirmative social interactions (i.e., those that satisfy needs for autonomy, competence, relatedness) are interactions in which the individual feels understood and appreciated by the other. Interestingly, conflict was not found to diminish feeling close and connected in daily interaction.

In interpreting this outcome, Reis emphasizes that while conflict may be affectively unpleasant, it does not necessarily undermine satisfaction of relatedness needs. The key point here is that emotional well-being is promoted by meaningful social ties, and these frequently are nurtured by how individuals cope constructively with negative emotion and relationship conflict. Thus, conflictual interactions may, paradoxically, be instrumental in generating enhanced closeness. Reis's work is especially valuable for illuminating at the microanalytic level the nature of social interactions that can accomplish these ends.

The program of group psychotherapy for women with breast cancer also gives explicit emphasis to negative emotion. Spiegel and Kimerling describe the expression of emotion as central to the therapeutic process. Patients are encouraged to access, express, and work through their emotional reactions to the stresses of cancer. Suppression of emotion, they emphasize, "reduces intimacy in families and social networks and limits opportunities for direct expression of affection, concern, and utilization of social support." Emotional expression, they show, decreases psychiatric and physical symptoms, reduces medical visits, and is linked with enhanced immune response and decreased viral replication.

Importantly, much of this expression is about negative or traumatic events, including the prospect of dying. Their quotes from cancer patients eloquently portray the intermingling of tears and laughter, their own and that of family members,' in dealing with the trauma of this disease. The families that adopt an atmosphere of open and shared problem solving help reduce anxiety and depression and thereby possibly influence both behavioral and biological pathways implicated in survival. Thus, the feeling of feelings and expressing them is a central message in this work, and such expression is fundamentally a journey between the negative and the positive.

Other chapters in this volume deal less explicitly with this distinction or follow more unitary formulations, wherein negative emotion is deemed bad for health (e.g., social conflict in the viral challenge paradigm, separation from mother in immune response, cumulative negative relationship pathways predicting allostatic load), and positive emotion is deemed good (e.g., social participation, recovery via return to a social group, positive relationship pathway). However, closer examination of some of these distinctions reveals leanings in the direction of the preceding observations. For example, the operationalization of the positive relationship pathway (chap. 5) includes emotional intimacy, which is measured with items that underscore whether the relationship allows for the expression of negative feelings. The important point is that future inquiry into the linkage of social relationships to health needs richer appreciation and characterization of the blends of positive and negative emotions.

It is perhaps worth noting that a long-standing idea in the social support/ health literature is that significant relationships can serve as important "buffers" against stress (Cohen, 1988; commentary by Robles). What the above observations suggest are two useful extensions of this thinking. First, sometimes stress itself ensues from the same social relationships that are the source of support, and second, emotional expression (positive and negative) may be a fundamental process through which such buffering occurs. Prior studies (Campbell, Connidis, & Davies, 1999; Cohen & Wills, 1985; Glass & Maddox, 1992; Seeman, Berkman, Blazer, & Rowe, 1994; Van-Tilburg, 1998) have distinguished between instrumental and emotional routes through which significant others can be supportive, but the preceding observations point to a much richer elaboration of emotional routes. And, although we have emphasized that negative emotion can sometimes be part of the process of attaining close, meaningful ties to others, this point does not overlook the ways in which significant others can be sources of negative input (Burg & Seeman, 1994; Thoits, 1995), which ultimately does not lead to richer intimacy.

Gender Differences

Mapping linkages among emotion, social relationships, and health requires attending to differences between men and women. Such differences are strongly evident at the phenomenological, behavioral, and social interactional levels (e.g., Fischer, 1995; Reis, 1998; Ryff & Singer, 1998a, 2000), and they are also implicated in building bridges to biology (e.g., Kiecolt-Glaser et al., 1996; Seeman, Berkman, Blazer, & Rowe, 1994) and in understanding the fundamental connection between social ties and mortality (House, Landis, & Umberson, 1988). Illustrating the first point, Gottman's program of research with married couples underscores differences between husbands and wives in the expression of emotions such as anger and affection as well as in regulating the affective balance in a marriage (Gottman & Levensen, 1992). He has found, for example, that an important element in marital dissolution may be the greater primacy of negative over positive affect among wives and the couple's tendency to escalate conflict.

The research on parental meta-emotion (e.g., Gottman, Katz, & Hooven, 1996) shows less emphasis on gender differences, either between mothers and fathers or in their ties with daughters versus sons, apart from noting that fathers show greater variability in their parenting. The commentary by Victoria von Sadovszky and Kathryn Angell considers the literature on gender stereotypes about emotion and asks whether parents might perceive emotion differently in sons and daughters. Might they be primed to detect more or different kinds of emotion in boys or girls? Might they label or problem solve about these emotions depending on whether the interaction was with a son or a daughter? And, at a more general level, what is the comparative time invested by mothers and fathers in emotion coaching? Given gender-role socialization, might mothers be expected to carry more of the responsibility in this realm of teaching self-regulation? If so, do mothers and, by their modeling perhaps, daughters differentially incur health-related costs or benefits in these familial social interactions?

The work by Reis points to gender similarities and differences. Regarding the former, he finds that both men and women report less loneliness when their interactions with confidantes are more intimate and satisfying. Alternatively, men's confidantes are overwhelmingly female, while women report confiding in both genders. Thus, men rely on women for their intimacy, showing significantly less intimate same-sex interactions than do women. Angela Cloninger's commentary raises further questions about possible gender differences. For example, do women more frequently initiate and maintain intimate interactions that involve disclosure (their own or others') and responses to it? From the the health perspective, what are the implications of these potential differences in emotion profiles for underlying biological pathways?

Ryff and Singer et al.'s national survey data find that men not only score significantly lower than women on positive relations with others but further show that this interpersonal aspect of well-being is the lowest rated of six aspects of psychological well-being for men. In the same study, members of both genders who reported more positive (and fewer negative) social ties to spouse, other family members, and friends also reported significantly lower levels of symptoms, fewer chronic conditions, and higher subjective health. Emphasizing cumulative relational profiles, Ryff et al. also found that being on a positive versus a negative relationship pathway was linked with having significantly lower allostatic load. This was true for both genders, but the effects were more dramatic for men. Alternatively, when allostatic load was linked with the positive-relations-with-others scale mentioned above, men but not women showed the predicted biological benefits of having higher relational well-being.

Seeman's work (Seeman, Berkman, Blazer, & Rowe, 1994; Seeman & McEwen, 1996) suggests that there may be greater costs associated with women's primary social relationships than with men's. For example, emotional support showed strong associations with neuroendocrine markers in positive directions for men but not for women. Women with higher levels of negative social interaction showed higher levels of urinary cortisol. Such findings converge with other recent studies (Kiecolt-Glaser et al., 1997) that show that women are more physiologically reactive to negative aspects of social relationships as assessed by marital conflict and neuroendocrine activity. These findings are all the more interesting when juxtaposed with epidemiological studies that show that social ties are more strongly associated with lower risk of mortality for men compared to women (House, Landis, & Umberson, 1988; Kaplan et al., 1988). Alternatively, women, on average, live significantly longer than men, and overall, they have significantly lower allostatic load than men. Clearly, putting pieces into the social relationship/health puzzle requires being closely attuned to the question of gender.

Some chapters in the volume do not address gender. Spiegel and Kimerling's chapter, for example, is focused exclusively on women with breast cancer. Nonetheless, Vicki Aken's commentary raises interesting questions as to whether psychotherapy interventions and the emphasis on emotional expression within them would work for men suffering from other forms of cancer or other terminal illnesses. Given Reis's work, which shows that men rely on women for intimacy and emotional disclosure, such interventions may be more challenging with men or may require mixed-gender groups. The viral challenge paradigm described by Cohen collects data on both men and women but analytically controls for gender. The commentary by Ted Robles discusses prior work that might justify making gender a focus of such analyses. Finally, the animal models described by Seeman and by Coe and Lubach are also largely silent on gender or are restricted exclusively to male samples. However, the commentary by Theresa Reyes notes controversy in the psychoneuroimmunology findings with regard to gender and suggests that it may be a worthwhile individual difference variable in future studies.

Mechanisms Linking Social Relationships to Health

A third primary, perhaps central, theme of this volume is mechanism, that is, how do social relationships (and, particularly, their emotional features) affect health? At the broadest level, this is a quest to understand process, and our contributors illustrate the scope and complexity of the task. Collectively, they implicate a chain, or progression, of mechanisms, which begins with phenomenological and behavior processes and ultimately intersects with biology, which then invokes additional cascades of unfolding influence. Gottman's work elaborates the beginnings of this larger progression. For him, the mechanism connecting parental meta-emotion to child self-regulation is the emotion-coaching or emotion-dismissing form of parenting. From these richly described parenting styles, children learn basic modes of experiencing and interpreting their own emotions. Gottman's formulation connects these parenting orientations not only to children's overall adjustment and well-being but also to their biology via an emphasis on vagal tone, through which Gottman suggests linkages to immune function and infectious illness. The steps in the latter process require empirical delineation (see commentary by von Sadovszky and Angell), as does the work pursued by Coe and Lubach, which connects social stress and emotional agitation in animal models to a host of immune processes.

Process, for Reis, is also at the phenomenological and behavioral level—

namely, the nature of day-to-day social interactions that lead people to feel validated and cared for. He hypothesizes and confirms that individuals with more affirmative social interactions will have greater emotional well-being, defined in terms of positive and negative affect. Although not explicitly concerned with health, Reis's microanalytic elaboration of social interaction is a potentially valuable new starting point for building linkages to biologically and epidemiologically oriented studies. The focus on affirmative social interaction (microanalytically assessed), for example, could prove a useful avenue for predicting differences in morbidity and mortality as well as variations in the response of neuroendocrine and immune markers.

Ryff and Singer et al.'s formulation of mechanism examines social relational histories and how they connect with allostatic load, and they note that the latter has been predictive of incident cardiovascular disease, decline in cognitive performance, and decline in physical functioning (Seeman, Singer, Rowe, Horwitz, & McEwen, 1997). What their perspective underscores is the need for long-term relational markers, to capture the recurring nature of particular kinds of social emotional experience believed to affect biology. Similarly, on the biological side, they invoke a construct conceptualized as an index of cumulative wear and tear on multiple physiological systems. Using assessments of early ties to mother and father as well as multiple dimensions of adult intimacy with spouse, they show lower allostatic load for those on the positive compared to the negative relationship pathway. This agenda could benefit from additional biological markers tied to positive relational experience, such as oxytocin, which would enrich our understanding of pathways through which positive social ties afford protection against morbidity and mortality (Carter, 1998; Panksepp, 1998; Ryff & Singer, 1998a, 2000; Uvnäs-Moberg, 1998; commentary by Wise).

Seeman's chapter is first and foremost about mechanism, that is, the routes through which social relationships get under our skin. Following a comprehensive review of studies that link social relationships to incidence, severity, and recovery—or mortality—from heart disease and stroke, she probes possible mechanisms. Evidence from both human and animal research documents a variety of endocrine correlates of style and quality of social interaction. Human studies further link social support to heart rate, blood pressure, cholesterol, epinephrine, and norepinephrine. Social interactions are also tied to autonomic activation, indexed by free fatty acid (FFA) levels and galvanic skin response. Taken as a whole, these studies illustrate the diverse routes through which the social world penetrates the skin. Perhaps a vital direction following from this work is the need to map the interrelationships among these various biological processes. As noted in a review of social support and physiology (Uchino, Cacioppo, & Kiecolt-Glaser, 1996), few studies to date have looked at multiple physiological mechanisms, despite the strong likelihood that they are, in fact, interactive.

Spiegel and Kimerling's formulation of the mechanism that underlies the nexus between psychotherapy with cancer patients and survival time incorporates multiple likely processes. As they suggest, the intervention may affect length of life by promoting improved health behaviors (diet, exercise, sleep) and better medical decision making (e.g., avoiding delays in seeking treatment) as well as by increasing adherence to treatment regimens (underscoring the educational benefits of the intervention). Also involved, however, are possible biological pathways, which address changes in the endocrine system that potentially moderate the rate of disease progression. Spiegel and Kimerling discuss three mechanisms by which a hyperactive hypothalamic-pituitary-adrenal (HPA) axis (linked to depression in cancer patients) could influence the rate of disease progression: differential control of gluconeogenesis in normal and malignant cells, growth stimulation of hormone-sensitive tumor cells, and steroid-induced immunosuppression. Components of the immune system that might mediate the effects of disease progression, such as natural killer cell activity, are also examined.

Cohen's approach to infectious disease susceptibility begins with social conflict or social participation, which are hypothesized to give rise, respectively, to negative or positive emotions and cognitions. These, in turn, are predicted to affect, adversely or beneficially, health practices and endocrine response, thereby leading to alterations in immune function and, ultimately, to susceptibility or resistance to upper respiratory infection. Following this richly elaborated process model, Cohen garners empirical support for some, but not all, of the hypothesized pathways. Health practices, for example, did not appear to play a major role in linking social environments to resistance to infectious illness. Regarding the links to endocrine and immune markers, Cohen calls for refinement in future measures, with regard to both temporal parameters and location of assessments (e.g., natural killer cell activity in the lung rather than the blood). The work is exemplary for its a priori formulation of mechanism and direct empirical tests.

Coe and Lubach's overview of PNI studies in humans shows immune alteration (decreased lymphocyte proliferation) as a function of psychological stress, from which they postulate two possible mediators: glucocorticoids and catecholamines, released from the HPA axis or SNS, respectively. Their developmental studies add to this literature by assessing whether changes in the social environment (e.g., separation from mother, reunion with social group) lead to changes in multiple immune parameters (e.g., number of immune cells in circulation, decreased lymphocyte proliferation, decreased cytolytic activity, decreased antibody response). These effects are further clarified by time trajectories, including social stresses occurring earlier versus later in development and for shorter versus longer periods of time. A main message of Coe's program of research is the importance of *when* in the developmental progression social stress occurs, with more lasting consequences shown when social disturbances occur in younger, more vulnerable organisms. Sharpening understanding of the criti-cal timing issues, lymphocyte proliferation was found to either increase or decrease depending on when, developmentally, a social stressor occurs. These results call for greater attention to another issue, namely, the importance of balance between processes of immune suppression and excessive immune activation.

Taken as a whole, these chapters reveal convergence in the broad categories of mechanism under scrutiny. However, each pursues select processes in particular detail. Collectively, they deepen appreciation of the wider territory that must be traversed to understand how emotion in social relationships affects health. The concluding message, yet again, is to integrate and merge the advances that are coming from the diverse corners of the larger field.

Cumulative Effects

How emotion in social relationships affects health is not likely a result of single, isolated interpersonal encounters but more likely follows from recurring patterns of affection, love, and nurturance, on the one hand, or conflict, anger, and disregard, on the other. This observation points to the importance of continuities and discontinuities in individuals' relational experiences, that is, the pile-up of emotional strain and difficulty through time or, on the salubrious side, the persistence of intimacy and meaningful connections. Parenthetically, the cumulation of flat affect—social relationships that lack significant expression of positive or negative affect—may constitute a unique and possible consequential category itself: the cumulative import of relational neutrality.

Ryff and Singer et al.'s chapter offers explicit emphasis on the idea of cumulation. They first operationalize it at a single point in time by combining assessments of relational quality across three categories of social ties: spouse, other family members, and friends. Using the MIDUS survey, they find that individuals in the top tertile of quality relations (summed across these types) reported better health (measured by chronic conditions, health symptoms, subjective health) than those in the bottom tertile. Moving to cumulation through time, they then constructed with a subsample of respondents from the Wisconsin Longitudinal Study relational histories via measures of early relationships with mother and father as well as aspects of adult intimacy with spouse. Using these sources of information, they created positive and negative relationship pathways, to differentiate between those who had had preponderantly good versus poor relational experiences. As noted before, these pathways were tied to differences in allostatic load, a biological marker conceptualized as cumulative wear and tear on multiple physiological systems. Underscoring the need for a richer portrayal of relationship histories, Ryff and Singer et al. also detail three biographical cases: the marriages of Leo and Sonya Tolstoy, Frida Kahlo and Diego Rivera, and Elizabeth Barrett Browning and Robert Browning.

Working at the other end of the life span, Coe and Lubach also address the long-term consequences of social relational experience, with a focus on implications for immune function. Importantly, when social disruptions are acute (e.g., a brief separation), immune alterations are transient. However, with earlier or more long-lasting social stressors (e.g., gestational stress, separation from mother at birth), the immune consequences are more long-lasting; some continued beyond two years. They conclude that certain aspects of maternal care, possibly including immune products in breast milk, may be essential to the normal development of immunity. The studies further show the difficulty of restoring normal physiology after it has been derailed.

The commentary by Reyes adds a further point, namely, that brief stressors that occur again and again, that repeat and cumulate over time, may also alter the developmental trajectories of immunity and other disease-causing processes. She notes that the immune system has a great deal of redundancy, such that the loss of one function is often compensated for by other cells in the immune system, but underscores that this capacity is not unlimited. Perhaps repeated insults over time could result in serious immune dysfunction.

These observations and findings are important vis-à-vis the human studies. What, for example, are the cumulative consequences of growing up with an emotion-dismissing parent? Gottman finds that such children, compared to those with emotion-coaching parents, have more infectious illnesses, but the mechanisms that underlie these effects have yet to be elucidated. Also pertinent to Gottman's work is continuity of emotional styles: do children raised by emotion-dismissing parents grow up to be emotion-dismissing adults, who perpetuate the same stance of disregarding their own feelings and those of their spouse and/or their children? Seen from this vantage point, parental meta-emotion may have long-term consequences both in terms of persistence of particular styles of emotion regulation and, perhaps even more important, for cumulation of underlying endocrinological and immunological sequelae. Does emotion-coaching or emotion-dismissing parenting in childhood predict allostatic load in adulthood? Is it part of the long-term, cumulative progression of influences that lead to later morbidity and mortality?

Empirically speaking, cumulation is perhaps most powerfully captured in the microanalytic details of daily life, which is the purview of the chapter by Reis. His method suggests that everyday events, social and otherwise, accumulate over time to predict levels of emotional well-being. Participants in these studies are required, over two-week periods, to report their relational highs and lows. This is invaluable information, composites of which could be fruitfully linked to more general relationship quality measures, such as those employed by Ryff and Singer, et al. Seeman, and Cohen. Moreover, the commentary by Cloninger notes that such daily data could be used to assess whether, and how much, people oscillate between positive and negative interactions with others. Such oscillation could be the emotional, phenomenological antecedent to the repeated physiological fluctuations hypothesized to result in higher allostatic load (McEwen & Stellar, 1993).

Spiegel and Kimerling's psychotherapy interventions with breast cancer patients ostensibly have less opportunity to demonstrate cumulative effects, given the shorter window of time over which the effects of emotional expressiveness and social support can accumulate. The interventive effects are, in fact, all the more dramatic given the shorter duration of treatment, perhaps underscoring the importance of the depth and intensity of experiences in these groups. Viewed in a wider time frame, one interesting issue raised by Aken's commentary is: what relational histories do individuals bring with them to these interventions? Perhaps those with more adverse histories (i.e., growing up with emotion-dismissing parents, married to nonsupportive spouses) are even more dramatically affected (emotionally and biologically), given the sharp discontinuity with their prior socioemotional experience. Aken also discusses, intersecting with the work of Reis, how individuals with different attachment styles might respond to Spiegel and Kimerling's psychotherapy interventions.

Cohen's viral challenge studies, while conducted over a period of only a few days, show that individuals who reported more chronic stressors (those enduring for more than six months) had greater susceptibility to the common cold. Importantly, it was not severe or acute stressors that mattered but the chronic difficulties. The animal studies reviewed by Seeman, particularly those focused on the free-living baboons in Kenya, also reveal cumulative biological advantages accruing to animals with a more dominant position in the social hierarchy. Added to these findings are the experimental studies, which manipulate group membership and social instability. A key finding in this work on position in a hierarchy, directly relevant to the idea of cumulation, is that animals exposed to repeated changes (i.e., social instability) have greater likelihood of developing cardiovascular disease.

Taken together, these chapters underscore the importance of tracking effects through time, particularly the recurrent, repetitive nature (deleterious or salubrious) of social interactional experiences.

Multiple Methods

The contributors to this volume represent a wide array of methodological orientations. Some study naturally occurring interactions (Gottman, Reis, Ryff and Singer et al., Seeman), while others focus on experimental or interventive studies (Coe and Lubach, Cohen, Spiegel and Kimerling). Many emphasize behavioral assessments of actual social interactions (Gottman, Reis, Spiegel and Kimerling, Coe and Lubach), while others utilize counts of relational ties and more extensive phenomenological ratings of relationship quality (Ryff and Singer et al., Seeman). Many have made explicit links among self-reported aspects of emotional, social, or event experiences and health outcomes, be they infectious illnesses, colds, cardiovascular disease, cancer progression, or survival or mortality (Gottman, Seeman, Ryff and Singer et al., Spiegel and Kimerling, Cohen). Finally, many address, conceptually or empirically or both, the endocrinological and immunological substrates of social and emotional experiences: Cohen's assessments of epinephrine and norepinephrine; Coe and Lubach's assessment of multiple immune parameters; Ryff and Singer et al.'s measure of allostatic load; Seeman's elaboration of multiple physiological sequelae; Spiegel and Kimerling's formulation of specific biological mechanisms.

What we underscore, looking at this array as a whole, is the need for integration of these diverse levels of analysis and types of data. Fortunately, the contributors to this volume are exemplars of investigators who have built programs of research that span the distance from phenomenology to behavior to biology, the pieces of which are all essential to penetrate the inner reaches of how emotion and social experience influence health.

Student Commentaries

A unique feature of this volume is the active involvement of students, both graduate and advanced undergraduate. These individuals were enrolled in a seminar of study prior to the hosting of the Third Annual Wisconsin Symposium on Emotion. During this semester, they read multiple works of all the symposium participants as well as other background studies pertinent to the theme of "Emotion, Social Relationships, and Health." And, during the conference itself, the students prepared and moderated discussion sessions after each presentation. This gave them the opportunity to interact directly with the distinguished conference participants.

In preparing this edited volume, the students assumed a further task, that of writing commentaries for each of the chapters. The objectives of the commentaries are essentially threefold. First, it was the students' task to distill the key messages from each chapter as they pertained to the focus of the volume. Benefiting from their prior readings, this distillation frequently includes references to other published works by each author, thereby linking the chapters herein with the researchers' prior programs of study.

Second, the commentaries provide detailed discussion of how each chapter intersects with the five themes of the volume described in the preceding section. Depending on the content of the chapter, some themes receive greater attention than others. Importantly, the students also utilize the themes to suggest useful avenues of future inquiry, particularly vis-à-vis issues (e.g., gender differences, cumulative effects) that have not been strongly evident in the prior program of study. This thematic evaluation across the various chapters provides coherence across the volume as a whole.

Finally, the student commentaries address cross-talk among the various chapters. That is, they examine how the various programs of research speak to, extend, and inform each other. This is a vital feature and a unique strength of this volume. At the outset, we acknowledged that the primary intent of this work was to bring together largely separate strands of empirical inquiry: those who study emotion in social relationships, those who study the epidemiology of social relationships and health, those who probe biological mechanisms and pathways. By explicitly addressing cross-talk from chapter to chapter, the student commentaries build vital bridges that link the various strands of the enterprise. Fundamentally, it is in the interstices of these programs of study that the ultimate strides will be made in understanding emotion, social relationships, and health.

References

Berkman, L. F. (1995). The role of social relationships in health promotion. *Psychosomatic Medicine, 57*, 245–254.
Berkman, L. F., & Breslow, L. (1983). *Health and ways of living.* New York: Oxford University Press.
Berkman, L. F., Leo-Summers, L., & Horwitz, R. (1992). Emotional support and survival after myocardial infarction: A prospective, population-based study of the elderly. *Annals of Internal Medicine, 117,* 1003–1009.
Berkman, L. F., & Syme, S. L. (1979). Social networks, host resistance, and mortality: A nine-year follow-up study of Alameda county residents. *American Journal of Epidemiology, 100,* 186–204.

Berscheid, E., & Reis, H. T. (1998). Attraction and close relationships. In D. T. Gilbert & S. T. Fiske (Eds.), *The handbook of social psychology* (Vol. 2, 4th ed., pp. 193–281). Boston: McGraw-Hill.

Buehlman, K. T., Gottman, J. M., & Katz, L. F. (1992). How a couple views their past predicts their future: Predicting divorce from an oral history interview. *Journal of Family Psychology, 5*(3–4), 295–318.

Burg, M. M., & Seeman, T. E. (1994). Families and health: The negative side of social ties. *Annals of Behavioral Medicine, 16*, 109–115.

Campbell, L. D., Connidis, I. A., & Davies, L. (1999). Sibling ties in later life: A social network analysis. *Journal of Family Issues, 20*(1), 114–148.

Carstensen, L. L., Gottman, J. M., & Levensen, R. W. (1995). Emotional behavior in long-term marriage. *Psychology and Aging, 10*, 140–149.

Carstensen, L. L., Graff, J., Levensen, R. W., & Gottman, J. M. (1996). Affect in intimate relationships: The developmental course of marriage. In C. Magai & S. H. McFadden (Eds.), *Handbook of emotion, adult development, and aging* (pp. 227–247). San Diego, CA: Academic.

Carter, C. S. (1998). Neuroendocrine perspectives on social attachment and love. *Psychoneuroendocrinology, 23*, 779–818.

Cassidy, J., & Shaver, P. R. (1999). *Handbook of attachment: Theory, research, and clinical applications.* New York: Guilford.

Coe, C. L. (1993). Psychosocial factors and immunity in nonhuman primates: A review. *Psychosomatic Medicine, 55*(3), 298–308.

Cohen, S. (1988). Psychosocial models of the role of social support in the etiology of physical disease. *Health Psychology, 7*, 269–297.

Cohen, S., Doyle, W. J., Skoner, D. P., Rabin, B. S., & Gwaltney, J. M., Jr. (1997). Social ties and susceptibility to the common cold. *Journal of the American Medical Association, 277*, 1940–1944.

Cohen, S., & Herbert, T. B. (1996). Health psychology: Psychological factors and physical disease from the perspective of human psychoneuroimmunology. *Annual Review of Psychology, 47*, 113–142.

Cohen, S., & Wills, T. A. (1985). Stress, social support, and the buffering hypothesis. *Psychological Bulletin, 98*, 310–357.

Fischer, A. H. (1995). Emotion concepts as a function of gender. In J. A. Russell, D. Fernandez, & M. Jose. (Eds.), *Everyday conceptions of emotion: An introduction to the psychology, anthropology and linguistics of emotion* (Vol. 81, pp. 457–474). Dordrecht, Netherlands: Kluwer Academic.

Fitness, J. (1996). Emotion knowledge structures in close relationships. In G. J. O. Fletcher (Ed.), *Knowledge structures in close relationships: A social psychological approach* (pp. 195– 217). Mahwah, NJ: Lawrence Erlbaum.

Fitness, J., & Fletcher, G. J. O. (1993). Love, hate, anger, and jealousy in close relationships: A prototype and cognitive appraisal analysis. *Journal of Personality and Social Psychology, 65*(5), 942–958.

Fitness, J., & Strongman, K. (1991). Affect in close relationships. In G. J. O. Fletcher & F. D. Fincham (Eds.), *Cognition in close relationship* (pp. 175–202). Hilldale, NJ: Lawrence Erlbaum.

Glass, T. A., & Maddox, G. L. (1992). The quality and quantity of social support: Stroke recovery as psycho-social transition. *Social Science and Medicine, 34*(11), 1249–1261.

Gottman, J. M., Katz, L., & Hooven, C. (1995). *Meta-emotion.* Hilldale, NJ: Lawrence Erlbaum.

Gottman, J. M., Katz, L., & Hooven, C. (1996). Parental meta-emotion philosophy and the emotional life of families: Theoretical models and preliminary data. *Journal of Family Psychology, 10*, 243–268.

Gottman, J. M., & Levensen, R. W. (1992). Marital processes predictive of later dissolution: Behavior, physiology, and health. *Journal of Personality and Social Psychology, 63*(2), 221–233.

Hazan, C., & Shaver, P. R. (1994). Attachment as an organizational framework for research on close relationships. *Psychological Inquiry, 5*(1), 1–22.

House, J. S., Landis, K. R., & Umberson, D. (1988). Social relationships and health. *Science, 241*, 540–545.

Kaplan, G. A., Salonen, J. T., Cohen, R. D., Brand, R. J., Syme, L., & Puska, P. (1988). Social connections and mortality from all causes and cardiovascular disease: Prospective evidence from eastern Finland. *American Journal of Epidemiology, 128*, 370–380.

Kiecolt-Glaser, J. K., Glaser, R., Cacioppo, J. T., MacCallum, R. C., Snydersmith, M., Kim, C., & Malarkey, W. B. (1997). Marital conflict in older adults: Endocrinological and immunological correlates. *Psychosomatic Medicine, 59*, 339–349.

Kiecolt-Glaser, J. K., Malarkey, W. B., Cacioppo, J. T., & Glaser, R. (1994). Stressful personal relationships: Immune and endocrine function. In R. Glaser & J. K. Kiecolt-Glaser (Eds.), *Handbook of human stress and immunity* (pp. 321–340). San Diego, CA: Academic.

Kiecolt-Glaser, J. K., Newton, T., Cacioppo, J. T., MacCallum, R. C., Glaser, R., & Malarkey, W. B. (1996). Marital conflict and endocrine function: Are men really more physiologically affected than women? *Journal of Consulting and Clinical Psychology, 64*, 324–332.

Knox, S. S, & Uvnäs-Moberg, K. (1998). Social isolation and cardiovascular disease: An atherosclerotic pathway? *Psychoneuroendocrinology, 23*(8), 877–890.

Lubach, G. R., Coe, C. L., & Ershler, W. B. (1995). Effects of early rearing environment on immune responses of infant rhesus monkeys. *Brain, Behavior, and Immunity, 9*(1), 31–46.

McEwen, B. S., & Stellar E. (1993). Stress and the individual: Mechanisms leading to disease. *Archives of Internal Medicine, 153*, 2093–2101

Panksepp, J. (1998). *Affective neuroscience.* New York: Oxford University Press.

Reis, H. T. (1998). Gender differences in intimacy and related behaviors: Context and process. In D. J. Canary & K. Dindia (Eds.), *Sex differences and similarities in communication* (pp. 203–231). Mahwah, NJ: Erlbaum.

Reis, H. T., & Franks, P. (1994). The role of intimacy and social support in health outcomes: Two processes or one? *Personal Relationships, 1*(2), 185–197.

Reis, H. T., & Patrick, B. C. (1996). Attachment and intimacy: Component processes. In A. Kruglanski & E. T. Higgins (Eds.), *Social psychology: Handbook of basic principles* (pp. 523–563). New York: Guilford.

Reis, H. T., & Shaver, P. (1988). Intimacy as an interpersonal process. In S. Duck (Ed.), *Handbook of personal relationships* (pp. 367–389). Chichester, England: John Wiley and Sons.

Ryff, C. D., & Singer, B. H. (1996). Psychological well-being: Meaning, measurement, and implications for psychotherapy research. *Psychotherapy and Psychosomatics, 65*, 14–23.

Ryff, C. D., & Singer, B. H. (1998a). The contours of positive human health. *Psychological Inquiry, 9*, 1–28.

Ryff, C. D., & Singer, B. H. (1998b). Middle age and well-being. In H. S. Friedman (Ed.), *Encyclopedia of mental health* (pp. 707–719). San Diego, CA: Academic.

Ryff, C. D., & Singer, B. H. (2000). Interpersonal flourishing: A positive health agenda for the new millennium. *Personality and Social Psychology Review, 4*: 30–44.

Seeman, T. E. (1996). Social ties and health: The benefits of social integration. *Annals of Epidemiology, 6*, 442–451.

Seeman, T. E., Berkman, L. F., Blazer, D., & Rowe, J. (1994). Social ties and support and neuroendocrine function: MacArthur studies of successful aging. *Annals of Behavioral Medicine, 16*, 95–106.

Seeman, T. E., Berkman, L. F., Kohout, F., LaCroix, A., Glynn, R., & Blazer, D. (1993). Intercommunity variation in the association between social ties and mortality in the elderly: A comparative analysis of three communities. *Annals of Epidemiology, 3*, 325–335.

Seeman, T. E., & McEwen, B. S. (1996). Impact of social environment characteristics on neuroendocrine regulation. *Psychosomatic Medicine, 58*(5), 459–471.

Seeman, T. E., Singer, B., Rowe, J. W., Horwitz, R., & McEwen, B. (1997). The price of adaptation: Allostatic load and its health consequences: MacArthur studies of successful aging. *Archives of Internal Medicine, 157*, 2259–2268.

Seeman, T. E., & Syme, S. L. (1987). Social networks and coronary artery disease: A comparative analysis of network structural and support characteristics. *Psychosomatic Medicine, 49*, 341–354.

Sheldon, K. M., Ryan, R., & Reis, H. T. (1996). What makes for a good day? Competence and autonomy in the day and in the person. *Personality and Social Psychology Bulletin, 22*, 1270–1279.

Singer, B., Ryff, C. D., Carr, D., & Magee, W. J. (1998). Life histories and mental health: A person-centered strategy. In A. Raftery (Ed.), *Sociological methodology* (pp. 1–51). Washington, DC: American Sociological Assoociation.

Spiegel, D. (1990). Facilitating emotional coping during treatment. *Cancer, 66*(6 Suppl), 1422–146.

Spiegel, D. (1993). Psychosocial intervention in cancer. *Journal of the National Cancer Institute, 85*(5), 1198–1205.

Spiegel, D. (1996). Cancer and depression. *British Journal of Psychiatry, 168*, 109–116.

Spiegel, D. (1998). Effects of psychosocial treatment in prolonging cancer survival may be mediated by neuroimmune pathways. *Annals of the New York Academy of Sciences, 840*, 674–683.

Spiegel, D., Bloom, J. R., & Yalom, I. (1981). Group support for patients with metastatic cancer: A randomized outcome study. *Archives of General Psychiatry, 38*, 527–533.

Thoits, P. A. (1995). Stress, coping, and social support processes: Where are we? What next? *Journal of Health and Social Behavior, extra issue*, 53–79.

Tidwell, M. O., Reis, H. T., & Shaver, P. R. (1996). Attachment, attractiveness, and social interaction: A diary study. *Journal of Personality and Social Psychology, 71*(4), 729–745.

Uchino, B. N., Cacioppo, J. T., & Kiecolt-Glaser, J. T. (1996). The relationship between social support and physiological processes: A review with emphasis on underlying mechanisms and implications for health. *Psychological Bulletin, 119*, 488–531.

Uvnäs-Moberg, K. (1998). Oxytocin may mediate the benefits of positive social interaction and emotions. *Psychoneuroendocrinology, 23*(8), 819–835.

Van-Tilburg, T. (1998). Losing and gaining in old age: Changes in personal network size and social support in a four-year longitudinal study. *Journals of Gerontology: Psychological Sciences and Social Sciences, 53B*(6), S313–S323.

2

Meta-Emotion, Children's Emotional Intelligence, and Buffering Children from Marital Conflict

John Gottman

$\mathcal{F}$or the past 13 years, my laboratory has been investigating the transfer of marital discord to the developing child. We have been searching for buffers against the deleterious effects of marital conflict on children. The question that motivated this research was: is there anything that parents can do if they are in an ailing marriage to buffer their children? Our longitudinal research suggests one potential answer to this question (Gottman, Katz, & Hooven, 1995).

The cornerstone of our research was a concept called meta-emotion. Just as the term *Meta-communication* refers to communication about communication, and the term *Meta-cognition* refers to how we think about our thinking, in a similar way, the term *Meta-emotion* refers to our emotions about our emotions. We had a much broader meaning in mind than just feelings about feelings. We were also interested in what can be called the "executive functions" of emotion, those things that regulate our emotional experience and expression.

We were interested in how people feel about an emotion like anger, what the history of their experience with anger has been (in their primary families and so on), what were their metaphors, associated concepts, and narratives about anger, and what their philosophy about emotion was. We interviewed people about their history, feelings and metaphors, narratives, philosophy about sadness, anger, and more recently, fear, pride, love, guilt, and embarrassment. We found that huge variation exists in people's meta-emotions. For example, some people said anger is from the devil, that they punished their children just for getting angry even if there were no misbehavior. Others viewed anger like clearing one's throat—a natural event. They said that one simply expresses one's anger and then goes on.

In brief, we discovered two basic types of parents: emotion dismissing and emotion coaching. Here are some of the characteristics of emotion-dismissing (ED) parents.

They

- don't notice lower-intensity emotions in kids or self
- see negative affects as if they were toxins
- want a cheerful child and see an unhappy child as a failing of their own parenting
- want to protect their child from ever feeling any negative affect
- believe that staying in a negative affect state a long time is even more harmful, and they are impatient with negative affect
- believe in accentuating the positive and deemphasizing the negative in life
- will try to distract, cheer up, tickle, use food, etc., to change the child's negative affect quickly
- see examining the negative affect as a waste of time or potentially destructive
- don't have a detailed language for emotions

Here are some examples. One emotion-dismissing father in our studies said about his son: "If one of his friends took his toy or hit him, I say, don't worry about it, he probably didn't mean it or he'll give it back, but just don't dwell on it. Roll with the punches." Another father said about his daughter, "If she is sad, I try to find out her needs. I say, what do you need? Do you need to go outside? Do you need to watch TV? Do you need to eat something? Just respond to her needs. But usually she is never sad." By "responding to her needs," this father is emphasizing a method of distraction for dealing with his daughter's sadness.

Being raised by emotion-dismissing parents has profound consequences. One particularly dramatic story concerns a couple I recently interviewed. I asked the woman if there was anything special about this relationship, and she said that she was recently unpacking a smiley-face calendar from her childhood. She explained that her parents would put a smiley-face sticker on each day if she had been cheerful that day. If she earned 20 smiley faces a month, she could get some special toy. She said that her husband seemed to be interested in being with her and interested in what she had to say no matter what mood she was in. Even if she were depressed or in a crabby mood, he still wanted to listen to her and be near her. That was a first in her life. By the way, she grew up to be a professional football cheerleader. Growing up in an emotion-dismissing home can have a dramatic impact on a child, as our research demonstrates.

Emotion-coaching (EC) parents have entirely different meta-emotions. They

- notice lower-intensity affects in their kids
- see the negative affect as an opportunity for intimacy or teaching
- see the child's experience of negative affect as healthy or even part of the growth of the child
- are not impatient with the negative affect
- communicate understanding and empathy
- help the child to verbally label feelings
- try to understand the feelings that underlie any misbehavior
- set clear limits on behavior, problem solve with the child, and discuss with a child what the child can do in these situations

We now think that these differences have implications for how a child's brain processes what are called the "withdrawal emotions" of sadness and fear. They are called withdrawal emotions because they make you want to withdraw from the world, unlike joy, interest, affection, and anger, which make you want to engage with the world. Another withdrawal emotion is disgust. Emotion coaching, we think, adds to the experience of the withdrawal emotions a sense of control and optimism. The child is still being sad or afraid, but he feels more in control and more optimistic about things as well. This may have profound implications for how the child's autonomic nervous system bounces back from physiological arousal, as mediated by the vagus nerve.

Thanks to a brilliant undergraduate honors thesis by Vanessa Kahen, we found that in the teaching situation, ED parents and EC parents teach in different ways. The following table is a summary of these dramatic differences.

Emotion-Coaching Parents	Emotion-Dismissing Parents
1. They give child little information, just enough to get started, in a calm manner.	1. They give child lots of information in an excited manner.
2. They are not involved with the child's mistakes.	2. They are very involved with the child's mistakes
3. They wait for the child to do something right, then praise child's performance specifically	3. They wait for the child to make a mistake, then criticize child's performance. Then, they escalate the criticism to insults, trait labels, mockery, belittling, intrusiveness.

These interactions have a profound impact on a child. I recently read a book called *Sons on Fathers* (Keyes, 1992), an edited book of the reminiscences of some successful sons about their fathers. One chapter was by a writer named Christopher Hallowell, whose major memory of his dad was an incident that happened when Christopher was about six years old. His father called him into his wood shop and said, "Son, today I am going to teach you how to make a box. If you can build a box, you can build anything in the wood shop." His father showed him how to use the angle vises and other tools. Young Christopher then worked by himself for a long time, and he built a box that he recalled was a bit shaky, but it even had a lid on it, and he proudly showed it to his dad. His dad said, "Son, this is a wobbly box. If you can't build a box, you'll never be able to build anything." To this day, Hallowell, who is now a father himself, keeps that box on his dresser. He wrote that he cannot open the box without seeing his father's face in the lid saying to him, "You'll never be able to do anything." His father actually never said that, but Hallowell's memory is powerful indeed.

Haim Ginott (1965, 1971, 1975) relates a story about a little boy named Stuart. Ginott was in a school one morning when an elementary school teacher told him that today she was going to read a compassionate poem to her class. She was having some trouble getting the class to sit down, and Stuart was clowning around. She said, "Stuart! What is wrong with you? Do you need a special invitation to sit down, or are you just naturally slow?" Stuart finally sat down, and the teacher then read this sensitive poem to the class. But, according to Ginott, Stuart was not listening because he was busy planning the details of his teacher's funeral. This example also illustrates the idea that process is everything in the area of emotion. You can only teach respect respectfully, and you can only teach compassion by being compassionate. That is how children learn: they learn both parts of the role, the way they feel and the way you express your feelings.

More about Parents

Emotion-dismissing parents can be very warm. We have seen many parents, in response to their child's sadness, say lovingly, "Sweetheart, cheer up. Just put a smile on your face. Now that's better, isn't it? There's my big girl." A parent can be caring and affectionate and still be dismissing of a child's negative emotions.

ED and EC parents have completely different metaphors about anger, sadness, and fear in their own lives. If we examine the metaphors, here is what we find:

	Emotion-Dismissing Parents	*Emotion-Coaching Parents*
Anger	Explosion metaphors. Losing control, they equate anger with aggression, violence, selfishness	Think of anger as natural, as a block to goals
Sadness	Wallowing in self-pity, inaction, passivity, even death	Something is missing. Slow down and figure out what it is
Fear	Cowardice, inaction, being a wimp, failure	Natural cues of danger are important. Find out how to make your world safe.
Negative Affect in General	Leads nowhere; you should roll with the punches; it only inflames a bad situation; like throwing gasoline on a fire.	Is productive to explore, not scary or harmful

What are these results telling us? The metaphors of emotion-coaching parents suggest that it is helpful to them to explore how they feel. The exploration of inner emotions provides valuable direction in life for these people. However, for emotion-dismissing parents, it is a waste of time and even terrifying. Although these results might suggest that these concepts are going to be resistant to change, that they are fundamental, lasting personality traits, we have not found this to be true in our parenting groups. On the contrary, when parents experiment with alternative ways of thinking about their children's emotions and try emotion coaching, they change how they view emotion in their own lives, including in their marriages.

Empirical Rediscovery of Ginott

Ginott was, in my view, our most brilliant child psychologist. Whereas most other parenting approaches focus on noncompliant children and discipline, Ginott noted that, if we were completely successful with these approaches, we would produce only obedient children. Also, he claimed, we would produce children whose morality was what Selma Fraiberg (1959) called a "bookkeeping" mentality, evaluating actions in terms of rewards and punishments. A purely external reward and punishment approach to morality interferes with the normal development of conscience, which is based on identifying with the parent. The child sometimes goes through reasoning like the following when contemplating an immoral act like hitting a younger child: "What will it cost me? What will I gain? Oh well, it's worth it." Morality becomes a cost-benefit analysis. There is no internal code based on ethics, values, or justice.

Ginott disagreed with many books on parental discipline, which advised parents to be unemotional when disciplining their child. Consistent with Ginott's admonitions, for the parents who use emotion coaching, the basis of discipline can be the parent's genuine anger or disappointment with the child when the child has done something the parent thinks is wrong. This is true as long as the anger does not get translated into insults of the child's character or personality. The strong emotional bond formed through emotion coaching is disrupted by these parental emotions, which follow the child's misbehavior, and the child wants to set things right again, to reestablish closeness. Hence, Ginott argued that the parent should not be unemotional when disciplining a child but should use these real emotions (in a noninsulting manner) to let the child know how the parent feels. The parent's anger and disappointment are the parent's most powerful tools in discipline, Ginott counseled. We have found that children tend to find an upset, angry, or disappointed parent who talks about punishment as perfectly understandable and natural, but children find a calm and punitive parent quite cold and terrifying.

Ginott teaches us that the most important and magical moments to focus on in parent-child interactions are the moments when the child is emotional. This is a big conceptual break from the psychoanalytic stress on projection through play. The child is not asked to recreate an event and then to discuss it, which was a real problem for the child therapist, who saw the child in a scheduled 50-minute period. The child might or might not have the salient emotions during that period. The psychoanalytic approach is to use play as the projective medium, but Ginott challenged this idea. The implications of his ideas are that therapy has to occur when the child has a genuine emotional experience, and this requires being with the child a great deal. The obvious candidates for learning from Ginott are, therefore, teachers and parents, not therapists. For these reasons, Ginott's ideas were never absorbed by the traditional therapeutic community.

His ideas, although quite simple, are still greatly misunderstood today. For example, many teachers who seek to teach children about emotion do so by taking a calm group of kids and asking them about when they felt angry. The teachers are saying implicitly, "Talk about anger but in a calm way. Don't get angry, please." Ginott argued that this is not how kids learn about anger. They learn about it when they are actually angry. Then, when they are angry once again, they will have access to this learning. Learning about emotion is state dependent. This hypothesis has yet to be tested empirically, because the hypothesis is really that learning that is organized by a particular emotion will be more accessible when in that emotional state again. The hypothesis is not that any learning (e.g., nonsense syllables) in an emotional state will be more accessible when in that emotional state again but rather that learning is relevant to that emotion. Ginott gave us a complete approach to parenting, not just an approach to discipline, and his insights have been corroborated by our research.

Avoid Judgments

Ginott asked, "What is different about the language I must use with children?" His answer: avoid expressions that judge (either positively or negatively) a child's character or ability. Instead, parents must describe what they see, what they feel. Describe the problem and suggest a solution. For example, after a common household accident, the parent's best response is "I see the milk spilled. Here is a rag." Not "You are so clumsy, clean it up or else" (self-fulfilling prophecy). Or, a girl draws something and asks if it is good. The preferred response is "I see a purple house and lots of flowers. It makes me feel like I am in the country" Not "This is wonderful. You are a talented artist."

One of Ginott's insights was that nonspecific praise can be as harmful as negative labeling of a child's character. Here is an example. For 20 minutes, during a car ride, Jason was quiet in the back seat of the car while mom, dad, and the baby rode in the front seat. Mom then turned around to Jason and said he was mom's perfect angel. Jason then proceeded to dump the full ashtray on her head. She did not understand his behavior. After she had been so nice to him, he was mean to her. But the truth is that Jason had been quiet for the previous 20 minutes because he was trying to imagine how the family could get into a car accident that would kill only the baby but leave him and his parents alive. He had been silently planning the baby's death when his mom called him a little angel. In general, nonspecific praise raises a child's anxieties by setting standards that are unreachable. So the child acts to relieve us of our unreasonable expectations.

Process is Everything

We can only teach kindness kindly. We can only teach respect by being respectful. We can only teach politeness by being polite with our children. It does not work to say, "You stupid idiot, I said to be polite!"

This is probably the most important principle that Ginott espoused, and it has to do with empowering a child. I have seen many parents dramatize to a child his or her own powerlessness. Kids are very aware that they are small and powerless. They worry about it all the time and constantly think of how old they are, of what they could not do last year but can do now. They want to be bigger, more competent, more capable, but they still want their parents to take care of them. So they feel somewhat ambivalent about growing up.

Empowering a child is important if we want children who will eventually be independent and be able to think for themselves. Parents can still set limits and yet empower their children by offering them real choices.

The building blocks of self-concept involve honoring a child's small preferences, which often begin around food choices. A young child is unlikely to say, "When I grow up, I will study astronomy and theoretical physics." Instead, the child is likely to say, "I'm not eating this. I hate it when the peas and the mashed potatoes touch." This is a test of a small bit of self. The child is saying, "I think that I'm the kind of kid who likes separate food. Let's see what my mom says about that." It is as if the child is trying on a self-concept like someone tries on a new shirt and then looks in the mirror. The child whose mom is agreeable, who takes the plate and rearranges the peas and the potatoes so they don't touch, then can say, "Hey, I am the kind of kid who likes separate food, and this is Ok with my mom, and it's me." The child is learning, "I am acceptable this way." These little experiments with self-concept empower the child; they do not create an obnoxious or "spoiled" child. They lead to a child who will later say to herself, "I'm the kind of kid who likes a challenge on the monkey bars and then I do it."

Validate Emotional Experience

Parents do enormous harm by invalidating a child's emotions, which causes children to doubt their own instincts. The principle is to validate a child's emotional experience. When the child complains, "My finger hurts," the best parental response is "A scratch can hurt," not "It couldn't hurt, it's just a little scratch." Or when your child says, "It's hot," a parent should answer, "It's hot in here for you," not "Don't be silly. It's freezing in here." Parents do not invalidate a child's emotions out of malice, but they seem to believe that one of their jobs as parents is to hold a mirror of reality up to the unrealistic child. This well-intentioned invalidation, however, can do a great deal of harm.

Words of Understanding Must Precede Words of Advice

Parents are very confused about what effect they will have if they are understanding of a child's fear. Emotions do not vanish by being banished; research shows that they intensify physiologically if their expression is suppressed. Kids do not become cowards if dad understands their fear. We had a father in one of our parenting groups whose six-year-old son was afraid of shadows in his room, and the boy had trouble sleeping in there. His father had checked and rechecked the room, and it was perfectly Ok. He told his son to stop being a wimp and go to sleep. But it did not work. The child just lay there tense and sleepless all night, and soon his school performance was a problem as well. The group had this man try an experiment. He was told to lie down in bed next to his son and ask for a tour of all the scary shadows. Then he was taught how to validate those feelings as if they made sense to him, to ask the boy for a solution, and to wait. The boy showed his father a shadow that looked just like Tyrannosaurus rex, and the father said, "It does look like a T-rex." The boy said, "That's what I've been trying to tell you." Then the father asked, "What should we do about it?" His son said, "Let's get our dinosaur book out and read it real loud." Although this made no sense to the father, he did it, and in a few moments, his son was fast asleep in his arms. He said that it was the first time in months he felt like a real father. The next night, the same solution was repeated, and the next, but on the fourth night the boy said he would read to the T-rex by himself. He had little trouble after that going to sleep in his room. Remember, not "Don't be a wimp," but "Show me those scary shadows."

A parent who sits with a sad child and is also sad and not impatient with the sadness communicates many profound things to the child:

- Being sad will not kill you. It's Ok to be sad.
- You are not alone. I understand, and I feel what you feel.
- It makes sense to feel what you feel. Trust your feelings.
- Even with these feelings, you are acceptable.

A parent who sets limits by communicating his real feelings of anger and disappointment (without insult) also communicates a great deal to the child. Discipline becomes part of sharing the values of the family and being close; these values are internalized. Emotional communication becomes two-way and real.

A parent who involves the child in the solution to a problem and not just in the problem also communicates a great deal:

- You have good ideas.
- You can solve problems.
- I trust your capability.
- You can be part of the solution, not just part of the problem.

Emotion Coaching Is Natural

These ideas do not involve social skill training of parents, usually. We do not need a detailed and time-consuming treatment program to get parents to be emotion coaching. The skills are usually in the repertoire of all adults, for example, in how we treat guests. We take care of guests' emotions respectfully. When a guest leaves an umbrella, we say "You forgot your umbrella. Here it is," not "What is wrong with you? If you keep forgetting things, you will never succeed in life. What am I, your slave?" When a guest spills some wine, we say, "The wine spilled. No problem. This will clean it. Would you like some more wine?" not "You are so clumsy. You have ruined my best tablecloth. I can never invite you again. If you keep being so careless, you will become a criminal and probably be executed."

Parental Agendas

So, if emotion coaching as easy as I say it is, and the skills are in most people's repertoire already, why don't they do it? This is a great question. Through our clinical work, we have found that the major obstacle to parents being able to follow the rule "understanding must precede advice" is the natural process of parental concern about various problems they worry about in each child. This leads parents to want to draw a moral lesson for each child in every situation, which we call the *parental agenda*. These agendas are usually healthy. Dad worries that his son is not generous enough, or mom worries that her daughter is too impulsive, and so on. Then, when a situation arises that dramatizes this parental worry, it is quite natural for the parent to try to draw a moral lesson from the disastrous situation.

Here is an example supplied by Dr. Alice Ginott-Cohen, Haim Ginott's widow. It is the holiday shopping season, and a mother warns a four-year-old child who she considers somewhat "spacey" to pay attention and stay close to her in the department store. Otherwise, he might get lost. Of course, he does get lost. After 45 frantic minutes, the parent and child are reunited by the store detective. What has been going on in the child's mind during this time? The separation has activated one of the terrors of this age. The boy is thinking, "I bet this is how kids wind up in orphanages. I just know it, they are going to take me and put me in an orphanage, and I'll never see my parents or my dog or my house again. My life is over." When the mother and child get together again, she is very likely to say, "I am never taking you anywhere again. You are never leaving your room. Didn't I tell you to stay close to me? Why are you so spacey?" Instead, the mother could say, " Come over here. That must have been very scary. Were you scared? Tell me. [pause while mom listens] Yes, I don't blame you for being scared. I was scared. Now let's calm down. [later] That was so awful. Let's talk about how we can prevent that from happening again. Any ideas?"

When I was in graduate school, I leaned against a loose railing on my friend Steve Asher's porch, fell, and broke my elbow. After five hours of surgery, I called my parents. My father was very quiet, and then he said, "How many times have I told you? Don't lean." Indeed, that was a parental agenda of his when I was growing up. He would typically pass me in the yard, leaning against a tree, and say, "Stand up straight. You're a young guy. Why you gotta lean?" So, after all those years, he had finally found a moral lesson in my broken elbow. It is a parental urge. How satisfying it is to be able to say, "I told you so, didn't I? Now will you listen at last?"

Society Is Emotion Dismissing

In many ways, our society has cultivated an emotion-dismissing philosophy in people by emphasizing achievement to evaluate a person's worth and by deemphasizing being in the moment with what one is feeling and instead, emphasizing a future orientation. The way a person moves through time with the peoples he loves makes life have meaning. My friend Ross Parke calls himself a "collector of moments"—as if these moments were pearls on a string. A collection of great moments of emotional connection do not go on anyone's resume, but they make it all worthwhile.

Our society does not reward a person for spending time with her children, for choosing to attend her daughter's soccer game on Sunday instead of playing golf with a client, as the boss has asked. In fact, sociological studies show that these parents make an average of around 25% less than those parents who choose work over family, and they get fewer promotions. And the situation of the workplace militating against families is worse in Japan than in the United States.

I think the motto of the Nike sneaker ad—Just do it!—exemplifies this value well. "Just do it" means do not think about it much, do not figure out whether you really want to do it, just get in there and compete. Do not think that you feel sad every time you do this sport and that maybe it is not for you. Do not pay attention to how you feel. Ignore your pain. Just achieve. If you do not do it, you will become a bum, a failure. No one will want you. That is the threat. And, what is the promise? If you just do it, everything will turn out all right. You will be honored and respected, you will receive the applause, you will be loved.

But it's a lie.

Research Findings

Based on Ginott's views, in our research, we have found that children who have EC parents have

- greater ability to calm their hearts after emotional upset (they have higher vagal tone)
- greater ability to focus attention.
- higher math and reading scores at age eight, even controlling age for IQ
- fewer behavior problems as rated by teachers
- better relations with other kids
- fewer infectious illnesses

These differences were only amplified as we followed the children into adolescence, and we had to conclude that the children are really developing an *emotional intelligence* (as Dan Goleman, 1995, has called it).

The very skills that EC teaches in early childhood, however, become a liability in middle childhood in the face of peer teasing and peer entry situations. The worst thing that a middle-childhood kid can say in response to teasing or upon entering a new group is "I don't like it when you do that." Talking about one's feelings and calling attention to one's self has become a liability by middle childhood. When we make tape recordings of middle-childhood kids talking to their friends, the major thing they are worried about is avoiding embarrassment. In effect, they act with their peers (not in private) as if they have had an "emotion-ectomy." The amazing thing is that kids who have been emotion coached early know this—and act accordingly. They have the ability to "psych out" social situations and to analyze them appropriately. At each major developmental period, this "psych out" involves different processes being prominent. In adolescence, it involves using friendships and love relationships for self-exploration. Again, kids who are emotion coached do well with these developmentally appropriate tasks. So, learning the skills of emotion coaching is not learning a set of splinter skills but involves developing a kind of emotional intelligence. These children become better social problem solvers.

How does it all work? We think that it is mediated by the greater ability of these children to self-soothe and to focus attention in the service of an external goal. Our path modeling suggests that this is mediated by the tenth cranial nerve, the vagus nerve.

Vagus Nerve

The autonomic nervous system consists of two branches, the sympathetic nervous system (SNS) and the parasympathetic nervous system (PNS), which mostly are mutually antagonistic in maintaining a dynamic homeostatic regulation in the body. The following table is a summary of the way these two branches generally work.

PNS	SNS
Slows heart	Speeds heart
Decreases how hard the heart contracts	Increases myocardial contractions
Puts sugar into liver as glycogen	Gets sugar into blood by converting glycogen

The vagus nerve (so called because it is the "vagabond" nerve that travels throughout the body) is the tenth cranial nerve; it innervates the viscera, heart, lungs, kidneys, gut, and liver. It has been assessed effectively through the pioneering work of Steve Porges (1972, 1973, 1984), who has measured respiratory variability versus heart rate variability. There is a respiratory rhythm in our heart rates because as we inhale the heart speeds up slightly, and as we exhale it slows down slightly. This connection between cardiovascular and respiratory systems is related to vagal activation, and it is also related to the focusing of attention. Children who are emotion coached have higher vagal tone. We do not yet know whether this is a causal link, and we are planning to do experiments to test this hypothesis. Right now, our operating assumption is that emotion coaching causes higher vagal tone, which makes emotional regulation and self-soothing easier and leads to all the better developmental outcomes we have observed in our longitudinal study. In addition, the vagus innervates the thymus gland, which is responsible for T-cell maturation, and so the better outcome on infectious illnesses confirms our hypothesis.

Emotion Regulation Theory

Precisely how do meta-emotions affect the functioning of families and act to affect child outcomes? We are particularly drawn to theories that attempt to integrate behavior and physiology, and so our hypotheses are oriented toward approaches that have emphasized the importance of balance and regulation, including the development of children's abilities to regulate emotion (Garber & Dodge, 1991) and the development of children's abilities to self-soothe strong, potentially disruptive emotional states (Dunn, 1977), focus attention, and organize themselves for coordinated action in the service of some goal.

Linkages between Family and Peer Worlds

It is now well known that the ability to interact successfully with peers and to form lasting peer relationships are important developmental tasks. Children who fail at these tasks, who are rejected by their peers, and who are unable to make friends are at risk for a number of later problems (Parker & Asher, 1987). The peer context presents new opportunities and formidable challenges to children. Interacting with peers provides opportunities to learn about more egalitarian relationships than parent-child relationships: to form friendships with agemates, negotiate conflicts, engage in cooperative and competitive activities, and learn appropriate limits for aggressive impulses. Peer interactions provide opportunities for learning that friends can be sources of great fun and adventure as well as comfort in times of need. Even very young children are able to obtain this kind of comfort in times of stress from their friends. For example, Kramer and Gottman (1992) found that the quality of friendships among three-year-olds was the best predictor of adjustment to becoming a sibling. On the other hand, children are typically less supportive than caregivers when their peers fail at these tasks.

In our research, the quality of the child's peer relationships forms the most important class of child outcome measures. A major goal of the research we undertook was to predict peer social relations in middle childhood from variables descriptive of the family's emotional life during preschool. The theoretical challenge is in predicting peer social relations across these two major developmental periods, from preschool to middle childhood. Major changes occur in peer relations in middle childhood, as children become aware of a much wider social network than the dyad. In preschool, children are rarely capable of sustaining play with more than one other child (see, for example, Corsaro, 1979, 1981). However, in middle childhood, children become aware of peer norms for social acceptance, and teasing and avoiding embarrassment suddenly emerge (see Gottman & Parker, 1986). Children become aware of clique structures, influence patterns, and social acceptance.

In middle childhood, some of the correlates of peer acceptance and rejection change dramatically, particularly with respect to the expression of emotion. One of the most interesting changes is that the socially competent response to a number of salient social situations, such as peer entry and teasing, is to be a good observer, somewhat wary, basically "cool," and emotionally unflappable. The child in middle childhood being teased needs to act as if he has undergone an emotion-ectomy, and indeed, a major concern of children in this developmental period is avoiding embarrassment (Gottman & Parker, 1986). Thus, we can see that the basic elements and skills a child learns through emotion coaching (labeling, expressing one's feelings, and talking about one's feelings) become liabilities in the peer social world in middle childhood, especially if they are simply transferred by the child from the home to the school. The model that describes the linking of emotion coaching in preschool to successful peer relations in middle childhood cannot be a simple isomorphic transfer of social skills model. Instead, it becomes necessary to identify a mechanism operative in the preschool period that makes it possible for the child to learn something during that time that underlies the development of appropriate social skills across this major developmental shift in what constitutes social competence with peers.

The major challenge in being able to make linkages from the family's affective world to the child's peer world is that, as the child develops, many of the child's peer social competencies become precisely the opposite of what children specifically learned from emotion-coaching parents. Even in the preschool period, entry into a peer group is successful to the extent that children do not call attention to themselves and their feelings; instead, they watch the peer group, understand what is going on, and quietly and nonintrusively do what they are doing, waiting to be invited in. These skills of observing, waiting, watching, and not expressing one's emotions nor discussing them are even more important in middle childhood, when teasing becomes central. Any theory we develop has to contend with the problem that the specific skills that children learn in emotion-coaching interactions with parents are precisely the wrong skills for succeeding with peers, and this is even more the case in middle childhood. We propose, therefore, that a social learning or modeling theory of the development of social competence is doomed to failure.

Emotional Intelligence

As an alternative, we suggest that, instead of a social skills theory for making developmental predictions and linkages from the family to the child peer system, we posit a set of general abilities that underlie the development of social and emotional competence with peers. These abilities form the basis of what Salovey and Mayer (1990) call *emotional intelligence*. While Salovey and Mayer's idea of emotional intelligence is a long list of skills, we thought that the link would be much simpler: the child's abilities to regulate emotions, to self-soothe, and to focus attention during emotionally trying peer situations. We predict that we will observe that the child's peer social competence will hold primarily in the inhibition of negative affect (Guralnick, 1981), particularly aggression, whining, oppositional behavior, fighting requiring parental intervention, sadness, and anxiety with peers. Being teased in middle childhood is the ultimate proving ground for the child's ability to inhibit negative affect.

Children's peer social competencies include the ability to resolve conflict, to find a sustained common play activity, and to empathize with a peer in distress (e.g., Asher & Coie, 1990; Gottman, 1983; Gottman & Parker, 1986). To see how these basic skills of emotion regulation might operate and support the more complex social skills that have been described as the child's peer social competence, consider children's peer social skills before age five, in which most of the child's interaction occurs in dyads. In one transcript of a play session in our research, two four-year-olds got into a conflict in which he wanted to play Superman and she wanted to play house. After shouting their wishes back and forth a few times, he calmed down and suggested that they pretend this was Superman's house; she had also calmed down and thought this was a great idea, and their compromise resulted in an enjoyable pretend play session for both children. It takes a lot of skill to be able to self-soothe in this situation and to both suggest and to accept a creative compromise.

What is different about children who can and cannot do this? We think there is a fundamental set of abilities that have to do with understanding one's own emotions and being able to regulate them, to soothe one's self physiologically, to focus attention, to listen to what one's playmate is saying, to take another's role and empathize, and to engage in social problem solving or, as Asher et al. (1990) has suggested, being able to relate one's goals to one's strategies. These are the skills children learn with emotion-coaching parents, but they are not applied isomorphically to the peer world. They involve the child knowing something about the world of emotion, her own as well as others. This knowledge arises only out of emotional connection being important in the home.

We suggest that the child in middle childhood who has been emotion coached by parents has developed a general set of skills that appear to have nothing to do with expressing and understanding one's own feelings. However, they have to do with the ability to inhibit negative affect, with being able to self-soothe, with being able to focus attention (including social attention), and with being able to regulate one's own emotions. In middle childhood, these abilities are manifested by the inhibition of displays of distress and by the inhibition of aggression when teased. Instead the child who has been emotion coached acts emotionally unflappable and is able to enter an ongoing peer group with ease and awareness instead of with the lumbering bravado of the socially rejected child.

We think that it will eventually turn out that these emotion regulation abilities are, to some extent, temperamental but to a greater extent, we think that they are shaped by parents—beginning in infancy. This shaping begins in parents' ability to deal with an infant's distress with affection and comfort (Dunn, 1977) and continues into the face-to-face play with the infant in the first year of life (Gianino & Tronick, 1988; Stern, 1985). This thinking is consistent with many current theorists' writings about social and emotional development in infancy and the role of face-to-face interaction of infants and parents, work we will review later in this chapter. We predicted and found pathways from our meta-emotion variables to the child's physiological responses during emotion-arousing situations in the laboratory parent-child interaction and in our emotion-eliciting films.

Child Regulatory Physiology and Child Health

In our research, we constructed an emotion regulation theory in which we discussed two opponent processes in the child's autonomic nervous system: the vagal *brake* and the sympathetic *accelerator*. Crudely speaking, the vagal brake slows many physiological processes, such as the heart's rate, down, while the sympathetic accelerator acts to speed them up. Each of these processes influences emotion regulation.

Research by Porges and his colleagues (1972, 1973, 1984) on the PNS indicates a strong association between high vagal tone and good attentional abilities, and there is evidence that these processes are related to emotion regulation abilities (e.g., Fox, 1989; Fox & Field, 1989). Porges also showed that baseline vagal tone is related to reactivity as well as to regulatory processes, and the suppression of vagal tone appears to be a necessary physiological state for sustained attention.

In a series of programmatic studies, Porges and his associates demonstrated that a child's baseline vagal tone is related to the child's capacity to focus attention, to react, and to self-regulate (Porges, 1972, 1973, 1984). Fox (1989) found that infants who had higher basal vagal tone were more likely to cry during mild arm restraint than infants lower in vagal tone. This relationship of basal vagal tone to reactivity is usually associated with greater regulatory abilities as well.

We found that basal vagal tone at age five was a predictor of fewer child illnesses at age eight, and the ability to suppress vagal tone at age five was a predictor of more child illnesses at age eight. This differential prediction of illness from the two vagal tone variables is interesting, particularly since the ability to suppress vagal tone may indicate a pattern of the child's active engagement with cognitively or affectively stressful events. The child who can suppress vagal tone may seek out challenges that imply a more stressful daily life, which has the cost of suppressing the child's production of T-cells

Adding to Ginott

We have refined Ginott's thinking through specificity and simplification. First, we have delineated the five steps of emotion coaching, which are all we think that we need to teach parents:

- awareness of less intense emotions in self and child
- seeing these emotions as an opportunity for intimacy or teaching
- communicating empathy and understanding of the emotions, even if these emotions underlie misbehavior
- helping the child verbally label the emotions
- Setting limits on behavior (not feelings or wishes) and problem solving

Second, we have supplied research data. These data have added a fundamental concept, the concept of meta-emotion. To this, we add the understanding of people's metaphors about emotion and how these guide a parent's response to the child's emotions.

Third, we have discovered the father's importance in the child's emotional development. In all of our path models, the father's variables were much more powerful in predicting child outcomes. This is because there was three times the variability in the father's behavior than in the mother's. Mothers tended to be more positive and have less variability. Fathers were capable of doing great harm as well as great good in their children's emotional and social development, and we think this means that there are emotionally intelligent fathers out there.

Fourth, we have understood the impact of the parental marriage on parenting. The amazing thing we discovered in this regard is that, when parents are emotion coaching, there is not a trade-off between the marriage and the parenting. They are all of one fabric, and we are beginning to find in our clinical work that training parents in EC helps marriages. Parents who are EC with their children become EC in their marriages. Also, fathers who are involved with their children's emotional worlds are more involved in the family in general, and the partnership between spouses is enormously strengthened. The linkages were strong between marital and parent-child interaction processes. Parents who coached their children were less likely to be contemptuous of their partners during conflict discussions and were generally more positive and more constructive than those who were dismissing of emotion. While we have explored only negative affects to date, we are now studying people's relationships with pride and love. These also seem to play a major role in families' emotional systems.

Fifth, we have expanded and corroborated Ginott's interest in teaching kids. We already discussed the two styles of teaching we discovered with Vanessa Kahen's coding of parent-child teaching interactions. These results parallel Ginott's ideas in working with teachers. Derogatory parenting, labeling the child's character, and intrusiveness, have strong negative effects on child outcomes.

Sixth, our focus on the child's regulatory physiology is entirely new, as is the seventh contribution we have made, which is a focus on attention. Attention is turning out to be the most sensitive lead indicator for school failure and for the development of a wide range of child psychopathologies.

Eighth is our emphasis on the child's peer world. We are interested in the development of the child's social competence, and emotional intelligence is our key construct in understanding this important developmental outcome. It has proven itself to be the best predictor of adult functioning that we can obtain from childhood assessments.

Finally, we have discovered that emotion coaching buffers children from nearly all the negative consequences of a hostile or a dissolving marriage, including school performance, peer relations, the development of behavior problems, and infectious illnesses. It does not, however, buffer children from sadness and anxiety in their daily moods. We think that it takes only one parent to be an emotion coach for these effects to be obtained, although we also discovered that discrepancy between parents in their philosophies of emotion coaching or dismissing is highly predictive of divorce.

References

Asher, S. R., & Coie, J. D. (Eds.). (1990). *Peer rejection in childhood*. New York: Cambridge University Press.

Asher, S. R., Parkhurst, J. T., Hymel, S., & Williams, G. A. (1990). Peer rejection and loneliness in childhood. In S. R. Asher & J. D. Coie (Eds.), *Peer Rejection in childhood* (pp. 253–273). New York: Cambridge University Press.

Corsaro, W. (1979). We're friends, right? Children's use of access rituals in a nursery school. *Language in Society, 8,* 315–336.

Corsaro, W. (1981). Friendship in the nursery school: Social organization in the peer environment. In S. Asher and J. M. Gottman (Eds.), *The development of children's friendships*. New York: Cambridge University Press.

Dunn, J. (1977). *Distress and comfort*. Cambridge, MA: Harvard University Press.

Fox, N. A. (1989). The psychophysiological correlates of emotional reactivity during the first year of life. *Developmental Psychology, 25,* 364–372.

Fox, N. A., & Field, T. M. (1989). Individual differences in preschool entry behavior. *Journal of Applied Developmental Psychology, 10,* 527–540.

Fraiberg, S. (1959). *The magic years*. New York: Scribner's.

Garber, J., & Dodge, K. A. (Eds.). (1991). *The development of emotion regulation and dysregulation*.New York: Cambridge University Press.

Gianino, A., & Tronick, E. Z. (1988). The mutual regulation model: The infant's self and interactive regulation and coping and defensive capacities. In T. M. Field, P. M. McCabe, & N. Schneiderman (Eds.), *Stress and coping across development* (pp. 47–70). Hillsdale, NJ: Lawrence Erlbaum.

Ginott, H. G. (1965). *Between parent and child*. New York: Avon.

Ginott, H. G. (1971). *Between parent and teenager*. New York: Avon.

Ginott, H. G. (1975). *Teacher and child*. New York: Avon.

Goleman, D. (1995). *Emotional intelligence*. New York: Bantam Books.

Gottman, J. M. (1983). How children become friends. *Monographs of the Society for Research in Child Development, 48*(2, Serial No. 201).

Gottman, J. M., Katz, L., & Hooven, C. (1995). *Meta-emotion*. Hillsdale, NJ: Lawrence Erlbaum.

Gottman, J. M., & Parker, J. (Eds.). (1986). *Conversations of friends*. New York: Cambridge University Press.

Guralnick, M. J. (1981). Peer influences on the development of communicative competence. In P. Strain (Ed.), *The utilization of classroom peers as behavior change agents* (pp. 31–68). New York: Plenum.

Keyes, R. (Ed.). (1992). *Sons on fathers*. New York: HarperCollins.

Kramer, L., & Gottman, J. (1992). Becoming a sibling: "With a little help from my friends." *Developmental Psychology, 28,* 685–699.

Parker, J. G., & Asher, S. R. (1987). Peer relations and later personal adjustment: Are low-accepted children at risk? *Psychological Bulletin, 102,* 357–389.

Porges, S. W. (1972), Heart rate variability and deceleration as indices of reaction time. *Journal of Experimental Psychology, 92,* 103–110.

Porges, S. W. (1973). Heart rate variability: An autonomic correlate of reaction time performance. *Bulletin of the Psychonomics Society, 1,* 270–272.

Porges, S. W. (1984). Heart rate oscillation: An index of neural mediation. In M. G. H. Coles, J. R. Jennings, & J. A. Stern (Eds.), *Psychophysiological perspectives: Festschrift for Beatrice and John Lacey*. New York: Van Nostrand Reinhold.

Salovey, P., & Mayer, J. D. (1990). Emotional intelligence. *Imagination, Cognition and Personality, 9,* 185–211.

Stern, D. N. (1985). *The interpersonal world of the infant: A view from psychoanalysis and developmental psychology*. New York: Basic.

Stifter, C. A., & Fox, N. A. (1990). Infant reactivity: Physiological correlates of newborn and 5-month temperament. *Developmental Psychology, 26*, 582–588.

Stifter, C. A., Fox, N. A., & Porges, S. W. (1989). Facial expressivity and vagal tone in 5- and 10-month-old infants. *Infant Behavior and Development, 12*, 127–137.

Commentary

Victoria von Sadovszky & Kathryn E. Angell

Gottman has proposed a theory of emotion regulation that links parents' feelings and thoughts about emotions (i.e., meta-emotion; Gottman, Katz, & Hooven, 1996) to children's competence level in peer relationships, infectious illnesses, and other important developmental outcomes. We first review this theory and the supporting evidence Gottman cites. Then, we place Gottman's research within the context of the larger body of research on emotions, social relationships, and health presented in this volume, giving special attention to the themes of the conference (emotion, gender differences, social relationships, mechanisms, and cumulative effects). In so doing, we evaluate Gottman's unique contribution to this emerging field. We also identify ways in which Gottman's theory might be extended or refined in light of other relevant findings and suggest how future research might be designed to rigorously test Gottman's hypotheses and address the new questions we raise.

Gottman's Contribution

After establishing a program of research in which he was able to predict divorce or marital stability with remarkable accuracy (Buehlman, Gottman, & Katz, 1992), Gottman embarked on a new direction, which is concerned with the effects of marital conflict on children. The stated purpose of this body of research is to search for "buffers against the deleterious effects of marital conflict on children." From this work, influential findings emerge that could have a considerable impact on the way we view emotion, social relationships, and health. First, Gottman has discovered that there are different parenting styles in terms of emotion. Second, he has found that parents with different styles teach their children about emotions differently, thus affecting their social relationships. Finally, Gottman makes some links to the physiological and psychological health of these children based on the different parenting styles.

The conceptual cornerstone of Gottman's work is meta-emotion, which he refers to as our emotions about our emotions or the feelings and thoughts about emotions. Gottman, from pilot work, found that parents had different philosophies when it came to communication about emotion with their children. From these observations of variations in the way parents view emotions, Gottman proposed two distinct parenting styles: emotion coaching and emotion dismissing. An emotion-coaching parent is more likely to notice lower intensity emotions in his children, to view negative affect as healthy and as an opportunity for teaching, to communicate understanding and empathy, to help his child to label emotions, and to set clear limits on behavior through problem-solving techniques. In contrast, emotion-dismissing parents are more likely not to exhibit or use these same characteristics. For example, ED parents will not notice lower intensity emotions in their children. They also see negative affect as toxic and harmful and, thus, try to protect their children from these emotions or ignore them altogether. ED parents do not have a detailed language of emotions and view exploration of negative emotions as a waste of time. Hence, in reference to the two parenting styles, the emphasis is on how the parent views and confronts the emotion.

Most interesting is how these two different parenting styles deal with negative affect, such as anger. The parents in each group, EC or ED, had different metaphors for anger. For instance, ED parents equate anger with losing control, violence, aggression, or selfishness; EC parents view anger as natural and as a block to goals. Thus, the way each person views emotion gives insight into how much exploration or time a parent will take in exploring that emotion with her child.

This is an important finding, which has great theoretical and practical application. However, this is primarily based upon pilot work. Gottman does not detail the number of observations he has made regarding parents who have these different styles, nor does he reveal how these different styles are measured. It appears that many of these observations were made in a laboratory setting, and application to naturalistic settings of daily life should be explored further.

The second intriguing finding Gottman has described is the different ways parents teach their children, which is also determined by their parenting style. Gottman sees his work as an empirical rediscovery of Ginott's insights on discipline and the teaching of children. Gottman highlights three points that Ginott (1965, 1971, 1975) made about parent-child teaching styles. Ginott hypothesized that parents who focused on discipline would raise children who contemplated immoral acts in a cost-benefit fashion or in a way in which there was no internal code based on ethics, values, or justice. Second, he theorized that children needed to be aware of their parents' emotions. This awareness of emotions, if not manifested as a character assault, would lead to a greater understanding of how emotions are experienced and ultimately serve to help discipline children. Finally, Ginott felt that the best way to learn about emotion was to learn while experiencing the emotion. These basic tenets of Ginott are often referred to in Gottman's work.

Gottman found that the parents in his study had different teaching styles, which would lend support to Ginott's claims. In a teaching situation, EC parents gave their child enough information to get started, presented it in a calm manner, were not involved in the child's mistakes, and then would praise the child's performance. Conversely, ED parents got overinvolved in the teaching situation by giving their child a lot of information in an excited manner, criticizing the child when he made a mistake, and escalating the criticisms to character attacks. What Gottman has substantiated of Ginott's theory is the concept of "teaching in the moment." In other words, teaching the emotion and demonstrating the behavior. While teaching children in a calm manner, EC parents are demonstrating to their children how to approach challenging situations positively. The ED parents, on the other hand, are teaching their children that challenging situations are negative and produce much frustration and embarrassment. How these parenting styles translate into discipline and moral reasoning by the child is unelucidated in this preliminary work. Furthermore, Gottman viewed these parents and children interacting in a lab and with one specific task, teaching a video game. Questions can be raised whether EC and ED parents always teach this way and if they exhibit these behaviors in different contexts. Further exploration of this is certainly warranted by the findings presented in Gottman's work. From anecdotal examples that Gottman cites, he seemingly has some evidence, albeit on that level, that these parenting styles are stable over time and do have profound effects upon the child, which can last into adulthood. Gottman illustrates the negative effects that an ED parent can have on the memory of children, even into their adulthood. He does not make any conclusions about the memories of children who have been emotion coached, nor does he refer to them.

Gottman claims that EC requires no special skills beyond treating people as you would a guest in your home. The reason why people do not practice this with their children is what Gottman calls the *parental agenda*. In other words, parents infuse a moral lesson into their interaction rather than coaching the child emotionally or attempting to understand the child's emotions at the moment. Gottman specifically cites an example of a mother who has lost her child in a store. In his example, the mother's parental agenda takes over, and she engages in emotion dismissing. The assumption, with this and other examples Gottman furnishes, is that parents can instantaneously regulate their own emotions in stressful situations. This may be the case, but under which contextual circumstances, including which variations of emotional intensity? These aspects have not been explored.

The last major finding that Gottman has contributed to our understanding is the links he makes to health. Gottman has discovered some exciting connections, which offer insight into the mechanisms of how parents' emotion philosophies can influence their children's health.

One of the many intriguing ideas that Gottman has put forth is that EC children have fewer infectious illnesses. Although the exact mechanisms by which this occurs is under exploration in his work, Gottman posits a theory. Building on Porges (1995), Gottman has found that children who are EC have higher baseline vagal tone. Gottman believes that this higher vagal tone leads to better innervation of the thymus, better T-cell maturation, and thus, more effective immunity to infectious illnesses. Porges (1973 to 1984) found that children who have a higher baseline vagal tone are able to focus attention and to regulate their emotions better than children with a lower vagal tone. Gottman believes that EC causes a better vagal tone, because children who are EC are better able to emotionally regulate themselves. According to Gottman, EC could act as a behavioral buffer against illnesses by teaching children which social situations will elicit more stress. For example, Gottman theorizes that EC children have a higher vagal tone and that they are also more aware of their environment. This awareness of their environment will lead to better emotional regulation in stressful situations and thus—because emotional regulation, vagal tone, and the thymus are interconnected, according to Gottman—a better T-cell maturation in the thymus. Conversely, children who are not emotion coached suppress their vagal tone, thereby causing them to seek challenges that will increase their stress, thus suppressing their T-cell maturation and leading to illnesses. Evidence to support these claims lies in the future. At this point, no clear link has been established between vagal tone and T-cell maturation or activity in infectious illnesses. The theoretical link that Gottman makes here is certainly interesting and justifies further exploration. However, this link should be explored along with others, such as the possibility that EC children, who are better at regulating emotion and stress, may have lower levels of glucocorticoids and neuroendocrine markers, which prior research has shown to influence natural killer cell function and to affect immunity.

Interestingly, Gottman states that the emotional regulation abilities he has studied are only somewhat related to temperamental traits. He believes that emotion regulation abilities are shaped from infancy by the child's parents. Certainly, he has evidence of this mutable regulatory function in adults. The evidence he gives to support this claim is that ED parents undergoing his emotion-coaching interventions in parenting groups do, in fact, change their views of emotion in their lives and marriages when they try emotion coaching. Gottman reveals this finding and interpretation without any other supporting evidence. It is an important finding and one that deserves much more attention as it has broad implications for clinical practice and further research.

Gottman also cites evidence about the cumulative effects of emotion coaching on children's lives. Beyond acute infectious illnesses, Gottman has found evidence that emotion coaching can have long-term effects on behavior, academic performance, and social relationships.

Gottman has found that children who have been emotion coached are able to focus attention better on tasks. They also have higher reading and math scores, when controlled for IQ. These children have fewer behavioral problems and better peer relations. Again, this is another interesting finding, which deserves more attention. Gottman does not elaborate on how long-lasting are the effects of EC on academic performance, behavioral problems, and social relationships. Longitudinal analyses would be interesting to see if EC can buffer children against deleterious behaviors, such as drug use, or if it can enhance future academic and professional performance and continue to assist with social relationships. Gottman does not offer the cumulative effects of an ED style on children and whether there are significant differences between EC children and ED children.

Gottman proposes that the reason EC children have better social relationships is based on development of an emotional intelligence as described by Goleman (1995). According to Gottman, EC children have developed a social awareness that allows them to "psych out" social situations and to act accordingly. EC children are better able to resolve conflicts, play for extended periods of time, and empathize with their peers. This gives them an edge when dealing with peers, even in middle childhood, when using EC skills, such as disclosing emotion, could potentially cause the child to be the object of teasing and embarrassment.

Gottman claims that these children have social awareness and are able to act like they have had an "emotion-ectomy" and maintain control in these social situations. However, these exact links are not elaborated upon and still need to be explored.

In sum, Gottman and colleagues have discovered stylistic philosophies of emotions that can have profound consequences on the psychological, academic, and physical health of children as well as salutary effects on marriages. Opportunities for future knowledge development are discussed in the final sections of this commentary.

Gottman and the Themes of this Volume

As with all exciting programs of research and discovery, there are often as many questions as answers posed by Gottman's work. This section outlines some opportunities for future research that are directly related to the themes of this volume: emotion, gender differences, social relationships, cumulative effects, and causal mechanisms. Opportunities where other researchers' work could add to Gottman's program of study are also discussed.

Emotion

Unlike many in his field, Gottman does not see negative emotion as fundamentally toxic. Instead, and to his credit, he has shown that it is how individuals stylistically approach and process negative emotions that is the critical factor. By defining the metaphors and styles of EC and ED parents and by showing how EC children have positive health effects, he has implied that negative emotions can actually be healthy. What is not clear from his work, however, is what happens with positive emotions. What are the metaphors used by both styles of parenting for positive emotions? Do EC and ED parents differ in their coaching or examination of positive emotions with their children and in their own relationships? And, specifically referring to Ginott (1965, 1971, 1975), is validation of positive emotions just as important as validation of negative ones?

Gottman's theory and findings have important implications for practitioners across many disciplines. One particularly useful finding, which has great implication for practice, is the ability to assess the EC and ED parenting styles, thereby affording directions for intervention. However, these assessments raise questions. How are they measured? What is the cross-time stability of these emotion-coaching and emotion-dismissing styles? Further, is having an EC style always conducive to positive outcomes, and does an ED style always contribute to negative outcomes?

Finally, Gottman's research does not provide a clear distinction between emotion regulation as a heritable trait and emotion regulation as a developmental process. Traditionally, temperament has been viewed as an inborn characteristic of how individuals regulate their emotions (Kagan, 1996; Rothbart & Ahadi, 1994); however, Gottman proposes a new theory of emotion regulation. He finds that children who are emotion coached have better regulation of emotion, and he draws a link to the way they have been taught. Furthermore, he has also found that adults in his parenting groups can change the way they view emotions, once taught, and act upon this change. This brings to the forefront the debate of trait versus developmental perspectives on personality, and on which side (if not both) does emotion regulation fall? For instance, do children who are emotion coached have better vagal tone and better emotion regulation because they have inherited such dispositional tendencies from their parents? Conversely, can those who are ED actually change their emotion regulation and thereby possibly change associated physiological mechanisms (vagal tone)? These are interventive questions of powerful significance. As a clinician, Gottman presumably believes such changes are possible, but they have as yet to be empirically demonstrated.

Gottman can add to his work by utilizing some of the other researchers' work in this volume, specifically Reis's work. For Gottman, *which* emotion is experienced seemingly is not as important as *how* it is experienced by the parent-child dyad. This connection is insightful, and, certainly, there is evidence to support that the cognitive processing, rather than a total focus on the emotional processing, of negative events is less stressful and conducive to a higher level of functioning (Johnson, Fieler, Jones, Wlasowicz, & Mitchell, 1997). The perception of the experience of the emotion between the parent and the child is the interactional component that is most significant in Gottman's work. However, Reis postulates that the emotion experienced can have an effect on intimacy and attachment in human relationships. Thus, what are the specific emotional end products of emotion-coaching and emotion-dismissing interactions, and how do they affect the next interaction and intimacy between the parent and child? Extrapolating when individuals emotion coach and/or dismiss, under what circumstances, and the effects of these styles are paramount in determining the broader applications of Gottman's work. Reis's technique of keeping diaries would be a strong self-report measure, which could be employed to answer several of these questions.

Another important aspect of the interaction of the emotion and parenting style is how the participants within the interaction experience the interaction, both in the moment and over time. More of this will be discussed in later sections.

Gender Differences

How does gender influence meta-emotion? In the context of parent-child interactions, both parent gender and child gender could potentially affect both parent behaviors and child behaviors. Gottman briefly discusses the greater variability of fathers' relative to mothers' behaviors and the resulting greater association of fathers' behaviors with child emotional development. Below we discuss two other ways in which gender and meta-emotion processes could intersect to affect health outcomes.

Emotion-Coach Gender: Potential Effects for Parent and Child   How much time do mothers versus fathers spend emotion coaching their children? Traditional gender roles would submit that emotion coaching is the mother's responsibility. Acting consistently with these gender role prescriptions could hold important social and health implications for both parents and children. For women, providing social support while receiving little in return is a potentially important source of stress (Belle, 1982; Kessler, McLeod, & Wethington, 1984). Seeman and McEwen (1996) suggest that, for women, these greater relationship costs may compromise the health benefits associated with social relationships. This would explain why (1) emotional support is significantly associated with lower endocrine activity in men but not in women (Seeman, Berkman, Blazer, & Rowe, 1994), and (2) social ties may be more strongly associated with lower mortality risks for men (House, Landis, & Umberson, 1988; Kaplan, et al., 1988). In addition, if mothers spend more time emotion coaching their children, then children may learn to associate emotion and emotion coaching with being female. Traditional gender roles could be perpetuated intergenerationally via role models, with girls taking greater responsibility for learning and implementing emotion coaching of peers and future children and disproportionately incurring the related health costs mentioned above. On the other hand, associating emotion with being female might counteract the lessons of emotion coaching for boys, such that health benefits (e.g., increased vagal tone) are abated.

Child Gender: Potential Moderator of Meta-Emotion Techniques Gottman and colleagues identified the five steps of emotion coaching:

> a) [parents being] aware of low intensity emotions in themselves and in their children; b) [parents viewing] the child's negative emotion as an opportunity for intimacy or teaching; c) [parents validating] their child's emotion; d) [parents assisting] the child in verbally labeling the child's emotions; and e) [parents problem solving] with the child, setting behavioral limits, and discussing goals and strategies for dealing with the situation that led to the negative emotion. (Gottman, Katz, & Hooven, 1996, p. 244)

How might child gender influence each of these steps? Plant, Hyde, Keltner, and Devine (2000) found that, of 19 emotions studied, women were stereotyped as experiencing nine (e.g., sadness, fear, love) more than men, and men were only stereotyped as experiencing one (pride) more than women.[1] Thus, baseline expectations that a given individual experiences an emotion are gender *and* emotion specific. These expectations may influence parents' judgments about whether their son or daughter is experiencing an emotion in Gottman's first step of emotion coaching.

As such, parents might be primed to detect many low intensity emotions, such as sadness, fear, and love, in daughters, whereas they might more easily perceive pride in sons. A parent cannot view an emotion as an opportunity for intimacy, teaching, or validating, as prescribed in steps *b* and *c*, if she has not acknowledged the emotion in step *a*. Moreover, emotion stereotypes can serve both descriptive and prescriptive functions. That is, these stereotypes imply both that males *are* less emotional than females, and that males *ought to be* less emotional than females. Consequently, emotion stereotypes may guide parents to unwittingly foster greater expression of emotion or expression of different emotions in daughters relative to sons.

In the fourth step of emotion coaching, the parent helps the child verbally label the emotion. Two studies provide evidence that people label others' emotions differently depending upon the gender, or perceived gender, of the other person. Plant and colleagues (2000) used the Facial Action Coding System (Ekman & Friesen, 1976, 1978) to create slides of men and women portraying physiologically equivalent facial expressions. Participants interpreted ambiguous (both sad and angry) facial expressions as displaying greater sadness for women than men and greater anger for men than women. Furthermore, the unambiguous anger-only expression was interpreted as mixed sadness and anger for women but predominantly as anger for men. Given the equivalent facial expressions, gender stereotypes apparently influenced the participants' interpretations of facial expressions. Similarly, Condry and Condry (1976) found that college students interpreted an infant's ambiguous behavior as indicating more anger if they thought that the infant was a boy and indicating more fear if they thought the infant was a girl. Since the same videotaped segment of the same infant was used for both the male and female target conditions, the difference in labeling emotions must necessarily stem from the presumed gender of the child. Plant et al. (2000) found a similar pattern of results using Lamaze class members—but only for male participants who had strongly held stereotypes and only for the perception of anger. Together, these studies indicate that, even once a behavior has been identified as reflecting emotion in general, children may be coached to label their emotions differently based upon their gender. This tendency may depend upon how strongly parents hold stereotypes.

Finally, in the fifth step of emotion coaching—problem solving and setting behavioral limits—the appropriate strategies and limits might be determined in part by the stereotype's prescription for boys' versus girls' behavior. That is, problem-solving guidance or the specific behavioral limits set for physical aggression or crying might be different depending upon the gender of the child.

The evidence and reasoning cited above suggest that parental EC processes may well be influenced by gender stereotypes. Parents are likely to exhibit lower thresholds in identifying a number of emotions for girls, preferentially validate gender-stereotype–consistent emotions, and be biased by gender stereotypes when labeling the emotions that underlie ambiguous behaviors.

How could gender bias in emotion coaching affect health outcomes? Gottman cited prior findings that children with emotion-coaching parents reap substantial social, cognitive, and health benefits. These include higher vagal tone and fewer infectious illnesses, greater attentional capacity and higher math and reading achievement scores, and fewer behavior problems and better relations with peers. To the degree that boys are perceived as less emotional in general than girls, they may receive less emotion coaching than girls. To the degree that girls' emotions are mislabeled, their emotion coaching may serve them less than optimally. In both cases, the social, cognitive, and health benefits of emotion coaching may be compromised.

Theories of emotion provide further clues about how emotion coaching could affect health. Several researchers have proposed that emotion functions to provide important feedback to the self and others (e.g., Clore, 1994; Frijda, 1994; Levensen, 1994). Averill (1994) further emphasizes that specific emotions serve different functions. For example, anger may prevent a triggering situation from recurring (Averill, 1982) whereas sadness might evoke nurturance. Consequently, when emotions go undetected or are misperceived, they are less likely to serve their functions. The resulting unmet needs may lead to decreased emotional or instrumental support, which may, in turn, have negative health implications. For example, if boys' sadness is not perceived, they may be less likely to receive the nurturance that sadness often evokes. If girls' anger is mislabeled as sadness, it may not function to prevent the triggering situation from recurring but may evoke nurturance instead. The miscommunication of emotion feedback could result in women receiving less instrumental support. For example, a women who expresses anger but is perceived as sad about an abusive relationship may receive comfort (nurturance) instead of help with procuring a restraining order (instrumental support). These examples depict how failures in emotion coaching can lead to decreased emotional or instrumental support. Lower emotional support has been associated with higher levels of self-reported health symptoms (Ryff and Singer et al., chapter 5) and greater atherosclerosis (Seeman & Syme, 1987). Lower instrumental support has been associated with greater atherosclerosis as well (Seeman & Syme, 1987). Thus, gender stereotypes could lead to gender-biased emotion coaching, which teaches individuals or observers to misinterpret feedback regarding the emotions experienced. This miscommunication may compromise instrumental and emotional support, thereby leading to negative health outcomes.

Social Relationships

Contributors to this volume have assessed social relationships in three different ways: (1) measures of the individual's social network, such as the number or type of life domains represented in the social network (Cohen, Seeman) or group membership (Spiegel and Kimerling); (2) participants' feelings and perceptions stemming from their social relationships, such as the feeling of being loved (Seeman), perceived intimacy and satisfaction (Reis), or feeling understood or supported (Ryff, Singer, Wing, and Love); (3) behaviors that occur within the context of social interactions (Gottman, Ryff and Singer et al., Seeman). Social behavior variables play the most vital role in Gottman's research: they are the foundation of his theory of meta-emotion, are assessed directly via third-party observation, and are coded using standardized coding schemes.

In their research on meta-emotion, Gottman, Katz, and Hooven (1996) examined parent behaviors, such as respecting the child's emotional experience and comforting the child, to determine whether the parent was coaching or dismissing the child's emotions. This distinction was then linked to social, cognitive, and health outcomes. Similarly, in research on long-term couples, Gottman and Levensen's behavior variables, such as assent, put-downs, and defensiveness, were used to predict health outcomes and risk of marital dissolution (Gottman & Levensen, 1992; Krokoff, Gottman, & Hass, 1989).

Cohen and Seeman both identify unresolved questions from their research involving social network variables. Could using Gottman's social behavior variables help demystify their results? Cohen found a positive association between range of social relationships and resisting viral infection. However, two findings were contrary to his predictions: (1) his social network range variables were not associated with epinephrine and norepinephrine levels, and (2) he found no evidence that natural killer cell activity mediated the link between social environment and susceptibility to colds. In reviewing the literature, Seeman found conflicting evidence regarding whether an association exists between social integration and coronary heart disease. She suggested that discrepancies may stem from the potential for greater social integration to sometimes produce greater interpersonal conflict, thereby leading to worse health outcomes. Would social behavior measures, such as those used by Gottman and colleagues, produce the same perplexing patterns of results for Cohen and Seeman?

Cohen and Seeman both point out that social relationships can serve both to provide support and to provoke distress. However, measures of social networks are based on counts of social relationships, without regard to whether a given relationship is distress provoking or supportive. Consequently, lumping together social stressors and sources of social support under a singular "social integration" (or social environment) heading could account for inconsistent findings, since social stressors and social support would likely exert opposing influences on both emotions and health. In contrast to these measures, Gottman's social behavior variables specifically characterize the nature of the social interactions and tease apart the social stress variables from social support variables.

If the critical variable is social behaviors—not social network size—why, then, was Cohen able to establish a relationship between social environment and viral infection? A larger social network may imply a broader range of social relationships from which to choose. Potentially, then, individuals with wider social networks may have the luxury of choosing to spend more time with those people who provide greater social support, and ultimately, this could contribute to better health outcomes.

More generally, Gottman's approach of examining the actual behaviors that occur within the context of social interactions is important for linking social relationships to emotions and health outcomes for several reasons: (1) Behavior is a key element of social relationships. Gottman argues that the behavioral content of the interaction, that is, EC or ED behaviors, may moderate the link between emotion and health. (2) Social psychology has repeatedly demonstrated that people are not always able to accurately identify factors that influence their own thoughts and perceptions. By neglecting to independently measure the social environment, key social relationship variables (such as marital relationship quality), which likely affect emotion and health, may be overlooked. (3) Observable and operationally defined behaviors represent a concrete modifiable target for focusing potential interventions designed to improve health. For example, Gottman suggests that employing the five steps of emotion coaching may actually improve children's vagal tone. (4) When the behaviors are coded by trained observers, a common metric is established, and social relationship characteristics are independent of current mood or health status. (5) Description of specific behaviors that occur within a relationship provide rich details regarding the nature of that social interaction. For example, Gottman and Levensen (1992) defined *nonregulated* married couples as having a greater number of specific negative (e.g., put-downs, defensiveness, escalating negative affect) relative to positive (e.g., assent, humor-laughter) interaction patterns. *Regulated* couples were defined as showing the reverse pattern. They found that nonregulated couples demonstrated greater risk for marital dissolution and reported worse health four years later than regulated couples. The significance of marital interaction quality could not have been detected from analyses using a simple marital status variable.

Gottman's social behavior variables may be able to elucidate links between social relationships and health where social network size measures cannot. Thus, the literature that links social relationships to emotions and health needs to extend beyond a description of the number and range of social relationships to include information about what actually occurs within the context of social relationships.

Because subjective feelings and perceptions about one's social network are likely linked—if not more proximal—to emotion and health outcomes, they represent important intervening variables to be examined. However, these feelings and perceptions represent a composite of the existing social environment and the individual's interpretation of it. How do individuals come to feel and perceive the way they do? The answer would likely involve independently examining the individual's social context using an approach such as Gottman's.

A complete description of the interplay of social relationships, emotion, and health, then, would need to include all three aspects of social relationships listed above: measures of the social network, standardized measurements of social interaction behaviors, and subjective perceptions and thoughts about the social relationships. Moreover, a more in-depth understanding would also include specification of how these aspects of social relationships relate to each other as well as to emotions and health. Do children who experience emotion coaching perceive greater social support than children who experience emotion dismissing? The answer requires comparing Gottman's EC behavior measures and Reis's relationship satisfaction variables. Spiegel and Kimerling suggest that emotional expression was a critical aspect of the breast cancer support groups. Could teaching group members to emotion coach each other increase longevity? Measuring group members' EC and ED behaviors in breast cancer support groups versus control groups matched on initial health status would be a first step in identifying the life-promoting elements of Spiegel's and Kimerling's group. Then, the potential of Gottman's EC and ED measures to predict longevity and other health outcomes could be tested. Is it the interactions within the closest relationships or the overall size and structure of one's social network that is more predictive of health outcomes? Gottman's EC and ED measures could be compared to Cohen's social environment measures in their ability to predict hormonal levels, natural killer cell activity, and, ultimately, susceptibility to viral infection. Establishing the interconnections among the different types of social relationship measures will help establish a common language for social relationships and foster theoretical links and cross-talk among the different research programs.

Cumulative Effects

The benefits that EC children experience appear to be extended over time as are the long-term effects on children who have been raised in ED home's. Gottman alludes to long-term psychological consequences in a variety of case studies. However, broader, more systematic evidence is not provided. For example, Gottman finds that children who have been emotion coached do have fewer illnesses; however, is this related to a parenting style that promotes a healthier lifestyle in general (e.g., regular, balanced meals, appropriate sleeping schedules)? Gottman could enhance his research in this area by linking emotion coaching to individuals with more pathological disorders like those studied by other authors in this volume (Spiegel and Kimerling, Seeman). Spiegel and Kimerling's study of women with breast cancer and the effects of support groups in increasing longevity may provide more support for Gottman's work. In fact, as previously mentioned, it may be that in Spiegel and Kimerling's groups, emotion coaching was being practiced by the participants. By longitudinally following a group of individuals with some pathology, Gottman may be able to see the effects of his therapy on a more dramatic scale. Seeman found that instrumental support was associated with lowered heart rate, systolic blood pressure, serum cholesterol, and urine norepinephrine. These are important physiological measures, which Gottman could use longitudinally to see the effects of emotion coaching on specific individuals or family units. Furthermore, as with Spiegel and Kimerling's work, Seeman's finding of instrumental support may indeed be closely linked with emotion-coaching styles of communication.

On the other side of this issue is: what are the negative health consequences of emotion coaching? For instance, Gottman claims that society is largely emotion dismissing. How does this affect emotion-coaching individuals? Are they able to maintain a lower stress level longitudinally? Ryff, Singer, Wing, and Love's work would overlap nicely here. Ryff, Singer, and colleagues study the cumulative effects of allostatic load. Gottman, again longitudinally, could employ some of these physiological measures along with Ryff's multidimensional model of well-being to see the physiological and psychological effects of emotion coaching in a society that does not support such a concept.

Mechanisms

Gottman offers interesting hypotheses about the mechanisms by which EC may influence health. Speaking to impressive multimethod strategies, the measures include not only observational and self-report data about the effects of EC on children but also some physiological assessments. That EC children have better vagal tone, better emotion regulation, and better attentional focusing is most promising, along with the data on infectious illnesses. Gottman hypothesizes that EC causes better vagal tone and, in the long run, through affecting innervation of the thymus, higher T-cell maturation. This proposed causal link is worthy of serious scientific scrutiny. First, the specific physiological links need to be explored. Second, it suggests that parents, through EC, can powerfully influence the health of their child, by enhancing the child's immune system. Gottman could use Coe and Lubach's and Cohen's work here to further explicate the physiological processes that may be enhancing the immune system. Coe and Lubach found that increased agitation in their nonhuman primate sample compromised the immune system as measured by increased lymphocyte proliferation, lowered cytotoxic activity, and lowered antibody responses. Similarly, Cohen used natural killer cells, a close cousin of T-cells, as a marker of immune function in his participants. Although using natural killer cells are not a direct measure of T-cells and thus not a direct measure of Gottman's theory on vagal function, these markers of immune function are more comprehensive. Hence, Gottman could use them on an exploratory basis to provide some empirical evidence to support his hypothesized link to actual immune function outcomes.

Conversely, Gottman could strengthen his association of parenting styles with health outcomes by examining the effects of ED parenting styles on children's negative health outcomes. The empirical differences between ED and EC groups need to be mapped. Are children who have been raised in an emotion-dismissing home more likely to be ill? What types of illnesses are occurring in these children? And are the illnesses actually related to emotion-dismissing styles or to other factors, such as a lack of health-promoting practices in the home? Again, referring to Coe and Lubach, negative experiences in infancy have strenuous effects on the immune system in monkeys up to one year. How this extrapolates to humans is another question. Gottman, however, has the basis to explore this link. Gottman does not provide evidence as to when emotion-coaching and emotion-dismissing styles start in the developmental trajectory of the family group. For instance, do these different parenting styles start before verbal communication, and if they do, how do they affect the immune system from the beginning? These are powerful questions, which could either enhance or change our current beliefs about neonatal immunity. Referring back to cumulative effects, measures throughout childhood, with comprehensive immune markers and allostatic load (Ryff and Singer et al.), could provide more of an understanding of which physiological processes are actually being influenced and the effects of emotion-dismissing parental styles on the health and long-term outcomes of their children.

Summary

Gottman's theory of meta-emotion is a substantial contribution to the field of emotion, social relationships, and health. His theory proposes that individuals learn to emote within social contexts and that parents' styles of teaching about emotion can have substantial impact on social, behavioral, academic, and health outcomes. The ability to self-soothe and to regulate emotions as represented physiologically by baseline vagal tone are proposed to mediate these effects. Vagal tone is hypothesized to influence innervation of the thymus, which in turn influences

T-cell maturation and, ultimately, immunity. Gottman uses self-report, observational, and physiological methodologies, and he reports on a range of child outcomes. Use of standardized third-party-observer–rated social behaviors represents a unique strength of Gottman's research.

Gottman has already provided some evidence for an association between emotion coaching and higher vagal tone as well as a range of child health outcomes. However, per his chapter, much of the evidence seems to be from pilot work. Capturing these links longitudinally and across naturalistic settings will produce exciting data, which can transform practice. We have made the following suggestions, which we hope will further advance the theory and research on meta-emotion: (1) We recommended that meta-emotion theory be expanded to include consideration of positive emotions and effects of both child and parent gender. (2) We advocated that other researchers (e.g., Cohen, Seeman) consider using Gottman's third-party-observer–rated social behavior variables in their own research. Measuring emotion-coaching and emotion-dismissing behaviors may help clarify links among social relationships and health in these research programs and foster constructive cross-talk among researchers. (3) Empirical support needs to be provided for each of the links in Gottman's hypothesized causal chain between vagal tone and immune function. (4) Physiological measures used could be expanded to include measures of immunity, such as lymphocyte proliferation, lowered cytotoxicity, lowered antibody responses, and natural killer cell activity. (5) Methodological designs should be created to rule out alternative plausible hypotheses: long-term longitudinal studies (with multiple time points) of EC and ED parenting and child outcomes will be critical; a comparison of ED parents randomly assigned to EC-training intervention groups and control groups will help rule out effects due to heritability of emotion regulation; and studying the effects of EC in a group such as Spiegel and Kimerling's breast cancer support group could produce interesting and dramatic results. Finally, the theories that Gottman proposes and their clinical implications, some of which Gottman has already observed in his practice and research, are both important and exciting. We hope to see more of his research results in the near future.

Note

1. These numbers are based upon the following criteria for establishing a gender difference in experience of emotion: (1) a significant omnibus F-test for experience and expression of the emotion and (2) a significant Tukey's test for gender differences in experience of that emotion. If the first criterion is dropped, then females are thought to experience ten emotions more than males and males, are thought to experience two emotions (pride and amusement) more than females.

References

Averill, J. R. (1982). *Anger and aggression: An essay on emotion.* New York: Academic.
Averill, J. R. (1994). Emotions are many-splendored things.. In P. Ekman, & R. J. David-

son, (Eds.), *The nature of emotion: Fundamental questions*. (pp. 99–102) New York: Oxford University Press.

Belle, D. (1982). The stress of caring: Women as providers of social support. In L. Goldberger & S. Breznitz (Eds.), *Handbook of stress: Theoretical and clinical aspects* (pp. 496–505). New York: Free Press.

Buehlman, K. T., Gottman, J. M., & Katz, L. F. (1992). How a couple views their past predicts their future: Predicting divorce from an oral history interview. *Journal of Family Psychology, 4*(3–4), 295–318.

Clore, G. (1994). Why emotions are felt. In P. Ekman, & R. J. Davidson, (Eds.), *The nature of emotion: Fundamental questions*. (pp. 103–111). New York: Oxford University Press.

Condry, J., & Condry, S. (1976). Sex differences: A study of the eye of the beholder. *Child Development, 47*, 812–819.

Ekman, P., & Friesen, W. V. (1976). Measuring facial movement. *Journal of Environmental Psychology and Nonverbal Behavior, 1*, 56–75.

Ekman, P., & Friesen, W. V. (1978). *Facial Action Coding System: A technique for measurement of facial movement*. Palo Alto, CA: Consulting Psychologists' Press.

Frijda, N. J. (1994). Emotions are functional most of the time. In P. Ekman, & R. J. Davidson, (Eds.), *The nature of emotion: Fundamental questions*. (pp. 112–122). New York: Oxford University Press.

Ginott, H. G. (1965). *Between parent and child*. New York: Avon.

Ginott, H. G. (1971). *Between parent and teenager*. New York: Avon.

Ginott, H. G, (1975). *Teacher and child*. New York: Avon.

Goleman, D. (1995). *Emotional intelligence: Why it can matter more than IQ*. New York: Bantam.

Gottman, J. M., Katz, L. F., & Hooven, C. (1996). Parental meta-emotion philosophy and the emotional life of families: Theoretical models and preliminary data. *Journal of Family Psychology, 10*(3), 243–268.

Gottman, J. M., & Levensen, R. W. (1992). Marital processes predictive of later dissolution: Behavior, physiology, and health. *Journal of Personality and Social Psychology, 63*, 221–233.

House, J S, Landis, K. R., & Umberson, D. (1988). Social relationships and health. *Science, 241*, 540–545.

Johnson, J. E., Fieler, V. K., Jones, L. S., Wlasowicz, G. S., & Mitchell, M. L. (1997). *Self-regulation theory: Applying theory to your practice*. Pittsburgh, PA: Oncology Nursing Press.

Kagan, J. (1996). Temperamental contributions to the development of social behavior. In D. Magnusson (Ed.) *The lifespan development of individuals: Behavioral, neurobiological, and psychological perspectives* (pp. 376–393). Cambridge, UK: Cambridge University Press.

Kaplan, G. A., Salonen, I. T., Cohen R. D., Brand, R. J., Syme, S. L., & Puska, P. (1988). Social connections and mortality from all causes and cardiovascular disease: Prospective evidence from eastern Finland. *American Journal of Epidemiology, 128*, 370–380.

Kessler, R. C., McLeod, J., & Wethington, E. (1984). The costs of caring: A perspective on the relationship between sex and psychological distress. In I. G. Sarason & B. R. Sarason (Eds.), *Social support: Theory, research and applications* (pp. 491–506). The Hague: Martinus Nihjof.

Keyes, R. (Ed.). (1992). *Sons on fathers*. New York: HarperCollins.

Krokoff, L. J., Gottman, J. M., & Hass, S. D. (1989). Validation of a global rapid couples interaction scoring system. *Behavioral Assessment, 11*, 65–79.

Levensen, R. W. (1994). Human emotion: A functional view. In P. Ekman, & R. J. Davidson, (Eds.), *The nature of emotion: Fundamental questions*. (pp. 123–126). New York: Oxford University Press.

Plant, E. A., Hyde, J. S., Keltner, D., & Devine, P. G. (2000). The gender stereotyping of emotion. *Psychology of Women Quarterly. 24*, 80–92.

Porges, S. W. (1973). Heart rate variability: An Automatic correlate of reaction time performance, *Bulletin of the Psychonomic Society, 1*, 270–272.

Porges, S. W. (1984). Heart rate oscillation: An index of neural medication. In M. G. H. Coles, J. R. Jennings, & J. A. Stern (Eds.), Psychophysiological perspectives: Festschrift for Beatrice and John Lacey, (pp. 229–241), New York: Van Nostraud Reinhold.

Porges, S. W. (1995). Cardiac vagal tone: A physiological index of stress. *Neuroscience and Biobehavioral Review, 19*(2), 225–233.

Rothbart, M. K., & Ahadi, S. A. (1994). Temperament and the development of personality. *Journal of Abnormal Psychology, 103*, 55–66.

Seeman, T .E., Berkman, L. F, Blazer, D., & Rowe, J. W. (1994). Social ties and support and neuroendocrine function: MacArthur studies of successful aging. *Annals of Behavioral Medicine 16*, 95–106.

Seeman, T. E. & McEwen, B. S. (1996). Impact of social environment characteristics on neuroendocrine regulation. *Psychosomatic Medicine, 58*, 459–471.

Seeman, T. E., & Syme, S. L. (1987). Social networks and coronary artery disease: A comparison of the structure and function of social relations as predictors of disease. *Psychosomatic Medicine, 49*, 341–354.

3

Relationship Experiences and Emotional Well-Being

Harry T. Reis

$\mathcal{F}$ew would argue with the proposition that social involvement is related in an intrinsic and profound way to happiness. Summarizing a sweeping review of the literature, Argyle (1987) concluded that "social relationships are a major source of happiness, relief from distress, and health" (p. 31). Shortly thereafter, Myers (1992) called the importance of social relations to human happiness a "deep truth." Most accounts of human motivation and development accord relational striving a similarly central role. Attachment theory, for example, regards the "capacity to make intimate emotional bonds with other individuals . . . as a principal feature of effective personality functioning and mental health" (Bowlby, 1988 p. 121). Indeed, it is difficult, if not impossible, to find theories that do not assign relationships a fundamental role in human development and adaptation. Even the emerging field of evolutionary psychology makes the "need to belong" (Baumeister & Leary, 1995)—that is, the pervasive desire to form and maintain enduring relationships with others—a central factor in the evolutionary design of mechanisms for perception, cognition, and action (Barkow, Cosmides, & Tooby, 1992; Kenrick & Trost, 1997).

In this light, it seems sensible that a symposium focused on emotion should be directly interested in the complex interplay of social relations, relationship processes, and emotional experience. Nevertheless, it would be generous to call the field's understanding of the mechanisms by which interpersonal relations and emotion influence each other rudimentary. Ekman and Davidson highlighted this gap in summarizing the views of a diverse set of emotion theorists, each of whom had been asked to comment on the function of emotion: "While interpersonal functions have generally been given short shrift in comparison to intrapersonal functions . . . [a]ll the contributors believe that emotions are brought into play most often by the actions of others, and, once aroused, emotions influence the course of interpersonal transactions" (1994, p. 139). In other words, although relationships

57

may be intrinsically and fundamentally involved with emotional experiences in everyday life, the research literature does not reveal a corresponding emphasis.

Nevertheless, surveys and epidemiological studies make plain the importance of social relations in human well-being. For example, there is widespread evidence that socially involved persons are happier, healthier, and live longer than socially isolated persons do (see Berscheid & Reis, 1998, for a review). The magnitude of this association is such that, when House, Landis, and Umberson (1988) computed the relative increase in mortality risk associated with social isolation, it was greater than that of cigarette smoking. Married people tend to be, on average, happier and healthier than unmarried people (e.g., Glenn & Weaver, 1988; Wood, Rhodes, & Whelan, 1989). Surveys of the relative importance of various life goals show that people who rank close relationships more highly display better mental health across diverse indicators (e.g., Campbell, Converse, & Rodgers, 1976; Kasser & Ryan, 1996). And, in another type of research, elderly individuals reminiscing about their lives usually cite gratifying relationships with family and close friends as their single most important source of life satisfaction (e.g., Sears, 1977). As one commentator put it, no one ever said on their deathbed, "I should've spent more time at the office."

Evidence from the "dark side" also attests to the deeply rooted link between relationships and emotional well-being. For example, Veroff, Douvan, and Kulka (1981) conducted telephone interviews of a representative sample of more than 2,000 Americans, asking them, among many questions, to describe the last "bad thing" that had happened. Fully 50% of the respondents explicitly cited interpersonal conflicts, problems, and losses, and many others had clear interpersonal components (e.g., legal problems, family illness). The same survey reported that interpersonal problems constituted 59% of the problems for which respondents sought help from a mental health professional and 67% of the problems for which clergy were consulted. Another survey found that the most frequent presenting problem among psychotherapy patients was "troubled relationships," indicated by nearly one-third of patients. Depression, self-image, anxiety, and phobias, which also tend to have interpersonal causes or implications, were less prevalent (Pinsker, Nepps, Redfield, & Winston, 1985).

Reviewing this and much more evidence led Berscheid and Reis to conclude that "despite the wealth of evidence that relationships are people's most frequent source of both happiness and distress, there is inadequate evidence of the causal mechanisms responsible and of the types of relationships that are most beneficial or harmful, even though these issues form the core of much theorizing and research" (1998, p. 243). My premise in this chapter derives from that conclusion. In order to begin the important task of delineating and understanding mechanisms by which relationships contribute to emotional well-being (a goal toward which several chapters in this volume are addressed), we must first identify the relational circumstances that promote or hinder emotional well-being. This is a call toward specificity in research. What sorts of interactions are more and less satisfying? Among the many facets of social experience, which are most critical? How do interpersonal processes contribute to emotional experience? How do personality dispositions and relational circumstances interact to influence emotional well-being? In the first part of this chapter, I will review research that my colleagues and I have conducted, which addresses these general questions. The second section uses these findings to outline a general theory of the role of relationships in emotional experience.

Studying Emotional Well-Being in the Context of Everyday Social Interaction

Before describing our research, a brief methodological diversion may help set the stage for our particular approach to these important questions. Relationships pose special problems for researchers. Because they exist over time and because partners typically interact repeatedly in widely varying circumstances, data collected at a given moment or in a particular setting may not be representative of the relationship. Furthermore, because two (or more) interdependent persons are involved in a relationship, it can be difficult to distinguish effects best attributed to their individual dispositions from those that depend on their interaction with each other (Kenny, 1990). Also, given the many cognitive and motivational biases that may compromise self-reports, especially retrospective self-reports (Ross, 1989; Schwarz, Groves, & Schuman, 1998), global descriptions of relationship experiences even over relatively brief time periods are likely to differ markedly from on-line accounts. In other words, people are not very good at recalling, summarizing, and specifying the details of their social activities.

To bypass these difficulties, our research strategy takes advantage of a family of procedures called daily experience methods, or event-sampling (Reis & Gable, 2000). These methods, designed to study everyday events as they occur in natural contexts, are becoming increasingly popular, bolstered by the recognition that experience is most accurately assessed immediately and in situ, as well as by rapid growth in the accessibility of the procedural and statistical tools needed to collect and analyze daily experience data. Relevant examples include the Experience Sampling Method (Larson & Csikszentmihalyi, 1983), Ecological Momentary Assessment (Stone & Shiffman, 1994), and the Rochester Interaction Record (Reis & Wheeler, 1991), all of which have become relatively commonplace in studies of emotion, stress, health and coping, and social interaction.

Researchers have been drawn to these methods primarily for the methodological advantage of lesser susceptibility to retrospection bias. Although this benefit is undoubtedly important, the equally significant conceptual rationale for these methods tends to be overlooked (Reis & Gable, 2000). The focus on everyday events examined in their natural, spontaneous context represents an important perspective often overlooked in the behavioral sciences. Consequently, the methodological overview that follows focuses on the conceptual rationale for our approach.

From the Perspective of Ongoing Experience

Traditionally, research on relationships and social interaction has relied on either of two general approaches (Reis, 1994). In the first, studies are conducted in specific, usually highly controlled settings, such as research laboratories, interview rooms, or offices. These settings are chosen for their inherent interest or because they allow researchers to create particular circumstances and controlled conditions free of artifact. A limitation of this approach is that, because the research context is inherently unique, findings may not generalize to other settings, particularly to those common in everyday life. It may then be difficult to determine the boundary conditions of a given phenomenon or to establish its pervasiveness or relevance in normal activity.

Alternatively, researchers study social relations through self-reported descriptions of experiences in particular situations or with specific partners. Questionnaires and interviews are two common examples of this approach. Although self-generated impressions are a valuable source of information about how people perceive matters of personal importance, they are likely to differ significantly from on-line, or itemized accounts. Many cognitive and motivational processes are known to affect the encoding, storage, retrieval, aggregation, and evaluation of episodic memories (Schwarz et al., 1998). Over and above people's limited abilities to recall and summarize past experiences, even over comparatively short intervals, processes serving such motivated functions as cognitive efficiency and self-esteem maintenance are likely to transform event-by-event or moment-by-moment memories. Responses to global, retrospective questions (e.g., "How satisfying have your social relations been during the past month?") therefore are better construed as motivated reconstructions of personal experience rather than as unbiased accounts.

Daily experience studies minimize the pitfalls of retrospection and aggregation by relying on reasonably contemporaneous, momentary reports. At each occasion, respondents report on relevant variables—be they thoughts, feelings, symptoms, or activities—as experienced at that moment or within a finite, well-defined, and easily recalled unit of time. Because such data are embedded within the flow of ongoing, spontaneous, and contextually determined activity, relatively accurate, detailed, and ecologically valid portraits of particular phenomena are obtained. In other words, rather than investigating processes whose relevance to a certain context is unknown or asking about recollections of the past, daily experience studies are concerned with natural activity (viewed from the respondent's perspective, of course). They are useful for establishing the scope, impact, and pervasiveness of a phenomenon for both descriptive and theory-testing purposes. They can also help to identify natural patterns of variation over time and contexts (e.g., to what extent do certain emotions or interactions tend to occur?) and co-variation with predictors and consequences (e.g., to what extent do these emotions and interactions tend to covary?).

Major versus Minor Events

Whereas the health and emotional consequences of major life events, such as marriage, bereavement, or unemployment, have received considerable attention, the influence of minor, or mundane, daily events are less well documented. Implicit in the latter is the assumption that, even if any single episode is negligible, recurrent patterns of stress, emotion, or interaction accumulated over many instances may be important in the long run. For example, everyday hassles affect health and well-being over time (e.g., DeLongis, Folkman, & Lazarus, 1988; Stone, Neale, & Shiffman, 1993). To be sure, major life events are important, but their significance may be limited both by their relative scarcity and because their impact tends to taper off over time. Suh, Diener, and Fujita (1996) found that only life events during the previous three months mattered for emotional well-being, a finding consistent with studies of adaptation to major traumas (Wortman & Silver, 1989). In contrast, mundane events, like minor conflict and friendly conversation, occur far more often, and therefore may exert continual influence on the individual. Because minor events are, by definition, routine and uneventful, they tend to be unmemorable, rendering retrospective methods problematic. Moreover, people are likely to have difficulty perceiving regularities or cyclical variations within a series of relatively inaccessible events, so that responses to global questions may be misleading. In contrast, repeated timely reports of even the most forgettable feelings or events allow researchers to identify whatever meaningful patterns may exist and whatever consequences these small occurrences may have. This approach is in keeping with the remark, attributed to Benjamin Franklin, that happiness "is produced not so much by great pieces of good fortune that seldom happen as by little advantages that occur every day."

Interaction, not Relationship

Although commonly treated as synonymous, relationships and social interactions are more appropriately conceptualized and studied at different levels of analysis (Hinde, 1997). The term *relationship* refers to an enduring association between two persons. The existence of a relationship implies that these persons have established an ongoing connection with each other; that their bond has special properties, including a sense of history and some awareness of the nature of the relationship; that they influence each other's thoughts, feelings, and behavior; and that they expect to interact again in the future. Relationships are best understood not in terms of single interactions or processes but rather as global representations of a multidimensional and somewhat unique bond between individuals that varies across time and contexts. *Interaction*, in contrast, may occur between related or unrelated individuals, and it refers to a single social event.

It is therefore important to distinguish the study of relationships from that of interactions. Retrospective methods typically favor the former because people may find it difficult to isolate one particular interaction from others in their recollections. In contrast, diary methods, such as the Rochester Interaction Record (Reis & Wheeler, 1991), isolate interactions from one another by obtaining reports about each event, one at a time. It is then possible to study interaction processes within ongoing relationships and, perhaps more important, to examine how individual events accumulate to create a more general, multifaceted entity: the relationship. Like Hinde (1997), we believe that researchers have often overemphasized the latter to the exclusion of the former. The global features of a relationship derive in considerable part from real-life transactions between persons, modified, of course, to some extent by idiosyncratic reactions and interpretations. In order to trace the link between health and emotional well-being back to social relations, therefore, its origins in interaction processes must be considered (see Reis and Collins, 2000, for an overview of such models).

Everyday Social Interaction and Emotional Well-Being

The research to be described in the remainder of this chapter uses event-sampling to relate everyday social activity to emotional well-being. This work is founded on two theoretical models—attachment theory (Bowlby, 1969/1982) and intimacy theory (Reis & Shaver, 1988)—which assign social interaction a central role in emotional well-being. Both models feature processes of responsive interaction, situationally appropriate emotional openness, and affective engagement, as I discuss shortly. A cautionary note: the studies to be presented are not designed to test these theories directly but rather to apply them within the domain of everyday activity. Theory provides our road map: it tells us where to look for the key elements of social activity and what sort of impact they may be expected to have. The data tell us whether these maps are accurate. Given the constraints of this volume, a full review of these theories is not possible; Reis and Patrick (1996) provide a more extensive account.

As originally postulated by Bowlby (1969/1982), attachment is a control system designed by evolutionary mechanisms to maintain proximity between infants and caregivers. Its central premise is that infants who kept in close proximity with adult caregivers, who displayed appropriate protest behaviors when separated or threatened, and whose caregivers responded appropriately to those protests were more likely to survive into adulthood. A core process in the operation of the attachment system is emotional regulation. When the bond between infant and caregiver is secure, the child's expressions of anxiety and distress usually result in sensitive, situationally appropriate responses from the caregiver. As a consequence, the developing child feels safe in using the attachment figure as a secure base from which to explore the environment. Through repeated interactions, positive internal working models of self as love-worthy are gradually internalized, and the child comes to view others as supportive and as a source of affection and comfort.

In contrast, insecure attachment arises when a caregiver's response is chronically inadequate or poorly matched to the infant's needs. One form of insecurity, avoidance, is thought to result from inattention or emotionally cold responses to the infant's distress and desire for comfort. Avoidance involves emotional distance from others and learning to cope with anxiety by distancing and self-reliance. A different type of insecurity, originally called anxious-ambivalence and now more commonly called preoccupation, is hypothesized as the consequence of inconsistent or unreliable caregiving, intrusive at one moment and unresponsive at the next moment. These individuals are prone to experience anxiety and other negative emotions, and they tend to be preoccupied with close relationships, such as through excessive vigilance for signs of acceptance and rejection.

Other consequences include emotional hypersensitivity and relatively volatile relationships; anxiously preoccupied individuals tend to become dependent on close others but also are easily angered and disillusioned with them. At its core, then, attachment is a theory about how people experience emotions such as love, fear, anger, jealousy, sadness, disappointment, anxiety, loneliness, and contentment in the context of their close relationships.

How do attachment processes inform studies of the link between social relations and emotional well-being? At least three inferences can be drawn. For one, attachment theory suggests that emotional experiences during social interaction should be central to emotional well-being, especially during interactions that activate the attachment system, that is, interactions with implications for relational security, such as with actual and potential romantic partners or when conflict occurs. Second, attachment theory implies that people's ability to fulfill needs for closeness and relatedness by establishing and maintaining satisfying close relationships is a key component of emotional health. Presumably, this is because both anxious preoccupation and avoidance interfere with normal relationship functioning. Finally, the capacity to rely on relationship partners during stressful periods and to effectively draw supportive resources from them is also important. Reliance on attachment figures in stressful circumstances is innate, according to attachment theory, suggesting that one's willingness and skill in mobilizing supportive resources may contribute to emotional well-being.

Our second theoretical guide, intimacy theory (Reis & Patrick, 1996; Reis & Shaver, 1988), derives in part from attachment theory in proposing that emotionally close adult relationships fulfill many of the same functions that attachment relationships do in childhood. This model conceives of intimacy as an interactive process with three components: one person's expression of self-relevant thoughts and feelings through verbal, nonverbal, and behavioral channels; the partner's response, in terms of appropriateness and supportiveness; and the person's perception of the partner's response. Intimacy is experienced when the sequence of self-expression and partner response leads one to feel understood, validated, and cared for. Although most intimate relationships are mutual and reciprocated, in that partners typically alternate these two roles, the model focuses on a single exchange for clarity.

Intimacy theory implies that the most emotionally potent interactions are those in which significant self-disclosure occurs. More important, the model stipulates that perceived partner responsiveness, predicated on the partner's actual behavior but filtered by various processes, which may modify perceptions of that response, is most central to intimacy. What matters most is not the details of self-disclosure or of the other's response, but rather how responsive the other is perceived to be to one's core psychological self. Thus, the experience of positive emotions, such as love, happiness, and acceptance, and negative emotions, such as sadness, anger, and loneliness, can be described as reactions to a partner's response to the self, as shown through self-revelatory actions and statements. A related prediction is that interactions that involve intimate partners should be more important to emotional well-being than interactions that involve less close partners, inasmuch as emotionally self-relevant exchanges are more likely to occur.

Patterns of Social Participation Associated with Emotional Well-Being

One way to examine the role of social interaction in emotional well-being is correlational. That is, given that there are well-known dispositional differences in emotional well-being—some people generally enjoy greater well-being than do others—to the extent that social activity matters, global self-assessments of emotional well-being should correspond systematically to individual differences in social participation.

Loneliness

Prototypically defined as the failure to attain satisfying levels of social involvement (Russell, Peplau, & Cutrona, 1980), loneliness represents one of the most common varieties of emotional distress in everyday life. Loneliness, in both state (i.e., short-lived and presumably situationally based) and chronic (i.e., trait-based) forms, is a major risk factor for morbidity and mortality from various causes and has been linked to poor subjective health, diminished immune function, unhealthy behaviors, and major depression (Peplau & Goldston, 1982; Uchino, Cacioppo, & Kiecolt-Glaser, 1996). Our studies in this area were designed to determine whether loneliness describes a primarily subjective sense of inadequacy or whether it reflects actual deficiencies in social activity—and if so, which particular deficiencies.

Loneliness is typically assessed by global questionnaires that ask participants to summarize their social experience across various circumstances or time spans. For example, the popular UCLA Loneliness scale includes 20 items, such as "I feel in tune with the people around me" and "I feel isolated from others" (Russell et al., 1980). As argued earlier, items of this sort cannot distinguish between biased self-reports and actual social experiences as explanations.

We investigated this question as part of a longitudinal study of change and consistency in adult social participation (Reis, Lin, Bennett, & Nezlek, 1993). In the first part of the study, 113 adults (57 men, 56 women) between the ages of 27 and 31 kept the Rochester Interaction Record (Reis & Wheeler, 1991) for two weeks. The RIR procedure requires that diary records be completed immediately after, or as soon as is reasonable, all interactions lasting ten minutes or longer. Each record in this study contained the following information: time of day and length of interaction; initials and sex of partners; subjective ratings of interaction features, including intimacy and satisfaction; and description of the activity. Composite ratings were then computed across several types of interaction (e.g., average levels of intimacy in all same-sex interactions or in all interactions involving one's romantic partner). Because these indices average across many interactions, they tend to provide highly reliable estimates of social experiences.

After the RIRs had been collected, participants completed a questionnaire battery, which included the UCLA Loneliness scale, and described their role-relationship with every person encountered during the study (e.g., romantic partner, same-sex friend, coworker). Each participant also was asked to nominate one partner as their confidante. This procedure allowed us to determine whether certain features of social participation, either generally or limited to specific partners, as tabulated from event-by-event descriptions of ongoing social activity, predict global self-assessments of loneliness.

Several findings stand out. First, interaction with confidantes mattered most. For both men and women, the more satisfying and intimate their interaction with confidantes, the less loneliness reported (all rs between .28 and .35, $ps < .05$). The amount of interaction with confidantes correlated significantly with loneliness only among men, however. Loneliness tended to be lower the more time spent with confidantes ($r = -.46$, $p<.01$) and the more often interactions with this person occurred ($r = -.52$, $p<.01$). Clearly, then, ongoing interaction matters, especially if it involves intimate partners, as we had hypothesized.

How do we make sense of this sex difference? Men's confidantes are overwhelmingly women, whereas women tend to name both men and women. This pattern implicates sex differences, which emerge consistently in the many RIR studies we have conducted. A recent meta-analysis of eight such studies (Reis, 1998) indicated that men's same-sex interactions tend to be significantly less intimate than women's same-sex interactions, yielding an effect size of $d =.85$ (which, in the metric of meta-analysis, is an exceptionally large effect). Opposite-sex interaction, in contrast, did not produce a reliable sex difference across these eight studies.

The importance of intimacy in avoiding loneliness was also evident in more general patterns of social activity. For example, men's interactions with all female partners counted most in avoiding loneliness: loneliness was lowest in men who interacted with women more often ($r = -.34$, $p<.05$) and for more time ($r = -.30$, $p<.05$). Among women, the quality of interaction with men was more critical (for perceived intimacy, $r = -.42$, $p<.01$; for perceived satisfaction, $r = -.37$, $p<.05$). We believe this is because women can interact intimately in other contexts, whereas men are more dependent upon female partners for intimacy (an asymmetry we have shown with other samples, e.g., Wheeler, Reis, & Nezlek, 1983).

These findings indicate that deficiencies in one specific feature of everyday social activity, namely the absence of intimacy, is implicated in loneliness. Whether or not these predictions extend to other aspects of poor emotional health awaits further research.

Attachment Processes

Another way to illuminate interpersonal processes in emotional well-being involves comparing individuals who regulate emotions differently in social contexts. Attachment style, the dispositional version of the normative process described by Bowlby (1969/1982), provides such a construct. Defined in terms of stable internalized views ("internal working models") of the self's relation to others, attachment styles are thought to underlie chronic patterns of emotional experience and regulation in social interaction (Shaver, Collins, & Clark, 1996). Several different models of attachment styles have been proposed. In this research, we relied on Hazan and Shaver's (1987) three-category model. One category, avoidance, describes individuals who tend to avoid intimacy and closeness and who are uncomfortable relying on others for support. Anxious-ambivalent persons, on the other hand, are often anxious about their social relations and tend to be preoccupied with establishing and maintaining closeness. Secure persons find a comfortable balance between preoccupation and distance, and they typically perceive close relationships as a source of pleasure and satisfaction. These very general portraits are based primarily on research that uses global self-report questionnaires or interviews, methods that, as discussed earlier, may not provide accurate accounts of social activity. To determine whether attachment styles reflect actual experiences, as Bowlby and most contemporary theorists have contended, it is useful to examine attachment-theory predictions in the context of ongoing behavior.

Tidwell, Reis, and Shaver (1996) examined emotional experience and expression in everyday social interaction as a function of attachment-styles. One hundred twenty-five college students at the State University of New York in Buffalo kept a version of the RIR for one week, modified to include items asking about social support, conflict, and emotion. Participants completed two attachment-style measures at each of three different times during one semester: Hazan and Shaver's (1987) self-categorization measure and a series of Likert scales based on the same wording (Levy & Davis, 1988). They were assigned to a category by consensus among the six assessments. The wording of the self-categorization measure was as follows:

Avoidant: I am somewhat uncomfortable being close to others; I find it difficult to trust them completely, difficult to allow myself to depend on them. I am nervous when anyone gets too close, and often, love partners want me to be more intimate than I feel comfortable being.

Anxious-Ambivalent: I find that others are reluctant to get as close as I would like. I often worry that my partner doesn't really love me or won't want to stay with me. I want to get very close to my partner, and this sometimes scares people away.

Secure: I find it relatively easy to get close to others and am comfortable depending on them. I don't often worry about being abandoned or about someone getting too close to me.

Space considerations limit me to highlighting several results that are particularly relevant to the present discussion (Tidwell et al., 1996, present a fuller report). First, do the interactions of secure, avoidant, and anxious-ambivalent persons differ in emotional quality? In a word, yes. Compared to secure and anxious-ambivalent persons, avoidant persons reported significantly lower levels of intimacy, enjoyment, support, and positive emotion and higher levels of negative emotion. These differences were small in same-sex interactions but pronounced in opposite-sex interactions. Thus, social context appears to moderate the influence of attachment predispositions on social experience. Perhaps because we studied college students, opposite-sex interactions were especially likely to activate concerns about closeness and security.

Second, we found evidence that avoidant persons may actively structure their social activity in ways that minimize intimacy. For example, only about 8% of their interactions involved romantic partners; the comparable figures for anxious-ambivalent and secure persons were 16% and 19%, respectively. Similarly, avoidant individuals averaged less time per opposite-sex partner (about 57 minutes per partner over the week) than the other groups did (about 100 minutes per partner), indicating relatively lower levels of engagement with the interaction partners they did have.

Third, we were interested in the relevance of role differentiation for adaptive emotional regulation. Normatively, the development of intimacy closely parallels acquaintance (Altman & Taylor, 1973): the better acquainted two individuals are, the more intimate their interactions tend to be. Reversals of this pattern—low intimacy in close relations, high intimacy with strangers—may indicate poor social functioning (Derlega, Metts, Petronio, & Margulis, 1993). To evaluate this proposition, we first sorted all interactions involving opposite-sex partners into two categories: interactions with romantic partners and with nonromantic partners. As expected, the average degree of difference in intimacy levels between romantic and nonromantic partners was greatest for secure persons (mean difference = 1.04 on a 1–7 scale), moderate among anxious-ambivalent persons (mean difference = 0.59), and smallest for avoidant persons (mean difference = 0.22; the attachment style x type of partner interaction is significant, $p < .05$). In other words, secure persons reported greater intimacy with romantic partners than the other two groups did, whereas with nonromantic others, avoidant participants reported somewhat higher levels than secure or anxious-ambivalent persons did. Perhaps avoidant individuals experience interaction with romantic partners as relatively distressing, whereas more superficial cross-sex contacts are relatively more comfortable.

Finally, attachment-related difficulties in emotion regulation may also be evident in emotional volatility. When we computed the variability of subjective emotion ratings from one interaction to another, anxious-ambivalent persons varied significantly more than avoidant or secure persons did. In other words, anxious preoccupation with closeness and social acceptance may enhance emotional reactivity—more positive feelings when the social environment seems secure and approving, more negative feelings when partners seem aloof or rejecting.

In short, these data demonstrate that feelings that arise during spontaneous, everyday socializing—and how one manages them when they do arise—contribute to the maintenance and perpetuation of attachment styles in adulthood.

Within-Person Level of Analysis

The results presented to this point show that participation in meaningful social activities is associated with psychological well-being. However, this evidence and nearly all of the evidence available in this vast literature derives from disposition-level effects, that is, persons high in some variety or characteristic of social activity report or display higher levels of well-being than persons low in the same social indicators. Although these demonstrations are interesting and important, because the evidence is correlational, questions about alternative causal interpretations must be considered.

Many researchers would like to conclude that social activity is responsible for increments and decrements in emotional states; indeed, several prominent theories are predicated upon this pathway. However plausible this notion may be, simple correlations of the sort described above cannot support this inferential burden. Among the more viable alternative explanations is the possibility that "third variables" may exert independent causal effects on social activity and emotional well-being, resulting in a spurious correlation between them. This is not an idle speculation. More than a few personality and temperamental variables have been hypothesized both to directly influence emotional states and to predispose persons to particular types of interactions (e.g., Lykken & Tellegen, 1996; Watson & Clark, 1994). The fact that personality traits such as extraversion, neuroticism, and agreeableness, which have well-established genetic determinants that account for as much as about half of their variance, have demonstrated associations with emotion and social activity makes this sort of dispositional alternative to the preferred social-experience-causes-emotion a reasonable option.

This ambiguity stems from the reliance on dispositional methods. There is a different level of analysis, however, that suggests an alternative—and causally less equivocal—conceptualization of the central phenomenon. Consider the two hypothetical individuals whose average daily mood for each of 14 days is displayed in figure 3.1. Although A's average level of well-being is higher than B's, both persons vary substantially from one day to another. To what extent can these fluctuations be attributed to corresponding variations in social activity? Or, in other words, do variations in well-being around one's personal mean (as distinct from mean differences between persons) relate to interpersonal experiences?

Substantial evidence indicates that within-person variability in emotional states is both theoretically meaningful and practically important. For example,

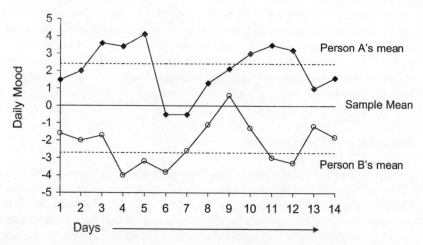

Figure 3.1 Comparing between-person and within-person effects.

mood variability relates systematically to a broad list of temporal and dispositional factors (Larsen & Diener, 1987). Studies of daily stressors and their impact
on mood and well-being are common in the stress and coping literature (e.g.,
David, Green, Martin, & Suls, 1997; Stone et al., 1998), and within-person variability in self-esteem has demonstrated consequences for self-perception and
social interaction over and above mean levels (Kennis, 1995). In this vein,
Moskowitz, Brown, and Côté (1997) argue that highlighting temporal and contextual variations in the expression of personality traits may provide new understanding of personality structure and its impact on behavior; that is, particular
personality characteristics will not be evident indiscriminately but rather will appear in the specific settings that make those traits salient.[1] Our research group has
adopted the strategy of examining within-person covariation between social activity and emotion—that is, to what extent do changes in social interaction covary
with changes in emotional state? In some research programs, within-person
analyses are conducted as a methodological device for controlling the influence
of between-person factors (i.e., to partial out dispositional differences or to
remove statistical nonindependence). These obvious benefits notwithstanding,
within-person strategies also shift the conceptual focus of research in a subtle but
important way (Gable & Reis, 1999). Consider the findings discussed earlier in
this chapter, which exemplify the between-person level of analysis. They address
the following general question: Do people with more positive social experiences
also have more positive emotional well-being?

I refer to this as a *personological question*, because it asks whether people who
differ in one domain also differ similarly in another domain. Note, however, that
personological theories did not suggest this question in the first place; rather, it
arose from consideration of processes thought to operate during social interaction, which, presumably, describe the impact of certain experiences on an individual. To better reflect this theoretical grounding, we might instead ask a somewhat different question: Do people experience more positive emotions when
engaging in more positive and less negative social events? This question, which I
label an *experiential question*, examines a within-person effect because it in-
quires whether variations in one aspect of experience reliably correspond to
variations in another dimension. Note that it refers to variability in a given person's experience and not to differences between people.

I propose that the experiential question is in many respects more compelling
than is the personological question, even though the former is far more common
in the literature. Most theorizing about the impact of social relations on emotional
well-being and health is not at its core personological; rather, theories tend to
focus on the impact of particular circumstances on emotional states, as mediated
by processes that, at least in theory, are orthogonal to dispositional differences.

That this perspective may be useful for studies of emotional well-being is suggested by evidence from subjective assessments of quality of life, which documents that evaluations of personal well-being at any given moment tend to emphasize within-person referents. For example, Kahneman (1999) summarized
several programs of research that indicated that judgments of personal well-being
tend to be based on the direction and magnitude of recent changes in one's cir-

cumstances, rather than objective assessments of existing circumstances (see also Suh et al., 1996). In other words, and notwithstanding the extensive literature on cross-person social comparison, comparisons that involve the self across time and situations may be prevalent and influential determinants of emotional states (see Gable & Reis, 1999, for more extensive discussion of this distinction and its ramifications for research and theory). Perhaps this is why, when acquaintances greet each other with the ubiquitous "How are you?" replies tend to focus on the impact of recent events.[2]

Because they generate repeated instances for each individual, event-sampling methods are ideal for investigating within-person processes, as long as sufficient and representative natural variation in relevant variables is incorporated (Reis & Gable, 2000). To study social support and symptoms, for example, researchers would need to assess a reasonably broad range of support-relevant contexts, aggregating data according to dimensions of interest—for example, by partners (to examine how different partners provide different levels and types of support); by time (to investigate the development and decay of support over time or to examine regular temporal cycles, such as days of the week); by settings (to contrast theoretically distinct contexts in which support is sought and received); or by features of the event itself, such as its stressfulness (to study covariation among event qualities and people's reactions).

Following this general line of reasoning, my colleagues and I have explored within-person processes that link social relations and affective well-being in two ways. One line of research examines event nature and valence. The second set of studies concerns the impact of interpersonal interactions on satisfaction of basic human needs and how this process relates to affective well-being.

Everyday Social Events and Emotional Well-Being

Although prior research has established clear connections between stressful daily events, irrespective of their specific content, and mood (e.g., Clark & Watson, 1988; Marco & Suls, 1993), we were interested in the impact of social events in particular. Furthermore, we simultaneously compared positive and negative events. Whereas prior research is largely limited to the presence or absence of negative events (e.g., stressors), growing evidence suggests that positive events may have substantial independent effects on well-being (e.g., Ryff & Singer, 1998; Taylor, 1991). The functional independence of positive and negative affect has received considerable support in studies of emotion (Cacioppo & Gardner, 1999), which suggests that, in daily life, each may be predicted by distinct events.

This research used an interval sampling scheme, in which participants completed one record at the end of each day for seven days. The record asked which of 71 events had occurred that day, and if so, what their impact had been. Four event types were listed, chosen from pilot research to include the most common everyday occurrences in college students' lives:

- positive social events (e.g., went out socializing with friends)
- negative social events (e.g., was left out by my group of friends)

- positive achievement events (e.g., completed work on an interesting project or assignment)
- negative achievement events (e.g., did poorly on a school or work task)

Participants also rated their mood for that day, with separate scales of positive and negative affect (Gable, Reis, & Elliot, 2000, provide additional details).

As mentioned earlier, our interest focused on within-person processes. We used Hierarchical Linear Modeling (Bryk & Raudenbush, 1992) to examine co-variation between event impact and daily mood. (Recall that this method isolates individual differences from these effects.) At the within-person level, the esti-mated effects are conceptually equivalent (but statistically superior) to computing for each participant the slope between event impact and well-being across the seven days of recording and averaging these values across all participants.[3] Figure 3.2 displays results from this analysis.

As expected, social events significantly predicted daily mood, as did achieve-ment events. Positive affect was higher on days in which people experienced more positive social events; similarly, negative affect was greater on days in which people experienced more negative social events. It is noteworthy that posi-tive and negative affect displayed excellent discriminant validity: positive events did not predict negative affect, and negative events did not predict positive affect, an important finding that goes beyond the oft-noted lack of correlation between positive and negative mood in establishing independent event-based predictors for each affect. This is a pattern that we have now replicated in several studies.

We also found that social events predicted both positive and negative mood. Existing studies tended to focus on only one or the other, and some researchers have suggested that social events relate primarily to positive mood (e.g., Clark & Watson, 1988). A possible source of the discrepancy stems from the relative scarcity of negative social events in everyday life. Our list was constructed to em-

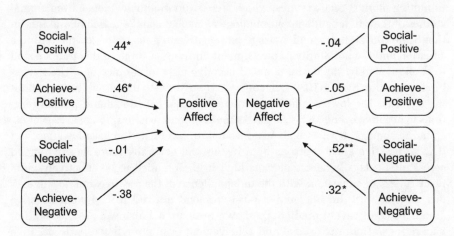

Figure 3.2 Predicting daily affect from event impact (within person). Coefficients are unstandardized. * $p < .01$; ** $p < .001$

phasize common events, including those that result from social exclusion or the absence of desired interactions. Demonstrating that negative social events predict negative affect—and not simply the absence of positive affect—supports our view that negative social emotions (such as loneliness, sadness, and jealousy) are discrete states with specific environmental antecedents.

On the other side, finding that positive interpersonal events had clear independent effects apart from negative events suggests that the field's emphasis on the impact of negative processes and events in health (Uchino et al., 1996), social cognition (Taylor, 1991), and marital functioning (Gottman, 1994; Notarius & Markman, 1993) may be unwarranted. As Ryff and Singer (1998) note, because health and well-being are sometimes construed in terms of the absence of illness or distress, existing theories may underestimate the importance of positive processes on well-being.

Although these analyses downplay the role of trait predispositions, traits are, of course, meaningful in determining reactions to everyday occurrences. Everyone does not react to the same event in the same way; some people feel challenged by failure, for example, whereas others withdraw. Trait processes can be integrated into the within-person perspective by considering how they moderate reactions to particular events. This is the core principle of the interactionist approach to personality: that situational factors and dispositions interact to produce behavior (Endler & Magnusson, 1976). An individual's standing on relevant traits may predispose her to be more reactive to certain environmental events and less reactive to others. In other words, behavior is not merely based on the events that occur but rather on how people react to those events.

The next study followed the same general design as the prior study with two exceptions: participants kept the daily diary for 14 days, and prior to the study, they completed Carver and White's (1994) Behavioral Activation and Inhibition scale. This measure has two parts, which assess traits that correspond to constructs introduced by Gray (1987). Gray postulated the existence of independent activating and inhibiting motivational systems, which were supported by evidence from animal studies of their independent neurobiological mechanisms. The Behavioral Inhibition Scale (BIS) reflects tendencies to be sensitive to potential risks inherent in a situation and the possibility of punishment. Individuals high in this trait are said to be motivated by the desire to avoid negative or painful outcomes. The Behavioral Activation System (BAS), in contrast, is sensitive to the possibility of obtaining rewards. The logic of these constructs suggests that BIS should predict reactions to negative events, whereas BAS should predict reactions to positive events.

In the simplest terms, this is what we found. BIS related to negative affect and BAS to positive affect. Persons high in BIS had generally more negative mood across all 14 days, whereas persons high in BAS tended to be affectively more positive. Again consistent with the independence of the positive and negative affect systems, BIS did not predict positive mood nor did BAS predict negative mood. The daily event predictions shown in figure 3.2 also were replicated: impact ratings of negative social and achievement events predicted daily negative mood, whereas impact ratings of positive social and achievement events predicted positive mood.

More compelling are the impact of BIS and BAS on reactions to daily events. BIS produced the predicted differential reactivity effect: the higher one's standing on the BIS trait measure, the stronger the effect of negative events on negative mood. In other words, the slope relating negative events and mood was greater to the extent that people were high in BIS. This differential effect was substantial: the slope for persons one standard deviation above the mean in BIS was about four times larger than the slope for persons one standard deviation below the mean (i.e., 1.02 versus .24). Positive events told a different story, however. BAS did not moderate the impact of positive events on positive mood. Instead, BAS predicted differential exposure to positive events: the higher one's standing on BAS, the more positive events that were reported and the higher one's daily mood. This asymmetry makes good conceptual sense. Whereas negative events typically occur in the pursuit of ordinary life activities without intentional instigation, positive events may require active initiation by the individual. Good outcomes are unlikely to occur without being sought, and traits like BAS predict positive-outcome (i.e., reward) seeking. Bad outcomes, on the other hand, follow normal activity, so that BIS would predict differential reactions to them. (Gable, et al., 2000, provide further details about these findings and their interpretation).

If nothing else, these results affirm a central principle of theorizing about emotion—that emotions reflect the perceived importance of environmental circumstances to personal concerns and goals (e.g., Frijda, 1994). Trait predispositions describe systematic differences in concerns and goals; hence it is reasonable that the impact of events on emotional states would depend differentially on predispositions. Thus, although the general implication of this work is that mundane events account for substantial amounts of the variability in everyday emotional well-being, it also shows that people differ systematically in the extent to which various events are likely to occur and the extent to which those events matter to them. Event-sampling is an ideal approach for testing models that emphasize spontaneous initiative and subjective construals in the natural environment. The final study to be discussed examines this process directly.

Satisfying Basic Needs in Everyday Activity

The notion that humans possess innate needs whose satisfaction is fundamental to effective functioning and well-being is scarcely novel. Most theories of motivation and personality begin with a set of assumptions about the intrinsic nature of human organisms and the drives that impel our behavior. When described as needs, these assumptions have been criticized for several reasons, notably the possibility of arbitrariness, in the sense that there often existed no compelling empirical or logical reason for positing the fundamental existence of one set of needs over another. With the advent of evolutionary and biological thinking in psychology (Barkow, Cosmides, & Tooby, 1992), however, as well as the reemergence of functionalist theorizing, the notion that humans may be innately endowed with certain core mechanisms, which operate to establish or maintain critical behaviors, has become far more plausible, grounded as it is in natural science knowledge about the human organism. These core mechanisms implicate particular needs as basic—that is, as drives that reside within the individual, the fulfillment of which is essential to adaptive functioning.

Exactly which needs are most basic is, of course, open to debate and investigation, as is a somewhat more tractable question: What are the emotional consequences of frustrating or satisfying these basic needs in everyday activity? This important question is sometimes addressed in theories of emotion, although empirical research is scarce. As discussed earlier, several definitions of emotion stress the relevance of environmental events to personal needs and goals as eliciting emotion, which then prepares the organism to respond appropriately. To Frijda, for example, "emotions signal the relevance of events to concerns" (1994, p. 113). If *concerns* are considered as proximal mental representations of innate or basic needs, as seems reasonable, it follows that need facilitation or obstruction in everyday activity should influence emotional states. A within-subjects approach is ideal for evaluating this proposition, inasmuch as it sidesteps chronic individual differences in affect, as well as likely related dispositional tendencies to feel generally fulfilled or not (as assessed by traits such as neuroticism and optimism). In other words, this research examined the hypothesis that good days and bad days— that is, day-to-day fluctuations around one's average level of emotional well-being—depend on one's ability to meet basic needs in everyday activity.

Our theoretical model relies on the work of Deci and Ryan (1991), who argue that three needs—autonomy, competence, and relatedness—are essential to individual growth, integrity, and well-being. In their view, these innate needs, each representing a behavioral and psychological orientation that had adaptive value over evolutionary time, describe specific and necessary conditions for optimal functioning and thereby have independent potential to influence well-being. Thus, activities that facilitate satisfaction of these needs should foster emotional well-being, whereas activities that thwart or inhibit need satisfaction should engender distress. This logic is consistent (although not isomorphic) with the emotion theories described earlier: needs such as autonomy, competence, and relatedness presumably underlie the most influential personal concerns and goals that engender emotions.

The present study extends our research by adding a more psychological dimension—the extent to which activities contribute to need satisfaction—to the prior focus on event types and valence. *Competence* refers to the feeling that one can act effectively to bring about desired outcomes; *autonomy* involves feeling that one's activities are self-chosen and concordant with intrinsic interests and values; and *relatedness* pertains to feeling close and connected to significant others. Our hypothesis is that daily activities that facilitate attainment of these three needs will enhance well-being, whereas activities that hinder realization will lessen well-being. Note that this hypothesis and the design to be used goes beyond the person-level prediction that individuals who exhibit high levels of competence, autonomy, and relatedness will tend to experience relatively high levels of well-being. The use of a within-subjects design, together with activity ratings, allows us to examine the more subtle but nevertheless important process of day-to-day fluctuation around one's own mean.

This study, described more fully by Reis, Sheldon, Gable, Roscoe, and Ryan

(2000), addressed two general questions. First, to what extent does satisfaction of autonomy, competence, and relatedness needs in daily activity relate to affective well-being? Second, what types of social experiences are more and less likely to engender affective well-being? Despite the extensive literature highlights the importance of feeling socially involved and connected (Baumeister & Leary, 1995; House et al., 1988), few studies have investigated the relative impact of different types of social events on such feelings.

For ten days, participants in this study completed an end-of-day diary record to describe several aspects of that day's activity, including:

Basic Need Satisfaction Participants first noted their three most time-consuming activities and their three most time-consuming social interactions. Using a protocol developed by Sheldon, Ryan, and Reis (1996), activities were evaluated for the extent to which participants felt autonomous and competent while engaging in them. Relatedness was assessed in terms of the degree to which participants felt "close and connected" with partners during social interactions.

Daily Emotional Well-Being Daily moods were assessed with an adjective checklist, which included both positive (joyful, happy, pleased, enjoyment/fun) and negative (depressed, worried/anxious, frustrated, angry/hostile, unhappy) terms, rated on 1 (not at all) to 7 (extremely) scales. Participants were asked to report the extent to which they had experienced each emotion on that day.

Nature of Social Interaction Participants described the extent to which their three most time-consuming interactions involved seven qualitatively different forms of engagement: talking about something meaningful; engaging in activities and concrete tasks; just "hanging out" with others; feeling understood and appreciated by others; doing things that were pleasant or fun; feeling self-conscious, judged, or insecure; and quarreling, arguing, or engaging in conflict. These seven categories were chosen on the basis of their centrality in the relationships literature and because each has been linked to emotional well-being by others.

We then aggregated across each day's ratings to create a daily composite for each variable, and we analyzed these composites by the same multilevel modeling strategy presented above. Once again, it bears mentioning that this analysis controls individual differences and is concerned only with identifying predictors of within-person variation.

As we had hypothesized, satisfaction of basic needs covaries with everyday fluctuation in emotional state. Table 3.1 shows that higher levels of autonomy and competence in daily activity were associated with higher levels of positive mood and lower levels of negative mood. Relatedness correlated positively with positive mood during social interaction but did not relate significantly to negative mood (discussed further below). In other words, on good days people feel more autonomous, competent, and related, whereas on bad days, people feel less autonomous and less competent.

We next examined which type of social activities contribute to feeling close and connected with others. These findings are displayed in figure 3.3. By far the

Table 3.1 Predicting Daily Well-Being from Day-Level Predictors

Predictors	Positive Emotion		Negative Emotion	
	B	t	B	t
Yesterday's well-being	.133	4.00**	.203	5.73**
Today's autonomy	.046	6.39**	−.023	3.34**
Today's competence	.250	5.17**	−.232	4.71**
Today's relatedness	.147	2.53*	−.053	1.04

$N = 76$
**$p < .001$
*$p < .05$

strongest predictor was feeling understood and appreciated by others. Meaningful talk, avoiding self-consciousness, and "hanging out" were also significant predictors, whereas concrete tasks and quarrels were unrelated. The apparent predominance of feeling understood, as well as the impact of meaningful talk and avoiding self-consciousness, supports our theoretical focus in this chapter on intimacy and attachment, and it begins to suggest details regarding what I will discuss in the final section of this chapter as "affirmative social interaction." Equally informative are those forms of social interaction that did not engender relatedness. Concrete tasks and activities, which some theorists have described as providing important bonding experiences for men (e.g., Tiger, 1969; Wood & Inman, 1993), had no significant effect. For that matter, on none of the activities were there sig-

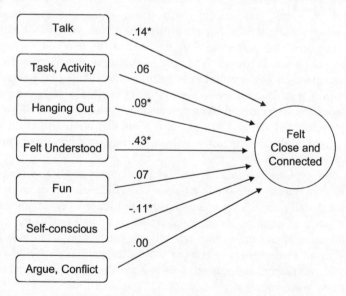

Figure 3.3 Predicting daily relatedness from social activity (within person). Coefficients are standardized. * $p < .01$

nificant interactions with sex; each form of social interaction predicted (or did not predict) relatedness need satisfaction equally well among men and women, counter to those theories that stress qualitative sex differences in relationships (but consistent with our own emphasis on the similarity of men's and women's social goals and values; Reis, 1998).

Why was conflict unrelated to feeling close and connected in daily social interaction? Substantial evidence relates interpersonal conflict to negative emotions and poor emotional well-being, and further, many relationship theorists propose that conflict is the sine qua non of relationship success (e.g., Christensen & Walczynski, 1997). Conflict, therefore, should diminish feelings of relatedness. But conflict may also contribute to enhanced feelings of relatedness, for two reasons: first, because conflict is most likely to occur in the context of relationships that are already close—between romantic partners or good friends, for example— and second, because conflict in ongoing relationships is often accompanied by active attempts to reconcile the contentious issue and to remain connected. Moreover, some theorists argue that conflictual interactions are most diagnostic of relationship well-being, since one can best determine how a partner regards the relationship when one's own and the partner's self-interests clash (Holmes, 1991). Thus, although conflict is affectively unpleasant, it need not diminish satisfaction of relatedness needs.

Although our results support a mediating role for relatedness needs in the association between social interaction and everyday moods, this last finding suggests that the emotional tenor of social activity may also affect well-being directly. To examine this possibility, we repeated the analyses displayed in figure 3.3 and added the seven forms of social interaction to the model after controlling for need satisfaction. This analysis examines nonmediated effects: do social relations contribute to daily well-being when satisfaction of relatedness needs is held constant? This speculation was supported in two cases. First, conflict was significantly related to end-of-day negative affect; as conflict increased, so did negative affect. Second, fun was significantly associated with positive affect; the more fun during socializing, the higher one's positive mood.

In sum, the impact of everyday social events on emotional states is complex. Social relations at times elicit powerful emotions that directly affect individual well-being. But psychological well-being involves more than simply maximizing positive affect and avoiding negative affect (Ryff, 1995); satisfying intrinsic organismic needs through ongoing activity is also essential. When ordinary social interaction fosters feelings of closeness and connection with significant others, individual well-being is enhanced relative to personal baselines; correspondingly, the absence of such activity diminishes well-being relative to baseline. Social interaction provides one important domain of activity in which everyday life events moderate the seemingly inflexible impact of trait predispositions.

Role of Affirmative Social Interaction in Emotional Well-Being

Arguing that positive social relations promote emotional well-being, both dispositionally and from one day to the next, and that poor relations impair emotional health is hardly controversial. Even a superficial search through *Bartlett's Quotations*, websites like www.quotes.com, the behavioral science literature, or popular bookstores is likely to generate widespread support for this general notion. Our role as researchers, of course, is to go beyond generalities, to establish what is actually true and what is false, and to determine the boundary conditions and mediating mechanisms for established phenomena. In other words, our task is to flesh out prevailing but imprecise beliefs with detailed empirical evidence. Exactly what is an affirmative social interaction? What sorts of social experience are distressing and injurious, and what sorts promote emotional well-being? These questions might also be phrased in a more process-oriented manner: how is it that socializing sometimes leads people to feel supported and uplifted, yet at other times leaves them isolated and dejected?

The research reported in this chapter pursues these questions within the domain of everyday social experiences. Methodological advantages aside, this approach emphasizes the manner in which affect arises during ordinary, natural activity. If behavior is contextually determined, as nearly all theories of motivation and behavior assume, then relationships—who one is with or thinking about—surely provide one of the most important and influential contextual variables (Reis, Collins, & Berscheid, 1999). And further, as mentioned in the introduction, if relationships are the predominant source of human emotion, then it is vital for emotion theorists to pay closer attention to the ways in which emotions spontaneously arise and subside in natural social contexts. I do not mean to imply that daily event methods are the only, or even the preferred, method for investigating these processes, but I do mean to suggest that they are likely to provide unique and informative insights for this critically important endeavor.

That daily event studies may be informative about the causes and consequences of emotional well-being can also be anticipated in other ways. Emotions, according to theorists like Frijda (1994), alert individuals to the existence of circumstances with potential relevance to personal goals and concerns. To Lazarus (1994), emotions embody appraisals of the personal significance of environmental conditions. He identifies a series of such appraisals, called "core relational themes," which are prototypic of the major human emotions, many of which reflect interpersonal events with significance for ongoing relationships. For example, anger indicates "a demeaning offense against me and mine," sadness denotes "having an irrevocable loss," and envy signifies "wanting what someone else has" (p. 164). Although social relations are more relevant to some emotions than to others, most of Lazarus's 15 emotional themes describe circumstances rooted in interpersonal activity and occurrences that often possess behavioral implications for ongoing relationships. Thus, many of the most important human emotions relate to interpersonal goals and desires, arise from events that involve the real or imagined behavior of others, stimulate interpersonal responses, and influence the subsequent course of relationships. Studying these event-appraisal-emotion sequences in their natural context would seem desirable.

Emotion is rooted deep in our evolutionary past, as is the predilection to seek and form enduring relationships. For example, Baumeister and Leary (1995) have theorized about the "need to belong"—the tendency to engage in lasting, affectively positive, and mutually caring relationships—which is similar in key respects to Deci and Ryan's (1991) relatedness need, which was discussed earlier. Based on the adaptive value of proximity with caregivers early in development, attachment theory (Bowlby, 1969/1982) proposed an innate homeostatic mechanism that engenders comfort and security when caregivers (and other attachment figures) are felt to be close or responsive and that engenders distress when they are perceived to be unavailable. Whereas the emotions generated during social relating (or its absence) serve as proximal, or mediating, motives in attachment theory, the more distal motive concerns the adaptive value of participating in stable, close relationships. Even the tendency for social life to revolve around small groups has been traced to the evolutionary survival advantages of this particular configuration (Brewer & Caporael, 1990). Regardless of specific propositions, in short, few theories would disagree that participating in stable, close relationships represents a fundamental human motive with emotional consequences.

These principles lead me to posit that (1) affirmative social interactions are those interactions in which innate needs for meaningful social ties are satisfied, and (2) positive emotions are experienced when these needs are fulfilled, whereas negative emotions result when they are thwarted. In what types of social activity are such needs most likely to be met? By examining emotion-relevant causes and consequences of various features of everyday social activity, the research described in this chapter highlights several variations on a common theme. All of the studies implicate participation in intimate, personally meaningful interactions; focusing one's activity on close others; feeling close and connected to partners and perceiving them as understanding of the self; and engaging in enjoyable events while avoiding negative events. Not coincidentally, these are themes emphasized by the intimacy model, which I have discussed elsewhere (Reis & Patrick, 1996; Reis & Shaver, 1988). As depicted in figure 3.4, this model de-

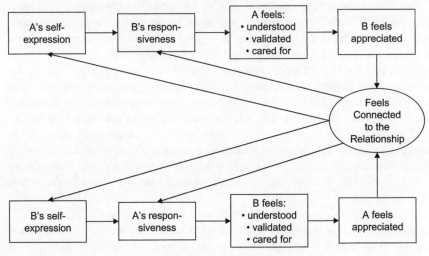

Figure 3.4 Reis and Patrick's (1996) intimacy model.

scribes the processes by which people come to feel intimately connected with their social partners.

Intimacy is conceptualized as an interactive process that begins when one individual expresses self-relevant thoughts, feelings, and personal information to another. Self-expression may be verbal or nonverbal, implicit or explicit, semantic or behavioral; all that matters is that the revealed content pertains to the emotional core of the self. The next step in the process depends on the partner's reaction. Responses perceived to be supportive and accepting tend to facilitate development of intimacy, whereas inappropriate, disinterested, or rejecting responses tend to deter intimacy. Responses that instill the perception that one is understood, validated, and cared for by a partner are most likely to foster intimacy. It is important to distinguish these three related characteristics in conceptual terms. *Understanding* refers to the belief that a partner "gets the facts right" and is important primarily in establishing a shared informational base. Feedback perceived as misinformed or irrelevant or that ignores one's self-understanding, no matter how favorable, is likely to be discounted. *Validation* refers to appreciation for one's dispositions, beliefs, or life circumstances. It contributes to intimacy and meaningful interaction by suggesting that the other values and respects the emotional core of the self. Feeling *cared for* matters because liking and concern are central to feeling comfortable and secure in a relationship and being willing to be self-expressive or responsive to a partner. Participating in this interactive process helps fulfill basic relatedness needs for both partners, as the far right arrows in figure 3.4 indicate.

Intimacy theory expands on earlier theories of self-disclosure and the acquaintance process in several respects: the priority given to emotional self-revelation through diverse modes of communication; the emphasis on perceived partner responses; the distinction among understanding, validation, and caring; and the simultaneous impact on intimacy of enacting either role in the process. Empirical support for the model is reviewed by Reis and Patrick (1996).

The link between intimate interaction and emotion may be clarified further by considering the role of attachment processes. According to attachment theory, over time and development, individuals generalize from their experiences in close relationships to form internalized mental representations of self in relation to others (Shaver et al., 1996). These mental models, comprising qualities such as social self-confidence, trust, perceived responsiveness, and comfort with closeness, influence social activity in several ways, prominently including the generation of expectations that regulate people's willingness to participate in intimate relationships and that color their perceptions of intimacy-related behavior. For example, an avoidantly insecure person who expects others to be cold and rejecting may be unlikely to initiate emotional self-revelation, may react with distance to a partner's self-disclosure, and may misconstrue behaviors intended to be helpful or supportive.

Furthermore, in adulthood, intimate relationships normally fulfill many of the functions characteristic of attachment relations (Hazan & Zeifman, 1999). For example, attachment figures often serve as a secure base—a supportive partner whose perceived availability facilitates exploration and mastery of the environment—and as a safe haven in distressing times. Also, like intimacy theory, attachment theory similarly stresses the role of feedback that is responsive to the person's needs in signaling that the self is valued. And, although attachment originates in the motivation to establish physical proximity, with increasing cognitive maturation, mental proximity—or perceived availability—becomes the functional representation of this drive. Perceived availability is phenomenologically similar to the subjective sense of closeness in intimate relationships. Finally, both theories propose that the strongest emotional reactions will occur when the self-concept is activated and vulnerable to feedback. These and other points of conceptual overlap led Bowlby (1988) to view intimate relations as the adult version of the attachment bond, which he described so eloquently for children and their caregivers.

In short, research on intimacy, attachment, and various other aspects of close relationships (Berscheid & Reis, 1998) implicate several processes, which form the heart of affirmative interaction. The value of identifying commonalities that reappear across different theoretical models and research programs resides in illuminating a common core of fundamental processes, which transcend any single way of thinking about or investigating these phenomena. Elsewhere, I have referred to these processes as component processes, in the sense that, together, they embody the many behavioral and emotional phenomena observed in affectively close relationships (Reis & Patrick, 1996). In no particular order, these processes are expressing the self to significant others; feeling securely connected to others and able to rely on them appropriately during stressful circumstances; being responsive and supportive to partners and open to their expressions of need; perceiving with reasonable accuracy a close partner's understanding, valuing, and caring for the self; experiencing genuine enjoyment during interaction with significant others; and coping constructively with negative emotions and interpersonal conflict. What makes such interactions affirmative is that they fulfill fundamental needs to relate to others, needs that have both distal-evolutionary and proximal-experiential roots. In our theorizing, frustration of these needs is likely to activate harmful processes (including negative emotions, maladaptive cognitions and behavior, and destructive psychophysiological reactions), whereas their satisfaction is likely to mobilize more beneficial response patterns.

It should be evident that our understanding of how these processes operate is at best elementary. Nevertheless, the current status of research into relationships, emotions, and human biopsychology provides ample evidence as to the vital importance of social relationships in any comprehensive model of human well-being (e.g., Berscheid & Reis, 1998; Ryff & Singer, 1998). A great deal more research is needed, of course, on both sides of this question: on the relationship side, to better understand the nature of these mechanisms and how they operate in close relationships; and on the well-being side, to identify specific mechanisms by which relational circumstances and feelings engender well-being (or its absence). Studies of these and related questions are likely to provide some of the most exciting, far-reaching, and important findings in the next generation of behavioral research.

Conclusion

The studies described in this chapter are consistent with four general principles:

1. Socially derived affect, both of the intense/transient and weak/enduring sort, is a core component of emotional well-being.
2. Social relations help regulate emotions, both by producing some emotions and by moderating emotions produced by other causes, and they influence the impact of events on emotional well-being.
3. The manner in which affects and emotions arise from ongoing activity within natural social networks is influential in determining both an individual's global sense of emotional well-being and day-to-day variations.
4. Full understanding of emotional well-being requires more comprehensive and detailed understanding of the impact of everyday interpersonal experiences.

The tantalizing notion that social relations are fundamental to human health and well-being has been a central element of folk wisdom for centuries, in nearly all recorded human societies and cultures. Behavioral science research has, however, been slow to pick up on this theme and begin the arduous but critical task of putting empirical flesh and scholarly meat on this skeletal notion. Recent developments, including, but not limited to, the work described throughout this volume, suggest that significant progress in understanding these processes may no be longer be a distant vision but may instead lie within the range of contemporary theories, methods, and technologies. It is hard to imagine an area of research with greater implications for knowledge and intervention.

Notes

1. Just in case it is not clear what I mean by within-person variation, here are two examples of within-person effects that are commonly studied. One type of study treats the degree of within-person variation as a phenomenon of interest: people differ in the extent of their mood swings. Some people's affect varies widely from moment to moment and day to day, whereas others' are more steady. Variability can be assessed through repeated measurement and then related to its presumed dispositional or contextual causes. For example, extroverted persons show larger mood variations across time than do introverted persons (Larsen & Kasimatis, 1990). A second type of study is concerned with identifying and explaining situational factors that produce variations around a person's baseline. For example, for most people, mood tends to be more positive on weekend days than weekdays. Reis et al. (2000) suggest that these differences might be due to activity differences: weekend days are more likely to involve activities that satisfy basic psychological needs than are weekdays.

2. Or, as Bernard Weiner is reported to have said, pithily, "Life is a within-subjects variable."

3. The statistical advantages come from maximum likelihood estimation and from weighting the obtained values by their variance and numerosity.

References

Altman, I., & Taylor, D. A. (1973). *Social penetration: The development of interpersonal relationships.* New York: Holt, Rinehart & Winston.

Argyle, M. (1987). *The psychology of happiness.* New York: Methuen.

Barkow, J. H., Cosmides, L., & Tooby, J. (1992). *The adapted mind.* New York: Oxford University Press.

Baumeister, R. F., & Leary, M. R. (1995). The need to belong: Desire for interpersonal attachment as a fundamental human motivation. *Psychological Bulletin, 117,* 497–529.

Berscheid, E., & Reis, H. T. (1998). Attraction and close relationships. In D. T. Gilbert, S. T. Fiske, & G. Lindzey (Eds.), *The handbook of social psychology* (4th ed., pp. 193–281). Boston: McGraw-Hill.

Bowlby, J. (1982). *Attachment and loss: Vol. 1. Attachment* (2d ed.). New York: Basic.

Bowlby, J. (1988). *A secure base.* New York: Basic.

Brewer, M. B., & Caporael, L. R. (1990). Selfish genes vs. selfish people: Sociobiology as origin myth. *Motivation and Emotion, 14,* 237–243.

Bryk, A. S., & Raudenbush, S. W. (1992). *Hierarchical linear models.* Newbury Park, CA: Sage.

Cacioppo, J. T., & Gardner, W. L. (1999). Emotion. *Annual Review of Psychology, 50,* 191–214.

Campbell, A., Converse, P. E., & Rodgers, W. L. (1976). *The quality of American life.* New York: Sage.

Carver, C. S., & White, T. L. (1994). Behavioral inhibition, behavioral activation, and affective responses to impending reward and punishment: The BIS/BAS scales. *Journal of Personality and Social Psychology, 61,* 132–140.

Christensen, A., & Walczynski, P. T. (1997). Conflict and satisfaction in couples. In R. J. Sternberg & M. Hojjat (Eds.), *Satisfaction in close relationships* (pp. 249–274). New York: Guilford.

Clark, L. A., & Watson, D. (1988). Mood and the mundane: Relations between daily life events and self-reported mood. *Journal of Personality and Social Psychology, 54,* 296–308.

David, J. P., Green, P. J., Martin, R., & Suls, J. (1997). Differential roles of neuroticism, extraversion, and event desirability for mood in daily life: An integrative model of top-down and bottom-up influences. *Journal of Personality and Social Psychology, 73,* 149–159.

Deci, E. L., & Ryan, R. (1991). *Intrinsic motivation and self-determination in human behavior.* New York: Plenum.

DeLongis, A., Folkman, S., & Lazarus, R. S. (1988). The impact of daily stress on health and mood: Psychological and social resources as mediators. *Journal of Personality and Social Psychology, 54,* 486–495.

Derlega, V. J., Metts, S., Petronio, S., & Margulis, S. T. (1993). *Self-disclosure.* Newbury Park, CA: Sage.

Ekman, P., & Davidson, R. J. (1994). Afterword: What is the function of emotions? In P. Ekman & R. J. Davidson (Eds.), *The nature of emotion* (pp. 137–139). New York: Oxford University Press.

Endler, N., & Magnusson, D. (1976). Toward an interactional psychology of personality. *Psychological Bulletin, 83,* 956–974.

Frijda, N. H. (1994). Emotions are functional, most of the time. In P. Ekman & R. J. Davidson (Eds.), *The nature of emotion* (pp. 112–122). New York: Oxford University Press.

Gable, S. L., & Reis, H. T. (1999). Now and then, them and us, this and that: Studying relationships across time, partner, context, and person. *Personal Relationships, 6,* 415–432.

Gable, S., Reis, H. T., & Elliot, A. (2000). Behavioral activation and inhibition in everyday life. *Journal of Personality and Social Psychology, 78,* 1135–1149.

Glenn, N. D., & Weaver, C. N. (1988). The changing relationship of marital status to reported happiness. *Journal of Marriage and the Family, 50*, 317–324.

Gottman, J. M. (1994). *What predicts divorce? The relationship between marital processes and marital outcomes.* Hillsdale, N.J.: Erlbaim.

Gray, J. A. (1987). *The psychology of fear and stress* (2d ed.). Cambridge: Cambridge University Press.

Hazan, C., & Shaver, P. R. (1987). Romantic love conceptualized as an attachment process. *Journal of Personality and Social Psychology, 52*, 511–524.

Hazan, C., & Zeifman, D. (1999). Pair bonds as attachment: Evaluating the evidence. In J. Cassidy & P. R. Shaver (Eds.), *Handbook of attachment: Theory, research, and clinical applications* (pp. 336–354). New York: Guilford.

Hinde, R. A. (1997). *Relationships: A dialectical perspective.* East Sussex, England: Psychology Press.

Holmes, J. G. (1991). Trust and the appraisal process in close relationships. In W. H. Jones & D. Perlman (Eds.), *Advances in personal relationships* (Vol. 3, pp. 57–104). London: Kingsley.

House, J. S., Landis, K. R., & Umberson, D. (1988). Social relationships and health. *Science, 241*, 540–545.

Kahneman, D. (1999). Objective happiness. In D. Kahneman, E. Diener, & N. Schwarz (Eds.), *Well-being: The foundations of hedonic psychology.* New York: Russell Sage.

Kasser, T., & Ryan, R. M. (1996). Further examining the American dream: Differential correlates of intrinsic and extrinsic goals. *Personality and Social Psychology Bulletin, 22*, 280–287.

Kennis, M. H. (1993). The roles of stability and level of self-esteem in psychological functioning. In Baumeister, R. F. (Ed.), *Self-esteem: The puzzle of low self-regard* (pp. 167–182). New York: Plenum.

Kenny, D. A. (1990). What makes a relationship special? In T. Draper & A. C. Marcos (Eds.), *Family variables: Conceptualization, measurement, and use* (pp. 161–178). Newbury Park, CA: Sage.

Kenrick, D. T., & Trost, M. R. (1997). Evolutionary approaches to relationships. In S. Duck (Ed.), *Handbook of personal relationships* (2d ed., pp. 151–177). Chichester, England: John Wiley and Sons.

Larsen, R., & Diener, E. (1987). Affect intensity as an individual difference characteristic: A review. *Journal of Research in Personality, 21*, 1–39.

Larsen, R. J., & Kasimatis, M. (1990). Individual differences in entrainment of mood to the weekly calendar. *Journal of Personality and Social Psychology, 58,* 164–171.

Larson, R., & Csikszentmihalyi, M. (1983). The experience sampling method. In H. T. Reis (Ed.), *Naturalistic approaches to studying social interaction* (pp. 41–56). San Francisco: Jossey-Bass.

Lazarus, R. (1994). Universal antecedents of the emotions. In P. Ekman & R. J. Davidson (Eds.), *The nature of emotion: Fundamental questions* (pp. 163–171). New York: Oxford University Press.

Levy, M. B., & Davis, K. E. (1988). Love styles and attachment styles compared: Their relations to each other and to various relationship characteristics. *Journal of Social and Personal Relationships, 5*, 439–471.

Lykken, D., & Tellegen, A. (1996). Happiness is a stochastic phenomenon. *Psychological Science, 7*, 186–189.

Marco, C., & Suls, J. (1993). Daily stress and the trajectory of mood: Spillover, response assimilation, contrast, and chronic negative affectivity. *Journal of Personality and Social Psychology, 64*, 1053–1063.

Moskowitz, D. S., Brown, K. W., Cote, S. (1997). Reconceptualizing stability: Using time as a psychological dimension. *Current Directions in Psychological Science, 6,* 126–131.

Myers, D. G. (1992). *The pursuit of happiness: Who is happy—and why.* New York: William Morrow.

Notarius, C., & Markman, H. (1993). *We can work it out: Making sense of matital conflict.* New York: G. P. Putnam's Sons.

Peplau, L. A., & Goldston, S. E. (1982). *Preventing the harmful consequences of severe and persistent loneliness.* Rockville, MD: National Institute of Mental Health.

Pinsker, H., Nepps, P., Redfield, J., & Winston, A. (1985). Applicants for short-term dynamic psychotherapy. In A. Winston (Ed.), *Clinical and research issues in short-term dynamic psychotherapy* (pp. 104–116). Washington, DC: American Psychiatric Association.

Reis, H. T. (1994). Domains of experience: Investigating relationship processes from three perspectives. In R. Erber, & R. Gilmour (Eds.), *Theoretical frameworks for personal relationships* (pp. 87–110). Hillsdale, NJ: Erlbaum.

Reis, H. T. (1998). The interpersonal context of emotions: Gender differences in intimacy and related behaviors. In D. J. Canary & K. Dindia (Eds.), *Sex differences and similarities in communication* (pp. 203–231). Mahwah, NJ: Erlbaum.

Reis, H. T., & Collins, N. (2000). Assessing relationship properties and interactions bearing on social support. In S. Cohen, B. Gottlieb, & L. Underwood (Eds.), *Social support: A guidebook for research and intervention.* New York: Oxford University Press.

Reis, H. T., Collins, W. A., & Berscheid, E. (2000). The relationship context of human behavior and development. *Psychological Bulletin, 126,* 844–872.

Reis, H. T., & Gable, S. L. (2000). Event-sampling and other methods for studying daily experience. In H. T. Reis & C. Judd (Eds.), *Handbook of research methods in social psychology* (pp. 190–222). New York: Cambridge University Press.

Reis, H. T., Lin, Y. C., Bennett, M. E., & Nezlek, J. B. (1993). Change and consistency in social participation during early adulthood. *Developmental Psychology, 29,* 633–645.

Reis, H. T., & Patrick, B. C. (1996). Attachment and intimacy: Component processes. In A. Kruglanski & E. T. Higgins (Eds.), *Social psychology: Handbook of basic principles* (pp. 523–563). New York: Guilford.

Reis, H. T., Sheldon, K. M., Gable, S. L., Roscoe, J., & Ryan, R. M., (2000). Daily well-being: The role of autonomy, competence, and relatedness. *Personality and Social Psychology Bulletin, 26,* 419–435.

Reis, H. T., & Shaver, P. (1988). Intimacy as an interpersonal process. In S. Duck (Ed.), *Handbook of personal relationships* (pp. 367–389). Chichester, England: John Wiley and Sons.

Reis, H. T., & Wheeler, L. (1991). Studying social interaction with the Rochester Interaction Record. In M. P. Zanna (Ed.), *Advances in experimental social psychology* (Vol. 24, pp. 269–318). San Diego: Academic.

Ross, M. (1989). Relation of implicit theories to the construction of personal histories. *Psychological Review, 96,* 341–357.

Russell, D., Peplau, L. A., & Cutrona, C. E. (1980). The revised UCLA loneliness scale: Concurrent and discriminant validity evidence. *Journal of Personality and Social Psychology, 39,* 472–480.

Ryff, C. D. (1995). Psychological well-being in adult life. *Current Directions in Psychological Science, 4,* 99–103.

Ryff, C. D., & Singer, B. (1998). The contours of positive human health. *Psychological Inquiry, 9,* 1–28.

Schwarz, N., Groves, R. M., & Schuman, H. (1998). In D. T. Gilbert, S. T. Fiske, & G. Lindzey (Eds.), *The handbook of social psychology* (4th ed., pp. 143–179). Boston: McGraw-Hill.

Sears, R. R. (1977). Sources of life satisfactions of the Terman gifted men. *American Psychologist, 32,* 119–128.

Shaver, P. R., Collins, N., & Clark, C. L. (1996). Attachment styles and internal working models of self and relationship partners. In G. Fletcher & J. Fitness (Eds.), *Knowledge structures and interaction in close relationships: A social psychological approach* (pp. 25–61). Mahwah, NJ: Erlbaum.

Sheldon, K. M., Ryan, R., & Reis, H. T. (1996). What makes for a good day? Competence and autonomy in the day and in the person. *Personality and Social Psychology Bulletin, 22,* 1270–1279.

Stone, A. A., Neale, J., & Shiffman, S. (1993). Daily assessments of stress and coping and their association with mood. *Annals of Behavioral Medicine, 15,* 8–16.

Stone, A. A., Schwartz, J. E., Neale, J. M., Shiffman, S., Marco, C. A., Hickcox, M., Paty, J., Porter, L. S., & Cruise, L. J. (1998). A comparison of coping assessed by ecological momentary assessment and retrospective recall. *Journal of Personality and Social Psychology, 74,* 1670–1680.

Stone, A. A., & Shiffman, S. (1994). Ecological momentary assessment (EMA) in behavioral medicine. *Annals of Behavioral Medicine, 16,* 199–202.

Suh, E., Diener, E., & Fujita, F. (1996). Events and subjective well-being: Only recent events matter. *Journal of Personality and Social Psychology, 70,* 1091–1102.

Taylor, S. E. (1991). Asymmetrical effects of positive and negative events: The mobilization-minimization hypothesis. *Psychological Bulletin, 110,* 109–128.

Tidwell, M. O., Reis, H. T., & Shaver, P. R. (1996). Attachment, attractiveness, and social interaction: A diary study. *Journal of Personality and Social Psychology, 71,* 729–745.

Tiger, L. (1969). *Men in groups.* New York: Vintage.

Uchino, B. N., Cacioppo, J. T., & Kiecolt-Glaser, J. K. (1996). The relationship between social support and physiological processes: A review with emphasis on underlying mechanisms and implications for health. *Psychological Bulletin, 119,* 488–531.

Veroff, J., Douvan, E., & Kulka, R. A. (1981). *Mental health in America: Patterns of help-seeking from 1957 to 1976.* New York: Basic.

Watson, D., & Clark, L. A. (1994). Emotions, moods, traits, and temperaments: Conceptual distinctions and empirical findings. In P. Ekman & R. J. Davidson (Eds.), *The nature of emotion* (pp. 89–93). New York: Oxford University Press.

Wheeler, L., Reis, H., & Nezlek, J. (1983). Loneliness, social interaction, and sex roles. *Journal of Personality and Social Psychology, 45,* 943–953.

Wood, J. T., & Inman, C. C. (1993). In a different mode: Masculine styles of communicating closeness. *Journal of Applied Communication Research, 21,* 279–295.

Wood, W., Rhodes, N., & Whelan, M. (1989). Sex differences in positive well-being: A consideration of emotional style and marital status. *Psychological Bulletin, 106,* 249–264.

Wortman, C. B., & Silver, R. C. (1989). The myths of coping with loss. *Journal of Consulting and Clinical Psychology, 57,* 349–357.

Commentary

Angela Cloninger

It has long been social scientists' goal to study the nature of human social interaction in situ, but few have achieved this aim. Harry Reis and colleagues take a microanalytic look at daily life by asking individuals to report on various features of ten-minute or more social interactions shortly after they have been experienced. Using this diary method, Reis focuses on the emotional substance of daily social interactions; his theory is that well-being is rooted in the emotional nourishment one obtains from the cumulation of daily contact with others. This approach makes significant contributions to the goal of linking emotion in social relations to health.

Reis's empirical approach is unique for several reasons. First, event-sampling measures like the Rochester Interaction Record (RIR) probe beyond the basic behavioral content of social interaction. The RIR takes a snapshot of "emotion in action" by requiring participants to indicate which emotions and levels of intimacy they experienced in each social interchange. In addition, the RIR avoids many of the methodological difficulties associated with retrospective self-reports as it requires participants to describe isolated minor interactions proximal to when they are occurring. The diary approach also minimizes self-report bias by requiring on-the-spot details about everyday social experiences. Last, by exploring the significance of social connections at the microanalytic level, Reis extends past social relational research which emphasized the emotional impact of major events only.

Much of Reis's work is driven by two theories: Bowlby's attachment theory (1969/1982) and Reis and Shaver's intimacy theory (1988). With regard to attachment, Reis seeks to develop Bowlby's postulation that the attachment bond a child develops with her caregiver is transmuted to adulthood and is manifest within adult intimate relations. He classifies an individual's attachment style as secure, anxious-ambivalent, or avoidant. With respect to intimacy, Reis and Shaver formulate intimacy as a sequence of self-expression and partner response. As illustrated in figure 3.4, an intimate interaction is defined as one in which the discloser-responder sequence encourages the discloser to feel "understood, validated, and cared for." Reis and Patrick (1996) elaborate that this sequence involves verbal and nonverbal sharing of meaningful thoughts, feelings, behaviors, desires, and needs. Both attachment and intimacy processes are thought to be "linked intrinsically to well-being," as they are thought to have "deep-seated and pervasive effects on social behavior and personal health and well-being"(Reis & Patrick, 1996, p. 525).

Reis contributes to the core ideas that guide this volume by drawing on these theories to characterize emotional interactions as fundamental to positive social relationships. "Affirmative social interactions" are accompanied by positive emotions, which function to satisfy inborn needs for meaningful social ties. Individuals involved in affirmative social interactions are securely attached, and they experience, to some degree, satisfaction of three basic needs: autonomy, competence, and relatedness. Among the social processes that Reis proposes as affirmative are "experiencing genuine enjoyment during interaction with significant others, being responsive and supportive to partners, and feeling securely connected to others."

In formulating the affirmative social interaction, Reis plays the role of psychological archaeologist by using a within-person approach to uncover what it means for an individual to "be well" over a series of daily social encounters. His analyses identify both the quantitative and qualitative dimensions of social interaction which feed into the daily experience of emotional well-being. With regard to quantity, Reis finds that the more individuals interact with confidantes, the less loneliness they report in a separate loneliness questionnaire administered in conjunction with the RIR. Reis further asserts that the valence of social events (positive or negative) and daily mood must be considered in linking emotion in social relations to health. Although little emphasis is placed on trait dispositions, Reis highlights that individual differences in emotional reactivity, as well as differences in the relevance of everyday events for satisfying individual basic needs (autonomy, competence, and relatedness) may influence how emotionally well one feels on a day-to-day basis. Finally, Reis discusses how attachment styles, or individual styles of emotional regulation, may indirectly determine levels of emotional well-being on a microanalytic level by sculpting both the quality and quantity of social interactions. His studies suggest that attachment styles not only affect emotional well-being via social interactions but, in a reciprocal fashion, they are preserved by the daily expression of one's attachment style within a social context.

Daily Social Relations and Themes of This Volume

Positive and Negative Emotions

Reis focuses extensively on the positive and negative aspects of daily social interactions, characterizing both as dimensions of the actual social interactions. He explicitly asks individuals to report the good and the bad emotions. Reis also distinguishes between positive and negative event types and attachment styles, secure (positive) versus insecure (negative). He goes beyond identifying good and bad parts of daily social interactions, however, by asking questions about the positive and negative meaning that individuals assign to such experiences. First, as depicted in figure 3.2, Reis's research suggests that different event types (positive social events, negative social events, positive achievement events, and negative achievement events) may have significant independent effects on positive and negative emotional experience. Previous work has mostly concentrated on the implications of negative social events for health and social functioning. His work is thus unique for suggesting that *both* positive and negative daily social interactions may have powerful, independent effects on one's well-being.

Reis writes that satisfaction of basic needs may mediate the connection between social interchanges and the positive and negative emotions derived from such interchanges. Specifically, individuals may feel both greater positive emotion and less negative emotion when their needs for autonomy, competency, and relatedness have been fulfilled in some way. These positive/negative findings improve on past work which has typically overlooked that positive and negative emotions are significant independent psychological entities. And, from a microanalytic perspective, such findings serve to support the goal of this volume for more comprehensive models of well-being, which incorporate the role of positive social experiences as well as negative ones.

Reis's look at the independent roles of positive and negative emotions in social experiences also suggests a key idea, namely, that negative life experiences can be made positive if they are viewed as opportunities for positive change. His studies have shown that conflict, ordinarily considered a negative activity, may result in increased negative affect in the short term, but in the long run may allow one to feel more intense positive emotions. He discusses how "coping constructively with negative emotions and relationship conflict" can paradoxically lead to close-ness, since conflict frequently erupts within close relationships and therefore is usually followed by reconciliation. He adds that conflictual interactions may be instrumental in generating affirmative social interactions. These points fit well with those of other social relational theorists, who consider negative interactions paramount for encouraging self-discovery, personal growth, and developing a sense of life meaning (King & Pennebaker, 1996). In the future, Reis could build on these claims by analyzing the frequency of and conditions under which con-flicts are healthy (i.e., significantly linked to high levels of emotional well-being). That negative daily interactions may allow for deeper positive relationships is relevant for understanding how, at the microanalytic level, social relations with significant others may serve to buffer individuals from stress, as discussed by Cohen, Spiegel, and Kimerling, and Seeman elsewhere in this volume.

How both positive and negative daily experiences affect well-being may also re-quire a more explicit definition of emotional well-being. Reis describes elsewhere (Sheldon, Ryan, & Reis, 1996) that daily well-being scores are computed from four daily well-being outcome measures included in the diary checklists, a positive and a negative mood checklist, a Psychological Vitality scale, and a physical symptom checklist. However, he does not provide a clear definition of emotional well-being, which is needed to explain why he included the four well-being outcome meas-ures. Moreoever, Reis might consider other psychological components of well-being, including aspects of Ryff's psychological well-being measures, such as per-ceived levels of personal growth or purpose in life (Ryff, 1989), or self-esteem levels. And, to validate the somatic complaints that respondents report in the physical symptom checklist, he might include a physician's assessment of each participant at some point during the two-week experimental periods.

Gender Differences

Reis's research has shown that men and women hold similar social goals and val-ues and that several types of social activities evoke similar degrees of close feel-ings for both genders. However, his work suggests several gender differences as well. First, although both men and women experience less loneliness when their interactions with confidantes are more intimate and satisfying, this correlation achieves significance only among men. Since men's confidantes are primarily women, it makes sense then that men who interact with women more often and for longer periods of time appear significantly less lonely than those who do not. Further, it appears that men rely on women for intimacy. For women, daily emo-tional interactions seem to affect mental health in a different manner. Reis's work suggests that when women interact with men, the quality of the interaction rather than the quantity of the interactions, may be significantly related to both per-ceived intimacy and satisfaction of social experience. Reis notes that this finding may indicate women's ability to interact intimately in many situations and with many people.

Reis's conclusions about gender differences are compelling and quite interesting, but they should be viewed with caution. That women are more skilled in the ability to engage in intimate, satisfying activities could be tested by conducting a gender analysis on the frequency with which each gender participates in high-intimacy interactions. In so doing, Reis may show that gender differences in general emotional experience and expression, which has been suggested in previous literature, can be partly explained by the fact that women on a daily basis more frequently initiate and maintain intimate interactions. If women, in fact, show greater levels of emotional well-being within interpersonal contexts, the implications of such a gender difference for physical health are all the more interesting. Further, although Reis acknowledges in another volume that his data suggest that gender differences in intimacy are influenced by cultural norms (Reis, 1998), his findings cannot be generalized across the entire population due to the limits imposed by his homogeneous participant samples, which consisted primarily of privileged young adults. His results on gender differences would pertain to more diverse peoples if he were to examine the effects of age, educational history, or socioeconomic status on daily intimacy levels (perceived with significant others) or daily quantities of affirmative social interactions.

To expand his current work, Reis can also research other hypothesized gender differences, which have accumulated in the recent proliferation of emotion literature. His methodology might be employed to explore whether women know more about the causes, characteristics, and consequences of emotions—not just because they more frequently experience them, but because they have learned to take emotions more seriously than do men (Fischer, 1995). Since his diary method requires participants to document emotions and their intensities over a broad range of social interactions, Reis could clarify whether women are more inclined than men to share their emotional troubles over a wider network of human relationships (Salokangas, Mattila, & Joukamaa, 1988). Finally, he may be able to probe why, at the microanalytic level, men report positive relations with others as the lowest rated of Ryff's six aspects of psychological well-being (see chap. 5).

Mechanisms and Methods

At the beginning of his chapter and at several later points, Reis refers to emotion as the nexus between social interaction and psychological health. Of interest to this volume is whether daily interactions with others and the emotions surrounding them penetrate the physiological routes to broader health outcomes. Accordingly, his microanalytic assessments of social experiences are usefully merged with other, more biologically oriented agendas outlined in this collection. As noted by Temoshok, "The term 'emotion' should be considered to cover at least three overlapping areas: expression (verbal or nonverbal behavior), physiological manifestations, and experiential phenomena" (1996, p. 39). The section on cross-talk describes possible avenues of communication among Reis and other contributors to this book, who address physiological mechanisms that link emotion in social relationships to health. These researchers also stand to benefit from the work in Reis's chapter, as they have not, for the most part, probed the day-to-day features of social interaction that may shape health outcomes.

Reis uses a single self-report approach to assess a wide range of daily emotional experience. The method provides an in-depth look at what an individual feels and experiences over the course of an average day. Uniquely, it taps experiences that are often forgotten shortly after they occur. Moreover, Reis's diary approach captures, at the self-report level, the daily frequency of affirmative social interactions, which foster emotional health. The RIR is also frequently used in conjunction with other self-report assessments, such as the UCLA Loneliness scale and Carver and White's (1994) Behavioral Activation and Inhibition scales.

The event-sampling method used by Reis asks participants to rate intimacy on a Likert scale from 1 (superficial) to 7 (meaningful). It would be useful to know how individuals that respond to this scale construe intimacy: what are their characterizations of it? Moreover, what other important needs (beyond competence, relatedness, and autonomy) might be served by these interactions? Maslow's need hierarchy, for example, suggests that over and above striving to satisfy belongingness and love needs, humans seek to fulfill self-esteem and self-actualization needs. These are commonly satisfied in an interpersonal arena (Maslow, 1971/ 1993). Reis, too, highlights that both attachment and intimacy theories "propose that the strongest emotional reactions will occur when the self-concept is activated and vulnerable to feedback." Hence, it may be informative to measure levels of self-esteem and self-actualization fostered by discrete daily social interactions. Such analyses could show how daily relational precursors influence emotional well-being via indirect influences on self-esteem or satisfaction of self-actualization needs.

Cumulative Effects

Reis's approach is, in itself, an accumulation of self-reports of a series of daily social interactions. His method invites examination of the extent to which many everyday minor events, rather than just salient events, accumulate to create a perceived level of emotional well-being. Essentially, his studies require participants to count up the small relational highs and lows that occurr over a random two-week period. This feature of Reis's work is invaluable because the accumulation of many small daily adversities and advantages may comprise core ingredients of the emotions that influence well-being. However, Reis does not explicitly address the role that total quantity of social interactions (including those with insignificant others) plays in contributing to emotional well-being. Extensive daily social interactions may be emotionally healthy to a point, but then interaction overload might exert a negative influence on one's well-being. Such frequency data could also be used to clarify whether some people tend to oscillate between positive and negative interactions more frequently than others.

The health implications of chronicity or great fluctuation in positive and negative daily interactions are of particular relevance to this volume. As Reyes discusses in her commentary on the chapter by Coe and Lubach, a stressor (e.g., separation from the mother) may not be harmful if it occurs infrequently, but it may adversely affect the immune system if repeated many times within a short period. Along these lines, it would be interesting to examine whether daily bombardment of wholly negative social interactions, or even extensive positive social interactions, take a toll on (or bolster) the mind and the body, the immune system in particular. Ryff and Singer et al.'s study of allostasis assumes that "healthy functioning requires ongoing adjustments and adaptations of the internal physiologic milieu." They suggest that an individual with emotionally satisfying human relationships may have lower allostatic load and thereby suffer relatively little "physiological wear and tear on organ systems and tissues." Reis could help substantiate this claim by showing that socioemotional relations influence allostatic load on the microanalytic level as well.

Prospective study designs would be particularly helpful in identifying how social interaction styles are learned or established, as well as whether intimacy or attachment styles change over time. Incorporating a life course scope also might specify factors (e.g., shifting roles or life crises) that may influence, at the microanalytic level, changes in intimacy levels with significant others or perceived levels of emotional well-being. From a developmental perspective, Erikson (1966) delineates the sixth stage of psychosocial development, which embodies the young adult's struggle with isolation and intimacy, and he suggests that intimacy may not mean the same thing for a young adult and a middle-aged person. Reis has the methodology to clarify whether the young adult's *daily* struggle with intimacy is perhaps distinct from the middle-aged adult's experience. How the intimacy characteristics of different life stages might affect health behaviors could also speak to the impact of social relationships on health, which is the focus of this volume.

Cross-Talk

Reis's research, in combination with the work of other contributors, may prove instrumental for the future exploration of emotions, social relationships, and health. First, communicative interchange between the research programs of Reis and Spiegel presents avenues for future study. Spiegel and Kimerling propose that increased emotional expression and emotional support derived from group therapy may slow progression of metastatic breast cancer among women. Reis's event-sampling strategy could provide a useful framework for studying the daily interactions that take place in Spiegel and Kimerling's cancer group therapy sessions. By asking patients to complete the RIR for the interactions that occur in a series of group meetings, Spiegel could pinpoint the health-promoting features of intimate group therapy interactions. In particular, it might be possible to specify the interactional processes that encourage a discloser to feel understood, validated, and cared for. Furthermore, Reis's attachment framework can inform the dynamics of the support groups by clarifying the attachment styles that individuals bring with them to the therapy. Drawing on attachment theory, Spiegel and colleagues could integrate a measurement of women's attachment styles into their formulation of emotional expression in cancer outcomes.

In turn, Reis could elaborate on the connections among emotion, relationships, and health by blending aspects of Spiegel's work into his own. Spiegel and Kimerling's studies emphasize that emotional expression is significant for the psychological well-being of women with metastatic breast cancer and show that those who participate in expressive support group therapy are "significantly less anxious and depressed" than those who do not. What is the role of daily emotional expression in social interactions for emotional well-being? This is a significant question for emotion researchers, who almost always draw a distinction between emotional experience and expression. Experiencing an emotion does not necessarily translate to expression of it. It could be informative for Reis to distinguish between emotions experienced and expressed in each daily interaction. Is emotion expression the stronger influence on well-being?

From the clinical perspective, as exemplified by the work of Gottman and Spiegel and Kimerling, much might be learned about an individual's daily emotional functioning from Reis's event-sampling method. As one of the main goals of psychotherapy is to increase emotional well-being, the RIR may serve as a unique tool for evaluating the therapeutic efficacy of existing cognitive and behavioral treatment techniques. Specifically, individuals learning Gottman's emotion-coaching techniques or those participating in Spiegel and Kimerling's expressive group therapy sessions could be studied with regard to their daily social interactions. So doing would clarify which types of individuals are most likely to benefit from the interventions and during which difficult life situations (e.g., health crises or work transitions). On a more general level, Reis's approach could be used to distinguish the daily social relational ingredients between normal and troubled, thereby advancing an understanding of daily intimacy among those who are psychologically healthy, compared with those suffering from varying degrees of dysfunction. Such knowledge could contribute to the development of novel educational or clinical interventions focused on social relational functioning at the daily level.

Adopting Gottman's clinical perspective is further valuable for learning more about how the experience of a negative emotion might have positive effects. As Gottman affirms, the emotion-coaching parent, who raises emotionally healthy children, does not "see negative affects as if they were toxins." Reis's daily experience surveys allow for a microanalytic depiction of how emotion coaching about negative affect in daily interactions can paradoxically lead to enhanced well-being, including a deeper sense of intimacy.

Seeman offers another investigative angle for Reis to pursue. Seeman's research explores the connection between social relational ties and neuroendocrine regulation. However, such work is based on global assessments of social relations. An interesting question is whether more microanalytic daily evaluations might show stronger ties to such measures as cortisol, epinephrine, or norepinephrine, especially when the day-to-day measures are combined to illustrate cumulative relational profiles.

There is also valuable complementarity between the research programs of Cohen and Reis. Cohen shows that introverts may be at greater risk for development of the common cold than extroverts. What are the daily interactional styles of introverts and extroverts, and are these patterns related to the influence of BIS

(Behavioral Inhibition System) versus BAS (Behavioral Activation System), as examined by Reis? Cohen's framework also offers a classification system for categorizing the many social interactions reported on the RIR, such as the three categories of conflict: interpersonal, work, and other. Ryff and Singer et al.'s relationship types (spouse, nonspousal family relationships, and friends) also provide categories for classifying the daily interactional data that comprise the RIR. In turn, Reis could expand the scope of Cohen by clarifying whether those with more diverse social relationships have less susceptibility to colds. Cohen measures social diversity by examining participation in 12 types of social relationships, using the Social Network Index questionnaire, but Reis's event-sampling approach would add qualitative texture to Cohen's definition of "diverse social relationships," probably as it does the emotional interactions that are responsible for the development of social relationships.

Future Directions

Clearly, there is much to be gained from linking Reis's microanalytic assessment of socioemotional experience to biological variables. This could begin with single components of allostatic load, such as cortisol or epinephrine, to measure both the emotional and physical wear and tear sustained in the cumulation of daily interaction. Panksepp (1978) has shown that social attachments may increase natural brain opiates, but Reis might investigate whether Panksepp's finding is valid at the microanalytic level. Uvnäs-Moberg's research (1998) suggests that the neuropeptide system, which contains oxytocin, may mediate the consequences of positive social interactions. According to her research, Reis might attempt to show that the cumulation of affirmative social interactions, which enable an individual to feel understood, validated, and cared for, is also linked to oxytocin. Or, Reis might even attempt to link intimacy and attachment to spirituality or healing capacities (illness duration) in order to probe more sensitively the effects that emotion in social relationships have on health on a day-to-day basis. Certainly, all such routes hold promise for the future and will provide opportunities to explore how "each emotion provides specific psychobiological information as part of a process of core psychological growth with parallel physiologic changes" (Dafter, 1996, p. 33) and, thereby, the dynamic blend of emotions and their meanings that facilitates optimal health and well-being.

Another major future avenue of research involves assessing both participants in the discloser-responder interactional sequence. If intimacy, an interdependent process, is to be used to understand emotional well-being, all actors in the social interactions should probably be investigated. That is, a more vivid picture of intimacy may result were Reis to administer the RIR to two or more of the social interactors. By sampling each participant, it would be possible to determine the amount of convergence or divergence in the extent to which each intimate partner feels understood, validated, and cared for. Such analysis would be relevant not only for determining what people receive from daily social interactions but also what they impart to the other partner in an intimate dyad.

In sum, Reis's comprehensive microanalytic look at the *experience* of emotions in social relations and their role in positive mental functioning is a significant and much-needed component of understanding how emotion in social relationships makes its way to health outcomes. Everyday socioemotional interchange is not likely the sole determinant of well-being, but Reis has convincingly demonstrated it as a powerful ingredient. By combining the event-sampling approach with longitudinal designs and physiological or clinical assessments, significant advances would be made in understanding how daily affirmative social interactions promote well-being of the mind and of the body.

References

Bowlby, J. (1982). *Attachment and loss: Vol. 1. Attachment* (2d ed.). New York: Basic.

Carver, C. S., & White, T. L. (12994). Behavioral inhibition, behavioral activation, and affective responses to impending reward and punishment; The BIS/BAS scales, *Journal of Personality and Social Psychology, 67,* 319–333.

Dafter, R. E. (1996). Why "negative" emotions can sometimes be positive: The spectrum model of emotions and their role in mind-body healing. *Advances, 12,* 6–18.

Erikson, E. H. (1966). Eight stages of man. *International Journal of Psychiatry, 2,* 281–300.

Fischer, A. H. (1995). Emotion concepts as a function of gender. In J. A. Russell et al. (Eds.), *Everyday conceptions of emotion* (pp. 457–474). The Netherlands: Kluwer Academic Publishers.

King, L. A. & Pennebaker, J. W. (1996). Thinking about goals, glue, and the meaning of life. In R. S. Wyer, Jr. (Ed.), *Ruminative thoughts: Advances in social cognition* (pp. 97–106). Mahwah, NJ: Lawrence Erlbaum.

Maslow, A. H. (1993). *The farther reaches of human nature.* (2d ed.). New York: Arkana/Penguin.

Panksepp, J. (1978). The biology of social attachments: Opiates alleviate separation distress. *Biological Psychiatry, 13,* 607–618.

Reis, H. T. (1998). The interpersonal context of emotions: Gender differences in intimacy and related behaviors. In D. J. Canary & K. Dindia (Eds.), *Sex differences and similarities in communication* (pp. 203–231). Mahway, NJ: Erlbaum.

Reis, H. T. and Patrick, B. C. (1996). Attachment and intimacy: Component processes. In A. Kruglanski & E. T. Higgins (Eds.), *Social psychology: Handbook of basic principles* (pp. 523–563). New York: Guilford.

Reis, H. T., and Shaver, P. (1988). Intimacy as an interpersonal process. In S. Duck (Ed.), *Handbook of personal relationships* (pp. 367–389). Chichester, England: John Wiley and Sons.

Ryff, C. D. (1989). Happiness is everything, or is it? Explorations on the meaning of psychological well-being. *Journal of Personality and Social Psychology, 57,* 1069–1081.

Salokangas, R. K. R., Mattila, V., and Joukamaa, M. (1988). Intimacy and mental disorder in late middle age. *Acta Psychiatrica Scandinavica, 78,* 555–560.

Sheldon, K. M., Ryan, R., and Reis, H. T. (1996). What makes for a good day? Competence and autonomy in the day and in the person. *Personality and Social Psychology Bulletin, 22,* 1270–1279.

Temoshok, L. R. (1996). On new-old myths and new-old models concerning the role of emotion in health and illness. *Advances, 12,* 38–41.

Uvnäs-Moberg, K. (1998). Oxytocin may mediate the benefits of positive social interaction and emotions. *Psychoneuroendocrinology, 23,* 819–835.

4

Group Psychotherapy for
Women with Breast Cancer

Relationships among Social Support,
Emotional Expression, and Survival

David Spiegel & Rachel Kimerling

*A*s oncological treatment has become more effective, cancer can be thought of more as a chronic than a terminal illness. However, given the progressive nature of the disease and the fact that approximately half of all people diagnosed with cancer will eventually die of it, a realistic approach to cancer care involves attention to emotional support for patients who are coping with the disease. In particular, the affective responses of patients and their families to life threat is often viewed as a problem rather than an opportunity for intervention. This review of psychosocial problems and interventions for cancer patients will emphasize attention to the management of emotion in the context of illness.

Supportive/expressive group psychotherapy, an empirically validated psychological intervention for breast cancer patients conducted at the Psychosocial Treatment Laboratory at Stanford University Medical Center, is presented as a means for facilitating emotional adjustment. First, we review the main components of the therapy and the empirical support for the relationship of these elements to psychological adjustment and health. We then review the literature regarding group psychotherapy interventions for cancer patients and their effects on psychological adjustment and survival. A critical analysis follows, which delineates potential mechanisms by which the social support and emotional expression facilitated in these interventions might affect the survival time of cancer patients. We propose that both the provision of social support and the opportunity for emotional expression are beneficial to health and psychological adjustment in cancer patients. We also propose that an interaction between these two factors— where relationships with similar others develop in an emotionally expressive context—may be especially potent in the impact on the psychological adjustment, medical adherence, and, potentially, the health status of individuals diagnosed with advanced cancer.

Supportive/Expressive Group Psychotherapy

Psychosocial intervention for cancer patients in our clinical research program, conducted in conjunction with appropriate psychopharmacological, medical, and surgical treatment, consists of seven components: social support, emotional expression, processing issues regarding death and dying, reordering life priorities, increasing family support, facilitating communication with physicians, and symptom control. Following is a brief review of these components:

Social Support

Psychotherapy, especially in groups, can provide a new social network built upon the common bond of facing similar problems (Spiegel, 1993a). Cancer patients often have to curtail social, vocational, and educational activities because of limitations imposed by the disease (Bloom & Spiegel, 1984). Symptoms of both depression and post–traumatic stress disorder have been documented in breast cancer patients (Alter et al., 1996; Cordova et al., 1995; Spiegel, 1996). Inherent in both of these syndromes are feelings of alienation and isolation and difficulties in close relationships. These psychological reactions to cancer diagnosis and treatment may decrease patients' ability to maintain and utilize their existing social support networks. Furthermore, disease-related dysphoria is more intense when amplified by isolation, leaving patients to feel that they are deservedly alone with the anxiety, loss, and fear that they experience. Being in a group where many others express similar distress normalizes their reactions, which makes them less alien and overwhelming.

Existing Social Networks Spouses, parents, children, or friends may also experience psychological reactions to the patient's diagnosis (Compas et al., 1994; Fuller, McDermott, Roetzheim, & Marty, 1992; Manne et al., 1995). Thus, terminal illness also places a strain on the patient's existing social network and may further disrupt social relationships (Aspinwall & Taylor, 1997). At a time when the illness may make a person feel removed from the flow of life, when many others withdraw out of awkwardness or fear, psychotherapeutic support provides new and important social connections. Constructing new social networks for cancer patients via support groups and other means is doubly important: it comes at a time in life when natural social support may erode, and when more support is needed to combat additional challenges and stresses (Mulder, van der Pompe, Spiegel, & Antoni, 1992). The universality (Yalom, 1995) created by interacting with others who share similar experiences with severe illness can be quite powerful for group participants and often provides an atmosphere of caring and support right from the beginning of the group.

Health Effects of Social Support There is strong evidence that social contact and support has not only positive emotional effects but health and survival benefits as well. Social contact has been demonstrated to reduce overall mortality risk (House, Landis, & Umberson, 1988) as well as that from cancer (Reynolds & Kaplan, 1990). Social isolation has been shown to be as strongly related to age-adjusted mortality as serum cholesterol levels or smoking (House et al., 1988). Prospective studies of cancer patients document elevated risks of mortality in individuals with smaller social networks and poorer social support satisfaction (Funch & Marshall, 1983; Reynolds & Kaplan, 1990), while reports of high satisfaction with emotional support is associated with longer survival time (Ell et al., 1992).

These striking effects of social support on health in cancer patients are hypothesized to stem from several pathways. For example, individuals in the patient's social network may reinforce positive health behaviors or treatment adherence or increase access to medical care and services through instrumental support (Richardson et al., 1990). Furthermore, positive mood states associated with social interaction and support have been linked to increased immune function and decreased stress-related physiological arousal (Cohen & Herbert, 1996), both of which can directly affect health status. However, studies that emphasize the health benefits of interactive and expressive aspects of social support, such as emotional support satisfaction, expressive social activities (Hislop, Waxler, Coldman, Elwood, & Kan, 1987; Waxler-Morrison, Hislop, Mears, & Kan, 1991), and intimate relationships, such as marriage (Goodwin, Hunt, Key, & Samet, 1987), point to the importance of emotional expression facilitated by supportive relationships in the effect of social support on health.

Emotional Expression

The expression of emotion is important in reducing social isolation and improving coping, yet it is not often a major focus of psychosocial treatment in cancer patients. By emotional expression, we refer to aspects of treatment that encourage participants to access, label, express, and work through emotional reactions to stressors relevant to cancer and other areas of their lives. Suppression of emotion, or lack of its expression, often reduces intimacy in families and social networks, limiting opportunities for direct expression of affection and concern and the utilization of social support.

Emotional Expression in Psychotherapy The lack of focus in treatment on this important process, in part, may be the result of literature that suggests that emotional distress is negatively related to survival in cancer patients (Gilbar, 1996; Molassiotis, Van Den Akker, Milligan, & Goldman, 1997; Weisman & Worden, 1976) and that periods of denial, or positive illusions (Taylor, Helgeson, Reed, & Skokan, 1991), may help individuals to come to terms with a chronic illness, such as cancer (Meyerowitz, 1980), and decrease chances of recurrence (Dean & Surtees, 1989). Thus, many treatments focus on facilitating changes in cognitive schemata and coping strategies by pathways other than the expression of emotion. However, the literature that supports such strategies is somewhat equivocal. Denial of emotional distress has also been associated with poorer psychosocial outcome (Carver et al., 1993). Thus, the role of emotional expression as an integral aspect of group therapy for survivors of cancer or other chronic illness is an important issue. Indeed, one randomized trial compared the effects of more emotionally expressive group psychotherapy with a skills-based intervention, which did not directly address emotion, among HIV-infected patients and found greater decreases in psychiatric symptoms and emotional distress for the more emotionally expressive approach (Kelly et al., 1993).

Health Effects of Emotional Expression   Studies of emotional expression in nonpatient populations have documented several health benefits of emotional expression without therapeutic intervention. In these research paradigms, participants are asked to write about a stressful or traumatic event for a designated period of time, on a single occasion. Such exercises have been associated with decreased reports of physical symptoms, fewer medical visits, enhanced immune responses, and decreased viral replication when compared with participants who wrote about neutral subjects (Smyth et al., 1999; Pennebaker, 1993; Pennebaker, Kiecolt-Glaser, & Glaser, 1988). Furthermore, when the words used by patients who wrote about stressful events were analyzed, those individuals who used a greater amount of negative emotion–laden words demonstrated enhanced health benefits (Pennebaker, 1993). These researchers hypothesized that the effort involved in the suppression of emotions and distress has deleterious somatic consequences, perhaps via the autonomic nervous, endocrine, and immune systems. Thus, though a large body of literature has drawn associations of increased psychological distress with disease states and poorer health (e.g., Cohen, Tyrell & Smith, 1991), the expression of emotions, particularly disease-related distress, may enhance management of negative affect and increase cognitive and affective states associated with better health, such as optimism (Carver, Pozo-Kaderman, Harris, et al., 1993).

The pattern of results found in research with cancer patients is similar. The suppression or avoidance of cancer-related thoughts and emotions has been associated with less adaptive methods of coping (Greer, 1991; Greer, Morris, & Pettingale, 1979), increased psychological distress (Miller et al., 1996), and greater likelihood of cancer recurrence (Epping-Jordan et al., 1994). Furthermore, the expression of emotion is associated with better adjustment in cancer patients (Classen, Koopman, Angell, & Spiegel, 1996). Patients who describe themselves as outgoing show decreased mortality risk from cancer as compared to patients who describe themselves as emotionally reserved (Stavraky, Donner, Kincade, & Stewart, 1988). Cancer patients who report being able to ventilate strong feelings directly cope more effectively with cancer (Derogatis, Abeloff, & Melisaratos, 1979; Greer, 1991; Greer et al., 1979; Pettingale, 1984; Spiegel, 1993b; Temoshok et al., 1985). Furthermore, researchers have hypothesized that one of the pathways that links social support to improved health status is the positive effect of the emotional expression facilitated by close relationships. For example, expres-

sive social activities have been linked to increased survival time in cancer patients (Hislop et al., 1987; Waxler-Morrison et al., 1991). Therefore, to the extent
that a support group directly addresses and encourages emotional expression, it
may enhance the benefits of the group for participants. Doing so seems to reduce
repressive coping, which limits the expression of positive as well as negative
emotions.

Reduced Suppression of Positive as well as Negative Emotion   Indeed, the expression of positive feelings often brackets the expression of painful sadness:

> A 20-year-old daughter was tearfully coming to terms with the sudden
> downhill pre-terminal course of her mother's breast cancer: "I see this black
> hole opening up in my life. I don't think I will want to live without my
> Mom. She would stay up at 2 A.M. and talk me through my misery for two
> hours. She won't be there, but I don't want to make her feel guilty for
> dying." Her father, also at the family group meeting, held her hand and tried
> to comfort her, but he clearly was overwhelmed by his own sadness and his
> lifelong fear of strong emotion and dependency on him by others. The hus-
> band of another woman whose breast cancer was progressing rapidly
> started to comfort her but found his voice choked with emotion: "I am sure
> you will get through this—there's so much love in your family." "Why are
> you crying?" the father asked. "I don't know," he replied, and everyone,
> tearful daughter included, found themselves laughing.

The use of the psychotherapeutic setting to deal with painful affect also provides an organizing context for handling the intrusive thoughts common to cancer patients (Alter et al., 1996; Cella, Mahon, & Donovan, 1990). When unbidden
thoughts involving fears of dying and death intrude, they can be better managed
by patients who know that there is a time and a place during which such feelings
will be expressed and explored (Spiegel, 1993a).

Processing Death and Dying

Death anxiety in particular is intensified by isolation, in part because we often
conceptualize death in terms of separation from loved ones. Feeling alone, especially at a time of strong emotion, makes one feel already a little bit dead, which
sets off a cycle of further anxiety. Such emotional and existential distress can be
powerfully addressed by psychotherapeutic techniques that explore these concerns in a setting of mutual support. This component of the therapy involves
looking the threat of death right in the eye rather than avoiding it. The goal is to
help those facing the threat of death to achieve a more adaptive cognitive framework by means of emotional expression. When fearful or anxiety-related emotions regarding death are processed by the individual, life-threatening problems
are acknowledged as real but not overwhelming (Spiegel, 1993a).

The diagnosis of cancer carries with it a heterogeneity of stressors, which can
range from impaired functional health status to threats to life and bodily integrity
to financial problems. As a result, individuals with cancer engage in a variety of

coping strategies (Jarrett, Ramirez, Richards, & Weinman, 1992). While investigations that attempt to correlate specific cancer-related coping strategies with improved outcome have reported inconsistent results, some researchers have interpreted such results as support for a matching hypothesis, in which strategies that appropriately match the demands of each illness-related stressor are more effective (Aspinwall & Taylor, 1997). In support groups, the exploration of emotional reactions to cancer-related stressors may help patients organize thoughts and feelings and choose appropriate coping strategies. Facing even life-threatening issues directly can help patients shift from emotion-focused to problem-focused coping (Moos & Schaefer, 1987; Spiegel, 1990). Once the fear is experienced directly, many patients find they can move beyond it to address related concerns. The process of dying is often more threatening than death itself. Direct discussion of death anxiety can help to divide the fear of death into a series of problems: loss of control over treatment decisions, fear of separation from loved ones, anxiety about pain. Discussion of these concerns can lead to means of addressing if not completely resolving each of these issues.

One woman with metastatic breast cancer described her group therapy experience in this way:

> "What I found is that talking about death is like looking down into the Grand Canyon (I don't like heights). You know that if you fell down, it would be a disaster, but you feel better about yourself because you're able to look. I can't say I feel serene, but I can look at it now" (Spiegel, 1993, p. 148).

Even the process of grieving can be reassuring at the same time that it is threatening. The experience of grieving others who have died of the same condition constitutes a deeply personal experience of the depth of loss that will be experienced by others after one's own death.

A treatment designed to foster mutual support and to facilitate emotional expression is necessary to process the strong feelings that emerge with discussions of dying and the experience of grief. Such loaded subjects cannot be adequately dealt with in an oblique manner. Patients are most reassured when therapists help them address these ultimate concerns directly and with acceptance and exploration of death-related anxiety and sadness.

Reordering Life Priorities

The acceptance of the possibility of illness shortening life carries with it an opportunity for reevaluating life priorities. When cure is not possible, a realistic evaluation of the future can help those with life-threatening illness make the best use of remaining time. Patients' ambitions and goals for the future may radically change with the onset or progression of terminal illness and may have a large impact on their adjustment to illness (Aspinwall & Taylor, 1997). A reordering of life priorities and goals may therefore need to occur to facilitate adequate coping and adjustment to illness. One of the costs of unrealistic optimism is the loss of time for accomplishing life projects, communicating openly with family and friends, and setting affairs in order.

The daughter referred to above expressed bitter regret that she had not discussed how much her mother meant to her before she slipped into a coma. The daughter had been afraid that discussing death openly would somehow "push" her mother toward death, but she now found herself hungering for even a few minutes of lucid conversation with her.

Thus, these issues must be overtly addressed in psychological treatment in order to help patients engage in emotional expression, receive support from their social network, and reduce avoidance and denial as coping strategies. Facing the threat of death can aid in making the most of life (Spiegel, Bloom, & Yalom, 1981). This can help patients perceive control in the aspects of their lives they can influence, while appropriately grieving and relinquishing those they cannot. Treatment that focuses on such existential issues has even demonstrated positive impact on the immune functioning of patients in the early stages of cancer (van der Pompe, Duivenvoorden, Antoni, Visser, & Heijnen, 1997), suggesting that addressing such issues openly has somatic as well as psychosocial consequences.

Family Support

Family relationships are often uniquely affected by chronic illnesses such as cancer. While social relationships with distant friends and acquaintances appear to be more adversely affected by patients' avoidance, denial, and reluctance to express their emotions regarding the illness (Dakof & Taylor, 1990; Fitzpatrick, Newman, Lamb, & Shipley, 1988), social support from family members can be disrupted by distress regarding their family member's condition (Tompkins, Schulz, & Rau, 1988). Also, the illness and its psychological sequelae may prevent the patient from meeting family members' own support needs (Cassileth, Lusk, Miller, Brown, & Miller, 1985; Hatchett, Friend, Symister, & Wadhwa, 1997). The illness may also lead to alterations in family routines and roles, requiring readjustment by family members.

Shared Problem Solving Psychotherapeutic interventions with family members can be quite helpful in improving communication, identifying needs, increasing role flexibility, and adjusting to new medical, social, vocational, and financial realities (Spiegel, 1993a). There is evidence that an atmosphere of open and shared problem solving in families results in reduced anxiety and depression among cancer patients (Spiegel, Bloom, & Gottheil, 1983). Thus, facilitating such open communication is a useful therapeutic goal. The group format is especially helpful for such a task, in that problems of interpersonal needs and emotions can be examined among group members as a model for clarifying communication in the family.

Encouraging Role Flexibility In addition to enhancing communication, both patients and family members are encouraged to develop role flexibility, a capacity to exchange roles or to develop new ones as the pressures of the illness demand. One woman, for example, who became unable to carry out her usual household activities, wrote an "owner's manual" for the care of the house so that her husband could better help her and carry on after her death. Other patients wrote letters to friends asking them to cook an extra bit of dinner on one evening a month to relieve them of the pressure of cooking.

Clearer and more open communication in the emotional domain is especially important. Men often cope with expressions of distress by their wives in a problem-focused manner, by trying to "fix" the problem through reassurance, offering to consult a doctor, or trying to find a new treatment. We have seen this response experienced by the patient as a trivialization of her distress: it is viewed as irrational, as too strong for a realistic assessment of the situation. This interaction can lead to escalation of distress and further failed efforts to stop it:

> Ed, a devoted husband, explained to other members of his family group what he had learned about comforting his wife about her breast cancer and her treatment: "I kept trying to help Janet understand that her problems were not that bad, and she got more and more upset. It turned out she was so weak from chemotherapy that she could not stand up, and I ran out of things to suggest, so I gave up and got down on the floor with her and hugged her and cried. It turned out that was the right thing to do."

Communication with Physicians

Support groups can be quite useful in facilitating better communication with physicians and other health care professionals. Research has shown that cancer patients are more satisfied with the results of medical intervention, such as lumpectomy versus modified radical mastectomy, to the extent that they have been involved in making the decision about which type of treatment to undergo (Fallowfield, Hall, Maguire, & Baum, 1990). Indeed, participation in the decision is more predictive of outcome than choice of procedure. One study of breast cancer patients found that approximately one-half of them reported problems communicating with physicians (Lerman et al., 1993). The most frequently reported problems included difficulties asking questions of their physicians, expressing feelings, and comprehending information provided. Such communication problems were associated with increased psychological distress, and this was statistically independent of baseline demographic, clinical, and psychosocial variables. Thus, patients who are able to ask questions, express emotions, and seek clarification of information may have better outcomes. In fact, interventions that help chronically ill patients to better communicate with physicians have demonstrated improved health outcomes (Kaplan, Greenfield, & Ware, 1989).

Support groups provide mutual encouragement to get questions answered, to participate actively in treatment decisions, and to consider alternatives carefully. Participants at different stages of the disease can provide information to other participants and modeling for making decisions regarding treatment options. Such groups must be careful not to interfere with medical treatment and decisions but rather should encourage clarification and the development of a cooperative relationship between doctor and patient.

Symptom Control

Many treatment approaches involve teaching cognitive techniques to manage anxiety. These include learning to identify emotions as they develop, to analyze sources of emotional response, and to move from emotion-focused to problem-focused coping. These approaches help the patient utilize more active coping strategies toward the illness. While emotions not examined nor expressed can seem overwhelming, while sharing their feelings with other group members, patients learn to divide problems into smaller and more manageable questions and to cognitively restructure existential issues. If I don't have much time left, how do I want to spend it? What effect will further chemotherapy have on my quality of life?

In addition, many group and individual psychotherapy programs teach specific coping skills designed to help patients reduce cancer-related symptoms, such as anxiety, anticipatory nausea and vomiting, and pain. The majority of women with metastatic breast cancer tend to report significant amounts of pain (Spiegel, 1993a), and this pain is more highly correlated with mood disturbance and pain beliefs than with cancer variables, such as site of the metastases (Spiegel & Bloom, 1983a, 1983b). While the decrease in cognitive and affective disturbance associated with group psychotherapy may serve to indirectly decrease pain perceptions, specific pain control skills are also taught to participants. Psychotherapy sessions conclude with a brief self-hypnosis exercise designed to induce physical relaxation and analgesia. This activity helps to provide closure to group sessions and teaches the relaxation/hypnosis skill, which can be practiced outside of group sessions and used for pain control (Spiegel, 1990; Spiegel & Bloom, 1983b). This approach can also be used to help patients manage other treatment-related symptoms, such as conditioned nausea and vomiting secondary to chemotherapy.

Format of Therapy Sessions

Supportive/expressive group psychotherapy sessions are comprised of eight to ten women and two co-leaders, who are mental health professionals. Groups are preferably relatively homogeneous for type and stage of disease, that is, women with metastatic or primary breast cancer. However, if a woman in a group for primary breast cancer relapses, it is critical that she continue in her group, providing reassurance to her and the other members of the group that, even if her disease progresses, she is important to the group and will continue to receive (as well as give) support.

Sessions last 90 minutes and tend to be relatively unstructured. Participants share thoughts and feelings spontaneously, and therapists facilitate discussion around the seven themes described above. Therapists encourage direct discussion of patients' thoughts and feelings related to cancer, such as fears related to disease progression and death, family problems, communication with physicians, and renegotiating goals and relationships for the rest of their lives. The purpose of the group is to provide a safe environment for women to freely express themselves among others who have shared concerns and experiences. Group members serve as models for overcoming difficulties, expressing emotions, and normalizing/universalizing common experiences among cancer patients and chronically ill individuals. The reciprocal nature of the support also serves to enhance participants' feelings of competence and self-efficacy by their experience of helping others in similar circumstances. The groups create a social network explicitly designated for support around issues of chronic illness, dying, and death. This provides participants with support often lacking in their existing social networks, even among individuals with many social contacts or close relationships. Thus, women can discuss these issues without fear of the burden or impact such disclosure may have on other close relationships, such as spouses or children.

Family Groups

Groups for family members of patients are held once per month. In these groups, eight to ten family members meet with two therapists. These groups are structured in a similar format to those for patients, and discussion centers around the same seven themes. The purpose of these groups is similar to those of the patients: to allow for emotional expression without fear of the burden or impact such disclosure would have on the patients. Family group members report that they attend the groups to "feel good about feeling bad," and they report positive consequences of the support and validation obtained in the groups. Though research at the Psychosocial Treatment Laboratory often includes the coping responses and health status of family members as well as patients, the discussion of the relationships between psychotherapy and health outcomes in the current chapter will be limited to our research and experiences with the patients.

Health Outcomes of Group Psychotherapy

Psychological Effects

There is now clear evidence that various psychotherapies for cancer patients are effective in reducing anxiety and depression (Ferlic, Goldman, & Kennedy, 1979; Gustafson & Whitman, 1978; Mulder et al., 1992; Spiegel et al., 1981; Spiegel & Bloom, 1983b; Wood, Milligan, Christ, & Liff, 1978), increasing active coping strategies (Fawzy et al., 1990; Turns, 1988), and reducing symptoms, such as pain, nausea, and vomiting (Cain, Kohorn, Quinlan, Latimer, & Schwartz, 1986; Forester, Kornfeld, & Fleiss, 1985; Morrow & Morrell, 1982). Supportive/expressive group therapy for metastatic breast cancer patients has been shown to result in better mood, fewer maladaptive coping responses, fewer phobic symptoms (Spiegel et al., 1981), and reduced pain (Spiegel & Bloom, 1983a).

Medical Effects

A provocative literature has emerged that indicates that group psychotherapy may also affect the quantity as well as the quality of life. Our research group found, to our initial surprise, that the breast cancer patients in our original trial who had undergone our supportive/expressive group therapy program lived significantly longer than did the randomly assigned control sample (Spiegel, Bloom, Kraemer, & Gottheil, 1989). These data were derived from a study of 86 women with metastatic breast cancer, randomized between a nonintervention control group (36 women) and a supportive/expressive psychotherapy group (50 women).

Ten years after the completion of this study, the researchers (Spiegel et al., 1989) collected additional medical outcome data on these subjects, including survival times. Women randomized to the support group lived an average of 36.6 months from entry into the study, while women randomized to the nonintervention control group lived an average of 18.9 months. By 48 months after the study had begun, all of the control patients had died, but a third of the treatment sample were still alive. These data must be interpreted with some caution, as they were yielded by a study of relatively small sample size, which was originally designed to test hypotheses other than the effects of intervention on health and survival. However, associations between psychosocial intervention and increased survival time to a statistically and clinically significant extent is notable and merits further investigation. These findings are further strengthened by additional analyses of the data, which indicate that associations between the intervention and increased survival occurred independent of differences between groups in subsequent medical treatment or health behaviors (Kogon, Biswas, Pearl, Carlson, & Spiegel, 1997). Studies are currently underway at Stanford and in Toronto (Goodwin et al., 1996) to replicate these findings with metastatic breast cancer patients and to investigate mediating variables in the relationship between psychotherapy and survival.

Other researchers have also documented increased survival time in samples of cancer patients who received psychotherapeutic interventions. Richardson and colleagues (1990) found that lymphoma and leukemia patients who were offered a combination of educational counseling and home visiting lived significantly longer than control patients, even when observed differences in adherence to medical treatment were controlled. This study examined 94 male and female patients who were randomized to a nonintervention control group (25 patients) or one of three treatment conditions, which focused on increasing adherence to medical regimens (a total of 69 patients). All treatment conditions involved an educational component in a group conducted by a nurse. This component of treatment consisted of a presentation that described the cancer, its treatments, and side effects and that encouraged active involvement by patients in their medical care and treatment adherence. The presentation also included discrete periods devoted to questions and discussion among patients. Behavioral interventions aimed at increasing adherence to medication schedules were also included in the treatment conditions. These behavioral interventions were administered by nurses and delivered either at the hospital or in the patient's home, and they involved shaping, behavioral contracts, and/or self-monitoring. Interventions delivered via home visit also elicited support for treatment adherence from one of the patient's family members.

These researchers found that participation in any of the intervention groups was associated with a significantly decreased risk of mortality (RR = .36) and that a significantly greater percentage of individuals in the intervention group survived for longer periods of time as compared to the control group. Average lengths of survival times were not reported in the study. Because this was an intervention that focused on increasing medical adherence, this would be the most likely mediator in the relationship of the intervention to survival. However, when researchers examined the relationship between the intervention and survival—controlling for demographic variables, illness severity, and medical adherence—the significantly decreased risk for mortality among individuals who participated in the intervention persisted (RR = .39). The authors hypothesized that the emphasis of the educational intervention on communication with health care professionals, symptom monitoring, eliciting family support, and taking an active role in their medical care was effective enough to contribute to better health and survival. The authors also posit that the active role that patients may have taken in medical care could also lead to a more general sense of control and decreased anxiety, which could have also affected health and survival. Elements of these interventions that pertained to social and family support were not emphasized in treatment delivery nor hypothesized to be a factor in the increased survival time of intervention group patients. In addition, specific interventions were not examined separately, so differential survival times in individuals who received treatment that specifically involved support from a family member (home visits) were not calculated.

Fawzy and colleagues at UCLA (1990) found that malignant melanoma patients who were randomly assigned to a series of six structured support group meetings were less anxious and depressed than control patients six months later and demonstrated decreased recurrence and increased survival time six years later (Fawzy et al., 1993). The study evaluated 68 men and women diagnosed with malignant melanoma randomized to either a nonintervention control group (34 patients) or a brief cognitive-behavioral group intervention (34 patients). This intervention was delivered in group format and combined education with stress management, coping skills training, and social support. The emphasis of the intervention was largely on cognitive coping and stress management techniques. Groups met once per week for six weeks in groups of seven to ten individuals. Sessions lasted 90 minutes and were co-led by two mental health professionals. No alterations in oncological care were made in association with the investigation.

At six-year follow-up, Fawzy and colleagues (1993) reported significantly lower rates of recurrence ($7/40$ vs. $13/40$) and mortality ($3/40$ vs. $10/40$) in the individuals who participated in the intervention when compared to the control group. Average lengths of time for survival or until recurrence were not reported in the study. The statistically significant relationship between support group participation and extended disease-free and survival time persisted when the severity of melanoma was controlled. These researchers also found that higher levels of mood disturbance, as measured by the Profile of Mood States, and greater reports of active behavioral coping were related to increased disease-free and survival time, but they did not report any interactions between intervention effects and these variables. As with the two other studies that demonstrated association between a psychotherapeutic intervention and survival with cancer, these results are striking and merit further investigation. However, this study does share some of the methodological drawbacks of the Spiegel study (Spiegel et al., 1989), including a design that was not originally intended to examine the effects of the intervention on survival times and a relatively small sample size.

The authors hypothesized several potential pathways by which participation in the intervention could have affected recurrence and survival. First, they cited the educational components of the program and their potential effect on promoting better health behaviors and increased treatment adherence. Second, improvements in coping efficacy as a result of the intervention could have resulted in a more positive attitude, better physician-patient relationships, or more active control of their medical care, all of which have demonstrated a positive impact on health status in cancer patients. The authors also posit that the stress-management components of the intervention may have substantially reduced psychological distress and physiological components of distress, thereby leading to better health status. Indeed, they found that participants in the treatment group had significantly higher alpha-interferon–augmented natural killer cell cytotoxicity (NKCC) at six-month follow-up than control patients. While this difference was not statistically related to survival time, baseline NKCC was predictive of relapse rates (Fawzy et al., 1990). Finally, the authors acknowledge that increased social support, which was provided by group meetings, may have had a direct effect on health or an indirect effect, through information sharing and modeling of problem solving or coping.

These three randomized trials have demonstrated an association of a group psychological intervention with survival time in cancer patients. Furthermore, these researchers have identified theoretically and empirically plausible mechanisms, which may account for the relationship. Though these studies require replication, examination of these data also yield new directions for research in an effort to delineate the relationship between these psychosocial variables and health status. However, several investigations of group psychotherapy for cancer survivors have failed to find extended disease-free or survival time.

Of the studies that have not demonstrated associations among psychological intervention and survival time, one study described the results of an individual therapy intervention, and two studies described the results of group interventions. The individual therapy intervention was conducted by Linn, Linn, and Harris (1982). These investigators conducted a randomized prospective trial of supportive psychotherapy based on the theories of Kubler-Ross (1969). The treatment goals were for patients to develop a supportive and trusting relationship with the therapists, reduce denial, increase perceptions of hope and control, complete "unfinished business," and explore the meaning of their lives and illness.

For the treatment group ($N = 62$), an unlimited number of counseling sessions were offered. Participants were 120 males recruited from a Veterans Administration hospital. Patients were heterogeneous with respect to cancer type, though the majority of patients ($N = 65$) were diagnosed with lung cancer. All participants were diagnosed with advanced metastatic disease with a prognosis of 3 to 12 months. The one-year follow-up compared the 62 treatment patients with the 58 control patients and documented decreased depressive affect and decreased feelings of alienation, increased life satisfaction, increased self-esteem, and increased internal locus of control. However, no differences were found between groups on hospital readmission, number of days in the hospital, or survival time. While the intervention appeared to enhance the quality of life, comparable gains were not observed in domains of physical functioning or survival. The authors cited the advanced stage of the disease of the patients (most of the patients had died within the initial year of the study) and their relatively uniform physical functioning. Thus, in a sample with a relatively uniform and preterminal prognosis, it is likely that little variance remains to be affected in disease progression, and effects of psychosocial intervention on health and survival may be difficult to achieve.

Siegel and colleagues (Gellert, Maxwell, & Siegel, 1993) evaluated a program of group psychotherapy for cancer patients, relatives, and friends. The treatment, the Exceptional Cancer Patients program (ECaP), is a national program that offers individual counseling, patient peer support, family therapy, and behavioral skills training in relaxation, mental imagery, and meditation. The program's goals are to facilitate acceptance of the disease and increase perceptions of control and hope. The program also proposes the idea that psychological factors may have caused cancer and that the patients can control the course of the disease through their attitudes toward their cancer. The study examined 34 program participants and a group of 102 nonparticipants matched on major prognostic factors of cancer, whose statistics were obtained from a national cancer tumor registry. The groups were followed from the date of cancer diagnosis and compared at ten-year follow-up. No differences in survival were found between program participants and registry controls. The authors cited a small sample size and a lack of randomized design as limitations of the study, which might have obscured a survival effect. However, the authors also acknowledge that the techniques of this program differ from other group psychotherapy studies, which have documented effects on survival, and that the possibility exists that the specific mental imaging and meditation proposed by this program is not sufficient to affect survival. Indeed, it may have adverse effects by inducing guilt in patients who believe they should be able to psychologically control the progression of the disease but find their illness advancing nonetheless (Spiegel, 1993a).

Ilnyckyj and colleagues (Ilnyckyj, Farber, Cheang, & Weinerman, 1994) also conducted support groups with cancer patients and reported survival data. This study describes the results of three types of group interventions as compared to a no-treatment control group. All interventions consisted of weekly one-hour sessions for a period of six months. Each group was composed of approximately 15 members and differed on the basis of group facilitators. One group was led by a social worker for the entire six-month period; one group was professionally led

for the first three months and then met for three months as a peer-led group; and
the third was peer led for the entire six-month period. Group leaders were not in-
structed in any specific theories or techniques, aside from instructions to be informative and supportive. Peer groups were given no agenda or instructions. Participants consisted of 127 cancer patients of a variety of tumor sites and stages of
cancer, though the majority of cancer patents were at the early stages of disease
progression. Survival data were analyzed at an 11-year follow-up. When the intervention groups were combined and compared to the control group, no differences
in the length of survival were found. However, there was also no demonstrable
psychological benefit from the intervention. Despite the adequate sample size in
this study, the inclusion of several different types of groups and varying types
of cancer and disease stages would make any existing survival effect extremely
difficult to detect. Furthermore, the lack of a replicable and effective intervention model would limit the generalizability of any findings obtained in such an
investigation.

Salient Components of Psychosocial Support

Common to all studies that demonstrated survival effects were professionally facilitated components of treatment, which focused on interpersonal support. Social support and emotional expression are among the primary goals of support-
ive/expressive psychotherapy, which was utilized in the studies by Spiegel and
colleagues and which was a central component of the Fawzy et al. (1990) intervention. Though the Richardson intervention was not designed to facilitate support, several components of the intervention, such as the initial group session, the
direct involvement of a family member in the treatment regimen, or home visits
by a professional nurse may have indirectly acted to provide or increase participants' social support.

In contrast, several elements of the other interventions may have served to diminish potential effects of social or group support for participants. For example,
the Ilnyckyj, Siegel, and Linn studies included patients either in varying stages
of disease or with varying tumor sites in the same support groups. Such heterogeneity lacks the advantage of the natural understanding and sense of community
that occurs in groups of similar patients. An initial supportive and trusting atmosphere is easier to establish when patients immediately understand and share each
other's experiences. In such an atmosphere, social support will be easier to maintain and to use therapeutically.

Theories, such as social learning theory, premise the effects of social relationships on health-related behaviors with a sense of belonging and intimacy. As the
closeness and intimacy of relationships increase, the greater is the positive impact of their reinforcement and support on behavior (Bandura, 1986). These same
aspects of a social network also serve to increase emotional disclosure in relationships. Emotional disclosure regarding cancer may serve to further strengthen ties
among group members, as well as to increase the health benefits of treatment.

However, behavioral changes that result from increased social support may not entirely account for the survival effects documented in effective interventions. Social support and emotional disclosure may provide evidence of direct effects on health status not mediated by affective or behavioral pathways. Specific components of interventions successful in affecting survival time may act directly on biological pathways involved in disease progression. Researchers have hypothesized that the concealment of negative thoughts and affect is an effortful process, which exacts a somatic toll on the individual (Pennebaker, 1993). Such hypotheses are supported by experimental studies in which individuals engage in emotional disclosure and display enhanced immune defense and decreased medical utilization (Smyth et al., 1999; Pennebaker et al., 1997; Pennebaker et al., 1988; Spiegel, 1999). In studies of healthy individuals, social support has been demonstrated to attenuate physiological reactivity to laboratory stressors in women (Kamark, Manuck, & Jennings, 1989). Social support appears to affect physiological reactivity independent of affective reactions to chronic and acute stressors in men and women (Kennedy et al., 1988, 1995; Uchino, Kiecolt-Glaser, & Cacioppo, 1992). In other studies, social support by a close other appears to have a direct effect on sympathetic nervous system activity, as shown by decreased catecholamines in men and women (Ely & Mostardi, 1986; Kirschbaum, Klauer, Filipp, & Hellhammer, 1995), which was not explained by reports of stress or affective symptoms. In studies of breast cancer patients not involved in interventions, perceptions of social support have been associated with increased NK cell activity (Levy et al., 1990) and emotional expression with slowed tumor growth (Temoshok et al., 1985). However, emotional disclosure in the context of a supportive relationship, presumably present in relationships with close others, may be necessary to achieve health benefits from support. Intervention studies with healthy individuals that focus on increasing social contact—but not intimacy or emotional disclosure—have not found such decreased reactivity or catecholamine levels as a result of increased social support (e.g., Arnetz et al., 1987). Thus, preliminary research suggests that the combination of a close supportive relationship with emotional disclosure may have direct benefits on the individual's ability to combat illness.

What Links Psychosocial Treatment to Survival?

Possible mediators in the relationship between psychotherapeutic intervention and survival would be behavioral, affective, or physiological alterations that result from treatment that affect the course of the disease. Thus, interventions may affect health status by (a) promoting improved health behaviors and medical decision making, (b) increasing adherence to medical treatment regimens, or (c) directly influencing specific activities in biological pathways that enhance health status.

Health Behaviors

Negative health behaviors, such as poor diet, excessive alcohol consumption, and poor sleep habits, have been associated with increased disease progression in breast cancer patients (Eberlein, Simon, Fisher, & Lippman, 1985; Garland, Willett, Manson, & Hunter, 1993; Schatzkin & Longnecker, 1994). Therefore, if treatment effects were to ameliorate these negative behaviors, disease progression might be slowed. The experience of a psychosocial treatment group might affect health behaviors in several different ways. For example, formal or informal educational components of treatments have been linked with beneficial changes in diet and exercise (Fawzy, Fawzy, Arndt, & Pasnau, 1995). Social support may be a necessary component for health-related behavior change. Social learning theory (Bandura, 1986) suggests that the self-efficacy necessary for individuals to alter existing behavioral patterns is built upon the social milieu. Specifically, naturalistic observation of others engaging in desired behaviors and receiving social reinforcement for approximations of desired behaviors, when it occurs within a group where members feel a sense of intimacy and belonging, are powerful determinants of behavior change. This process has been observed in our own treatment groups (Spiegel et al., 1981). For example, such constant contact with topics related to cancer may help patients to avoid delays in treatment seeking, which is associated with poorer outcome (Facione, 1993). In addition, support provided within group intervention likely aids patients in thinking through treatment decisions and makes advice available from others who may have encountered a variety of similar treatment experiences.

Medical Adherence

Cancer treatments have many uncomfortable side effects, which can make adherence to medical regimens difficult for patients (Barofsky, 1984; Given & Given, 1989). Psychological reactions to the diagnosis or the side effects, such as fear and loss of perceptions of control have been associated with nonadherence (Hoagland, Morrow, Bennett, & Carnrike, 1983), and improved adherence has been associated with increased survival time in breast cancer patients (Bonadonna & Valagussa, 1981). Educational components of interventions with cancer patients may strengthen perceptions of control, decrease fears related to the disease and treatment side effects, and provide support for treatment adherence, thereby increasing adherence to medical regimens (Ayres et al., 1994; Given & Given, 1989). This is established by the Richardson et al. (1990) study, in which the intervention met its stated goal of increased adherence and resulted in an associated increase in survival time. The components of interventions that provide education and assist in the adjustment and adherence to difficult treatment regimens is extremely important for cancer patients. However, these gains in survival time may not be due entirely to medical factors (Kogon et al., 1997). Some studies have documented that adherence to a placebo treatment has resulted in increased survival time (Epstein, 1984; Pizzo et al., 1983). Therefore, additional factors appear to partially mediate the association between these psychosocial interventions and survival time. For example, social support may affect medical adherence in a similar manner to how it affects other health-related behaviors. Modeling provided by other group members may increase patients' self-efficacy with respect to withstanding aspects of treatment with particularly deleterious side effects or may emphasize the health benefits of good treatment adherence.

All effective psychosocial interventions demonstrated effects that could not be accounted for by educational effects (e.g., choices regarding cancer treatment) or treatment adherence. For example, Spiegel and colleagues (Kogon et al., 1997; Spiegel et al., 1989) in the original reports and subsequent reanalyses of these data have demonstrated that the longer survival times in metastatic patients who receive therapy were not accounted for by differences in medical treatment, stage of cancer, or health behaviors between the experimental and control groups. In the studies by Fawzy and colleagues (1993), while initial health status did not account for group differences in survival, increases in active behavioral coping associated with the intervention were related to recurrence status and survival time. In the Richardson et al. (1990) study, though the intervention was designed primarily to increase medical adherence, the authors found that the extended survival time in the intervention group was not accounted for by increased medical adherence. Thus, the effects on survival of these interventions do not appear to be due entirely to access to information regarding medical treatment choices, increased medical adherence, or better health behaviors.

Endocrine System

Stress and support-induced changes in the endocrine system have the potential to modulate the rate of disease progression. The role of endogenous corticosteroids in breast cancer progression is worthy of further exploration since: (1) steroid hormone levels are responsive to psychosocial stressors (Hofer, Wolff, Friedman, & Mason, 1972; Irwin, Daniels, Risch, Bloom, & Weiner, 1988; Hofer et al., 1972 a,b), through the HPA via CRF, ACTH, and the response of the adrenal gland in producing them; and (2) the HPA is hyperactive in depressed cancer patients (Nemeroff et al., 1984). Stressful marital interaction has been shown to increase secretion of ACTH, epinephrine, and norepinephrine but not cortisol (Malarkey, Kiecolt-Glaser, Pearl, & Glaser, 1994) among couples classified as high in negative behaviors, such as hostility and criticism (Weiss & Summers, 1983).

There are at least three mechanisms by which a hyperactive HPA axis could influence the rate of disease progression: (1) differential control of gluconeogenesis in normal and malignant cells (Sapolsky & Donnelly, 1985); (2) growth stimulation of hormone-sensitive tumor cells (Rowse, Weinberg, Bellward, & Emerman, 1992); and (3) steroid-induced immunosuppression (Irwin et al., 1988).

Although there are many theories about the mechanisms by which stress may influence physiological vulnerability to disease, there are conflicting data regarding the tumor-promoting effects of stress in humans (Barraclough et al., 1992; Geyer, 1991; Ramirez et al., 1989). Evidence from animal studies indicates that stress both elevates cortisol and promotes tumor progression (Jiang, Weinberg, Wilkinson, & Emerman, 1993; Sapolsky, Krey, & McEwen, 1983). In particular, older animals are sensitive to the effects of chronic stress, showing far slower return to baseline levels of cortisol.

Conversely, there is evidence that social support can buffer stress-induced cortisol elevation. Levine, Coe, and Wiener (1989) found in squirrel monkeys that the elevation in plasma cortisol seen when an animal is stressed alone is reduced by 50% when the animal has one "friend" with him, and there is no elevation in cortisol at all in response to the same stressor when the animal has five friends present. Thus, a change in social environment profoundly alters the physiological consequences of a stressor. This would plausibly apply to humans coping with stressors as well.

Immune System

Similarly, there is reason to believe that components of the immune system could mediate psychosocial effects on disease progression. For example, natural killer (NK) cells have been implicated as having a role in cancer progression (Andersen et al., 1994; Bovbjerg, 1989; Herberman, 1985). NK cells are known to kill tumor cells of many different types when tested either in vitro or in animal studies (Herberman, 1985). NK cells are similar to lymphokine-activated killer (LAK) cells in having antitumor activity without recognition of tumor-specific antigens (Rosenberg & Lotze, 1986). In a series of studies, Levy, Herberman, and colleagues (1985, 1987, 1990, 1991) have demonstrated an association among breast cancer progression, axillary lymph node and estrogen receptor status, sustained psychosocial stress, and decreased NK cell activity. Levy et al. found that high-quality emotional support from a spouse or intimate other, perceived social support from one's physician, and actively seeking social support were related to higher NK activity. Similarly, patients with squamous cell carcinoma of the cervix have reduced NK activity compared with normal controls, the reduction increasing with tumor load (Radhakrishna et al., 1989). Thus, there is some evidence that immune system functioning, which is affected by psychosocial variables, could modulate the rate of breast cancer progression.

Summary

Supportive/expressive psychotherapy groups for breast cancer survivors aim to address educational and existential issues relevant to breast cancer patients. The primary goal is to establish a supportive and cohesive social network for patients, which fosters an atmosphere conducive to emotional expression and the giving and receiving of emotional support. Such an atmosphere is established by providing consistent and ongoing weekly support groups for patients, grouping patients of like medical diagnoses together (e.g., metastatic vs. primary cancer), and using therapeutic techniques that directly focus on the expression of affect and discussion of existential issues.

Such a supportive network of individuals who are facing similar medical stressors is not only necessary for the therapeutic benefits we describe but provides health and survival benefits to patients as well. This support network has the ability to model and reinforce positive alterations in health-related behaviors, coping behaviors, and medical adherence. These behavioral changes have been associated with better health in cancer patients but do not entirely account for the health and survival benefits demonstrated by cancer patients in group treatment. We propose that the increased emotional expression and emotional support that results from the new social network and group therapy participation may also directly slow disease progression and lengthen survival time. A growing research literature continues to illuminate the interplay among social support, emotional expression, and health. Applications of this literature will not only delineate specific mechanisms that link psychotherapy to health in cancer patients but will will help to provide more comprehensive and efficacious health care to these patients. When we rediscover the role of care as well as cure in medicine, we will help patients and their families better cope with disease, and we may also better mobilize the mind and body's resources to fight illness.

References

Ader, R., Felten, D., & Cohen, N. (1990). Interactions between the brain and the immune system. *Annual Review of Pharmacology and Toxicology, 30*, 561–602.

Alter, C. L. Percovitz, et al. (1996). Identification of PTSD in cancer survivors *Psychometrics, 37*, 137–143.

Anderson, B. L., Kiecolt-Glaser, J. K., et al. (1994). A biobehavioral model of cancer stress and disease course. *American Psychology, 49*(5), 389–404.

Arnetz, B. B., Wasserman, J., Petrini, B., Brenner, S. O., Levi, L., Eneroth, P., Salovaara, H., Hjelm, R., Salovaara, L., Theorell, T., et al. (1987). Immune function in unemployed women. *Psychosomatic Medicine, 49*, 3–12.

Aspinwall, L. G., and Taylor, S. E., (1997). A stitch in time: Self-regulation and proactive coping. *Psychological Bulletin, 121*(3), 417–436.

Ayres, A., Hoon, P. W., Franzoni, J. B., Matheny, K. B., Cotanch, P. H., & Takayanagi, S. (1994). Influence of mood and adjustment to cancer on compliance with chemotherapy among breast cancer patients. *Journal of Psychosomatic Research, 38*(5), 393–402.

Bandura, A. (1986). The explanatory and predictive scope of self-efficacy theory. *Journal of Social and Clinical Psychology, 4*(3), 359–373.

Barofsky, I. (1984). Therapeutic compliance and the cancer patient. *Health Education Quarterly, 10 Suppl.*, 43–56.

Barraclough, J., Pinder, P., Cruddas, M., Osmond, C., Taylor, I., & Perry, M. (1992). Life events and breast cancer prognosis. *British Medical Journal, 304*(6834), 1078–1081.

Bloom, J. R., & Spiegel, D. (1984). The relationship of two dimensions of social support to the psychological well-being and social functioning of women with advanced breast cancer. *Social Science and Medicine, 19*(8), 831–837.

Bonadonna, G., & Valagussa, P. (1981). Dose-response effect of adjuvant chemotherapy in breast cancer. *New England Journal of Medicine, 304*(1), 10–15.

Bovbjerg, D. (1989). Psychoneuroimmunology and cancer. In J. C. Holland & J. H. Rowland (Eds.), *Handbook of psychooncology* (pp. 727–754). New York: Oxford University Press.

Burish, T. G., & Lyles, J. N. (1981). Effectiveness of relaxation training in reducing adverse reactions to cancer chemotherapy. *Journal of Behavioral Medicine, 4*(1), 65–78.

Cain, E. N., Kohorn, E. I., Quinlan, D. M., Latimer, K., & Schwartz, P. E. (1986). Psychosocial benefits of a cancer support group. *Cancer, 57*(1), 183–189.

Carver, C., Pozo-Kaderman, C., Harris, S., Noriega, V., Scheier, M., Robinson, D., Ketcham, A., Moffat, F., & Clark, K. (1993). Optimism versus pessimism predicts the quality of women's adjustment to early stage breast cancer. *Cancer, 73*(4), 1213–1220.

Cassileth, B. R., Lusk, E. J., Miller, D. S., Brown, L. L., & Miller, C. (1985). Psychosocial correlates of survival in advanced malignant disease? *New England Journal of Medicine, 312*(24), 1551–1555.

Cella, D. F., Mahon, S. M., & Donovan, M. I. (1990). Cancer recurrence as a traumatic event. *Behavioral Medicine, 16*(1), 15–22.

Classen, C., Koopman, C., Angell, K., & Spiegel, D. (1996). Coping styles associated with psychological adjustment to advanced breast cancer. *Health Psychology, 15*(6), 434–437.

Coates, T. J., McKusick, L., Kuno, R., & Stites, D. P. (1989). Stress reduction training changed number of sexual partners but not immune function in men with HIV. *American Journal of Public Health, 79*(7), 885–887.

Cohen, S., & Herbert, T. B. (1996). Health psychology: Psychological factors and physical disease from the perspective of human psychoneuroimmunology. *Annual Review of Psychology, 47*, 113–142.

Cohen, S., Tyrell, D. A., et al. (1991). Psychological stress and susceptibility to the common cold [see comments]. *New England Journal of Medicine, 325*(9), 606–612.

Compas, B., Worsham, N., Epping-Jordan, J., Grant, K., Mireault, G., Howell, D., & Malcarne, V. (1994). When mom or dad has cancer: Markers of psychological distress in cancer patient, spouses, and children. *Health Psychology, 13*(6), 507–515.

Cordova, M. J., Andrykowski, M. A., Redd, W. H., Kenady, D. E., McGrath, P. C., & Sloan, D. A. (1995). Frequency and correlateds of posttraumatic-stress-disorder–like symptoms after treatment for breast cancer. *Journal of Consulting and Clinical Psychology, 63*(3), 981–986.

Dakof, G. A., & Taylor, S. E. (1990). Victims' perceptions of social support: What is helpful from whom? *Journal of Personality and Social Psychology, 58*(1), 80–89.

Dean, C., & Surtees, P. G. (1989). Do psychological factors predict survival in breast cancer? *Journal of Psychosomatic Research, 33*(5), 561–569.

Derogatis, L. R., Abeloff, M. D., & Melisaratos, N. (1979). Psychological coping mechanisms and survival time in metastatic breast cancer. *Journal of the American Medical Association, 242*(14), 1504–1508.

Derogatis, L. R., Morrow, G. R., Fetting, J., Penman, D., Piasetsky, S., Schmale, A. M., Henrichs, M., & Carnicke, C. L., Jr. (1983). The prevalence of psychiatric disorders among cancer patients. *Journal of the American Medical Association, 249*(6), 751–757.

Eberlein, T., Simon, R., Fisher, S., & Lippman, M. E. (1985). Height, weight, and risk of breast cancer relapse. *Breast Cancer Research and Treatment, 5*(1), 81–86.

Ely, D. L., & Mostardi, R. A. (1986). The effect of recent life events: Stress, life assets, and temperament pattern on cardiovascular risk factors for Akron city police officers. *Journal of Human Stress, 12*(2), 77–91.

Epstein, L. H. (1984). The direct effects of compliance on health outcome. *Health Psychology, 3*(4), 385–393.

Facione, N. C. (1993). Delay versus help seeking for breast cancer symptoms: a critical review of the literature on patient and provider delay. *Social Science and Medicine, 36*(12), 1521–1534.

Fallowfield, L., Hall, A., Maguire, G. P., & Baum, M. (1990). Psychological outcomes in women with early breast cancer [letter; comment]. *British Medical Journal 301*(6765), 1394.

Fawzy, F. I., Cousins, N., Fawzy, N. W., Kemeny, M. E., Elashoff, R., & Morton, D. (1990). A structured psychiatric intervention for cancer patients. I. Changes over time in methods of coping and affective disturbance. *Archives of General Psychiatry, 47*(8), 720–725.

Fawzy, F. I., Fawzy, N. W., Arndt, L. A., & Pasnau, R. O. (1995). Critical review of psychosocial interventions in cancer care. *Archives of General Psychiatry, 52*(2), 100–113.

Fawzy, F. I., Fawzy, N. W., Hyun, C. S., Elashoff, R., Guthrie, D., Fahey, J. L., & Morton, D. L. (1993). Malignant melanoma: Effects of an early structured psychiatric intervention, coping, and affective state on recurrence and survival 6 years later. *Archives of General Psychiatry, 50*(9), 681–689.

Fawzy, F. I., Kemeny, M. E., Fawzy, N. W., Elashoff, R., Morton, D., Cousins, N., & Fahey, J. L. (1990). A structured psychiatric intervention for cancer patients. II. Changes over time in immunological measures. *Archives of General Psychiatry, 47*(8), 729–735.

Ferlic, M., Goldman, A., & Kennedy, B. J. (1979). Group counseling in adult patients with advanced cancer. *Cancer, 43*(2), 760–766.

Fitzpatrick, R., Newman, S., Lamb, R., & Shipley, M. (1988). Social relationships and psychological well-being in rheumatoid arthritis. *Social Science and Medicine, 27*(4), 399–403.

Forester, B., Kornfeld, D. S., & Fleiss, J. L. (1985). Psychotherapy during radiotherapy: Effects on emotional and physical distress. *American Journal of Psychiatry, 142*(1), 22–27.

Fuller, S. M., McDermott, R. J., Roetzheim, R. G., & Marty, P. J. (1992). Breast cancer beliefs of women participating in a television-promoted mammography screening project. *Public Health Reporter, 107*(6), 682-690.

Funch, D. P., & Marshall, J. (1983). The role of stress, social support and age in survival from breast cancer. *Journal of Psychosomatic Research, 27*(1), 77–83.

Ganz, P. A., Schag, A. C., Lee, J. J., Polinsky, M. L., & Tan, S. J. (1992). Breast conservation versus mastectomy: Is there a difference in psychological adjustment or quality of life in the year after surgery? *Cancer, 69*(7), 1729–1738.

Garland, M., Willett, W. C., Manson, J. E., & Hunter, D. J. (1993). Antioxidant micronutrients and breast cancer. *Journal of the American College of Nutrition, 12*(4), 400–411.

Gellert, G. A., Maxwell, R. M., & Siegel, B. S. (1993). Survival of breast cancer patients receiving adjunctive psychosocial support therapy: A 10-year follow-up study. *Journal of Clinical Oncology, 11*(1), 66–69.

Geyer, S. (1991). Life events prior to manifestation of breast cancer: a limited prospective study covering eight years before diagnosis. *Journal of Psychosomatic Research, 35*(2–3), 355–363.

Gilbar, O. (1996). The connection between the psychological condition of breast cancer patients and survival: A follow-up after eight years. *General Hospital Psychiatry, 18*(4), 266–270.

Given, B. A., & Given, C. W. (1989). Compliance among patients with cancer. *Oncology Nursing Forum, 16*(1), 97–103.

Goodwin, J. S., Hunt, W. C., Key, C. R., & Samet, J. M. (1987). The effect of marital status on stage, treatment, and survival of cancer patients. *Journal of the American Medical Association, 258*(21), 3125–3130.

Goodwin, P. J., Leszcz, M., et al. (1996). Randomized trial of group psychosocial support in metastatic breast cancer: The BEST study—Breast-Expressive Supportive Therapy study. *Cancer Treatment Review, 22*((Supp. A), 91–96.

Greer, S. (1991). Psychological response to cancer and survival. *Psychology of Medicine, 21*(1), 43–49.

Greer, S., Morris, T., & Pettingale, K. W. (1979). Psychological response to breast cancer: Effect on outcome. *Lancet, 2*(8146), 785–787.

Gustafson, J., & Whitman, H. (1978). Towards a balanced social environment on the oncology service. *Social Psychiatry, 13*, 147–152.

Hatchett, L., Friend, R., Symister, P., & Wadhwa, N. (1997). Interpersonal expectations, social support, and adjustment to chronic illness. *Journal of Personality and Social Psychology, 73*(3), 560–573.

Herberman, R. (1985). Natural killer cells: Characteristics and possible role in resistance against tumor growth. In A. E. Reif & M. S. Mitchell (Eds.), *Immunity to cancer* (pp. 217–229). San Diego: Academic Press.

Hilgard, E. R., & Hilgard, J. R. (1975). *Hypnosis in the relief of pain*. Los Altos, CA: William Kauffman.

Hislop, T. G., Waxler, N. E., Coldman, A. J., Elwood, J. M., & Kan, L. (1987). The prognostic significance of psychosocial factors in women with breast cancer. *Journal of Chronic Diseases, 40*(7), 729–735.

Hoagland, A. C., Morrow, G. R., Bennett, J. M., & Carnrike, C., Jr. (1983). Oncologists' views of cancer patient noncompliance. *American Journal of Clinical Oncology, 6*(2), 239–244.

Hofer, M. A., Wolff, C. T., Friedman, S. B., & Mason, J. W. (1972a). A psychoendocrine study of bereavement. I. 17-Hydorxycorticosteroid excretion rates of parents following death of their children from leukemia. *Psychosomatic Medicine, 34*(6), 481–491.

Hofer, M. A., Wolff, C. T., Friedman, S. B., & Mason, J. W. (1972b). A psychoendocrine study of bereavement. II. Observations on the process of mourning in relation to adrenocortical function. *Psychosomatic Medicine, 34*(6), 492–504.

Holland, J. C. (1989). Fears and abnormal reactions to cancer in physically healthy individuals. In J. C. Holland & J. H. Rowland (Eds.), *Handbook of psychooncology* (pp. 13–21). New York: Oxford University Press.

House, J. S., Landis, K. R., & Umberson, D. (1988). Social relationships and health. *Science, 241*(4865), 540–545.

Ilnyckyj, A., Farber, J., Cheang, M., & Weinerman, B. (1994). A randomized controlled trial of psychotherapeutic intervention in cancer patients. *Annals of the Royal College of Physicians and Surgeons of Canada, 27*(2), 93–96.

Irwin, M., Daniels, M., Risch, S. C., Bloom, E., & Weiner, H. (1988). Plasma cortisol and natural killer cell activity during bereavement. *Biological Psychiatry, 24*(2), 173–178.

Irwin, M. R., & Strausbaugh, H. (1991). Stress and immune changes in humans: Biopsychosocial model. In J. M. Gorman & R. M. Kertzner (Eds.), *Psychoimmunology update*. Washington, DC: American Psychiatric Press.

Jarrett, S. R., Ramirez, A. J., Richards, M. A., & Weinman, J. (1992). Measuring coping in breast cancer. *Journal of Psychosomatic Research, 36*(6), 593–602.

Jiang, Y., Weinberg, J., Wilkinson, D. A., & Emerman, J. T. (1993). Effects of steroid hormones and opioid peptides on the growth of androgen-responsive Shionogi carcinoma (SC115) cells in primary culture. *Cancer Research, 15*(18), 4224–4229.

Kaplan, S. H., Greenfield, S., & Ware, J. E. (1989). Assessing the effects of physician-patient interactions on the outcomes of chronic disease. Henry J. Kaiser Family Foundation Second Conference on Advances in Health Status Assessment (1988, Menlo Park, CA). *Medical Care, 27*(3, Suppl.), S110–S127.

Kelly, J. A., Murphy, D. A., et al. (1993). Outcome of cognitive-behavioral and support group brief therapies for depressed, HIV-infected persons. *American Journal of Psychiatry, 150*(11), 1679–1686.

Kennedy, S., Kiecolt-Glaser, J. K., & Glaser, R. (1988). Immunological consequences of acute and chronic stressors: Mediating role of interpersonal relationships. *British Journal of Medical Psychology, 61*(pt. 1), 77–85.

Kirschbaum, C., Klauer, T., Filipp, S. H., & Hellhammer, D. H. (1995). Sex-specific effects of social support on cortisol and subjective responses to acute psychological stress. *Psychosomatic Medicine, 57*(1), 23–31.

Kogon, M. M., Biswas, A., Pearl, D., Carlson, R. W., & Spiegel, D. (1997). Effects of medical and psychotherapeutic treatment on the survival of women with metastatic breast carcinoma. *Cancer, 80*(2), 225–230.

Kubler-Ross, E. (1969). *On death and dying*. New York: Macmillan.

Lerman, C., Daly, M., Sands, C., Balshem, A., Lustbader, E., Heggan, T., Goldstein, L.,

James, J., & Engstrom, P. (1993). Mammography adherence and psychological distress among women at risk for breast cancer. *Journal of the National Cancer Institute, 85*(13), 1074–1080.

Lerman, C., & Schwartz, M. (1993). Adherence and psychological adjustment among women at high risk for breast cancer. *Breast Cancer Research and Treatment, 28*(2), 145–155.

Levine, S., Coe, C., & Wiener, S. G. (1989). Psychoneuroendocrinology of stress: A psychobiological perspective. In F. R. Brush & S. Levine (Eds.), *Psychoendocrinology* (pp. 341–377). San Diego: Academic Press Inc.

Levy, S. M., Fernstrom, J., Herberman, R. B., Whiteside, T., Lee, J., Ward, M., & Massoudi, M. (1991). Persistently low natural killer cell activity and circulating levels of plasma beta endorphin: Risk factors for infectious disease. *Life Scence, 48*(2), 107–116.

Levy, S. M., Herberman, R. B., Lee, J., Whiteside, T., Kirkwood, J., & McFeeley, S. (1990). Estrogen receptor concentration and social factors as predictors of natural killer cell activity in early-stage breast cancer patients: Confirmation of a model. *Natural Immunity and Cell Growth Regulation, 9*(5), 313–324.

Levy, S., Herberman, R., Lippman, M., & d'Angelo, T. (1987). Correlation of stress factors with sustained depression of natural killer cell activity and predicted prognosis in patients with breast cancer. *Journal of Clinical Oncology, 5*(3), 348–353.

Levy, S. M., Herberman, R. B., Maluish, A. M., Schlien, B., & Lippman, M. (1985). Prognostic risk assessment in primary breast cancer by behavioral and immunological parameters. *Health Psychology, 4*(2), 99–113.

Linn, M. W., Linn, B. S., & Harris, H. (1982). Effects of counseling for late stage cancer. *Cancer, 49*, 1048–1055.

Malarkey, W. B., Kiecolt-Glaser, J. K., Pearl, D., & Glaser, R. (1994). Hostile behaviors during marital conflict alters pituitary and adrenal hormones. *Psychosomatic Medicine, 56*(1), 41–51.

Manne, S. L., Lesanics, D., Meyers, P., Wollner, N., Steinherz, P., & Redd, W. (1995). Predictors of depressive symptomatology among parents of newly diagnosed children with cancer. *Journal of Pediatric Psychology, 20*(4), 491–510.

Mantell, J., & Hamovitch, M. (1992). Social relations, social support and survival among patients with cancer. *Journal of Psychosomatic Research, 36*(6), 531–541.

Meyerowitz, B. E. (1980). Psychosocial correlates of breast cancer and its treatments. *Psychological Bulletin, 87*(1), 108–131.

Miller, W. C., Thielman, N. M., Swai, N., Cegielski, J. P., Shao, J., Ting, D., Mlalasi, J., Manyenga, D., & Lallinger, G. J. (1996). Delayed-type hypersensitivity testing in Tanzanian adults with HIV infection. *Journal of Acquired Immune Deficiency Syndrome Human Retrovirology, 12*(3), 303–308.

Molassiotis, A., Van Den Akker, O. B. A., Milligan, D. W., & Goldman, J. M. (1997). Symptom distress, coping style and biological variables as predictors of survival after bone marrow transplantation. *Journal of Psychosomatic Research, 42*(3), 275–285.

Moos, R. H., & Schaefer, J. A. (1984). The crisis of physical illness: An overview and conceptual approach. In R. H. Moos (Ed.), *Coping with physical illness. 2: New perspectives* (pp. 3–25). New York: Plenum.

Morrow, G. R., & Morrell, C. (1982). Behavioral treatment for the anticipatory nausea and vomiting induced by cancer chemotherapy. *New England Journal of Medicine, 307*(24), 1476–1480.

Mulder, C., van der Pompe, G., Spiegel, D., & Antoni, M. (1992). Do psychosocial factors influence the course of breast cancer? A review of recent literature, methodological problems and future directions. *Psychooncology, 1*, 155–167.

Nemeroff, C. B., Widerlov, E., Bissette, G., Walleus, H., Karlsson, I., Eklund, K., Kilts, C. D., Loosen, P. T., & Vale, W. (1984). Elevated concentrations of CSF corticotropin-releasing factor–like immunoreactivity in depressed patients. *Science, 226*(4680), 1342–1344.

Pennebaker, J. W. (1993). Putting stress into words: Health, linguistics, and therapeutic implications. *Behavioral Research Therapy, 31*(6), 539–548.

Pennebaker, J. W., Kiecolt-Glaser, J. K., & Glaser, R. (1988). Disclosure of traumas and immune function: Health implications for psychotherapy. *Journal of Consulting Clinical Psychology, 56*(2), 239–245.

Pennebaker, J. W., Mayne, T. J., et al. (1997). Linguistic predictors of adaptive bereavement. *Journal of Personality and Social Psychology, 72*, 863–871.

Pettingale, K. W. (1984). Coping and cancer prognosis. *Journal of Psychosomatic Research, 28*(5), 363–364.

Pizzo, P. A., Robichaud, K. J., Edwards, B. K., Schumaker, C., Kramer, B. S., & Johnson, A. (1983). Oral antibiotic prophylaxis in patients with cancer: A double-blind randomized placebo-controlled trial. *Journal of Pediatrics, 102*(1), 125–133.

Radhakrishna, P. M., Balaram, P., Hareendran, N. K., Bindu, S., Abraham, T., Padmanabhan, T. K., & Nair, M. K. (1989). Immune reactive proteins as prognostic and clinical markers in malignant cervical neoplasia. *Journal of Cancer Research and Clinical Oncology, 115*(6), 583–591.

Ramirez, A. J., Craig, T. K., Watson, J. P., Fentiman, I. S., North, W. R., & Rubens, R. D. (1989). Stress and relapse of breast cancer [comments]. *British Medical Journal, 298*(6669), 291–293.

Reynolds, P., & Kaplan, G. A. (1990). Social connections and risk for cancer: Prospective evidence from the Alameda County study. *Behavioral Medicine, 16*(3), 101–110.

Richardson, J. L., Shelton, D. R., et al. (1990). The effect of compliance with treatment on survival among patients with hematologic malignancies. *Journal of Clinical Oncology, 8*(2), 356–364.

Rose, R. M. (1984). Overview of endocrinology of stress. In G. M. Brown (Ed.), *Neuroendocrinology and psychiatric disorder* (pp. 95–122). New York: Raven.

Rosenberg, S. A., & Lotze, M. T. (1986). Cancer immunotherapy using interleukin-2 and interleukin-2-activated lymphocytes. *Annual Review of Immunology, 4*, 681–709.

Rowse, G. J., Weinberg, J., Bellward, G. D., & Emerman, J. T. (1992). Endocrine mediation of psychosocial stressor effects on mouse mammary tumor growth. *Cancer Letters, 65*(1), 85–93.

Sapolsky, R. M., & Donnelly, T. M. (1985). Vulnerability to stress-induced tumor growth increases with age in rats: Role of glucocorticoids. *Endocrinology, 117*(2), 662–666.

Sapolsky, R. M., Krey, L. C., & McEwen, B. S. (1983). The adrenocortical stress-response in the aged male rat: Impairment of recovery from stress. *Experiments in Gerontology, 18*(1), 55–64.

Schatzkin, A., & Longnecker, M. P. (1994). Alcohol and breast cancer: Where are we now and where do we go from here? *Cancer, 74*(3 Suppl.), 1101–1110.

Smith, G., Jr., Monson, R. A., & Ray, D. C. (1986). Psychiatric consultation in somatization disorder: A randomized controlled study. *New England Journal of Medicine, 314*(22), 1407–1413.

Smyth, J. M., Stone, A. A., et al. (1999). Effects of writing about stressful experiences on symptom reduction in patients with asthma or rheumatoid arthritis. *Journal of the American Medical Association, 281*(14), 1304–1309.

Spiegel, D. (1985). The use of hypnosis in controlling cancer pain. *California Cancer Journal Clinic 35*(4), 221–231.

Spiegel, D. (1990). Facilitating emotional coping during treatment. *Cancer, 66*(6 Suppl.), 1422–1426.

Spiegel, D. (1991). Mind matters: Effects of group support on cancer patients. *Journal of NIH Research, 3*, 61–63.

Spiegel, D. (1993a). *Living beyond limits: New help and hope for facing life-threatening illness.* New York: Times Books/Random House.

Spiegel, D. (1993b). Psychosocial intervention in cancer. *Journal of the National Cancer Institute, 85*(5), 1198–1205.

Spiegel, D. (1996). Cancer and depression. *British Journal of Psychiatry, 168*(Suppl. 30), 109–116.

Spiegel, D. (1999). Healing words: Emotional expression and disease outcome. *Journal of the American Medical Association, 281,* 1328–1329.

Spiegel, D., & Bloom, J. R. (1983a). Group therapy and hypnosis reduce metastatic breast carcinoma pain. *Psychosomatic Medicine, 45*(4), 333–339.

Spiegel, D., & Bloom, J. R. (1983b). Pain in metastatic breast cancer. *Cancer, 52*(2), 341–345.

Spiegel, D., Bloom, J. R., & Gottheil, E. (1983). Family environment as a predictor of adjustment to metastatic breast carcinoma. *Journal of Psychosocial Oncology, 1*(1), 33–44.

Spiegel, D., Bloom, J. R., Kraemer, H. C., & Gottheil, E. (1989). Effect of psychosocial treatment on survival of patients with metastatic breast cancer. *Lancet, 2*(8668), 888–891.

Spiegel, D., Bloom, J. R., & Yalom, I. (1981). Group support for patients with metastatic cancer: A randomized outcome study. *Archives of General Psychiatry, 38*(5), 527–533.

Spiegel, D., Morrow, G. C., Riggs, G., Stott, P., Mudaliar, N., Pierce, H., Flynn, P., & Heard, L. (1996). Effect of group therapy on women with primary breast cancer. *Breast Journal, 2*(1), 104–116.

Stavraky, K. M., Donner, A. P., Kincade, J. E., & Stewart, M. A. (1988). The effect of psychosocial factors on lung cancer mortality at one year. *Journal of Clinical Epidemiology, 41*(1), 75–82.

Taylor, S. E., Helgeson, V. S., Reed, G. M., & Skokan, L. A. (1991). Self-generated feelings of control and adjustment to physical illness. *Journal of Social Issues, 47*(4), 91–109.

Temoshok, L. (1985). Biopsychosocial studies on cutaneous malignant melanoma: Psychosocial factors associated with prognostic indicators, progression, psychophysiology and tumor-host response. *Social Science Medicine, 20*(8), 833–840.

Temoshok, L., Heller, B. W., Sagebiel, R. W., Blois, M. S., Sweet, D. M., DiClemente, R. J., & Gold, M. L. (1985). The relationship of psychosocial factors to prognostic indicators in cutaneous malignant melanoma. *Journal of Psychosomatic Research, 29*(2), 139–153.

Tompkins, C. A., Schulz, R., & Rau, M. T. (1988). Post-stroke depression in primary support persons: Predicting those at risk. *Journal of Consulting and Clinical Psychology, 56*(4), 502–508.

Turns, D. M. (1988). Psychosocial factors. In W. L. Donegan & J. S. Spratt (Eds.), *Cancer of the breast* (3d ed., pp. 728–738). Philadelphia: W. B. Saunders.

Uchino, B. N., Kiecolt-Glaser, J. K., & Cacioppo, J. T. (1992). Age-related changes in cardiovascular response as a function of a chronic stressor and social support. *Journal of Personality and Social Psychology, 63*(5), 839–846.

van der Pompe, G., Duivenvoorden, H. J., Antoni, M. H., Visser, A., & Heijnen, C. J. (1997). Effectiveness of a short-term group psychotherapy program on endocrine and immune function in breast cancer patients: An exploratory study. *Journal of Psychosomatic Research, 42*(5), 453–466.

Watson, M., Pruyn, J., Greer, S., & van den Borne, B. (1990). Locus of control and adjustment to cancer. *Psychological Reporter, 66*(1), 39–48.

Waxler-Morrison, N., Hislop, T. G., Mears, B., & Kan, L. (1991). Effects of social relationships on survival for women with breast cancer: A prospective study. *Social Science Medicine, 33*(2), 177–183.

Weisman, A. D., & Worden, J. W. (1976). The existential plight in cancer: Significance of the first 100 days. *International Journal of Psychiatry in Medicine, 7*(1), 1–15.

Weiss, R. L., & Summers, K. J. (1983). *Marital interaction coding system III.* Beverly Hills, CA: Sage.

Wood, P. E., Milligan, M., Christ, D., & Liff, D. (1978). Group counseling for cancer patients in a community hospital. *Psychosomatics, 19*(9), 555–561.

Yalom, I. (1995). *Theory and practice of group psychotherapy.* New York: Basic.

Zeltzer, L., & LeBaron, S. (1982). Hypnosis and nonhypnotic techniques for reduction of pain and anxiety during painful procedures in children and adolescents with cancer. *Journal of Pediatrics, 101*(6), 1032–1035.

Commentary

Vicki Aken

In the past, physicians have focused on treating the mind or the body. The contributors to this volume look at how the mind and the body interact, instead of treating them as two separate entities. Collectively, they propose that emotional expression and social relationships may play a significant role in determining health outcomes.

David Spiegel seeks to build a bridge between those who take a mechanistic approach to treating disease and those who believe that a problem will be automatically fixed in the body if it is somehow fixed in the mind. He believes that the "mindless materialism" approach ignores the patient's psychological adjustment to illness while the "mind over matter" approach places blame on the patients by implying that they failed to exert proper mental control over their disease (Spiegel, 1993). Spiegel's work is helping to promote the idea that what is going on in our minds and our hearts affects the health of our bodies. This commentary will examine Spiegel's contributions to the field of social relations, emotions, and health, as well as suggest how Spiegel and other researchers in this field can complement and enrich each other's work.

Review of Research

Studies have emerged in recent years to indicate that social support may affect the quality as well as the quantity of life. Spiegel's work evaluates the effects of psychosocial intervention on the health outcomes of women with metastatic breast cancer. The psychosocial intervention consisted of randomized trials of supportive/expressive weekly group therapy. The group therapy sessions stressed seven themes: (1) building strong supportive bonds, (2) encouraging emotional expression, (3) dealing directly with fears of death and dying, (4) reordering life priorities, (5) improving relationships with family and friends, (6) enhancing communication with physicians, and (7) learning self-hypnosis for pain control.

Spiegel and Kimerling found that patients in the intervention sample showed an improvement in mood while patients in the control group suffered a statistically significant worsening of their mood. Symptoms included anxiety, depression, fatigue, confusion, and loss of vigor (Spiegel, 1993). Women in the control group also had a statistically significant survival advantage, even after controlling for baseline differences in initial staging, days of radiation, age, and disease-free interval (Spiegel, 1995).

Spiegel discusses three possible mediating mechanisms that may account for the relationship between psychosocial intervention and health outcomes: (1) promotion of improved health behaviors and medical decision making, (2) increased adherence to a medical treatment regimen, and (3) direct influence of specific activity in biological pathways.

Health behaviors, such as excessive alcohol consumption and poor diet and sleeping habits, have been linked to increased disease progression in breast cancer patients. Patients who participate in group therapy may receive social support that reinforces positive health behaviors. In one of his earlier studies, Spiegel found that patients may adopt positive health behaviors after observing others engaged in desired behaviors and after receiving social reinforcement for approximations of desired behaviors (Spiegel, Bloom, & Yalom, 1981).

Cancer patients may have difficulty adhering to treatments because of the uncomfortable side effects. Psychosocial treatment may increase a patient's knowledge about the treatments, either from other group members or from the enhanced communication with her physicians. Observing how others in the group deal with their treatments may also increase a patient's self-efficacy. Increased knowledge and self-efficacy may lead to increased adherence to treatment regimens.

Although improved health behaviors and increased medical adherence are both logical mechanisms for improving health outcomes, Spiegel has found that the longer survival times in metastatic breast cancer patients were not accounted for by differences in medical treatment, stage of cancer, or health behaviors between the experimental and control groups.

The third possibility for a mediating mechanism is that psychosocial intervention directly influences specific activity in biological pathways. One possible method for this is psychoneuroendocrinology. Hormones influenced by stress and depression, such as cortisol and prolactin, influence tumor proliferation. Cortisol is potently immunosuppressive. Extreme physical stress, such as having surgical procedures, causes the body to secrete prolactin. Because the dopamine system, which regulates prolactin's secretion, is widely distributed in the basal ganglia and the frontal lobes, it is involved with intentional activity, arousal, and mood regulation. Researchers have shown prolactin to promote breast tumor growth and tissue culture (Spiegel, 1993). A study done by Spiegel found that people whose cortisol levels do not go down during the diurnal cycle do not live as long (Spiegel, 1997).

Psychoneuroimmunology is another possible biological pathway. Stress and depression may influence components of the immune system. Major depression is associated with reduced natural killer (NK) cell activity, a subset of T-cells involved in cancer surveillance. Stress triggers the release of norepinephrine. This could alter NK cell activity and function because norepinephrine and other neurotransmitters, such as endorphins, influence cell adhesion molecules on lymphocytes. Researchers who looked at melanoma patients found that patients who participated in intensive group psychotherapy had increased NK cell activity and lower recurrence rates than the control group (Fawzy et al., 1993).

The research indicates that the mediating mechanisms for psychosocial intervention likely stem from direct influence of specific activity in biological pathways. However, it may be possible that different mediating mechanisms are present for different components of the intervention. One possible avenue of future studies could be to trace the pathways that different components of the psychosocial intervention follow. Are different mediating mechanisms present? Enhancing communication with physicians may improve medical decision making while encouraging emotional expression may have direct biological effects. Are some components of the intervention more effective than others? If so, which? Is there an interaction among different aspects of the intervention? For example, does encouraging emotional expression improve patients' relationships with family members? Answers to these questions could help in the design of future psychosocial interventions.

Links to Other Contributors

Spiegel and Kimerling's work can complement and become enriched by the work of other contributors to this volume, both conceptually and empirically. In keeping with the themes of this volume, this section will discuss how the work of Spiegel and the other contributors can be strengthened in the areas of attending to both positive and negative emotions, examining gender differences, looking at cumulative effects, determining mediating mechanisms, and using multiple methods.

Gottman's research looks at parenting styles and their effect on children. Like Spiegel, Gottman proposes that the expression of negative emotions can play as significant a role as the expression of positive emotions in determining well-being. Parents who follow the emotion-coaching philosophy are more aware of emotions in themselves and their children, view negative emotion as an opportunity for intimacy, and validate their child's emotions. Emotion-dismissing parents view negative emotions as harmful and feel that it is their job to eliminate these emotions as quickly as possible (Gottman, Katz, & Hooven, 1996). Gottman found that emotion-coached children have increased vagal tone, do better in school, have better relations with their peers, have better behavior, and have fewer infectious diseases (Gottman, 1997).

Spiegel notes that the expression of emotion is key to getting the most out of social networks, reducing social isolation, and improving coping skills. Gottman's emotion-coaching approach could be integrated into interventions to improve interaction among patients and their families, physicians, and therapists. Gottman suggested that emotion-coaching fathers also make better husbands (Gottman, 1997). Teaching emotion-coaching techniques to the families of women with breast cancer may help them to be more aware of the emotions that their wife, mother, or daughter is experiencing, to validate those emotions, and to increase intimacy.

Physicians and therapists could also benefit from some emotion-coaching intervention. Spiegel has indicated that doctors often share the qualities of emotion-dismissing parents. Physicians are trained to treat crying as if it were bleeding: apply direct pressure until it stops (Spiegel, 1995). Experiencing negative emotions when faced with a life-threatening illness is a perfectly normal reaction. Patients and physicians need to understand that. Not only will receiving emotional support from a physician validate the patient's emotional experience, it will also increase patient trust, openness, confidence, and feelings of control, and it will enable the patient to elicit the information she needs.

Spiegel has done extensive work to show the link between psychotherapy and disease progression. Differences in survival rates have been shown between patients who received therapy and the control group. Future research could examine who succeeds and who does not *within* the group that receives treatment. Do women who express more emotion in the group benefit more? Does outcome relate to the amount of positive or negative emotion expressed? Gottman's observational coding technique could provide another method of analyzing affect and interaction, which would help to determine exactly what is going on in the groups.

Using Ryff and Singer et al.'s life history approach, Spiegel could examine if what the women bring—in terms of prior life history—to the group therapy has an impact on the way they respond to the psychotherapy. Their life history approach has five organizing principles. The first states that adversity and its cumulation over time have negative consequences. The life history approach tracks negative experiences in multiple life domains, including work and family (see chap. 5). Some women in Spiegel's groups may have accumulated a great deal of adversity over time. Do these women receive the same, or perhaps more, benefits from group therapy as other women? Researchers may want to examine how psychosocial intervention can help neutralize or overcome the negative health consequences of accumulated adversity.

The second principle states that advantage and its cumulation over time have positive health advantages. Advantages include starting resources, personal capacities and abilities, and positive events (chap. 5). Because Spiegel and Kimerling's samples have consisted mostly of middle- and upper-middle-class women, this may be a key variable to examine in future work. Replication of the intervention with a focus on women with lower socioeconomic status may help to determine if the intervention is comparably effective across education and lower income groups.

The third organizing principle of the life history approach states that reactions to adversity and advantage can exacerbate or ameliorate the impact of life experiences. This is similar to the coping style approach; it looks, however, not only at reactions to stressful life experiences but broadens the approach to include reactions to chronic conditions, normative life transitions, and general life evaluations (chap. 5). If group differences cannot be explained by cumulation of adversity or advantage, perhaps they can be explained by the different styles in which women cope with these cumulations.

Singer and Ryff (1997) also suggest that position in social hierarchies across life domains has health consequences. Social stratification encompasses race and class, hierarchies of ability, positions of power and influence in the family and community, and degree of autonomy and authority in the workplace (Ryff &

Singer). A measure of where the women who participate in group therapy are in the social hierarchy or, perhaps more important, where they perceive they are, could help determine if social position influences health outcome. Could group therapy improve health outcomes for those low in the social hierarchy? A more diverse intervention sample would enrich Spiegel and Kimerling's findings.

Finally, social relationships can exacerbate or ameliorate the impact of life experience and enduring conditions. Ryff and Singer et al. examine the buffering effects of quality relationships in the face of difficult life experiences and the role of quality ties with significant others in facilitating processes that protect and maintain the quality of the organism (chap. 5). Spiegel's psychotherapy groups encourage the building of quality relationships with other cancer patients. What was the quality of the patient's relationship with her significant others both prior to and after diagnosis? Does the quality of the patient's relations with her spouse or children affect her ability to build quality relationships within the group? Another possible avenue is to look at whether women with high-quality relationships outside of the group have better health outcomes.

In Reis's model of intimacy, emotional expression in disclosure is a better indicator of intimacy than the disclosure of personal facts. Furthermore, in his model, intimacy is an interactional process. It depends not only on a person's self-expression but also on the other person's response. The person doing the disclosing must feel that she is being understood, meaning that she feels that the other person has accurately comprehended the discloser's self-conception; the discloser must feel validated, meaning that she senses that the other values and respects her attributes and world view; and the discloser must feel cared for (chap. 3).

Reis's research implies that, while expression of emotion may be an important component of group therapy, the discloser's perception of group members' reactions may be just as important. The event-sampling method, such as that used by Reis, could help ascertain group members' perceptions. In this method, patients would provide data immediately after the group session, which would compensate for the vicissitudes of retrospection. This method could also provide richer detail about what exactly is going on in the groups and may provide insight into why some people benefit and others do not.

In reviewing gender differences in intimacy, Reis found that women self-disclose more and were more often the targets of self-disclosure; women were better at interpreting nonverbal cues; and women provided more emotion support. Given these findings, would mixed-gender interventions work? Would women be giving more than they are receiving in these groups? Would this be emotionally draining for them or would they receive some altruistic benefit? Would the psychosocial intervention work in a men-only group? If men rely on women for emotional disclosure, how would they interact in an all-male group?

Reis has examined the relationship between a person's attachment style and his interactions with others. An avoidant person is characterized by discomfort with closeness. Preoccupation with, and desire for, heightened closeness characterize an anxious-ambivalent person. A secure person is characterized by comfort with closeness and general trust of others (Reis, Tidwell, & Shaver, 1996). Determining the attachment styles of group participants may provide insight into how different members interact with the group. Spiegel may find that avoidant persons are underrepresented in his intervention sample. These persons may choose not to participate in therapy because of their discomfort about getting close to other people.

Reis also found that secure persons reported more positive emotions than avoidant, while ambivalent participants fell in between these groups. Secure and ambivalent persons reported roughly comparable levels of negative emotion, which were lower than those reported by avoidant persons. Furthermore, Reis found that avoidant individuals eschew extended social contact (Reis et al., 1996). If negative emotion combined with low positive affect and social isolation leads to poor health outcomes, as research suggests, then avoidant individuals may be the ones most in need of the social network–building skills taught and encouraged in Spiegel's group therapy. If Spiegel and Kimerling find that avoidant persons self-select out of group therapy, then finding a way to get them to participate should be developed.

As mentioned previously, Spiegel believes that the expression of emotions, both negative and positive, can help increase intimacy as well as have a positive impact on health. Looking at not only whether or not subjects felt positive or negative emotions but also how they were expressed and to whom they were expressed may help Reis derive a fuller understanding of emotional well-being.

In her work, Seeman has found that social network ties, particularly the instrumental and emotional support provided by these ties, may influence health outcomes (Seeman & Syme, 1987). Seeman examines the effects of existing social support networks, such as family and friends. How do the existing social networks influence a patient's ability to create and utilize new networks through group therapy? Do women with strong existing social networks reap more benefits from group therapy or vice versa? One might hypothesize that women with strong preexisting social ties might be better at building new networks and know more about how to utilize social networks. On the other hand, women without strong existing social networks might have a greater need for group therapy and thus receive more benefit from it.

Cohen suggests that many different variables may affect how people utilize and benefit from social support. What is considered social support and how it is used may vary among different cultures or social classes. Social support may be more useful to people with certain social skills and personality factors. People with a greater sense of personal control may use their networks more than people who feel they cannot control their outcomes (Cohen, 1988). Again, more diverse samples and detailed profiles of group participants could enrich Spiegel's work and provide insight into who is benefiting from his intervention.

Seeman's and Cohen's measures of social integration consist mainly of the quantity of existing social ties. Spiegel states that psychological reactions to a diagnosis, such as cancer, may decrease a person's ability to utilize their existing social networks. His psychosocial intervention provides women with the tools (e.g., encouraging emotional expression) to get more out of their social relationships. This suggests that it is not the quantity of ties that affect health outcomes but rather a person's ability to utilize those ties. Seeman did measure "feeling loved" as a way of getting at the emotional quality of the social relationships. But again, as Spiegel has shown, a patient may feel loved but still not get the emotional support she needs from her existing social network.

Cohen suggests that educational interventions are more effective than group discussion interventions. Cohen has found that group discussion interventions can have negative effects. They have the potential to negatively affect self-esteem and optimism about the future. Group members may bring up frightening and uncomfortable topics. Some members may not feel validated by others in the group, which could affect their self-esteem (Cohen & Helgeson, 1996). Spiegel has found that confronting fears in group therapy actually helps group members. However, measuring whether or not a group member feels validated may help determine whether or not group therapy is damaging anyone's self-esteem.

Cohen suggests that group discussion may reduce perceived control among some patients. He states that one way for some people to maintain control over the illness experience is to deny its existence (Cohen & Helgeson, 1996). Does breaking down denial in group discussion lead to higher distress in patients and, therefore, cause more harm than good? Or does denial negatively affect health outcomes in the long run?

Cohen also suggests that emotional support from existing social network members, such as family and friends, may have a greater influence on adjustment than emotional support from other cancer patients (Cohen & Helgeson, 1996). Examining the quality of existing networks may help determine if this is true. Could the positive effects of psychosocial intervention be neutralized by a woman whose outside social network exerts a negative influence? Also, is there some unique support that only fellow cancer patients can give to each other?

In his research on social relationships and the common cold, Cohen quarantines his subjects after they are exposed to the cold virus. This is done because social interactions may increase the probability of being exposed to infectious agents. Spiegel's work, however, indicates that this might be the time when social interaction can be most beneficial. When subjects are isolated, they do not have the opportunity to express emotion, nor can their network members reinforce positive health behaviors.

Future Directions

The previous section suggested some future directions for Spiegel by indicating how other contributor's insights could inform his own. This section will suggest other possible avenues for future research.

In his remarks at the Third Annual Wisconsin Symposium on Emotion, Spiegel mentioned that after something very sad is said in the group, there will often be some genuine, nonescapist laughter. Researchers have found both physical and psychological benefits of humor. Stress tends to weaken the immune system. Research indicates that people who have a strong sense of humor show little change in immune function when subjected to stressors. Psychological benefits of humor include enhancing self-esteem, promoting creativity, improving negotiation and decision-making skills, maintaining a sense of balance, improving performance, bestowing a sense of power, relieving stress, and improving coping abilities (Hafen, Karren, Frandsen, & Smith, 1996).

Laughter can also have physiological and psychological health benefits. Laughter stimulates the sympathetic nervous system, the pituitary gland, the cardiovascular system, and the hormones that relieve pain and inflammation. Laughter also boosts the production of immune enhancers and suppresses the production of stress hormones. Laughter can also diminish fear, calm anger, and relieve depression (Hafen et al., 1996).

Examining whether or not people in the group with a strong sense of humor have better health outcomes may be one future research topic. Is there a difference in health outcomes between people who use humor as a stress reliever and those who use it as a defense mechanism? Do people who laugh, not just smile, at humorous remarks made in group therapy report less pain? Also, is there a way to incorporate and encourage humor in group therapy?

Evidence suggests that altruism can boost health. Emotions related to altruism, such as compassion, may help stabilize the immune system against the immuno-suppressing effects of stress. Altruistic actions may also decrease pain by stimulating the brain to release endorphins, which are powerful natural painkillers (Hafen et al., 1996). What role does altruism play in group therapy, and what specific effects does it have on group members' health outcomes?

Spiegel's work on psychosocial interventions has primarily been with women with metastatic breast cancer. At this point in the disease, chances of long-term survival are minimal. While Spiegel's research has shown increased survival rates, his interventions may reap even more benefits if implemented earlier in the disease stage. Interventions could target those with high psychosocial risk, such as people with low socioeconomic status (SES) or those suffering from social isolation. Spiegel is involved with new intervention studies that target women with the breast cancer gene or who are at high risk for getting breast cancer (Spiegel, 1997). Intervention at this point may help women avoid metastatic breast cancer.

Would Spiegel and Kimerling's psychosocial intervention work as well for people with illnesses other than breast cancer? In their study of illness representations in on-line support groups, Davison and Pennebaker (1997) examined the expressive styles of patients and their beliefs about their illness in groups that dealt with heart disease, breast cancer, prostate cancer, arthritis, diabetes, and chronic fatigue syndrome. They found that people with certain illnesses are more emotional and personal while people with other illnesses tend to be more concerned with objective data surrounding their disease. In particular, they found that people in breast cancer groups were the most engaging, and the women had a nurturing quality toward each other. In contrast, diabetes patients carried a much more strident tone, were sensitive to criticism, and were occasionally outright hostile toward one another (Davison & Pennebaker, 1997). What does this imply about the generalizability to other illnesses of the psychosocial intervention?

What role does culture play in the way people deal with emotion? Is emotional expression universally good or could it actually be more stressful for people from different cultures? Cultural norms about openness and self-disclosure vary. Cultures develop rules to govern human interactions in specific contexts. Anthropologist Edward T. Hall categorizes cultures as either high- or low-context. In low-context (e.g., American and northern European) cultures, communication is direct and explicit; the verbal message contains most of the information. In high-context (e.g., Japanese, Arab, Greek) cultures, communication is often indirect and implicit; most of the information lies either in the physical context or within the people who are part of the interaction (Hall, 1978). Given the emphasis on verbal exchange in group therapy, would these interventions work as well for people from high-context cultures?

In future intervention studies, additional methods could be used to gather richer data; which may help account for within-group differences. Determining who succeeds and why within the group becomes more important as finding a true control group to compare results with becomes more difficult. Support groups are much more prevalent than they were when Spiegel first started his research. Spiegel noted that up to a third of the control group participated in other support groups, and a substantial portion of the women who received the intervention also participated in other support groups (Spiegel, 1997). Having more detailed information about what is going on in the group may help in finding out what those who succeed have in common and what those not helped by group therapy have in common.

Conclusion

Spiegel and Kimerling have found that encouraging people to express affect related to disease, to build a support network and strengthen existing ones, and to face, anticipate, and cope with the threats that lie ahead are helpful both physiologically and psychologically.

Spiegel's work adds to the growing evidence that psychosocial variables can influence the body's ability to resist disease progression. His work is part of a growing body of literature that indicates that the era of mind-body dichotomy in medicine is over. His interventions, along with the research of other contributors to this volume, demonstrate that emotional expression and social relationships can improve health outcomes.

References

Cohen, S. (1988). Psychosocial models of social support in the etiology of physical disease. *Health Psychology, 7,* 269–297.

Cohen, S., & Helgeson, V. (1996). Social support and adjustment to cancer: Reconciling descriptive, correlational and intervention research. *Health Psychology, 15,* 135–148.

Davison, K. P., & Pennebaker, J. W. (1997). Virtual narratives: Illness representations in online support groups. In R. J. Petrie & J. A. Weinman (Eds.), *Perceptions of health and illness* (pp. 465–486). Amsterdam: Harwood Academic.

Fawzy, F. I., Fawzy, N. W., Hyun, C. S., Elashoff, R., Guthrie, D., Fahey, J. L., & Morton, D. L. (1993). Malignant melanoma: Effects of an early structured psychiatric intervention, coping, and affective state on recurrence and survival 6 years later. *Archives of General Psychiatry, 50*(9), 681–689.

Gottman, J. (1997, May 2–3). Marital and parent-child relationships and child and adult health: A theory and some preliminary data. Paper presented at the Third Annual Wisconsin Symposium on Emotion, University of Wisconsin, Madison.

Gottman, J., Katz, L. F., & Hooven, C. (1996). Parental meta-emotion philosophy and the emotional life of families: Theoretical models and preliminary data. *Journal of Family Psychology, 10,* 243–268.

Hafen, B. Q., Karren, K. J., Frandsen, K. J., & Smith, N. L. (1996). *Mind/body health: The effects of attitudes, emotions and relationships.* Boston: Allyn and Bacon.

Hall, E. T. (1978). *Beyond culture.* Garden City, NY: Doubleday.

Reis, H. 1998. Gender differences in intimacies and related behaviors: Context and process. In D. Canary & K. Dindia (Eds.), *Sex differences and similarities in communication* (pp. 203–231). Mahwah, NJ: Lawrence Erlbaum Associates, Inc.

Reis, H., Tidwell, M. O., & Shaver, P. R. (1996). Attachment, attractiveness and social interaction: A diary study. *Journal of Personality and Social Psychology, 71,* 729–745.

Singer, B., & Ryff, C. (1997). Racial and ethnic inequalities in health: Environmental, psychosocial and physiologic pathways. In B. Devlin, S. E. Feinberg, K. Roeder, & D. Rasnich (Eds.), *Intelligence and success, is it all in the genes? Scientists respond to the bell curve.* New York: Springer-Verlag.

Seeman, T. E., & Syme, L. (1987). Social networks and coronary artery disease: A comparison of the structure and function of social relations as predictors of disease. *Psychosomatic Medicine, 49,* 341–354.

Spiegel, D. (1993). Psychosocial intervention in cancer. *Journal of the National Cancer Institute, 85,* 1198–1205.

Spiegel, D. (1995). Minding the body: Psychotherapy for extreme situations. *Strecker Monograph Series, 22,* 9–32.

Spiegel, D. (1997, May 2–3). Having a good cry: Group expression of emotion and health outcome among breast cancer patients. Paper presented at the Third Annual Wisconsin Symposium on Emotion, University of Wisconsin, Madison.

Spiegel, D., Bloom, J. R., & Yalom, I. (1981). Group support for patients with metastatic cancer: A randomized outcome study. *Archives of General Psychiatry, 314*(5), 527–533.

5

Elective Affinities and Uninvited Agonies

Mapping Emotion with Significant Others onto Health

Carol D. Ryff, Burton H. Singer, Edgar Wing, & Gayle Dienberg Love

Goethe's *Elective Affinities*, written in 1809, is a love story that celebrates themes of the romantic era: individuality, immediacy, passion. Love itself was hardly a novel topic, given centuries of prior literature and poetry on matters of the heart (see Singer, 1984a, 1984b). What was unique was Goethe's depiction of powerful longing for another in the context of a society characterized by strict marital customs. The novel pulled love out of the romantic haze, so to speak, and brought it into the prosaic routines of the country gentry. It challenged a view of human relationships governed by social convention and, instead, portrayed love selected by the heart; hence, he called his work *elective* affinities. He did not overlook, however, the complexity, pain, and turmoil that frequently accompany such a passionate response to another. Our phrase, *uninvited agonies*, draws attention to love's counterpoint and, more generally, to the observation that significant human relationships, lived out over the long term, frequently include a panoply of positive and negative emotions.

The purpose of this chapter is to probe the emotional features, both good and bad, of significant human relationships and to consider their import for human health. We draw on multiple data sources to probe connections among the quality of social relationships and various health outcomes. These include a national survey, which is valuable for assessing population profiles on the positive and negative emotions that are associated with key social relationships. Such survey data elaborate the range of variability in people's evaluations of the quality of their ties to significant others. In addition, the survey findings point to preliminary linkages between the presence of good (or poor) relationships and various measures of self-reported health.

This inquiry emerges from and extends a large body of literature that documents positive ties between social support and health (Berkman & Breslow, 1983; House, Landis, & Umberson, 1988; Seeman, 1996; Seeman, Berkman, Blazer, & Rowe, 1994; Uchino, Cacioppo, & Kiecolt-Glaser, 1996). Such research has frequently emphasized the structural features of social relationships, such as the size and proximity of one's social network (e.g., whether one is married or living alone, whether one has close confidantes, number of close friends or relatives, and frequency of contact with them). Less explicit concern has been given to the emotional texture and depth of such social relations, although questions are sometimes asked about levels of emotional support (e.g., Berkman, Leo-Summers, & Horwitz, 1992; Blumenthal et al., 1987; Glass & Maddox, 1992). The emotions that comprise such support are rarely elaborated. However, when probing more specific emotions, Seeman and Syme (1987) found that those who scored highest on "feeling loved" had the lowest levels of coronary artery disease.

To emphasize the need for greater attention to *emotion* in social relationships, we examine the record of emotional dynamics in the lives of three famous couples. These capture the lived experiences of connection to others and, in so doing, underscore the importance of tracking cumulative, indeed chronic, aspects of emotional experience with others. It is this cumulation of enduring love and affection, or bitterness and torment, that we suggest is consequential for health. These observations are then brought back to the empirical realm via life histories of relational data collected in the Wisconsin Longitudinal Study (WLS), a large cohort of men and women who have been studied from their senior year of high school to their late fifties. Our aim is to create relationship pathways of the WLS respondents, which combine information about the quality of early ties with parents (mother and father) and the quality of emotional ties to significant others in adulthood. For a subsample of respondents, we then link these cumulative relationship profiles to aspects of biology, which are viewed as possible intervening mechanisms between relational life histories and health outcomes. Our specific focus is on allostatic load, a measure of the physiological wear and tear on organ systems and tissues (Seeman, Singer, Rowe, Horowitz, & McEwen, 1997). Consistent with our aim of advancing knowledge of positive human health (Ryff & Singer, 1998a), we give particular emphasis to the role of emotionally rich, gratifying human relationships in keeping allostatic load low. The larger aim is to begin mapping linkages from long-term social relationship quality through biological mechanisms to unfolding profiles of morbidity and mortality.

Quality of Social Relations in the U.S. Population

In 1995, the MacArthur Research Network for Successful Midlife Development conducted a survey (known as MIDUS) based on a national probability sample of English-speaking adults aged 25 to 74, who resided in the 48 contiguous states. Data were collected by telephone interviews and self-administered questionnaires. The response rates for these different parts of the study were 68% and 87%. The data summarized here, pertaining to quality of social relationships (e.g., spouse, family, friends), involve 1,880 respondents on whom complete data are available.

Two evaluative aspects of social relationships are examined. The first pertains to the assessment of positive relations with others, one of six dimensions of psychological well-being formulated by Ryff (1989a). This global evaluation of the quality of one's ties to others is then augmented with assessments about the positive and negative aspects of three specific relationships: spouse, other family relationships, and friends.

Global Evaluation of Positive Relations with Others

Conceptual formulations in clinical and developmental psychology and the mental health literature converge in their depiction of psychological well-being as a multifaceted phenomenon (Ryff, 1985). Among the diverse components that comprise optimal human functioning, the most universally agreed-upon feature is that of having quality relations with others (Ryff & Singer, 1998a). While the particular ways in which good relationships are expressed may vary across cultures, it is universally true that all people everywhere deem connections with others as a core feature of optimal human existence.

Positive relations with others, as an aspect of well-being, has been operationalized with structured self-report scales, which probe the extent to which individuals feel that they experience warm, trusting, meaningful ties with others (Ryff, 1989a). This component of well-being, along with five other dimensions of positive functioning, was assessed in MIDUS, the MacArthur national survey. The six dimensions have been shown to be factorially distinct not only from each other but from other frequently used indicators of well-being (Ryff & Keyes, 1995). In MIDUS, the well-being dimensions were measured with three-item scales, which correlated from .70 to .89 with their longer parent scales and had internal consistency coefficients ranging from .39 to .59. The lower alpha coefficients followed from the decision to select short-form items that reflected the multifactorial structure of each parent scale, rather than selecting those that maximized internal consistency (see Ryff & Keyes, 1995).

Shown in figure 5.1 are mean-level scores for each of the six scales of well-being, plotted separately for three age groups of men and women. The general life-course story is that some aspects of well-being show incremental patterns with age (autonomy, environmental mastery), others show decremental patterns (purpose in life, personal growth), and still others show little age variation (self-acceptance, positive relations—only for women). Such patterns have replicative consistency across multiple studies (Ryff, 1989a, 1991; Ryff & Keyes, 1995; Ryff & Singer, 1998b). Of particular significance for the present inquiry is the finding that positive relations with others shows stable age profiles for women from young adulthood through midlife into old age, while for men the pattern is one of slight age increment, particularly from midlife to old age, perhaps tied to the Jungian notion that as men age, they become more aware of their affiliative needs and capacities (Jung, 1933). What is more striking, however, is the notable difference in overall levels of positive relations with others: men consistently score

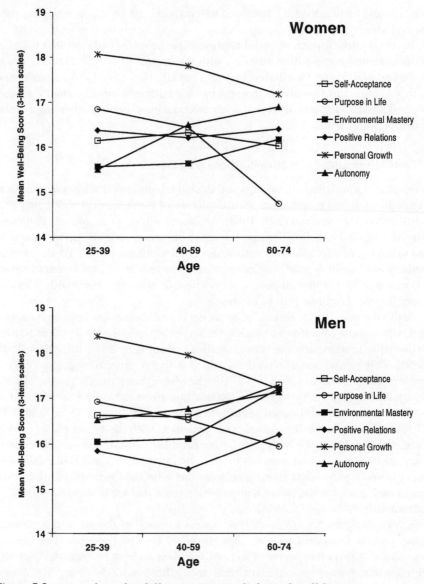

Figure 5.1 Age and gender differences in psychological well-being.

lower on this aspect of well-being than women, a finding that has been replicated with numerous samples with diverse socioeconomic and cultural groups (Ryff & Singer, 1998b). Further, positive relations with others is, for men, the lowest rated of all of their six dimensions of well-being.

Such a finding might suggest that the relational realm has less priority and importance for men compared to women, with perhaps other features of well-being (e.g., environmental mastery, autonomy) being more central to men. However, a prior study of "lay conceptions" of well-being (Ryff, 1989b) showed that both men and women gave highest priority to having quality relations with others in their spontaneously generated definitions of well-being. Taken together, these findings indicate that men may have less of the comparably valued relational goods than do women. If such quality relations are, indeed, linked with health, these gender differences may have significant consequences. The nearly eight-year differential in life expectancy between men and women (Spirduso, 1995) adds poignancy to the task of tracking gender differences in the connection between quality relations and health.

Specific Social Relationships and Health

The MIDUS national survey also probed the quality of specific social relationships, such as with one's spouse, with other family members, and with friends. Questions were asked about the positive and negative aspects of each of these relationships. For example, with regard to spousal relations, respondents were asked, "How much does your spouse really care about you?" "How much does he or she understand the way you really feel about things?" "How much can you open up if you need to talk about your worries?" Six positive items were included, and their internal consistency (coefficient alpha) was .91. Sample items to assess negative aspects of respondents' spousal relations were: "How often does he or she argue with you?" "How often does he or she get on your nerves?" Internal consistency (alpha) for these six items was .88. Similar questions were asked about respondents' evaluations of their ties to other family members (i.e., children, parents) as well as ties to friends. Four items each were asked about the positive and negative aspects of relationships with family and friends. Alpha coefficients showed high internal consistency (range = .79–.91).

Reports of the quality of these relationships are linked to three aspects of self-reported health: *symptoms* that the respondent had experienced over the last 30 days (measured as number times frequency), the number of *chronic conditions* (diagnosed by a physician) they reported during the last 12 months, and a general *subjective evaluation of their overall health*. Findings are first examined with regard to links between specific relationship items and health variables and then for aggregated relationship profiles and their ties to health.

Figure 5.2 summarizes, separately for married men and women, the frequency distribution of responses to the question: "How often does your spouse argue with you?" The modal response, which accounted for about half of men and slightly less of women, was "rarely." About 40% of men and 35% of women said "sometimes," with another 10% of women and slightly less of men reporting that their spouse argued "often" with them. At the other extreme, about 7% of men and 10% of women say their spouse "never" argues with them. The smaller percentages, when extrapolated to the larger U.S. population (of which this sample is representative) account for large numbers of people existing at the ends of these distributions. The line graph superimposed over the bars indicates the average report of health symptoms (number times frequency, see right vertical axis) for individuals in each response group. The graph shows that women overall report

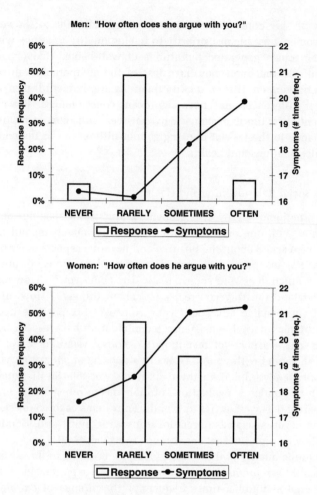

Figure 5.2 Negative spousal item (response distribution) and health symptoms.

higher levels of symptoms, but for both genders, there is an incremental pattern of symptoms following increments in frequency of arguing with spouse. Highest levels of symptoms for men are evident among those who say their wife argues often with them, while for women, highest symptom levels are evident for those who say their husband argues with them sometimes or often.

Figure 5.3 shows the response distributions for a positive spousal item: "How much does he or she understand the way you feel about things?" About 55% of men, but only 40% of women say "a lot." Slightly more than 40% of women and slightly less than 40% of men say "some," while about 7% of women and only 2% of men say "not at all." Again, superimposed over these response groups are reported levels of symptoms (number times frequency). Those who indicated that their spouse does not understand them much, or at all, have the highest levels of health symptoms (with women again reporting higher levels overall). The lowest levels of health symptoms for both men and women are reported for those who say their spouse understands them a lot.

Figure 5.4 again shows responses for "How often does he or she argue with you?" but now superimposed on the distribution are average numbers of chronic conditions reported by respondents. The data for men show that those who are at the extremes (i.e., they *never* argue with their wives, or they do so *often*) report the highest levels of chronic conditions. The former may comprise husbands who suffer from emotionally repressed anger or frustration, thereby connecting to the literature on emotional inhibition (e.g., suppressed anger or hostility) and its links to disease (Pennebaker & Traue, 1993) as well as to studies that show gender differences in patterns of emotional expression or inhibition and health symptoms (Malatesta & Culver, 1993). The data for women show a more linear pattern, which links frequency of arguing with reported chronic conditions, although they

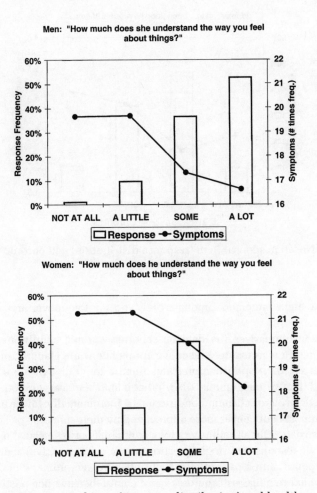

Figure 5.3 Positive spousal item (response distribution) and health symptoms.

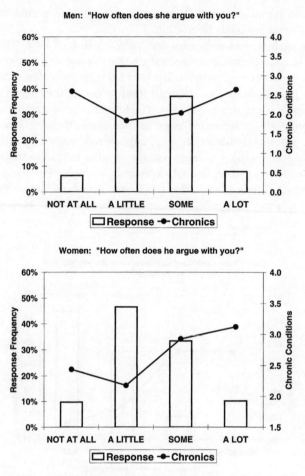

Figure 5.4 Negative spousal item (response distribution) and chronic conditions.

also show a slight increment among wives who say they never argue with their husbands.

Figure 5.5 summarizes the data on reported chronic conditions vis-à-vis a positive item: "How much does he or she appreciate you?" Happily, most married respondents say their spouse appreciates them a lot, although more so for men (about 70%) than women (about 55%). What is notably clear, for both genders, is that reported levels of chronic conditions are incrementally lower as husbands and wives report feeling ever more appreciated by their spouses.

The above data offer a preliminary look at the link between social relationships and health via responses to single questions (negative or positive) about a specific social tie (spouse) and a particular aspect of health (symptoms or chronic conditions). The next two figures provide a more comprehensive perspective; they incorporate the idea of cumulative relational impact by creating composite indices,

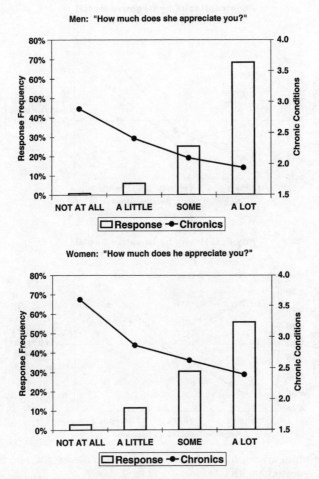

Figure 5.5 Positive spousal item (response distribution) and chronic conditions.

which were summed across positive versus negative items of relational quality and summed over three types of social relationships (spouse, nonspousal family relationships, friends). The sample is then divided into tertiles of relationship quality for this composite measure. Figure 5.6 summarizes the data—separately for married men and women in MIDUS—for the three measures of health (chronic conditions, physical symptoms, subjective health ratings) among those in the low, middle, and high tertiles on the composite negative relationship measure. The health measures are plotted as standardized z-scores. For men, those in the highest tertiles of negative social relationship ratings have significantly higher levels of chronic conditions ($F(2, 1074) = 7.6$, $p < .001$), higher number of health symptoms ($F(2, 1028) = 27.9$, $p < .001$), and significantly lower levels of subjective health ratings ($F(2, 1069) = 9.3$, $p < .001$) than those in the lowest tertile. Those in the middle tertile are also significantly different from those in the highest tertile on

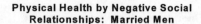

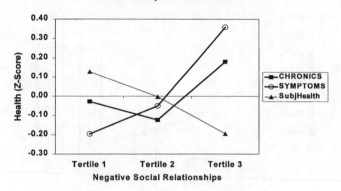

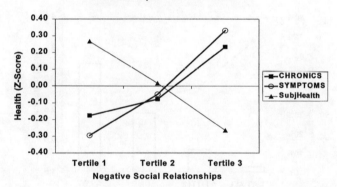

Figure 5.6 Cumulative relational profiles (negative items for spouse, family, friends) and reported health.

two of the three health measures (symptoms, subjective health). For women, the patterns are similar: those in the highest tertile of negative relations have significantly higher levels of chronic conditions ($F (2, 924) = 14.9$, $p < .001$), higher numbers of health symptoms ($F (2, 864) = 31.3$, $p < .001$), and significantly lower levels of subjective health ($F (2, 916) = 23.2$, $p < .001$) than those both in the middle and high tertile groups. Those in the middle group are also significantly different from those in the high group on all three health measures.

Figure 5.7 provides the counterpoint data, when married respondents report on the positive aspects of the social relationships with spouse, family, and friends. These data show strong patterns for both genders: those in the highest tertile of positive relationships have significantly lower levels of chronic conditions (men: $F (2, 1071) = 5.1$, $p < .001$; women: $F (2, 927) = 8.6$, $p < .001$), fewer health symptoms (men: $F (2, 1027) = 21.6$, $p < .001$; women: $F (2, 866) = 17.9$, $p < .001$), and higher levels of subjective health (men: $F(2, 1066) = 10.1$, $p < .001$; women: $F(2,919) = 26.0$, $p < .001$) than those with lower-quality relations.

Taken together, these findings indicate that both the presence of the good and the absence of the bad in social relationships are linked with better self-reported health profiles. Such data converge with prior survey and epidemiological studies that link social relationships to health and/or mortality (Berkman & Breslow, 1983; House, Landis, & Umberson, 1988; Seeman, 1996; Seeman, Berkman, Blazer, & Rowe, 1994; Seeman & Syme, 1987; Uchino, Cacioppo, & Kiecolt-Glaser, 1996). What they add, however, is more detail about positive and negative aspects of the emotional features of social relationships. That is, prior studies have tended to focus on simply relationship counts (number of significant others) or the instrumental features of social relationships (i.e., what others do for the respondent). While emotion is sometimes probed, questions have been general (e.g., "Do you receive emotional

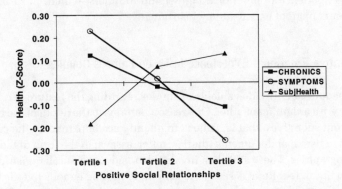

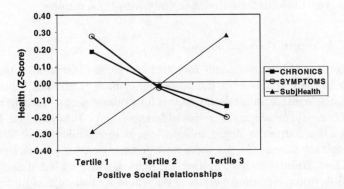

Figure 5.7 Cumulative relational profiles (positive items for spouse, family, friends) and reported health.

support from your spouse?") or have asked only about single emotions (e.g., "Do you feel loved?"). More differentiated dimensions of emotional interaction (e.g., understanding, opening up, criticizing, arguing) are infrequently probed. Certainly, the extensive literature on adult attachment (Cassidy & Shaver, 1999; Hazan & Shaver, 1994) and intimacy and close relationships (Barnes & Sternberg, 1997; Berscheid & Reis, 1998; Hatfield & Rapson, 1993) addresses these more emotional features of significant social relationships, but these studies rarely intersect with scientific agendas that link social relationships to health (see Ryff & Singer, 2000).

The preceding cross-sectional findings, and others like them, offer little insight about *how* such relationship patterns unfold or persist over time. Also, the dynamics between relational assessments and health (what causes what?), including possible reciprocities between the two, cannot be discerned. Further, issues of cumulative relationship impact over time cannot be assessed. To push forward questions regarding the long-term persistence of positive relations, or the chronicity of negative interaction, we will briefly consider the long-term relationships of three famous couples. These examples illustrate ideas of cumulative emotional experience in key relationships. These works also add texture and detail about the lived experience of emotional connection to others, which, in turn, has import for refinement of extant survey instruments.

Cumulative Emotional Experience in Three Famous Couples

Famous people can provide valuable examples regarding the texture of one's emotional life with a significant other. One reason pertains to the depth of the historical record about such lives, that is, fame is frequently accompanied by the compiling of extensive personal documents (diaries, letter, essays) in the form of biographies or autobiographies. These afford an invaluable inside look at relationship dynamics played out in real time. A second reason for exploring famous lives is that they frequently embody strong emotion. Indeed, the powerful yearnings of the artist, poet, writer, or musician frequently fuel the creative products from which their fame ensues. These features—detailed historical records and strong emotional expression—were the basis for selecting the following three couples.

Enduring Anguish: Leo and Sonya Tolstoy

The Tolstoys provide a remarkable look inside a stormy marriage, as both wrote copiously in their diaries from the beginning of their relationship through the next 48 years. William Shirer describes this long portrayal of feelings in his book, *Love and Hatred: The Stormy Marriage of Leo and Sonya Tolstoy* (1994). Both Leo and Sonya (fig. 5.8) were strong-willed, fiercely independent individuals, and even as their relationship began, there were signs of trouble. A week before their wedding, Leo shared with his betrothed his diaries, which included details of his passionate love for a peasant woman with whom he had an illegitimate child. Sonya was shattered. A fortnight after her marriage to Leo, she wrote in her diary: "Ever since yesterday, when he told me he didn't trust my love, I have been feel-

Figure 5.8 Leo Tolstoy (top), and Sonya Tolstoy (bottom).
Photographs from Shirer, 1994.

ing truly terrible. . . . He loves to torment me and see me weep. . . . What is he doing to me? Little by little I shall withdraw completely from him and poison his life" (Shirer, 1994, p. 26; all quotations in this section are from this work).

One month after the birth of their first child, Leo's diary entry read: "Her character gets worse . . . with her grumbling and spiteful taunts . . . her unfairness and quiet egotism frighten and torment me. . . . I've looked through her diary— suppressed anger with me glows beneath words of tenderness. . . . If this is so, it's all a mistake on her part—it's terrible—I'm terribly depressed" (pp. 28–29). Leo was deeply troubled that Sonya was not nursing the child. Later, in the fall of that year, she wrote, "He wants to wipe me off the face of the earth because . . . I'm not doing my duty. . . . How can one love an insect which never stops stinging? I am left alone morning, afternoon, and night. I am to satisfy his pleasure and nurse his child. I am a piece of household furniture. I am a woman" (p. 30).

The Tolstoys went on to have a very large family together: Sonya had 16 pregnancies, 3 of which were miscarriages; of the 13 remaining children, 10 survived into adulthood. "Yasnaya Polyana" was their home for 48 years, and it was there that Leo Tolstoy wrote *War and Peace, Anna Karenina*, and other famous works. During these years, Sonya not only had many children, she provided carefully written copies of his manuscripts; she copied somewhere around 21,000 pages of text. Recurrent depressions and tumultuous emotions characterized many of their years together. About 20 years after their wedding, Sonya's diary entry read: "Today he shouted at the top of his voice that his dearest wish was to leave his family. I shall carry the memory of that heartfelt heartrending cry of his to the grave. I pray for death, for without his love I cannot survive. . . . I cannot sleep in the bed he has abandoned. Lord help me, I long to take my life. . . . the clock is striking four" (p. 91). His diary two years later included these thoughts upon joining his family for tea: he found them all "so repulsive, pathetic, and degrading to listen to, especially the poor, mentally sick Tanya" (his name for Sonya) that he took to bed. He concluded, "it would have been better for me to have had no children at all" (p. 109).

Around age 50, Leo wrote about his tormented mind and soul in *Confession*, a book about his own midlife crisis. This was the period of life when he renounced his wealth and property, and he began dressing as a peasant and working with them in the fields. He took on a deeply religious and moral stance, even preaching abstinence to the Russian peasants. Sonya vented considerable anger about the hypocrisy of this position, as she found herself constantly pregnant with his children. Much was recorded by both husband and wife about their sensual attraction to each other, which was accompanied by feelings of depravity for succumbing to their desires. Leo's novella, *The Kreutzer Sonata*, published in 1889, offered a harsh diatribe against women, marriage, marital love, sex, and having children. Sonya was humiliated by it. During this time, she began having terrible nightmares, attempted to leave home, and even tried to kill herself. The loss of two of her younger children to scarlet fever during these years affected her deeply, and another child died of pneumonia in 1906. From those years until Leo's death in 1910, their marital relationship disintegrated into an unbearable hell for both of them.

The photo in figure 5.9 was taken on their 48th wedding anniversay. Leo wrote in his diary that he felt ashamed to be photographed as a loving couple. Growing old, they became two enemies, who spied on each other and read each other's diaries. Sonya was tormented by his relationship with a young man named Chertkov, to whom Leo was secretly arranging to leave his literary treasure. In October 1910, she wrote, "Everyday there are fresh blows that scorch my heart, shorten my life, and torment me unendurably" (p. 327). Leo, at age 82, with a heart condition, found life with her so unbearable that he arranged an escape from their home in the middle of the night. He boarded a train and traveled third class as far as the small town of Astapovo. By this point, he was wheezing and coughing up blood and had to be moved onto a table at the train station. On learning of his escape, Sonya tried to drown herself twice, but she was rescued by her children. The sadness of their final days is captured by the photo in figure 5.10, which is Sonya standing on tiptoe outside the Astapovo train station, trying to catch a glimpse of her dying husband, who did not want to see her. Sonya died nine years later.

Thus, the Tolstoys represent a marriage of marked emotional negativity, which not only cumulated but escalated over time. This relational torment seems to have been linked primarily with mental, rather than physical, health difficulties.

Figure 5.9 Last photograph taken of Leo and Sonya Tolstory (from Shirer, 1994).

Figure 5.10 Sonya Tolstoy standing on tiptoe outside the stationmaster's house at Astapovo (from Shirer, 1994).

Both parties suffered bouts of depression and had suicidal tendencies over the course of their lives together. Leo Tolstoy's ultimate demise was likely quickened by his need to escape his wife's presence when his health was deteriorating. For their historical time, however, both Tolstoys were quite long lived, suggesting the presence of other compensating factors, such as the pluses afforded by their high-class lifestyle (e.g., good nutrition, optimal living conditions) or the emotional strengths derived from other relationships (e.g., children, close ties to others outside their marriage) or simply strong biological constitutions. This combination of factors, which underlay their emotional dynamics and their health, underscores the complexity of the task of linking emotion in social relationships to health.

From Sequestered Illness to the Full Cup of Life: The Brownings

An equally dramatic couple of the positive variety is the story of Elizabeth Barrett and Robert Browning, written about by Julia Markus in *Dared and Done* (1995). The two met in 1845, when young Robert, then in his early thirties, began writing to the invalid poet; she was aged 39. Elizabeth was the daughter of a wealthy British gentleman, who was a widower with nine children. Domestic tyrant that he was, her father allowed none of his adult children to marry. Elizabeth's mother had died when Elizabeth was 21. As a young woman, Elizabeth suffered from lung problems and was given her first prescription of morphine as a teenager to calm down her "irritable restlessness." At the time Robert contacted her, she was living a life reduced to her upstairs room in the Wimpole Street house of her father. From her couch, she lived, in her words, "only inwardly" while Robert seemed to her to have "drunken from the cup of life full" (Markus, 1995, p. 28; all quotations in this section are from this work).

As the months passed, the reclusive poet agree to receive Robert as a visitor. Through the next year, visits occurred regularly, and Elizabeth experienced a burst of well-being. She wrote, "I had done living, I thought, when you came and sought me out" (p. 35). This woman, with the heart of a romantic poet and the body of an ailing invalid, had lived in one of the most repressive households of the Victorian period. Looking back, she wrote, "A thoroughly morbid and desolate state it was, which I look back now to with the sort of horror with which one would look to one's gravesclothes, if one had been clothed in them by mistake during a trance" (p. 83).

At the age of 40, she walked down the stairs of her father's house and out the door to a nearby chapel, where she and Robert were secretly married; they then left for Europe. In Paris, she wrote that they were "thinking one thought, pulsing with one heart" (p. 81) and described her new life as like "riding an enchanted horse" (p. 81). They settled in Pisa, Italy, where after two miscarriages, she gave birth to a healthy, fair-skinned baby boy on March 9, 1849. She was 43, Robert 37.

Her *Sonnets from the Portuguese* were written around 1850. The best of these have been rendered stale by their popular usage. However, one can imagine how Elizabeth's expressions evoked poignant response from Robert, upon his first reading of these lines:

How do I love thee?
Let me count the ways.
I love thee to the depth and breadth and height
My soul can reach, when feeling out of sight
for the end of Being and ideal Grace.

The Brownings shared nearly 20 years together in their beloved Italy before she died, at age 56, from recurrent lung problems. The photos in figure 5.11 are of Robert and Elizabeth shortly before her death. Robert lived for another 28 years and never remarried. While Elizabeth Barrett Browning was far from healthy from childhood onward, the ways in which their love brought vigor and engagement to her reclusive, somber world were unmistakable and remarkable. Theirs is a story of the power of deep connection to awaken the will to experience life fully, when health seemed to have been lost. Escaping to Italy for a new existence, complete with family and writing achievements for both of these talented individuals, did not fully overcome Elizabeth's long-term respiratory ailments nor her difficulties with morphine addiction, which was set in motion by her parents when she was a child. Robert did, nonetheless, take her away from a life described by herself as deathlike, and they shared 20 remarkable years together.

Expressions of Pain: Frida Kahlo and Diego Rivera

Emotional experience, both exhilarating and agonizing, is a well-known catalyst for creative expression. Frida Kahlo's art dramatically illustrates emotion trans-

Figure 5.11 Robert Browning (top), photograph by Alessandri, Rome, 1860, and Elizabeth Barrett Browning (bottom), photograph by Alessandri, Rome, May 27, 1861. Courtesy of the Armstrong Browning Library, Baylor University, Waco, Texas.

Figure 5.12 *Frieda and Diego Rivera* or *Frieda Kahlo and Diego Rivera*, 1931. © 2001 Banco de México Diego Rivera and Frida Kahlo Museums Trust. Av, Cinco de Mayo No. 2, Col. Centro, Del. Cuauhtémoc 06059, México, D. F., México. Reproduction authorized by the National Institute of Fine Arts and Literature, Mexico.

lated to canvas (Kettenmann, 1993). Frida met Diego Rivera, the renowned Mexican artist, in the 1920s, and they married in 1929. He was 21 years her senior. Rivera, established in the art world, recognized her talent and described her as "the first woman in the history of art to treat, with absolute and uncompromising honesty, one might even say with impassive cruelty, those general and specific themes which exclusively affect women" (Kettenmann, 1993, p. 51).

Frida came to this relationship with a history of health problems. As a child, she had had polio, which stunted the growth of her right leg and foot and led to the cruel nickname "Peg-Leg Frida." At the age of 19, she was severely injured in a bus accident, while traveling with her youthful boyfriend. Spinal injuries confined her to bed for months, which was when she began to paint in earnest.

Figure 5.12 is a work painted in 1931. Frida floats beside her corpulent husband, who at the time of their marriage was internationally acclaimed; she was artistically unknown. During the 1930s, while in the United States, Frida had an abortion for medical reasons related to her fractured pelvis. She became pregnant again and wanted to carry the child to term, but Diego was not interested in having a child. She had another miscarriage, her emotions about which are depicted in *The Flying Bed* (not shown), a painting completed in 1932. Her small body is lying on an enormous bed; the sheets are soaked with blood. She is surrounded by a vast, forlorn, desolate plain. Numberous symbols of the child (fetus, umbilical cord) and Rivera (the orchid he brought her in the hospital) are included.

Diego, a philanderer of monumental proportions, had repeated affairs with other women, including Frida's sister Cristina. A painting in 1935, *A Few Little Pricks*, was linked to a newspaper report of a woman murdered as a result of a man's jealousy. The wounds caused by the brutal male violence may have symbolized Frida's own emotional injuries at the time. In 1939, Frida divorced Rivera and painted *The Two Fridas* (see fig. 5.13), again expressing the emotions surrounding her separation and marital crisis. The person who was respected and loved by Diego was the Mexican Frida in Tehauna costume; the other Frida wore European dress. The hearts of both women are exposed; there is blood dripping

Figure 5.13 *The Two Fridas*, 1939. © 2001 Banco de México Diego Rivera and Frida Kahlo Museums Trust. Av, Cinco de Mayo No. 2, Col. Centro, Del. Cuauhtémoc 06059, México, D. F., México. Reproduction authorized by the National Institute of Fine Arts and Literature, Mexico.

from the freshly severed artery. This was followed by her *Self-Portrait with Cropped Hair* (see fig. 5.14), which was painted in 1940. Her feminine clothes have been replaced with a dark man's suit, and she has cut off her long hair. The verse across the top reads, "See if I loved you, it was for your hair, now you're bald, I don't love you any more." These words of a Mexican song captured Frida's feelings that she was loved by Diego only for her female attributes.

The two artists remarried in 1940, and for the next 14 years, Frida endured continuing physical and emotional pain. Her severe and chronic back problems became a recurrent topic for artistic expression. *The Broken Column* (1944, not shown) reveals the excruciating back brace she was forced to wear. Spinal surgery did not cure this world of pain, also depicted in *Wounded Deer* (fig. 5.15). The physical torment was compounded by the emotional trauma of Diego's continuing affairs with other women. The man, nonetheless, came to dominate her mind and heart, as depicted in her self-portrait entitled *Diego in My Thoughts* (fig. 5.16) and again in 1949 (*Diego and I*, not shown), while he was having an affair with a famous film star. In the latter, she looks mournfully at the viewer, long hair wrapped around her neck, with Diego central in her mind.

Figure 5.14 *Self-portrait with Cropped Hair*, 1940. © 2001 Banco de México Deigo Rivera and Frida Kahlo Museums Trust. Av, Cinco de Mayo No. 2, Col. Centro, Del. Cuauhtémoc 06059, México, D. F., México. Reproduction authorized by the National Institute of Fine Arts and Literature, Mexico.

Figure 5.15 *The Wounded Deer* or *The Little Deer* or *I am a Poor Little Deer*, 1946. © 2001 Banco de México Diego Rivera and Frida Kahlo Museums Trust. Av, Cinco de Mayo No. 2, Col. Centro, Del. Cuauhtémoc 06059, México, D. F., México. Reproduction authorized by the National Institute of Fine Arts and Literature, Mexico.

Frida Kahlo died at the age of 47 after 25 years of marriage to Diego Rivera. He died three years later at the age of 71. His health had been markedly less problematic than hers; whether his emotional/relational experiences were also less anguished is unclear. Given the health difficulties she brought to the relationship, Frida Kahlo's early death was certainly not solely attributable to having married a man who caused her great pain. Whether she would have longer withstood her health afflictions had she married a nurturing, loving, and devoted husband is an interesting but unanswerable question.

The lives of these three couples are notably unique, not only for the extremes they represent in terms of relational experiences, but also because each involved individuals of unusual expressive talents (in prose, poetry, art). Their writings and paintings give poignant insight into the nature of the recurring, cumulative emotions they shared, or inflicted, on each other. Unfortunately, limited information is available regarding their specific health trajectories as well as what their early-life relational experiences were about. Despite the missing pieces, these examples point to the importance of understanding emotion, social relational, and health linkages from a life-history perspective (Singer, Ryff, Carr, & Magee, 1998).

The final segment of our chapter returns to the lives of "ordinary" persons who have been studied over a long expanse of time. Our objective is to carry this emphasis on cumulative relational histories to the realm of longitudinal survey data. A second major objective is to explore biological variables, which may constitute

Figure 5.16 *Self-portrait as a Tehuana* or *Diego in My Thoughts* or *Thinking of Diego*, 1943. © 2001 Banco de México Diego Rivera and Frida Kahlo Museums Trust. Av, Cinco de Mayo No. 2, Col Centro, Del. Cuauhtémoc 06059, México, D. F., México. Reproduction authorized by the National Institute of Fine Arts and Literature, Mexico.

mechanisms, or bridges, that connect relational histories to health outcomes (i.e., morbidity, mortality).

Cumulative Relational Profiles and Biological Mechanisms

This section highlights recent empirical findings from a longitudinal study in which we examine relationships among multiple categories of social ties (e.g., spouse, mother, father) and various biological markers that reflect cumulative wear and tear on the body. For each individual, social relationships are represented by profiles, which incorporate information across different phases of life and multiple forms of connection with others (e.g., emotional, intellectual, sexual, recreational).

Our general hypothesis is that persons having larger amounts of negative relational experience relative to positive are also those having biomarkers of excessive wear and tear on multiple physiological systems. If so, these individuals are at elevated risk of later-life cardiovascular disease (CVD) and early decline in physical and cognitive functioning (Seeman, Singer, Rowe, Horwitz, & McEwen, 1997). Persons with profiles that show positive relationships with their parents from early life as well as close engagement with a spouse and friends in midlife are hypothesized to show biomarkers of wear and tear within normal operating range and thereby to be at reduced risk of later-life chronic conditions.

We first describe the sample in which these hypotheses are assessed and then summarize our specific measures of relationships and biological markers. The final section presents the empirical results that link the two realms.

Wisconsin Longitudinal Study (WLS)

The WLS is a long-term survey of a random sample of 10,317 men and women who graduated from Wisconsin high schools in 1957. Survey data were collected from the original respondents in 1957, 1975, and 1992–1993. Data have been collected on respondents' family background, starting resources, academic abilities, youthful aspirations, social support, social comparisons, and the timing and sequencing of adult educational and occupational achievements, work events and conditions, family events, and physical and mental health. For a comprehensive overview of WLS and many of the findings from it, see Hauser et al. (1993).

Our specific aim in this chapter is to investigate the relationship between cumulative adversity and advantage—in the realm of social relationships—over the life course and biological indicators implicated in later-life health. For a small subsample of WLS respondents, we have collected new data on the nature of early-life relationships with parents as well as their connections to significant others in adulthood. For these individuals, we have also obtained biological measures previously shown to predict later-life cardiovascular disease and decline in physical and cognitive function (Seeman et al., 1997). This inquiry is part of a broader agenda designed to link cumulative adversity and advantage across multiple life domains—including but not restricted to social relationships—to health outcomes, both mental and physical (Ryff & Singer, 1998a; Singer & Ryff, 1997; Singer, Ryff, Carr, & Magee, 1998).

Our biological subsample was selected to maximize variation in prior profiles of adversity and advantage as well as psychological well-being. This variation was designed to provide favorable circumstances for demonstrating a priori hypothesized differences in biomarker levels. The underlying philosophy was that clear, interpretable differences in biomarker distributions as a function of adversity and advantage profiles (relational and otherwise) would demonstrate the utility of conducting similar assessments on more extensive and representative samples. Specifically, we contacted sample members within geographic proximity to the location of the biological data collection and, to the extent possible, sought to maximize diversity with regard to levels of psychological well-being as well as levels of prior adversity (e.g., childhood poverty, growing up with an alcoholic parent, low occupational status in adulthood) or advantage (e.g., high socioeconomic status (SES) parents, upward occupational mobility).

Each person completed a social relationship questionnaire, which is described in detail below. They also participated in a physical health examination and contributed blood and urine samples, from which laboratory assays provided the requisite biomarker measurements. The social relationship measures focus on emotional features of key social ties, which were expected to be associated with the frequency with which biomarkers were (or were not) in normal operating ranges.

Relationship Measures

Caring, supportive, and affectionate relationships between parents and children are hypothesized to be important components of cumulative advantage profiles, which ultimately are linked with good physical and mental health in later life. Conversely, the experience of uncaring and even abusive interactions with one or both parents is anticipated to be a defining feature of a negative social relationship pathway, which would be associated with physiological indicators operating outside of normal ranges in later life.

Table 5.1 lists the 12 "caring" items in the Parental Bonding scale (Parker, Tupling, & Brown, 1979), which are the basis for discriminating in the parent-child bond between genuine caring and warmth and indifference and rejection. The WLS respondents were asked about their relationships with their mother and father separately, specifically, "When you were growing up, how much did she (he) behave in each of the following ways?" Response options were: never, a little, some, or a lot. With the exception of possibly two items (no. 5, no. 12), these questions probe explicitly emotional, affectional, caring features of one's relationship to mother and father.

Shifting attention to midlife relationships, four aspects of connection to a spouse or significant other are hypothesized to contribute to cumulative relationship profiles that should, in turn, be associated with later-life physiological indicators of wear and tear on the body. We assessed different aspects of intimacy by using four subscales of the PAIR (Personal Assessment of Intimacy in Relationships) Inventory

Table 5.1 Parental Bonding Scale

(+)	1. She (he) spoke to me with a warm and friendly voice.
(+)	2. She (he) was affectionate to me.
(−)	3. She (he) seemed emotionally cold to me.
(+)	4. She (he) appeared to understand my problems and worries.
(+)	5. She (he) helped me as much as I needed.
(+)	6. She (he) enjoyed talking things over with me.
(+)	7. She (he) frequently smiled at me.
(+)	8. She (he) seemed to understand what I needed or wanted.
(−)	9. She (he) made me feel I wasn't wanted.
(+)	10. She (he) could make me feel better when I was upset.
(+)	11. She (he) communicated with me very much.
(+)	12. She (he) took an active interest in my habits and school activities.

(+) Positively scored item
(−) Negatively scored item
Mother caring alpha = .95
Father caring alpha = .75

(Schaefer & Olson, 1981). The emotional and sexual subscales were included because of their focus on the most intimate forms of connection between two people. The intellectual and recreational subscales emphasize mutually enjoyed experiences, companionship, and the scope of shared communication. We did not use the social subscale of the PAIR because it concentrates on the mutual friends of the couple. Similarly, the conventionality subscale was deleted in our pathway constructions because it focused on efforts to create a good impression. Neither of these latter subscales were explicitly tapping feelings and connections between marital partners.

The PAIR seeks to (a) identify the degree to which each partner presently feels intimate in each specific relational area considered and (b) identify the degree to which each partner would like to be intimate. The items comprising the emotional, sexual, intellectual, and recreational subscales are listed in table 5.2. For

Table 5.2 Personal Assessment of Intimacy in Relationships (PAIR) Subscale Statements

Emotional (alpha = .89)

(−) I often feel distant from my partner.
(+) My partner can really understand my hurts and joys.
(−) I feel neglected at times by my partner.
(+) My partner listens to me when I need someone to talk to.
(+) I can state my feelings without him/her getting defensive.
(−) I sometimes feel lonely when we're together.

Sexual (alpha = .85)

(+) I am satisfied with our sex life.
(−) I feel our sexual activity is just routine.
(+) I am able to tell my partner when I want sexual intercourse.
(−) I "hold back" my sexual interest because my partner makes me feel uncomfortable.
(+) Sexual expression is an essential part of our relationship.
(−) My partner seems disinterested in sex.

Intellectual (alpha = .87)

(+) My partner helps me clarify my thoughts.
(−) When it comes to having a serious discussion it seems that we have little in common.
(−) I feel "put down" in a serious conversation with my partner.
(−) I feel it is useless to discuss some things with my partner.
(+) We have an endless number of things to talk about.
(−) My partner frequently tries to change my ideas.

Recreational (alpha = .85)

(+) I think that we share some of the same interests.
(−) I share in very few of my partner's interests.
(−) We seldom find time to do fun things together.
(+) We enjoy the same recreational activities.
(+) We enjoy the out-of-doors together.
(+) We like playing together.

(+) Positively scored item
(−) Negatively scored item

each statement, the respondent answers on a five-point scale from strongly agree to strongly disagree.

A more general measure of social relationship quality, the 14-item Positive Relations with Others scale, from Ryff's multidimensional model of well-being (1989a; Ryff & Keyes, 1995), was also utilized. A short-form version (three items) of this instrument that was included in the MIDUS national survey showed strong gender differences. Items for the 14-item scale are presented in table 5.3. Respondents answered on a six-point scale from strongly agree to strongly disagree. A high scorer on positive relations with others is described as having warm, satisfying, trusting relationships with others; being capable of strong empathy, affection, and intimacy; and understanding the give and take of human relationships. A low scorer is described as having few close, trusting relationships with others; finding it difficult to be warm, open, and concerned about others; being isolated and frustrated in interpersonal relationships; and not willing to make compromises to sustain important ties with others.

Biological Measures

Allostasis, meaning "stability through change" (Sterling & Eyer, 1988, p. 638), is a concept that emphasizes the dynamism of internal physiology and the fact that healthy functioning requires ongoing adjustments and adaptations of the internal physiologic milieu. Normally functioning physiological systems exhibit fluctuating levels of activity as they respond and adapt to environmental demands. Through allostasis, the autonomic nervous system the hypothalamic-pituitary-adrenal (HPA) axis, and the cardiovascular, metabolic, and immune systems protect the body by responding to internal and external stress.

The long-term, or cumulative, effect of physiological accommodations to stress

---

Table 5.3 Positive Relations with Others

(+) 1. Most people see me as loving and effectionate.
(−) 2. Maintaining close relationships has been difficult and frustrating for me.
(−) 3. I often feel lonely because I have few close friends with whom to share my concerns.
(+) 4. I enjoy personal and mutual conversation with family members or friends.
(+) 5. It is important to me to be a good listener when close friends talk to me about their problems
(−) 6. I don't have many people who want to listen when I need to talk.
(+) 7. I feel like I get a lot out of my friendships.
(−) 8. It seems to me that most other people have more friends than I do.
(+) 9. People would describe me as a giving person, willing to share my time with others.
(−) 10 I have not experienced many warm and trusting relationships with others.
(−) 11. I often feel like I'm on the outside looking in when it comes to friendships.
(+) 12. I know that I can trust my friends, and they know they can trust me.
(−) 13. I find it difficult to really open up when I talk with others.
(+) 14. My friends and I sympathize with each other's problems.

(+) Positively scored item
(−) Negatively scored item
alpha = .88

represent a price paid by the body to maintain systems within normal operating ranges. We conceptualize this price with the term *allostatic load*. It is a measure of the wear and tear that results from chronic overactivity or underactivity of the stabilizing allostatic systems (McEwen, 1998; McEwen & Stellar, 1993). The first operationalization of allostatic load was designed to summarize levels of physiologic activity across a range of regulatory systems pertinent to disease risks (Seeman et al., 1997). Allostatic load for an individual was defined as the number of indicators from the list in table 5.4 for which an individual's assessed value satisfies the stated inequality.

Cortisol, the catecholamines norepinephrine and epinephrine, and DHEA are mediators of physiological responses to adverse challenge. In particular, 12-hour urinary cortisol excretion is an integrated measure of HPA axis activity, while DHEA-S is a functional HPA axis antagonist, which serves to reset elevated cortisol levels to basal conditions following stressful challenge. Twelve-hour urinary norepinephrine and epinephrine are integrated measures of sympathetic nervous system activity. Blood pressure, waist-hip ratio, total and HDL cholesterol, and glycosilated hemoglobin are viewed as reflecting secondary consequences of stressful challenge. Systolic and diastolic blood pressure are indices of cardiovascular activity. Waist-hip ratio is an index of long-term levels of metabolism and adipose tissue deposition, thought to be influenced by glucocorticoid activity (Despres et al., 1990). Serum high density lipoprotein (HDL) and total cholesterol levels are indices of cardiovascular risk. Total glycosilated hemoglobin is an integrated measure of glucose metabolism over a period of several days.

The allostatic load measure, which is based on counting the number of indices in table 5.4 for which a person's assessed value satisfies the stated inequality, has been shown to be predictive of incident cardiovascular disease and later-life decline in physical functioning and memory loss (Seeman et al., 1997). Recent findings over a 7.5-year period also show that high allostatic load was predictive of subsequent mortality (Seeman, Singer, Wilkinson, & McEwen, 1999). The same protocol that was used to operationalize allostatic load in this initial work was also employed with the WLS biological subsample. We view the full array of biomarkers and their summary via allostatic load scores as intermediate outcomes in

Table 5.4 Indicators of High Allostatic Load

Indicator	Criterion Cutoff
Systolic blood pressure	≥ 148 mm Hg
Diastolic blood pressure	≥ 83 mm Hg
Waist-hip ratio	≥ 0.94
Total cholesterol–HDL ratio	≥ 5.9
Total glycosilated hemoglobin level	$\geq 7.1\%$
Urinary cortisol level	≥ 25.7 µg/g creatine
Urinary norepinephrine level	≥ 48 µg/g creatine
Urinary epinephrine level	≥ 5 µg/g creatine
HDL cholesterol level	≤ 37 µg/dl
DHEA	≤ 35 mg/dl

a cohort study (Munoz & Gauge, 1998). That is, they are measurements assessed after exposure—to cumulative adversity and advantage—but prior to the clinical appearance of disease. They therefore quantify early biological and/or altered structure/physiological function prior to pronounced declines in physical and cognitive functioning and incident chronic disease.

Constructing Relationship Pathways

Our relational histories are constructed via an incremental process wherein we first examine distributions on the various social relationship measures, then create composite profiles within measures (e.g., put together information about mother and father), and, finally, build pathways across measures. These analyses are presented for the 106 WLS respondents (57 men, 49 women) on whom biological data are currently available (data collection on additional respondents is ongoing).

Scores on Mother Caring and Father Caring from the Parental Bonding Scale can range in each instance from 0 to 36. Table 5.5 shows the five-number summaries suggested by Tukey (1977). We see that fathers are evaluated as substantially less caring than mothers. Indeed, the *upper* quartile of Father Caring (FC) is between the *lower* quartile and median of the Mother Caring (MC) distribution. There are some minor differences in these summaries when male and female respondents are considered separately. Men tend to have slightly higher scores on both FC and MC, with larger disparities between the lower quartile and minimum of the MC distribution.

To examine the relationships with both parents simultaneously, we cross-classify individuals as positive (+) or negative (−) on Father Caring and Mother Caring according to whether their score on the respective scale is above or below the median. These cross-classifications are presented separately for men and women in table 5.6.

For men and women, it is substantially more likely that both parents have the same valence (i.e., −,− or +,+) in their relationship with the respondent, which underscores the theme of cumulative relational experiences. This similarity in valence is somewhat more the case for men's perceptions of their parental relationships than for women's. This can be quantified by the odds ratio in both tables.

Table 5.5 Summaries of Scores on Parental Bonding

Scores	Father Caring (FC)	Mother Caring (MC)
Maximum	32	36
Upper quartile	27	33
Median	23	29
Lower quartile	20	24
Minimum	0	1

Table 5.6 Cross-Classifications on Father Caring
and Mother Caring

Father Caring (FC)	Mother Caring (MC)	
	−	+
Women		
−	14	9
+	7	16
Men		
−	17	7
+	10	21

$$\text{Odds ratio} = \frac{\#\,(+,+)\;\#\,(-,-)}{\#\,(-,+)\;\#\,(+,-)}$$
$$\text{Odds ratio (women)} = 3.56$$
$$\text{Odds ratio (men)} = 5.1$$

Both odds ratio are statistically significant ($p < .05$).

Scores on each of the subscales—emotional (E), sexual (S), intellectual (I), and recreational (R)—from the PAIR inventory can range from 6 to 30. We viewed emotional and sexual items as probes of the most personal and intimate aspects of spousal ties and thus combined these subscales in the concatenation E + S. Intellectual and recreational items were viewed as probing more companionate and cognitive forms of spousal connection and thus were combined in the concatenation of subscales I + R. Scores on each of the combined scales could range from 12 to 60.

Our data showed virtually no difference between men and women in their scores on the combined emotional/sexual (E + S) and intellectual/recreational (I + R) scales. The five-number summaries, presented separately for men and women, are shown in table 5.7. These summaries show slightly higher distributions on both combined scales for men compared to women. The differing aspects of spousal intimacy did not show notably different response distributions for either men or women.

We assess consistency of responses on both forms of intimacy by classifying

Table 5.7 Summaries of Scores on Emotional/Sexual
(E + S) and Intellectual/Recreational (I + R) Subscales

Scores	Women		Men	
	E + S	I + R	E + S	I + R
Maximum	54	56	60	58
Upper quartile	43	44	48	46
Median	39	39	43	41
Lower quartile	31	28	31	34
Minimum	12	14	12	12

persons as positive (+) or negative (–) on E + S and I + R according to whether they are above or below the median on each scale. This leads to the cross-classifications shown in table 5.8. The data show that it is more common to see concordance between both forms of intimacy than disparity. This is quantitatively expressed by the odds ratio.

$$\text{Odds ratio} = \frac{\#\ (+,+)\ \#\ (-,-)}{\#\ (-,+)\ \#\ (-,-)}$$
$$\text{Odds ratio (women)} = 18.7$$
$$\text{Odds ratio (men)} = 16.1$$

Both odds ratios are statistically significant ($p < .01$).

Our construction of relational pathways involved putting together the above assessments from early parental ties and adult spousal connections. We define an individual to be on a negative pathway if s/he scores (–,–) on Father Caring *and* Mother Caring (FC, MC) and/or on emotional/sexual *and* intellectual/recreational (E + S, I + R). Thus, these individuals experienced negative relationships with *both* parents and/or negative interaction with a spouse on *both* combined aspects of intimacy described above. Among men, 21% experienced negative relationships (with both mother and father) only in childhood; another 18% reported negative ties to spouse on all dimensions in adulthood; and the rest (61%) showed some combination of negative relational experience in childhood *and* adulthood. Among women, three respondents showed negative relational experience only in childhood; another two reported negative ties only in adulthood; and the rest (74%) showed some combination of negative relational experience in both periods.

We define an individual to be on a positive pathway if s/he has at least one + on FC or MC, i.e., (+, –), (–, +), or (+,+) *and* at least one + on E + S or I + R. Thus, the positive path requires some positive relational experience with one or both parents in childhood and at least one of the two combined forms of intimacy in adulthood. Again, this pathway underscores the cumulative nature of positive emotional experiences with significant others in childhood and adulthood.

To probe whether these pathways, which were generated on the basis of spe-

Table 5.8 Cross-Classifications on Emotional/Sexual and Intellectual/Recreational Scales

	Intellectual/Recreational (I + R)	
Emotional/Sexual (E + S)	–	+
Women		
–	16	3
+	6	21
Men		
–	22	6
+	5	22

cific familial relations, show consistency with the more general ratings from the Positive Relations with Others scale (Ryff, 1989a), we divided scores on this measure into tertiles and examined these tertile distributions along the positive and negative relationship pathways. Figure 5.17 shows the percentages of individuals (separately for men and women) in the top (T_1), middle (T_2), and bottom (T_3) tertiles of positive relations with others among individuals classified in the positive (26 men, 22 women) and negative (29 men, 24 women) pathways, as defined above.[1] The figure shows that, for women, there is essentially no difference in the distribution of positive and negative pathways across the three tertiles of positive relations with others. However, for men on the positive pathway, only 12% are in the lowest tertile and 62% are in the highest tertile on the more general relational measures. Conversely, on the negative pathway, 57% of men are in the lowest tertile and only 11% in the highest tertile on positive relations with others. Thus, evaluations of the general quality of one's relationships with others is, for men but not for women, closely linked with the type of pathway classification derived from specific relationship (parents, spouse) assessments. We will return to this distinction in presentation of the allostatic load data below.

Linking Allostatic Load to Relationship Pathways

Figure 5.18 shows the overall distribution of allostatic load scores, which is defined as the number of indicators from the list in table 5.4 for which an individual's assessed value satisfies the stated inequality. The study of Seeman et al. (1997) indicates that scores of 3 and above indicate elevated risk of subsequent incident cardiovascular disease and decline in physical functioning and memory loss. Thus, we define high allostatic load to mean a score of ≥3. Low allostatic load is defined as a score of 0–1, and intermediate load is defined as a score of 2. Using these designations, figure 5.19 shows gender-specific distributions of allo-

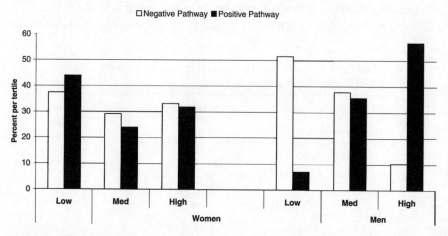

Figure 5.17 Distribution of pathway types among tertiles of positive relations with others.

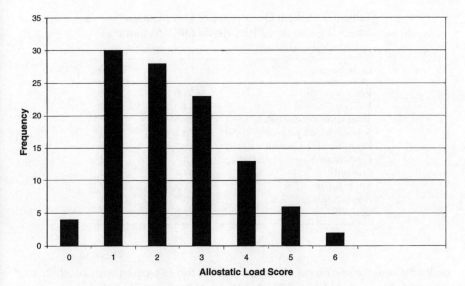

Figure 5.18 Frequency distribution of allostatic load scores.

static load scores. The figure reveals that men have a substantially higher percentage (50.9%) at high load than do women (30.6%).

There are also gender differences in the frequency with which particular components of allostatic load are outside of normal operating range. These are summarized in table 5.9. In addition to biological markers considered individually, it is useful to identify sets of markers that simultaneously contribute to the allosta-

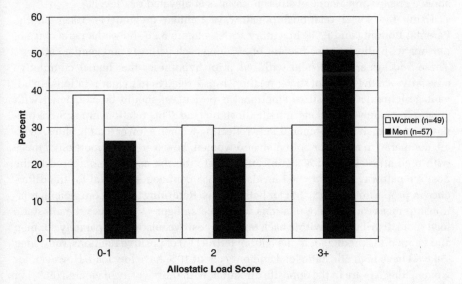

Figure 5.19 Frequency of low (0–1), medium (2), and high (3+) allostatic load by gender.

Table 5.9 Percent Occurrence of Components
Satisfying Elevated Risk Criteria for Contribution to
Allostatic Load Score

Component	Men	Women
Waist-hip ratio	52.6	8.2
HDL cholesterol	33.3	12.2
Total cholesterol–HDL ratio	24.6	12.2
Systolic blood pressure	28.1	16.3
Diastolic blood pressure	49.1	18.4
Glycosilated hemoglobin	3.5	8.2
Cortisol	54.4	67.3
Epinephrine	3.5	8.2
Norepinephrine	5.3	18.4
DHEA-S	7.0	34.7

tic load scores for persons at high load. Among the 15 women with allostatic load scores of ≥3, one-third have cortisol paired with the ratio of total cholesterol over HDL cholesterol outside the normal range; one-third have cortisol paired with norepinephrine; and one-third have cortisol paired with DHEA-S. The latter two groups also include a single woman with cortisol, norepinephrine, and DHEA-S all outside the normal range. Among the 29 men with allostatic load scores of ≥3, 38% have waist-hip ratio together with both systolic and diastolic blood pressure outside the normal range; 41% have waist-hip ratio paired with cortisol; and 38% have waist-hip paired with HDL cholesterol. Taken as a whole, these data suggest that men have more elevated levels of cardiovascular risk factors, while women show a greater prevalence of stress hormones at elevated risk levels.

Using the social relationship pathways defined previously—based on the Parental Bonding and PAIR Inventory scales—figure 5.20 shows the percentage of persons with allostatic load scores of ≥3 along each pathway and gender category. These findings are consistent with our prior hypotheses that higher cumulative adversity—in the realm of social relationships—relative to higher relationship advantage (cumulative positive emotional experiences) should be associated with greater frequency of persons at high allostatic load. This relationship is more pronounced for men than women, likely reflecting women's lower load profiles, overall, compared to men. For both men and women, however, the proportion of those with high allostatic load is significantly greater on the negative compared to the positive pathway at the $p < .05$ level. The 95% confidence interval for the difference in proportions is (.13, .61) for both groups. Returning to the more general relationship measure (positive relations with others), figure 5.21 shows the allostatic load score distributions within each tertile of positive relations, separately, for men and women. As predicted, in the bottom tertile (T_3) of positive relations, most men (58.8%) have high allostatic load and only about 10% have low load. However, for women, the data are in the opposite direction, with the majority of women (55%) in the bottom tertile of positive relations showing low allostatic load and about 15% showing high load. Alternatively, among those in the top tertile (T_1) of positive re-

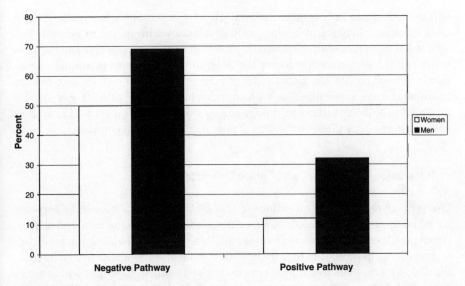

Figure 5.20 Percentage having high allostatic load on negative and positive relationship pathways.

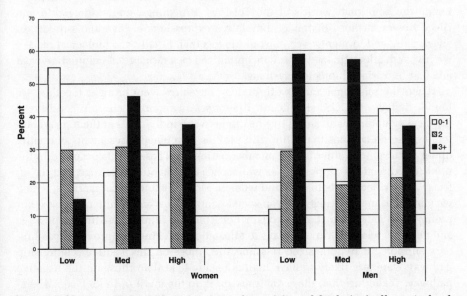

Figure 5.21 Percentage of low (0–1), medium (2), and high (3+) allostatic load within tertiles of positive relations with others.

lations, both genders show mixed allostatic load distributions, thereby showing no clear biomarker benefits of having positive relations with others in general. The contrast of these data with the allostatic load profiles vis-à-vis positive and negative relationship pathways underscores the need to obtain diverse relational assessments focused on not just global sense of connectedness but also on high-quality emotions, intimacy, and affection with key others. Such observations are especially pertinent to building bridges to biology among women, who appear to show differential patterns depending on the type of relational assessment employed.

Integration, Conclusions, and Future Directions

We have covered extensive territory in this chapter, moving from links between social relationships and health in a recent national survey to the cumulative emotional profiles of three famous couples and, finally, to data that link long-term social relationship profiles to biology in a subsample of respondents from a longitudinal study. Our objective in this concluding section is to highlight what we see as the main points from prior sections and to formulate needed directions for future inquiry.

A recurrent theme across the above three sections is the idea of *cumulation*, that is, the notion that the health sequelae of significant social relationships and intervening biological processes, require a long-term perspective that maps the recurring, chronic nature of social emotional experience in multiple key relationships across time. To address this theme, we created composite scores across multiple relationship types (spouse, family, friends) in the national survey data as well as positive and negative emotional pathways with the WLS data. A glimpse inside the emotional worlds of the Tolstoys, Brownings, and Frida Kahlo and Diego Rivera further illustrated cumulative expressions of love and support, or anger, pain, and torment, over years of life together. Finally, the biological marker we invoked, allostatic load, was conceptualized as a measure of cumulative wear and tear on various biological systems.

When the relational and health/biology measures were brought together, we found, first via MIDUS, significant differences in reported chronic conditions, physical symptoms, and subjective health between individuals at the top and bottom tertiles on composite relationship profiles (combined assessments of quality of ties with spouse, other family members, friends). These effects occurred in the predicted directions for positive as well as negative emotional ratings, and the effects were evident for both men and women. Moving to biological markers, which we viewed as mechanisms between social relationships and health outcomes, our preliminary data from the Wisconsin Longitudinal Study then linked positive and negative relationship pathways to allostatic load. Findings provided preliminary support for hypothesized relationships: those on the positive relationship pathway were less likely to have high allostatic load than those on the negative pathway. Taken together, these analyses speak to the merit of linking social relations and health—via a focus on cumulation—across types of emotion, types of relationships, and biological war and tear on the organism.

Prior avenues of research have, either implicitly or explicitly, emphasized the idea of cumulation. The adult attachment literature (Cassidy & Shaver, 1999; Hazan & Shaver, 1994), for example, probes the long-term reach of socioemotional ties between infant and caregiver to the quality of attachment relationships in adulthood. Focusing on physical health outcomes, a study by Russek and Schwartz (1997) found a strong positive link over a 35-year period between college students' reports of having had warm relationships with their parents and midlife health profiles (i.e., fewer diagnosed diseases, such as coronary artery disease, hypertension, duodenal ulcer, and alcoholism). Mental health researchers have also explored cumulative adversity as an antecedent to adult psychological disorders (Turner & Lloyd, 1995), and emotion researchers have explored the long-term health effects of "chronic emotions" (Pennebaker & Traue, 1993). Our prior work (Singer, Ryff, Carr, & Magee, 1998) organizes life-history information in terms of cumulative adversity and advantage, the pathways of which are then connected to psychological resilience.

In this chapter, the aim has been to bring ideas of cumulation to the emotion, social relations, and health nexus—specifically, to provide operational definitions of cumulative emotional experience in significant social relationships and to link them to an empirical formulation of cumulative biological wear and tear. In so doing, we acknowledge that much remains to be done—in many directions—such as expanding the scope of cumulative relational experience. Most adults, for example, spend the largest segment of daily life in the work setting, thus calling attention to the socioemotional climate of the workplace. Employment that involves critical and demeaning versus supportive and appreciative supervisors or rewarding versus draining coworkers may comprise significant realms of chronic emotional experience. Much that constitutes stress, or benefits, of the workplace may, in fact, be socioemotional in nature. Thus, mapping the intersections of emotional experience in work *and* family life is a critically needed future direction for research that connects social relations to health.

The links between positive and negative relationship pathways and allostatic load are also clearly in need of expansion to larger and more representative samples. Moreover, while high allostatic load has been predictive of subsequent cardiovascular disease, decline in physical function, memory loss (Seeman et al., 1997), and, more recently, mortality (Seeman et al., 2001), further studies are needed to replicate these effects and to connect allostatic load to other health outcomes. Such inquiries evoke fundamental questions regarding the nature of the causal relationships among social ties, allostatic load, and health outcomes. Throughout our discussion, we have suggested that emotional experience in social relationships affects health (via allostatic load), but it is also plausible that health conditions affect the quality of social relationships. The health problems of both Elizabeth Barrett Browning and Frida Kahlo were likely influences on the qualities of their marital relationships. Thus, reciprocal effects between relationship dynamics and health conditions (physical and mental) may well be prominent in the unfolding of directional effects. Whatever the nature of causal relationships, much is to be gained from tracking the co-occurrence of particular social relational profiles and attendant allostatic load markers in predicting subsequent morbidity and mortality.

Gender differences have been prominent throughout our findings. At the outset, we saw that men rate the quality of their relationships with others as significantly lower than women—in fact, the social relational realm was the *lowest* of all of their self-rated dimensions of well-being. In building bridges to biology, we also saw that, for men, there was more coherence or consistency between their general ratings of relationship quality (i.e., positive relations with others) and more emotionally specific measures of relationships with mother, father, and spouse. For men, links between these various relational measures and allostatic load were consistently in line with guiding hypotheses: allostatic load was lower for those on positive versus negative relationship pathways.

The data for women were more complicated. Although they rate the relational features of well-being consistently higher than men and while their relationship-specific assessments are tied in meaningful and predictable ways to their self-reported health, the bridges to biology were less consistent. On the one hand, the relationship pathways showed higher allostatic load among those on negative compared to positive paths, although the differences were less marked for women than men. Curiously, women's *general* relational evaluations (i.e., positive relations with others) showed links to allostatic load that were contrary to predictions: more than half of those with the poorest reported relationships had low, not high, allostatic load. Alternatively, among those in the top tertile on general relationships, there was no discernible benefit with regard to increased likelihood of having low allostatic load. These data underscore the importance, at least for women, of distinguishing between measures of social relationships that are global in content from those that are specific to particular emotions and key significant relationships. Further, among those women who showed poor global relational ratings and low allostatic load, we wonder whether the findings might suggest a kind of emotional *disengagement*, that is, a nonreactive response to unsatisfying relationships and, perhaps, to stress, more generally. Assessments of emotional reactivity via new directions in affective neuroscience (Davidson, 1992, 1995) provide avenues to test these ideas.

We note that numerous investigations have also shown gender differences in links between emotional support and neuroendocrine parameters (Seeman, Berkman, Blazer, & Rowe, 1994), endocrinological and immunological correlates of relationship conflict (Kiecolt-Glaser et al., 1997), interrelations of affect and physiology in long-term marriages (Levensen, Carstensen, & Gottman, 1994), and relations between physical symptoms and emotional expression (Malatesta & Culver, 1993). These findings assume ever-greater significance in light of the paucity of major longitudinal studies of women's health, along with the notable differentials in life expectancy between males and females. Clearly, gender will be center stage in the future mapping of the linkages among emotion, social relationships, and health (see Ryff & Singer, 2000).

At the beginning of the chapter, we emphasized the need to advance understanding of the positive aspects of social relationships. Our analyses thus made distinctions between positive and negative emotions in specific social relationships as well as between positive and negative pathways of cumulative emotional experience. These distinctions proved meaningful in establishing connections to self-rated health and to allostatic load. Nonetheless, we see numerous future avenues for sharpening assessment of the positive, with regard to both relational experience and its underlying biology (Ryff & Singer, 1988a, Ryff & Singer, 2000). One important direction emerges from studies of positive affiliation in animals (Carter, 1998; Panksepp, 1998).

Primary emphasis in the neurobiology and physiology of attachment has been given to the caregiver-infant and adult-heterosexual pair bondings. Attachment, viewed as a component of most, if not all, definitions of human love (Hatfield & Rapson, 1993; Sternberg & Barnes, 1988), can be operationalized in animals as selective social or emotional bonds and thus can facilitate observation and experimentation that connects the phenomenon to physiological substrates. At present, brain oxytocin, opioids, and prolactin systems appear to be key participants in experiences of social solidarity, warmth, and nurturance. Oxytocin, in particular, has been shown to increase in response to onset of pair-bonding in adults, maternal attachment, infant attachment, maternal responsivity, positive social behaviors or contacts, onset of sexual behavior, and exploration or approach to novelty (see Carter, 1998; Panksepp, 1998; Uvnäs-Moberg, 1998).

Concerning the cumulative effects of positive social interactions—positive social relationships when extrapolated to humans—it is important to note that the antistress effects of oxytocin become more pronounced after repeated exposure. That is, social bonds lead to repeated exposures to positive social stimuli and, thereby, to repeated release of oxytocin (Uvnäs-Moberg, 1998). In humans, such positive social experiences can be stored in memories, which in themselves may reactivate physiological processes. Thus, psychological processes can reinforce or extend the physical benefits of social relationships. Evidence from animal models further suggests that chronic oxytocin release is capable of producing long-term reductions in blood pressure and heart rate (Petersson, Alster, Lundeberg, & Uvnäs-Moberg, 1996). These findings point to a host of new directions at the human level to link positive emotions in social relationships to neurobiological substrates and, ultimately, to health outcomes.

Advancing these frontiers must, however, be accompanied by gains in how to probe the relevant depths of our significant social relational experiences. While the structured survey items employed here offer promising steps toward more emotionally rich assessment instruments and constitute much-needed additions to social relations construed as the size and proximity of one's network (House et al., 1988), there is room for improvement. More qualitative, idiographically tailored accounts of significant relationship experiences seem particularly promising future directions. The diaries of the Tolstoys and letters of the Brownings speak to the limited nature of strictly structured instruments. Although most persons lack the expressive capacities of those with literary fame, even routine data collection could incorporate such stems as "Today, my spouse made me feel ———" or "Today, time with my child left me feeling ———" or "Today, interactions with my boss (or coworkers) created feelings of ———." Such responses can be coded for emotional valence, strength, and complexity, the cumulative record of which may facilitate a portrait of more meaningful, personally relevant data about the emotional dynamics of daily life and, thereby, provide routes to biology.

Finally, as evidence mounts that social ties to key others are, indeed, consequential for biology and health, then a critical direction for the future is positive relational interventions, such as teaching effective emotion coaching to parents (Gottman, Katz, & Hooven, 1996) or facilitating emotional intelligence (Goleman, 1995) in social life. Fostering emotional know-how in key social relations thus becomes a primary avenue of health promotion. Arguably, the importance of nurturing social ties and maximizing opportunities for valued, emotionally rewarding, and meaningful interactions with significant others may be as consequential for long-term health and well-being as widely promulgated messages regarding proper nutrition and adequate exercise.

Notes

This research was supported by the John D. and Catherine T. MacArthur Foundation Research Networks on Successful Midlife Development (CDR) and Socioeconomic Status and Health (BHS), the National Institute on Aging (R01-AG13613-01), and a grant to the General Clinical Research Center of the University of Wisconsin (M01-RR03186).

1. 106 people are in the biology sample, 57 men and 49 women, although only 101 of these people (55 men, 46 women) also have complete data on relationship measures.

References

Barnes, M. L., & Sternberg, R. J. (1997). A hierarchical model of love and its prediction of satisfaction in close relationships. In R. J. Sternberg & M. Hojjat (Eds.), *Satisfaction in close relationships* (pp. 79–101). New York: Guilford.

Berkman, L. F., & Breslow, L. (1983). *Health and ways of living.* New York: Oxford University Press.

Berkman, L. F., Leo-Summers, L., & Horwitz, R. (1992). Emotional support and survival after myocardial infarction: A prospective, population-based study of the elderly *Annals of Internal Medicine, 117*, 1003–1009.

Berscheid, E., & Reis, H. T. (1998). Attraction and close relationships. In D. T. Gilbert, S. T. Fiske, & G. Lindzey (Eds.), *Handbook of social psychology* (Vol. 2, 4th ed., pp. 193–281). Boston: McGraw-Hill.

Blumenthal, J. A., Burg, M. M., Barefoot, J., Williams, R. B., Haney, T., & Zimet, G. (1987). Social support, type A behavior, and coronary artery disease. *Psychosomatic Medicine, 49*, 331–340.

Carter, C. S. (1998). Neuroendocrine perspectives on social attachment and love. *Psychoneuroendocrinology, 23*, 779–818.

Cassidy, J., & Shaver, P. R. (1999). *Handbook of attachment: Theory, research, and clinical applications.* New York: Guilford.

Davidson, R. (1992). Emotion and affective style: Hemispheric substrates. *Psychological Science, 3*, 39–43.

Davidson, R. (1995). Cerebral asymmetry and emotion: Conceptual and methodological conundrums. In R. J. Davidson & K. Hugdahl (Eds.), *Brain asymmetry.* Cambridge, MA: MIT Press.

Despres, J. P., Moorjani, S., Lupien, P. I., Tremblay, A. J., Nadeau, A., Bouchard, C. (1990). Regional distribution of body fat, plasma lipoproteins, and cardiovascular disease. *Arteriosclerosis, 10*, 497–511.

Fredrickson, B. L. (1998). What good are positive emotions? *Review of General Psychology, 2*, 300–319.

Glass, T., & Maddox, G. L. (1992). The quality and quantity of social support: Stroke recovery as psycho-social transition. *Social Science and Medicine, 34*, 1249–1261.

Goethe, J. W. (1971). *Elective affinities*. London: Penguin. (Original work published 1809.)

Goleman, D. (1995). *Emotional intelligence*. New York: Bantam.

Gottman, J. M., Katz, L. F., & Hooven, C. (1996). Parental meta-emotion philosophy and the emotional life of families: Theoretical models and preliminary data. *Journal of Family Psychology, 10*, 243–268.

Hatfield, E., & Rapson, R. L. (1993). *Love, sex, and intimacy*. New York: Harper Collins.

Hauser, R. M., Carr, D., Hauser, T. S., Hayes, J., Krecker, M., Hsiang-Hui, D. K., Magee, W., Presti, J., Shinberg, D., Sweeney, M., Thompson-Colon, T., Noah, U., & Warren, J. R. (1993). The class of 1957 after 35 years: Overview and preliminary findings. Working paper no. 93-17, University of Wisconsin Center for Demography and Ecology, Madison.

Hazan, C., & Shaver, P. R. (1994). Attachment as an organizational framework for research on close relationships. *Psychological Inquiry, 5*, 1–22.

House, J. S., Landis, K. R., & Umberson, D. (1988). Social relationships and health. *Science, 241*, 540–545.

Jung, C. G. (1933). *Modern man in search of a soul*. New York: Harcourt.

Kettenmann, A. (1993). *Frida Kahlo (1907–1954): Pain and passion*. Koln, Germany: Benedikt Taschen Verlag.

Kiecolt-Glaser, J. K., Glaser, R., Cacioppo, J. T., MacCallum, R. C., Snydersmith, M., Cheongtag, K., & Malarkey, W. B. (1997). Marital conflict in older adults: Endocrinological and immunological correlates. *Psychosomatic Medicine, 59*, 339–349.

Levensen, R. W., Carstensen, L. L., & Gottman, J. M. (1994). The influence of age and gender on affect, physiology, and their interrelations: A study of long-term marriages. *Journal of Personality and Social Psychology, 67*, 56–86.

Malatesta, C. Z., & Culver, C. (1993). Gendered health: Differences between men and women in the relation between physical symptoms and emotion expression behavior. In H. C. Traue & J. W. Pennebaker (Eds.), *Emotion inhibition and health* (pp. 116–144). Seattle, WA: Hogrefe & Huber.

Markus, J. (1995). *Dared and done: The marriage of Elizabeth Barrett and Robert Browning*. New York: Alfred A. Knopf.

McEwen, B. (1998). Protective and damaging effects of stress mediators. *New England Journal of Medicine, 338*(3), 171–179.

McEwen, B. S., & Stellar, E. (1993). Stress and the individual: Mechanisms leading to disease. *Archives of Internal Medicine, 153*, 2093–2101.

Munoz, A., & Gauge, S. (1998). Methodological issues for biomarkers and intermediate outcomes in cohort studies. *Epidemiologic Reviews, 20*(1), 29–42.

Parker, G., Tupling, H., & Brown, L. B. (1979). A parental bonding instrument. *British Journal of Medical Psychology, 52*, 1–10.

Panksepp J. (1998). *Affective neuroscience*. New York: Oxford University Press.

Pennebaker, J. W., & Traue, H. C. (1993). Inhibition and psychosomatic processes. In H. C. Traue & J. W. Pennebaker (Eds.), *Emotion inhibition and health* (pp. 146–163). Seattle, WA: Hogrefe & Huber.

Petersson, M., Alster, P., Lundeberg, T., Uvnäs-Moberg, K. (1996). Oxytocin causes a long-term decrease of blood pressure in female and male rats. *Physiology and Behavior, 60*, 1311–1315.

Russek, L. G., & Schwartz, G. E. (1997). Feelings of parental caring predict health status in midlife: A 35-year follow-up of the Harvard Mastery of Stress Study. *Journal of Behavioral Medicine, 30*, 1–13.

Ryff, C. D. (1985). Adult personality development and the motivation for personal growth. In D. Kleiber & M. Maehr (Eds.), *Advances in motivation and achievement: Motivation and adulthood* (Vol. 4, pp. 55–92). Greenwich, CT: JAI Press.

Ryff, C. D. (1989a). Happiness is everything, or is it? Explorations on the meaning of psychological well-being. *Journal of Personality and Social Psychology, 57,* 1069–1081.

Ryff, C. D. (1989b). In the eye of the beholder: Views of psychological well-being among middle and old-aged adults. *Psychology and Aging, 4,* 195–210.

Ryff, C. D. (1991). Possible selves in adulthood and old age: A tale of shifting horizons. *Psychology and Aging, 6,* 286–295.

Ryff, C. D., & Keyes, C. L. M. (1995). The structure of psychological well-being revisited. *Journal of Personality and Social Psychology, 69,* 719–727.

Ryff, C. D., & Singer, B. (2000). Interpersonal flourishing: A positive health agenda for the new millennium. *Personality and Social Psychology Review, 4,* 30–44.

Ryff, C. D., & Singer, B. (1998a). The contours of positive human health. *Psychological Inquiry, 9,* 1–28.

Ryff, C. D., & Singer, B. (1988b). Middle age and well-being. In H. S. Friedman (Ed.), *Encyclopedia of mental health* (pp. 707–719). San Diego, CA: Academic.

Schaefer, M. T., & Olson, D. H. (1981). Assessing intimacy: The PAIR inventory. *Journal of Marital and Family Therapy, 7,* 47–60.

Seeman, T. E. (1996). Social ties and health: The benefits of social integration. *Annals of Epidemiology, 6,* 442–451.

Seeman, T. E., Berkman, L. F., Blazer, D., & Rowe, J. (1994). Social ties and support and neuroendocrine function: MacArthur studies of successful aging. *Annals of Behavioral Medicine, 16,* 95–106.

Seeman, T. E., Singer, B., Rowe, J. W., Horowitz, R., & McEwen, B. (1997). The price of adaptation: Allostatic load and its health consequences: MacArthur studies of successful aging. *Archives of Internal Medicine, 157,* 2259–2268.

Seeman, T. E., Singer, B., Rowe, J., & McEwen, B. (2001). *Exploring a new concept of cumulative biological risk: Allostatic load and its health consequences. Proceedings of National Academy of Sciences* (in press).

Seeman, T. E., & Syme, S. L. (1987). Social networks and coronary artery disease: A comparative analysis of network structural and support characteristics. *Psychosomatic Medicine, 49,* 341–354.

Shirer, W. L. (1994). *Love and hatred: The Stormy marriage of Leo and Sonya Tolstoy.* New York: Simon and Schuster.

Singer, B., & Ryff, C. D. (1997). Racial and ethnic inequalities in health: Environmental, psychosocial, and physiological pathways. In B. Devlin, S. E. Feinberg, D. Resnick, & K. Roeder (Eds.), *Intelligence, genes, and success: Scientists respond to the bell curve* (pp. 89–122). New York: Springer-Verlag.

Singer, B., Ryff, C. D., Carr, D., & Magee, W. J. (1998). Life histories and mental health: A person-centered strategy. In A. Raftery (Ed.), *Sociological methodology, 1998* (pp. 1–51). Washington, DC: American Sociological Association.

Singer, I. (1984a). *The nature of love. Vol. 1: Plato to Luther* (2d ed.). Chicago: University of Chicago Press.

Singer, I. (1984b). *The nature of love. Vol. 2: Courtly and romantic* (2d ed.). Chicago: University of Chicago Press.

Spirduso, W. W. (1995). *Physical dimensions of aging.* Champaign, IL: Human Kinetics.

Sterling, P., & Eyer, J. (1988). Allostasis: A new paradigm to explian arousal pathology. In J. Fisher & J. Reason (Eds.), *Handbook of life stress, cognition, and health* (pp. 629–649). New York: John Wiley and Sons.

Sternberg, R. J., & Barnes, M. I. (1988). *The psychology of love.* New Haven, CT: Yale University Press.

Tukey, J. W. (1977). *Exploratory data analysis.* Reading, MA: Addison-Wesley.

Turner, R. J., & Lloyd, D. A. (1995). Lifetime traumas and mental health: The significance of cumulative adversity. *Journal of Health and Social Behavior, 33,*, 360–376.

Uchino, B. N., Cacioppo, J. T., & Kiecolt-Glaser, J. K. (1996). The relationship between
social support and physiological processes: A review with emphasis on underlying
mechanisms and implications for health. *Psychological Bulletin, 119,* 488–531.

Uvnäs-Moberg, K. (1998). Oxytocin may mediate the benefits of positive social interaction and emotions. *Psychoneuroendocrinology, 23,* 819–835.

Commentary

Meg Wise

The chapter by Ryff, Singer, Wing, and Love embraces many methods to understand the emotional and social pathways to physiological health. In three distinct
sections, the authors report on findings from a national survey, biographical descriptions of emotions in the intimate relationships of three famous couples, and
finally, how psychosocial variables might influence allostatic load (wear and tear
on biological systems) with data from a longitudinal study. By connecting the social and biophysical sciences with the arts and humanities, Ryff and Singer's
methodology echoes the recent conceptual acknowledgment that it is time to
correct Descartes's error (Benson, 1996; Damassio, 1994; Ornish, 1998). In other
words, the mind, body, heart, and spirit must be interconnected. This insight suggests the benefit of combining logical and intuitive research perspectives for the
stereoscopic vision needed to map the complex relationships between emotions
and health. Ryff and Singer et al.'s chapter suggests numerous ways—from phenomenology to physiology—to extend the current scientific horizon into the new
territory of cross-disciplinary investigation.

The first section of this commentary discusses Ryff and Singer's multimethod
research findings in the context of their prior work and as they contribute to the
other themes of this volume (gender differences, the role of positive and negative
emotions, the cumulation of advantage and adversity, and mechanisms for how
emotions and social relationships affect health). A second section systematically
addresses these themes to discuss the opportunity for cross-fertilizing the concepts and methods of Ryff and Singer et al. with those of the other investigators in
this volume. The final section discusses the implications and possible new directions for this line of research.

Summary and Discussion of the Work

Theoretical Background

In this chapter, Ryff and Singer implement the multidisciplinary research agenda
that they introduced in their recent theoretical work, "The Contours of Positive

Health" (1998a). From philosophers as diverse as Bertrand Russell and Viktor Frankl, Ryff and Singer identified a set of common features that embody health as a positive construct, or human flourishing. These include love, creativity, passion, spirituality, and happiness, in essence, integration or wholeness (which is the original meaning of the word *health*). Ryff and Singer observe that these features derive from a deeply felt purpose in life, positive and loving relationships with others, and high self-regard, which contribute to the six positive dimensions of Ryff's (1995, 1996) well-being scales. Ryff and Singer's notion of optimum health and well-being goes well beyond the dominant, long-standing metaphor of health maintenance as "repair shops and the return to neutral" (1998a, p. 7). Operationalizing health and well-being as positive constructs adds stereoscopic vision to the dominant practice of measuring psychological well-being and physical health as the absence of symptoms. Ryff and Singer conclude "The Contours of Positive Health" with a call for multimethod and collaborative research to map how cumulating life's advantages or adversities influences health throughout the life span. Their chapter in this volume answers that call by focusing on the pathways that link the dimension of positive relationships with others to health.

The MacArthur National Survey of Successful Mid-life Aging (MIDUS), a cross-sectional study, investigated the associations among Ryff's (1996; Ryff & Singer, 1996) six-dimension well-being scales, spousal relationship quality, friend and family relationship quality, and self-reported health status (symptoms, chronic conditions, and subjective health) in a representative U.S. sample. The key MIDUS finding was that general positive relationships with others and positive spousal relationships correlated with positive health. However, a gender difference emerged that warrants further investigation. That is, compared to men, women reported more overall symptoms and better general relationship quality despite their lower perception of spousal appreciation or understanding. This raises several questions for future investigations about gender differences in the perception and denial of symptoms and in the criteria used to define relationship quality. For instance, do women really have more symptoms, or are they just more aware and willing to report them? Conversely, are men less sensitive to symptoms and more likely to deny them? Do men and women use different criteria to define positive or negative spousal relationships? And finally, how might women "pay" for their positive relationships?

In summary, the MIDUS study breaks new ground by probing for emotional experience within significant relationships, rather than by focusing on the more traditional measurement of social network size. However, cross-sectional studies cannot illuminate how cumulative emotional advantage or adversity in intimate relationships influences health. Furthermore, the self-reported data used in this study cannot address the underlying mechanisms that link emotions, social relationships, and health.

The Wisconsin Longitudinal Study (WLS) section addresses these limitations by mapping relationship quality onto physiological health in a midlife (58 years) sample. The authors correlated individuals' relationship life histories with their multidimensional measures of physiological wear and tear (allostatic load). Relationship life histories assessed mother and father caring (Parental Bonding scale) and spousal intimacy and intellectual compatibility (PAIRS). Both positive *and* negative relationship pathways were determined by specific combinations of qualities in measured parental and spousal relationships (see chap. 5). Allostatic load is determined by a battery of physiological markers, which indicate wear and tear on several body systems, such as the central nervous, endocrine, and cardiovascular systems (McEwen & Stellar, 1993).

Gender Differences in Response to Cumulative Advantage and Disadvantage As in the MIDUS study, gender differences emerged in WLS. Again, women were less predictable. Ryff's generalized positive relationship scores correlated with positive relationship pathways and lower allostatic load for men, but not for women. Men had much more extreme positive and negative pathway scores between tertiles. By contrast, women's positive and negative pathway scores (see fig. 5.17) were close together in all three tertiles. In fact, in the top tertile, women's negative pathway score was somewhat higher than the positive pathway score. Despite this, women had lower allostatic load than men, which indicates that women's positive relationship pathways may be health protective even in the face of negative relationship pathways. This finding underscores Ryff and Singer's call for measuring positive along with negative dimensions of health and well-being.

However, four commonly acknowledged gender differences may also be operative in this WLS sample. They warrant a brief discussion here and more detailed assessment in future research. These include gender differences in the age of onset of cardiovascular disease, the role of midlife steroidal hormone changes in health and well-being, gender differences in health and social behavior, and possible salutogenic biomarkers, which are not measured by allostatic load. First, men with high allostatic load scores had greater indicators for cardiovascular disease (CVD). However, men at age 58 are fully in the window for CVD, whereas women are not (Kannel & Wilson, 1995). CVD onset for women is delayed by 15 years while the cardioprotective effects of estrogen taper off after menopause. Thus, future investigations may benefit from determining the menopausal and estrogen replacement status of female research participants.

Second, steroidal hormones, including estrogen, testosterone, and DHEA, affect male and female libido, mood, and several domains of quality of life, including relationships. These may be especially influential as hormone levels diminish during and after the midlife. Thus, emotions research could benefit by integrating ongoing investigations about how steroidal hormones affect emotions, social relationships, and health throughout the adult life span. This line of inquiry will be even more important in studying the "baby boomer" cohort of women now entering menopause, who, compared to the WLS sample, are more likely to have different lifestyles, roles, and expectations, along with greater options to manage their biological aging.

Third, women in the WLS sample may be more emotionally resilient and more likely to rally support from friends, family, or peers to compensate for their negative parental and spousal relationships. Women use support groups more often and with greater emotional involvement and self-disclosure than do men. In a study of on-line support groups across several illnesses, the breast cancer or chronic fatigue syndrome (>95% women) groups logged significantly greater volume and more supportive and empathic content than did the predominantly male groups, such as those focused on prostate cancer or heart disease (Davison & Pennebaker, 1997).

Finally, women may also have higher levels of positive biological markers (not measured), which either cancel out or mitigate the effects of negative parental and spousal relationships on allostatic load. One salutogenic biomarker is oxytocin, a hormone released in greater amounts during lactation, which is also associated with nurturing, love, general social well-being, and physiological relaxation (Uvnäs-Moberg, 1998).

Other Questions Raised by the WLS Findings These WLS results contribute much to understanding how emotional quality in long-term significant relationships may affect wear and tear on the body, but they raise several questions about the direction of causality. Do positive relationships cause better health? Does better health maintain positive relationships? Or, are there reciprocal relationships between positive relationships with others and good health, and, if so, how might these be empirically mapped and linked to underlying physiological mechanisms? While intimate social relationships are central to emotional experience, they may be complicated by larger social and economic factors, such as job downsizing,poverty, racial or other discrimination, a poor health diagnosis, war or displacement, or an unexpected life tragedy. Positive social ties can help individuals weather such challenges, but it is also notable (and lamentable) that the cumulative effects of such challenges can wreak havoc with marriage and family relationships and can, therefore, affect group-level health outcomes. Thus, studying the emotions experienced in a variety of challenging contexts could enlighten several public health issues, such as the effects of race or poverty on health (Anderson & Armstead, 1995; Johnson et. al., 1995).

In sum, the WLS study provided a broad framework to examine how relationships affect health but, as the authors acknowledge, did not probe actual emotional experiences in relationships.

The biographies of three famous couples expand this vision by describing the long-term relationships of Leo and Sonya Tolstoy, Robert and Elizabeth Barrett Browning, and Frida Kahlo and Diego Rivera. All three relationships, seen primarily through the woman's eye, were highly engaged and passionate and left a powerful artistic legacy. The emotions experienced ranged from erotic love and tormented hatred into old age in the first; to a sweet empowering love that defied a domineering father, chronic pain, and disability in the second; to tortured endurance of chronic emotional abuse, which exacerbated the chronic pain of a preexisting illness in the third. These examples provide different configurations of the effects of emotional experience in intimate relationships and their relationship to health and longevity. In so doing, they raise many questions.

Leo and Sonya Tolstoy, who both lived into their eighties, had high levels of negative but also high levels of positive emotional expression. Did their passionate love and hatred lengthen their lives and spur creativity? Did they live long lives despite their adversity? Or, did they just have good genetic endowment? Do certain people, like the Tolstoys, thrive in the face of adversity and therefore seek it? How do they differ from those who seek and create harmony in relationship, like the Brownings? How does adversity kindle artistic creation? Frida Kahlo accumulated adversity by staying with a tormenting, philandering spouse, but she used her agony to create powerful images. Adversity also spurred creativity for Elizabeth Barrett Browning whose poetry provided escape from a repressive father and her own invalidism. But her love for Robert helped her throw off her father and her invalidism—and continued to spur her creativity.

This section of the chapter, filled with art, poetry, and narrative, appears between the two empirical studies discussed above. Its centrality in a scientific paper is a strong message to pay attention to the complexity, depth, and texture of the uniquely individual emotional experience in long-term relationships. Social science and biological research methods cannot currently provide the whole picture about how passion affects our health. The standard assessment procedures rarely address what it means to be creative or to live with contradiction and paradox. Nor do they help us to understand what compels some to forgo safe relationships to engage in exciting but emotionally painful ones, or why some pursue negative goals, which leave legacies of beauty and meaning. This discussion reflects back to a possible dynamic tension among Ryff's dimensions of well-being. How do individuals negotiate between making a difference in their careers (autonomy, environmental mastery) and fostering positive relationships? When are these motivations in accord, and when are they in discord? Certainly, the answers differ by how individuals define their life purpose, and also by how different cultures and age cohorts interpret and value the various dimensions of well-being.

In conclusion, the take-home message from these descriptive relationship biographies is the need for collaboration across epistemologies, across methods, and across disciplines—to connect, as Ryff has suggested, phenomenology with the scientific method. The next section will discuss how Ryff and Singer's work could inform and be informed by the other contributors to this volume.

Cross-Fertilization: Ryff and Singer et al. and Other Contributors

As a general statement, Ryff and Singer's broad perspective and holistic research agenda can inform and be informed by all of the contributors to this volume. This section will first focus on how Ryff and Singer et al.'s approach to studying the effects of cumulative adversity and advantage on health can inform the work of other volume contributors. Second, it will examine how others' perspectives might inform the work of Ryff and Singer in areas of positive and negative emotions, gender differences, physiological substrates of emotions, and methodology.

Potential Influence of the Ideas of Cumulative Adversity and Advantage on Other Researchers

Ryff and Singer's work on how cumulative life adversity and advantage affects health could enrich several research programs, including those of Gottman, Reis, Spiegel, and Cohen.

Gottman used an intervention study to teach parents in troubled marriages how to emotionally coach their young children, with a follow-up component through adolescence. The intervention focused on teaching parents how to help their children understand and appropriately regulate their negative emotions— similar to what Goleman (1995) calls *emotional intelligence*. Emotionally coached children followed into adolescence were found to have higher vagus nerve activation (which affects emotional regulation and self-soothing) and the emotional intelligence to adapt the skills learned in young childhood to the different peer demands of adolescence.

Ryff and Singer's methods (well-being and spousal scales, parental relationship life histories, and physiological markers) could further Gottman's multifaceted program by assessing the intragroup variability at baseline. That is, what balance of adversity and advantage do divorcing mothers and fathers bring into the intervention? How might this affect which parents embrace or reject, or succeed or fail at, emotion coaching? And, how do parents' experience with emotion coaching influence children's subsequent emotional experience in intimate relationships and physical health? How did Gottman's intervention affect parental emotional health and marriage outcomes? Finally, adding allostatic load or other biomarkers could shed light on the health costs and benefits of the intervention for the parents and children.

Ryff and Singer's multimethod approach could also inform Reis's research on intimacy in young adult relationships. Using event-sampling diaries, Reis obtained a detailed account of the quality and level of intimacy in daily social interactions among college students. Adding childhood parental relationship histories, such as those used by Ryff and Singer, could further understanding of how cumulative advantage or adversity contributes to these daily social interactions and to the development of intimate relationships in young adulthood. Combining the historical and daily diary approaches could more powerfully test Reis's intimacy model, which includes understanding, validation, and caring. That is, how does a history, or lack thereof, of parental bonding in childhood later influence Erikson's (1963) developmental task of intimacy in young adulthood? Furthermore, these methods could help to address the issue of psychological resilience by identifying how specific well-being dimensions (e.g., autonomy or environmental mastery) could influence individuals' ability to overcome negative parental pathways and to later develop sustained intimate relationships.

Ryff and Singer's longitudinal studies emphasize how Ryff's six dimensions of well-being interact with the cumulation of adversity and advantage over the life span. This approach has been especially helpful for understanding midlife and old age life tasks, which were conceived by Erikson (1963) as generativity (as expressed by personal growth, autonomy, and environmental mastery) and ego integrity (as expressed by purpose in life and self-acceptance). Likewise, using Ryff's well-being scales could also address which dimensions are important in Erikson's central life task for young adults: the development of intimate relationships. Furthermore, following this sample over time could illuminate how dimensions of well-being in young adulthood provide the resilience to maintain intimate relationships through the inevitable challenges of the life and career course. Finally, assessing well-being and biological markers (e.g., allostatic load, immune function, or neuropeptides) could enrich understanding of how attachment style relates to psychological well-being and physiological pathways. For instance, how do anxious-ambivalent or avoidant individuals' scores differ from those of secure individuals on the well-being dimensions of relationships with others, environmental mastery, or autonomy? Finally, how might these variables influence physiological pathways?

Ryff and Singer's methods of measuring psychological resilience and allostatic load could also enrich Spiegel's work with emotionally expressive support groups for women with metastatic breast cancer. Coping with and overcoming a life-threatening illness is fundamentally about psychological resilience, where the balance of an individual's cumulation of life advantage and adversity is powerfully tested. One's purpose in life and relationships come into high relief: sense of purpose may be renewed or lost; relationships may get better or worse. Thus, understanding the well-being profiles and life histories in the support and control groups could further elucidate the characteristics of those who gain more (or less) from the groups, what roles they play as support givers and receivers, and how they take on the challenge of their illness in their broader lives and relationships. While Spiegel and Kimerling may learn these things about their study participants over the course of the year-long group, systematic collection of such data at baseline and follow-ups would provide insight into who benefits most and in what ways from support groups. Additionally, such data could also provide insight into how individual characteristics and circumstances influence coping with illness and how different well-being dimensions predict or influence quality of relationships throughout the course of the illness. Finally, follow-up data collection could identify how participation in support groups affect well-being.

Cohen's studies (chap. 7; Cohen et al., 1995; Cohen, Tyrell, & Smith, 1993), which intentionally exposed individuals to cold viruses, found that higher levels of stressful events, negative affect, and perceived stress were associated with greater susceptibility to having clinical viral symptoms. But negative affect and perceived stress provide only part of the picture, thus raising several questions that might be addressed with Ryff and Singer's cumulative advantage approaches to assessing individuals' well-being and life histories. This could address such questions as: To what extent did subjects' cumulative relationship or emotional adversities influence negative affect and perception of stress? On the other hand, what dimensions of advantage or resilience were present for those subjects who did not get sick? Finally, how does the relative duration of adversity dispose one toward health or toward chronic or acute illnesses?

Other Researchers' Possible Influence

Other volume contributors could inform the work of Ryff and Singer in these four themes: deeper empirical understanding of the role of positive and negative emotions in relationships, gender differences, physiological pathways of social and emotional experience, and methodology.

Positive and Negative Emotions in Relationships   Spiegel and Gottman both developed clinical interventions that help participants honor and use their emotions to cope with and thrive amidst life's adversities. Thus, it is not surprising that they offer the most toward our understanding of the role of positive and negative emotions in relationships. Both researchers developed programs to help individuals respond to what they lament as the repression of negative emotions in this culture (chaps. 2 and 4; Spiegel, 1995). Thus, having a good cry or being angry may be the appropriate and useful reaction to life threat, pain, or loss. It is through facing pain and death and dying that life becomes more precious and appreciated—its meaning is enriched.

It is through the mutual expression of fear, anger, and despair *and* the consequent understanding, validation, and caring of others that support groups build intimacy (see chap. 3). Thus, says Spiegel (1997), "Being able to share a good cry also enables us to share a good laugh." Such intimacy may then lead to the building and practice of courage, a fighting spirit, loving, a deeper commitment to living life fully and with meaning, and the experience and expression of other positive emotions (chap. 4; Ornish, 1998; Spiegel, 1995). These, in turn, can improve or maintain positive relationships. Finally, fully integrated emotional expression and social relationships can improve survival time and quality of life among women with metastatic breast cancer (Spiegel, Bloom, Kraemer, & Gottheil, 1989).

Like Spiegel, Gottman (chap. 2) also notes that honoring and expressing both negative and positive emotions is needed to maintain good relationships and personal well-being. To Gottman, anger is not a sin, but contempt, or not understanding, validating, or caring for the other, is. Thus, his program teaches parents in troubled marriages first how to reframe their own negative emotions and then how to coach their children. Coaching consists of helping children to acknowledge and be with their natural negative feelings and to express and act on them appropriately. This is especially challenging for fathers given a culture that labels the experience of negative emotions as a sign of men's personal weakness. But fathers who become successful emotion coaches have more positive effect on their children than do mothers.

To Spiegel and Gottman, then, the experience and expression of negative emotions can help individuals make meaning of the situation, and thus negative emotions can be healing (see also Dafter, 1996; Ornish, 1998). What can be learned from Spiegel and Gottman is that human experience is rich and varied in its sorrows and joys. Living in full awareness and expression of them may be what toughens immunity and improves relationships and emotional well-being. As Ryff and Singer have demonstrated, a multimethod approach can provide better understanding of how these complex dimensions of emotional experience in intimate relationships interact with individuals' relationship quality, health, and well-being.

What do these observations mean for Ryff and Singer's work? First, the above findings can be combined with the insights gleaned from the marriage biographies of famous couples to design studies that point the way to more complete assessments of specific emotional experiences for men and women and how they influence health over time. Such investigations could also be extended to other types of significant adult relationships, such as those in the workplace. Additionally, observational research methods may be useful in assessing the social and physiological effects that specific emotions (laughter, poignancy, excitement and desire, anger, jealousy, etc.) have on relationships.

Gender Differences   While Spiegel's support groups were beneficial to women with breast cancer, other research suggests that social relationships and intimacy may also have costs for women. Seeman and colleagues (Seeman, Berkman, Blazer, & Rowe, 1994; Seeman & Syme, 1987) found that women get fewer health benefits from having large social networks or certain kinds of social and emotional support. Likewise, Reis (chap. 3) reports that women are more often than men the recipients of men's and women's self-disclosure; women also provide men with more intimacy than they receive. These findings may suggest that deeply ingrained social expectations—that women take care of the emotional issues in marriage, child rearing, and extended families—may discourage the acknowledgment or reporting of unsatisfactory social relationships, despite the costs of those relationships. This may partially explain why, despite their higher scores for generalized positive relationships in the MIDUS study, women reported more symptoms than did men. Along these lines, Seeman et al. (1994) and Seeman and Syme (1987) found that those reporting no social support had lower incidence of atherosclerosis.

These findings raise questions about whether positive relationships are unilaterally health enhancing for women (or, for that matter, for individuals with social expectations that value self-reliance over social contact or with avoidant attachment styles). Evidence of the health-protective value of positive relationships may be confounded by the fact that women suffer more chronic conditions that reduce their quality of life, despite their longer lives and generally more positive relationships. For instance, women have greater incidence of obesity, diabetes, autoimmune diseases such as lupus and arthritis, chronic pain and fatigue syndrome, depression, and osteoporosis—and, contrary to common myth, equal incidence of cardiovascular disease by age 65. Seeman and Syme's (1987) finding that those reporting no social support had lower incidence of atherosclerosis may make sense in light of societal values on self-reliance, which tie self-worth to material gain and social status. Finally, Reis's work with attachment styles in young adulthood may also elucidate the finding: perhaps avoidants with high autonomy and environmental mastery scores thrive more with lower social connection than do individuals with secure or anxious attachment styles.

In sum, the health-emotions connection may be more complex for women than for men, requiring greater refinement in research. While gender differences is a huge area in matters of the heart, mind, and body, it will be equally important to learn how race, class, and culture might affect the variability within each gender's experience.

Physiological Substrates of Emotions and Social Relationships   The study of the physiological mechanisms that underlie emotions in social relationships is relatively new but holds great promise. The work of Cohen and of Coe (chaps. 7 and

8) suggest that measuring immune function in addition to allostatic load could generally enrich Ryff and Singer's future investigations into the relationship between emotions and health. Additionally, Coe and Lubach found that stress has more negative impact on the immune system early in the life span, when the immune system is quickly developing, and late in the life span, when the immune system begins to lose momentum. This finding may be useful in refining how physiological markers relate to the cumulation of advantage and adversity throughout the life span.

Furthermore, work by other investigators into the relationships among the salutogenic physiological markers, social relationships, and health holds great promise for the work of Ryff and Singer. This approach is more theoretically consistent with Ryff and Singer's (1998a, 1998b) positive constructs of health and well-being than is the measurement of allostatic load (which measures biological stressors). Oxytocin, a hormone that is associated most specifically with maternal nursing of infants and with general positive social relationships, warrants further attention (Uvnäs-Moberg, 1998). Its effects include lowered blood pressure, reduced adrenaline, higher sense of well-being, and improved digestion. To date, the studies of oxytocin in humans have been limited to its short-term effects. Therefore, integrating the assessment of oxytocin into longitudinal studies, such as those of Ryff and Singer, may illuminate how this physiological pathway operates in sustained positive relationships and how it contributes to health maintenance and the survival of illness.

This discussion concludes with the acknowledgment that, while there are several promising lines of investigation into the biological substrates of emotions in long-term relationships, much remains to be done in order to understand how they influence health and illness.

Methodology Ryff and Singer already use a rich multi-method approach, but the methods of a few other contributors might enrich their work. For instance, Gottman's observational approach might confirm or find discrepancies in self-reported information about relationships. Reis's microanalytic events sampling could expand the life histories and self-report data with more detailed daily accounts. This method may be especially useful during major life transitions, such as relocation, grieving the loss of a loved one, or facing a serious illness. Spiegel and Gottman's rich descriptive work, like Ryff and Singer's use of the biographies, underscores the value of narrative research and phenomenological analysis. In addition, Spiegel and Gottman's intervention research suggests that Ryff and Singer's findings might make a difference if they were applied in action research to education, psychotherapy, or health care policy.

Implications for Further Research

The work of Ryff and Singer raises many questions and possibilities for future directions in the investigation of emotions, social relationships, and health. Two will be discussed here: action or intervention research and integrating spirituality and non-Western health beliefs into the study of emotions, social relationships, and health.

Action or Intervention Research

Ryff and Singer's findings can contribute to the development and evaluation of educational and clinical programs. These can be accomplished through education programs that help adults deal with major life transitions, workplace training, and changing health care policy. Focusing on the last point, Ryff and Singer's research indicates that a health care system that invests in programs to promote emotional well-being may in the end provide better care and cost less than one that continues to operate under the "body as a sick machine" metaphor. The WLS data found that men with poor relationship pathways had high cardiovascular disease markers in their allostatic load. Yet, despite evidence that loneliness and depression contribute to CVD (Lesperance, Frasure-Smith, & Talajic, 1996), managed health care continues to cut psychotherapy services for marital problems and doctors' time with patients. Paradoxically, it is as if the more mind-body research proclaims that Descartes was wrong, the more for-profit managed health care proclaims that Descartes was right.

Nowhere is this more poignant (and ironic) than in heart care. Universally, across cultures and epochs, the metaphor for the heart is the emotional and spiritual center of humanity (Ornish, 1990). Yet, in medical care, the heart is simply the central oxygen exchange system in the body machine. In the emotional metaphor, a broken heart is healed or made whole again through love and purposeful living, while in the mechanistic view, the malfunctioning heart is fixed with powerful drugs and bypass surgery. According to Dean Ornish (1990, 1998), bypass surgery is well named—for it bypasses the heart and soul of the problem. Operating on the premise that people can heal their hearts by opening up to love, self-acceptance, and a commitment to purposeful living, Ornish has developed a rigorous lifestyle program that centralizes emotional and social relationships while minimizing medications and surgery. In an experiment, the control group received the American Heart Association usual care plan, including heart medications, exercise, and a moderately low-fat diet but little emotional or social support. Patients following Ornish's program had actual heart disease reversal and lower health care costs, while the control group got slightly worse (Gould et al., 1995). Yet few health care organizations cover the costs for Ornish's program or for psychotherapy to improve spousal or family relationships.

A central message from this volume is that helping marital (or significant other) relationships can improve health and may lower health care costs. A fundamental shift in perspective may be needed before the health care organizations will follow the more cost-effective and health-promoting methods. How can such a shift in perspective and treatment occur? Perhaps by collaboration among researchers, such as Ryff and Singer, and those involved in developing medical school curriculums and continuing medical education. As more physicians and patients are trained to trust in and practice from this perspective, health care organizations may be pressured from within to change their care delivery.

Spirituality, Belief Systems, and Complementary Medicine

Spirituality is most broadly conceived of as a life force energy that gives meaning to existence and as a sense of connection to humanity and the universe. In a health sense, it has been conceived of as a unifying force, which integrates the physical, mental, emotional, and social aspects of health (Benson, 1996; Hafen, Karren, Frandsen, & Smith, 1996). The relationship between spirituality and health has captured the public's imagination—despite the dearth of it in routine medical practice—as illustrated by bestselling books by Herbert Benson, Joan Borysenko, Dean Ornish, Rachel Naomi Remen, and Jon Kabat-Zinn. But the current public fascination with spirituality and health is consistent with the ancient connection between spirituality and healing (Benson, 1996), in which healers were often priests or priestesses. Ryff and Singer (1998b) touch on many spiritual aspects of health, especially with the well-being dimension of purpose in life. Future exploration of the power of beliefs in healing could enrich understanding of how matters of the mind and heart influence physiological healing.

Complementary medicine is a broad term, which includes a wide range of practices outside Western medicine, including acupuncture, herbs, and homeopathy. Weil (1983, 1995) explores numerous Western and Eastern healing systems. Inherent in their success is the body's innate ability to heal and the patient's and practitioner's belief in the intervention. Like spirituality, complementary medicine has captured the public's imagination—as shown by the amount of money people spend on it, a 1998 issue of *JAMA* devoted to it, and the establishment of the National Center for Complementary and Alternative Medicine. Thus spiritual and non-Western health belief systems offer other avenues to understanding the underlying mechanisms that link emotional, social, and physical health.

Conclusion

In sum, *Elective Affinities and Uninvited Agonies: Mapping Emotion with Significant Others Onto Health* pilots a broad, multimethod, cross-disciplinary research program for understanding the interrelationships among emotions, social relationships, health, and well-being. The examples of the famous couples' love stories and life histories tell us that the interplay among emotions, relationships, and health is a complex one. Negative emotions may have a positive role in life, but how and for whom? We must be careful as we forge understandings of the mechanisms among emotions, social relationships, and health to remember that the life well lived will not be defined in the same way for everyone: we must study multiple pathways across gender, class, culture, and race. Physical health and longevity may not be the final arbiter: some people with chronically poor health lead powerful, meaningful lives. Some people live tortured existences but leave the rest of us great artistic legacies. Yet others live long lives but meet their deaths with unresolved fears and unmet ambitions. The benefits of studying in detail the physiological substrates of purpose in life and other dimensions of well-being will be myriad.

References

Anderson, N., & Armstead, C. (1995). Toward understanding the association of socio-economic status and health: A new challenge for the biopsychosocial approach. *Psychosomatic Medicine, 57*(3), 213–225.

Benson, H. (1996). *Timeless healing: The power and biology of belief.* New York: Fireside.

Borysenko, J. (1996). *A woman's book of life: The biology, psychology and spirituality of the feminine life cycle.* New York: Riverhead.

Cohen, S., Doyle, W. J., Skoner, D. P., Gwaltney, J. M., Jr., & Newsom, J. T. (1995). State and trait negative affect as predictors of objective and subjective symptoms in respiratory viral infections. *Journal of Personality and Social Psychology, 68*, 159–169.

Cohen, S., Tyrell, D., & Smith, A. (1993). Life events, perceived stress, negative affect and susceptibility to the common cold. *Journal of Personality and Social Psychology, 64*, 11–140.

Damassio, A. (1994). *Descartes' error: Emotion, reason, and the human brain.* New York: Grosset/Putnam.

Dafter, R. (1996). Why "negative" emotions can sometimes be positive: The spectrum model of emotions and their role in mind-body healing. *Advances, 12*, 6–19.

Davison, K. P., & Pennebaker, J. W. (1997). Virtual narratives: Illness representations in on-line support groups. In K. J. Petrie & J. A. Weinman (Eds.), *Perceptions of health and illness* (pp. 463–485). Amsterdam: Harwood Academic Publishers.

Erikson, E. (1963). Eight stages of man. In E. Erikson, *Childhood and society* (chap. 7). New York: Norton.

Goleman, D. (1995). *Emotional intelligence.* New York: Bantam.

Gould, K. L., Ornish, D., Scherwitz, L., Brown, S., Edens, R. P., Hess, M. J., Mullani, N., Bolomey, L., Dobbs, F., & Armstrong, W. (1995). Changes in myocardial perfusion abnormalities by position emission tomography after long-term, intense risk factor modification. *Journal of the American Medical Association, 274*(11), 894–901.

Hafen, B., Karren, K., Frandsen, K., & Smith, N. (1996). *Mind body health: The effects of attitudes, emotions and relationships.* Boston: Allyn and Bacon.

Johnson, K., Anderson, N., Bastida, E., Kramer, B., Williams, D., & Wong, M. (1995). Macrosocial and environmental influences on minority health. *Health Psychology, 14*(7), 601–612

Kabat-Zinn, J. (1990a). *Full catastrophe living.* New York: Delta.

Kabat-Zinn, J. (1990b). *Wherever you go there you are.* New York: Hyperion.

Kannel, W., & Wilson, P. (1995). Risk factors that attenuate the female coronary disease advantage. *Archives of Internal Medicine, 155*, 57–61.

Lesperance, F., Frasure-Smith, N., & Talajic, M. (1996). Depression before and after myocardial infarction: Its nature and consequences. *Psychosomatic Medicine, 58*, 99–110.

McEwen, B. S., & Stellar, E. (1993). Stress and the individual: Mechanisms leading to disease. *Archives of Internal Medicine, 153*, 2093–2101.

Ornish, D. (1990). *Dr. Dean Ornish's program for reversing heart disease.* New York: Ballentine.

Ornish, D. (1998). *Love and survival.* New York: Harper Collins.

Remen, R. N. (1996). *Kitchen table wisdom.* New York: Riverhead.

Ryff, C. (1995). Psychological well-being in adult life. *Current Directions in Psychological Science, 4*, 99–104.

Ryff, C. (1996). Psychological well-being. *Encyclopedia of Gerontology, 2*, 365–369.

Ryff, C., & Singer, B. (1996). Psychological well-being: Meaning, measurement, and implications for psychotherapy research. *Psychotherapy and Psychosomatics, 65*, 14–23.

Ryff, C., & Singer, B. (1998a). The contours of positive health. *Psychological Inquiry, 9*(11), 1–28.

Ryff, C., & Singer, B. (1998b). The role of purpose in life and personal growth in positive health. In P. T. P. Wong & P. S. Fry (Eds.), *The human quest for meaning: A handbook of psychological research and clinical applications.* Mahwah, NJ: Lawrence Erlbaum.

Seeman, T., Berkman, L., Blazer, D., & Rowe, J. (1994). Social ties and social support and neuroendocrine function: The MacArthur studies of successful aging. *Annals of Internal Medicine, 50A*, M177–M183.

Seeman, T., & Syme, L. (1987). Social networks and coronary artery diseases: A comparison of the structure and function of social relations as predictors of disease. *Psychosomatic Medicine, 49*, 341–345.

Spiegel, D. (1995). *Minding the body: Psychotherapy for extreme situations.* Strecker Monograph Series no. 32. Philadelphia: Institute of Pennsylvania Hospital.

Spiegel, D. (1997, May 2–3). Having a good Cry: Group expression and health outcome among breast cancer patients. Paper presented at the Third Annual Symposium on Emotion, University of Wisconsin, Madison.

Spiegel, D., Bloom, J., Kraemer, H., & Gottheil, E. (1989). Effect of psychosocial treatment on the survival of patients with metastatic breast cancer. *Lancet, 2/8668*, 888–891.

Uvnäs-Moberg, K. (1998). Oxytocin may mediate the benefits of positive social interaction and emotions. *Psychoneuroendocrinology, 23*, 819–835.

Weil, A. (1983). *Health and healing.* Boston: Houghton Mifflin.

Weil, A. (1995). *Spontaneous healing.* New York: Fawcett Columbine.

6

How Do Others Get under Our Skin?

Social Relationships and Health

Teresa Seeman

As highlighted by the various chapters in this volume, there has been a growing recognition and interest in the role of social relationships in health and well-being throughout life. Indeed, over the past several decades, a considerable body of research has documented associations between the extent and quality of an individual's social relationships and better health and longevity (Broadhead et al., 1983; Cohen & Syme, 1984; House, Landis, & Umberson, 1988). While the evidence linking social isolation or lack of social support to increased risks for morbidity and mortality continues to grow rapidly, important questions remain concerning the precise mechanisms or pathways by which such social circumstances influence health outcomes. Various hypotheses have been offered (and supporting data found) for mediating pathways through social network influences on attitudes and behaviors that are known to have an impact on health and longevity, for example, evidence for associations between more healthful lifestyles and more successful risk-reduction efforts, such as reducing dietary fat, exercising, and smoking cessation (Bovbjerg et al., 1995; Cohen, 1991; Duncan & McAuley, 1993; House, Robbins, & Metzner, 1982; Sallis et al., 1989; Seeman, Seeman, & Sayles, 1985; Umberson, 1987). Social ties and support, however, have also been found to remain significant predictors of morbidity and mortality in their own right, independent of any associations with other risk factors (Broadhead et al., 1983; Cohen, 1991; Henry, 1983; Seeman et al., 1993; Seeman, Kaplan, Knudsen, Cohen, & Guralnik, 1987; Seeman & Syme, 1987). One area that has not received a full exploration is the hypothesis that there are more direct biological effects of social ties on human physiology, which may contribute to the observed associations between such ties and differential morbidity and mortality risks (Bovard, 1961, 1962, 1985; Cassel, 1976; Williams, 1985).

In this chapter, evidence that links social relationships to various health outcomes, including overall longevity and coronary heart disease (CHD), is outlined.

In light of the volume of existing literature that relates social ties to these various outcomes, a complete review is beyond the scope of this chapter. Rather, specific endpoints discussed here were selected because of their salience as major health outcomes; they are meant to be illustrative of the general pattern of findings. The latter half of the chapter outlines research that focuses on the question of possible biological pathways through which social relationships "get under our skin" to influence risks for such health outcomes. Particular attention is given to evidence that relates social environment characteristics (e.g., presence of social ties and/or social support characteristics) to patterns of hypothalamic-pituitary-adrenal (HPA) axis and sympathetic nervous system (SNS) activity in light of their central roles in the ongoing, homeostatic regulatory processes of the body in the face of changing environmental stimuli (McEwen & Stellar, 1993; Sapolsky, 1992; Williams, 1985) and their known links to pathophysiologic processes, such as elevated blood pressure, serum cholesterol, and diabetes (Brindley & Rolland, 1989; Eliot, Buell, & Dembroski, 1982; Findley, 1949; Henry, 1983; Krantz & Manuck, 1984; Matthews et al., 1986; Munck & Guyre, 1991; Munck, Guyre, & Holbrook, 1984; Troxler, Sprague, Albanese, Fuchs, & Thompson, 1977; Truhan & Ahmed, 1989).

Social Relationships and Health

Mortality

During the 1980s and 1990s, a considerable body of epidemiologic research documented consistent associations between greater social integration and lower risk for mortality. Figure 6.1 illustrates the pattern of these findings with data on nine-year mortality for men and women in the Alameda County study (Berkman & Breslow, 1983). The data presented show the relationship between levels of reported social integration at baseline and subsequent mortality. As shown, for both men and women and across all age groups, decreasing levels of social integration (as measured by a summary index that reflects ties with a spouse, close friends, and relatives and participation in churches and other types of groups) are associated with increasing mortality. And, as has generally been found in studies that examine this relationship, these differences in mortality risk remain significant independent of other sociodemographic characteristics and measures of health status and functioning.

Subsequent analyses of other community-based prospective studies, including Tecumseh, Michigan (House, Robbins, & Metzner, 1982); Durham, North Carolina (Blazer, 1982); and Evans County, Georgia (Schoenbach, Kaplan, Fredman, & Kleinbaum, 1968), as well as studies from Sweden (Orth-Gomer & Johnson, 1987; Welin et al., 1985) and Finland (Kaplan et al., 1988), provide further evidence for the protective effects of social integration with respect to longevity. Though measures of social integration used in these studies vary in their specific item content, all reflect assessments of the individual's ties with others (e.g., marital status, ties with friends and relatives, membership in groups). One interesting

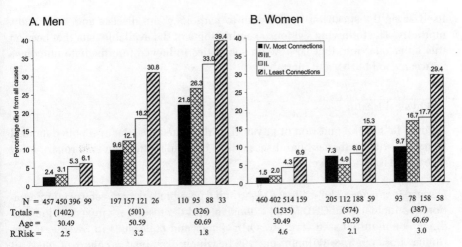

Figure 6.1 Alameda County study: 9-year mortality by level of social integration (reprinted from Berkman, L. F., Breslow, L. (1983). *Health and Ways of Living*. New York: Oxford University Press with permission). Mortality from all causes: Social Network Index, age and sex-specific rates (per 100), 1965–1974.

difference from the Alameda County results lies in the evidence from several of these studies (House, Robbins, & Metzner, 1982; Kaplan et al., 1988), which suggests that this protective effect may be stronger in men. Closer examination of the data, however, suggests that such a conclusion may be premature. These community-based studies largely represent more middle-aged cohorts, in which the average age is below 65. As a result, a large portion of the women are premenopausal and thus not yet into their period of highest mortality risk. The smaller number of events among women in these studies may thus have reduced their power to detect differences in risk by level of social integration.

Analyses of social integration and five-year mortality risk in three older cohorts from the National Institute on Aging's Established Populations for the Epidemiologic Study of the Elderly (EPESE studies) provide support for this interpretation of observed gender differences in the earlier studies. All participants in the EPESE studies were 65 years of age or older at baseline, which resulted in more comparable event rates for men and women (Seeman et al., 1993). Social integration was associated with reduced five-year mortality risk for both men and women in the New Haven, Connecticut, cohort. Interestingly, no significant effects were found for either men or women living in the East Boston, Massachusetts, community—a finding that may reflect the inadequacy of our measure of social integration (based on marital status, ties with "close" friends/relatives, group membership, church involvement) in capturing the full range of informal social connections that exist in this geographically circumscribed and ethnically homogeneous community (see Seeman et al., 1993, for more detailed discussion of these findings).

While this body of evidence, which relates social integration to mortality risks, has led to general acceptance of the idea that social ties influence health, there is less consensus regarding the question of where and how this influence manifests itself along the spectrum from health to pathology and disease and, ultimately, mortality. The following sections examine some of the available data that bear on this latter question, that is, how do social ties influence intermediate outcomes between good health and mortality?

Physical Health

Turning first to the question of physical health outcomes, the available data deal primarily with cardiovascular disease, with particular attention to coronary heart disease (CHD) and stroke.

Disease Incidence   The evidence regarding a possible link between social integration and incidence of CHD is not extensive, and the results are mixed. A longitudinal, community-based study by Orth-Gomer and colleagues in Sweden (Orth-Gomer, Rosengren, & Wilhelmsen, 1993), which examined a cohort of men, all aged 50 at the inception of the study, found a significant protective effect of social integration with respect to incidence of CHD (defined as either nonfatal myocardial infarction [MI] or death attributed to CHD in those found to be free from heart disease at the baseline examination). Subjects in the lowest tertile of social integration (i.e., the more socially isolated) experienced significantly greater six-year incidence of CHD, independent of other standard CHD risk factors. In another study of members of a health maintenance organization, Vogt and colleagues also found a protective effect of social integration (as indexed by the scope or range of different types of ties): those reporting a wider range of social ties experienced significantly lower 15-year incidence of MI (based on reviews of medical records), again independent of standard CHD risk factors (Vogt, Mullooly, Ernst, Pope, & Hollis, 1992). No significant associations with incident MI, however, were found for alternative measures of social integration based on network size or frequency of contacts. In addition, there were no significant associations with incidence of other disease outcomes, such as hypertension, stroke and cancer. Other studies, such as the Japanese-American study in Hawaii (Reed, McGee, Yano, & Feinleib, 1983), have not found significant effects of overall social integration (based on marital status, ties with children and parents, social activities with coworkers, and group memberships) with respect to incidence of heart disease (based on examination and review of medical records). Interestingly, however, a significant protective effect was found for two specific aspects of social integration—marital status and not living alone—a pattern of associations that parallels findings (discussed below) from studies of the impact of such factors on survival post-MI (Case, Moss, Case, McDermott, & Eberly, 1992; Williams et al., 1992).

One possible reason for the lack of a consistent association between level of social integration and incidence of CHD is suggested by findings from a study of Israeli men, in which those reporting higher levels of family problems were found to be at significantly increased risk of developing angina pectoris (Medalie & Goldbourt, 1976). As these data highlight, greater social integration, to the extent that it is accompanied by greater interpersonal conflict or other interpersonal problems, may not be uniformly associated with health benefits, including reduced risk of heart disease. However, the mixed findings regarding social integration and incidence of CHD permit no firm conclusions at this point. This is particularly true with respect to questions about risk relationships for women since a number of the studies included only men (Orth-Gomer, Rosengren, & Wilhelmsen, 1993; Reed, McGee, Yano, & Feinleib, 1983).

Disease Severity Other research has examined possible relationships among aspects of the social environment and the development of coronary atherosclerosis. The hypothesis in this case is that social environment characteristics might be related more strongly to the progressive accumulation of coronary atherosclerosis over time than to the onset of acute MI. Such a pattern of association could result from ongoing, cumulative social environment influences on biological parameters, such as blood pressure (BP) and stress hormones, such as norepinephrine (NE), epinephrine (E), and cortisol. If, for example, poorer social integration and support are associated with greater exposure to elevated levels of such physiologic stress parameters in response to environmental stimuli, those elevations would be hypothesized to result in potentiation of the development of atherosclerosis.

To test this hypothesis, we assessed levels of social integration and support in a sample of 161 men and women scheduled for coronary angiography to determine the extent of their coronary artery disease (CAD) (Seeman & Syme, 1987). Participants' reports of levels of instrumental support provided by others were found to predict levels of CAD: individuals who reported higher levels of support were found to have significantly less coronary atherosclerosis during subsequent angiography testing (see fig. 6.2). A similar pattern of findings was seen for re-

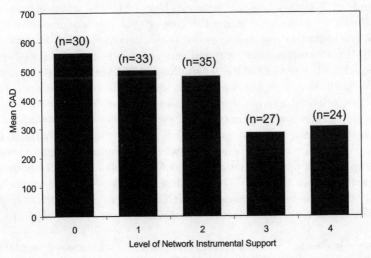

Figure 6.2 Mean coronary atherosclerosis by levels of instrumental support (adapted from Seeman, T. E., Syme, S. L. (1987). Social networks and coronary artery disease: a comparative analysis of network structural and support characteristics. *Psychosomatic Medicine, 49,* 341–354).

ported levels of "feeling loved": subjects scoring highest on feelings of being loved had the least CAD, and average CAD increased with decreasing levels of feeling that one is loved by others. A second study of angiography patients also found a significant inverse association between levels of emotional support and extent of atherosclerosis (particularly among type A patients) (Blumenthal et al., 1987). In contrast to these findings relating levels of support to CAD, level of social integration (based on marital status, ties with close friends/relatives, and group memberships) has not been related to the extent of coronary atherosclerosis (Seeman & Syme, 1987). One reason for this lack of association between level of social integration and the extent of CAD may relate to the findings of Medalie and Goldbourt (1976), which showed that men who reported higher levels of family problems were significantly more likely to develop chest pain (angina pectoris). As indicated, data such as these suggest that greater social integration may not have uniformly positive effects on risks for CHD if it is accompanied by greater interpersonal conflict or other such problems.

Recovery post-MI   Studies of patient populations provide the most consistent evidence of protective effects of social integration with respect to prognosis post-MI. Analyses of data from the B-HAT trial by Ruberman, Weinblatt, Goldberg, and Chaudhary (1984) were among the first to indicate that relatively more socially isolated men were at increased risk of death post-MI. This finding has been confirmed more recently by Williams et al. (1992), who found that individuals who were not married and had no confidant experienced significantly worse survival post-MI over a five-year follow-up period. In a similar vein, Case et al. (1992) found that subjects who lived alone experienced significantly greater risk of fatal or nonfatal recurrent coronary events over a follow-up period of up to four years.

A study by Berkman, Leo-Summers, and Horwitz (1992), which also examined survival post-MI, provides evidence that suggests that levels of emotional support may be one important reason why social isolation conveys greater mortality risk in post-MI patients. Emotional support was measured prospective to the actual MI as all subjects were part of the longitudinal EPESE study in New Haven, Connecticut. Subjects who reported having no sources of emotional support prior to their MI experienced nearly threefold greater six-month mortality than those reporting one or more sources, controlling for age, severity of MI, and other comorbidity. More recently, analyses of subjects hospitalized for congestive heart failure show a parallel pattern of association between prehospitalization levels of emotional support and post-hospitalization risk for recurrent hospitalization or mortality (Krumholz et al., 1998). Over a 12-month follow-up, those reporting no sources of emotional support were at threefold greater risk for such events compared with those reporting one or more available sources of such support.

Recovery post-Stroke   Additional analyses of data on incidence and recovery from stroke from the New Haven EPESE study have revealed a similar pattern of associations between social integration and incidence versus recovery from stroke. As in the Berkman et al. study of MIs (1992), strokes among cohort members were identified through hospital monitoring for all cohort members. Level of social integration was not a significant predictor of incident stroke in this older cohort, though the direction of the effect was toward increased incidence among the less socially integrated (Colantonio, Kasl, & Ostfeld, 1992). By contrast, post-stroke recovery was related to pre-stroke level of social integration (Colantonio, Kasl, Ostfeld, & Berkman, 1993). Among subjects who experienced a stroke, those who were more socially isolated exhibited significantly poorer functional status six months post-stroke as indexed by greater impairment in activities of daily living (ADL) and more frequent nursing home placement. Several studies have also found that levels of emotional support post-stroke are predictive of better recovery (Friedland & McColl, 1987; Glass & Maddox, 1992; McLeroy, DeVellis, DeVellis, Kaplan, & Toole, 1984), which suggests that greater available emotional support may be one reason that increased social integration predicts better post-stroke outcome.

Overall, the data regarding associations between social integration and physical health outcomes are generally supportive but mixed, the strongest evidence for such effects appearing to be with regard to prognosis after disease onset (at least with respect to cardiovascular disease).

Mental Health

With regard to mental health outcomes, the data are more consistent in showing the generally protective effects of social integration and the increased risks for psychological distress that result from social isolation and/or, as seen in the literature on bereavement, the loss of important ties, such as a spouse or parent (Biegel, McCardle, & Mendelson, 1985; Bowling, 1987; George, 1989; Kessler & MacLeod, 1985; Stroebe & Stroebe, 1987; Umberson & Chen, 1994). For example, studies of the impact of social ties on the risk of depression show consistent protective effects associated with greater social integration, particularly as reflected in the presence of what are generally seen as more intimate ties with spouse, children, and/or supportive significant others (Biegel et al., 1985; Broadhead et al., 1983; Dean, Kolody, & Wood, 1990; George, 1989; Johnson, 1991). The increased risks for psychological distress that result from disruption of such ties, particularly marital disruption (either through bereavement or marriage dissolution) have also been extensively documented (Aseltine & Kessler, 1993; Bloom, Asher, & White, 1978; Bowling, 1987; Moritz, Kasl, & Berkman, 1989; Stroebe & Stroebe, 1987). A report from the New Haven EPESE cohort, which examines three-year changes in depression, clearly illustrates the temporal patterning of the association between social integration and psychological symptomatology (Oxman, Berkman, Kasl, Freeman, & Barrett, 1992). Three-year changes in CES-D (Center for Epidemiologic Study of Depression scale) scores were examined in relation to baseline social network characteristics. Baseline measures of social integration, including reporting more contacts with children and with close friends, were associated with declines in depressive symptomatology. Available data on changes in social network ties also illustrate the negative consequences of losing important ties: subjects who lost their spouse during the three-year interval were more likely to exhibit increases in their levels of depressive symptomatology.

While the aforementioned data suggest the important mental health benefits that can accrue through social connections, it is also true that research has demonstrated the potential for social relationships to generate increased psychological distress through their demands or criticism (Kessler, MacLeod, & Wethington, 1985; Rook, 1984; for reviews, see Burg & Seeman, 1994; Wortman & Conway, 1985). Recent data from the MacArthur Studies of Successful Aging have provided similar evidence for possible negative effects on physical health (Seeman, Bruce, & McAvay, 1996). In analyses predicting onset of ADL disability in a cohort of older men and women, higher baseline levels of instrumental assistance are associated with increased risk of new ADL disability over a two-year follow-up among the men—again highlighting the possibility of negative impacts from our complex social relationships.

Social Relationships: Getting under Our Skin

As outlined above, social ties appear to have the potential to positively or negatively influence our physical and mental health. So, how do they get under our skin?

One of the primary ways through which social relationships are thought to modulate our internal physiology is through their influence on cognitive-emotional interpretations of stimuli, interpretations which then influence neuroendocrine activity via neocortical and limbic centers (Bovard, 1961, 1962, 1985; Schneiderman, 1983; Williams, 1985). Information regarding the external social (and nonsocial) environment is processed first by the sensory systems of the neocortex and fed via the temporal lobe (especially the entorhinal cortex) to the amygdala and hippocampus, which, in turn, signal the HPA axis and the noradrenergic and serotonergic systems (Bovard, 1961, 1962; Gray, 1995; McEwen, 1995). This processing of information ultimately results in emotional and behavioral responses to environmental stimuli (LeDoux, 1995; McEwen, 1995), including the responses of fear and anxiety, with their attendant patterns of more general bodywide neuroendocrine arousal (Gray, 1995; LeDoux, 1995; Phillips & LeDoux, 1992). While factors such as genetics and prior experience influence the brain's processing of stimuli, our focus here is on the impact of the social environment. To the extent that social cues influence the processing and ultimate interpretation of other incoming data regarding the external (or internal) environment, the social environment is hypothesized to influence the relative frequency with which the brain's processing of information results in emotional states, such as fear or anxiety, and their associated profiles of neuroendocrine arousal. In the following sections, evidence from both human and nonhuman primates is reviewed, which illustrates the physiological impact of social relationships.

Nonhuman Primates

Like humans, nonhuman primates are social animals, and research on monkeys and baboons, among others, provides perhaps the most extensive evidence of the effects of social relationships on specific health outcomes (such as coronary atherosclerosis); it also serves as a useful model for understanding more about the actual biological pathways through which social relationships can have positive or negative effects on risk for such health outcomes. A series of studies from Bowman Grey University have elegantly demonstrated the effects of experimentally induced social stress on coronary disease (Clarkson, Kaplan, Adams, & Manuck, 1987; Kaplan, Manuck, Clarkson, Lusso, & Taub, 1982; Kaplan et al., 1983; Shively & Kaplan, 1984). In these studies, social stress was induced by periodic reshuffling of group membership, which created ongoing social instability. As shown in figure 6.3, the socially stressed group developed greater atherosclerosis (Kaplan et al., 1983).

Importantly, these studies also demonstrate that where you are in the social hierarchy of your group (and, perhaps the cognitive/emotional and behavioral implications of your social position) also appears to affect your disease risks. As shown in figure 6.4, development of CAD was found to be significantly greater for dominant animals as compared with more subordinate animals in the *unstable* groups (i.e., groups exposed to repeated membership changes) (Kaplan, Adams, Clarkson, Manuck, & Shively, 1991). By contrast, under stable social conditions (when group membership remained constant over time), the dominant males appear to experience somewhat less atherosclerosis (though, as the authors note, these latter differences are not statistically significant). One interpretation of these data might be that, under conditions of social instability, social relationships of dominance versus subordination are more frequently being challenged. This puts greater stress on the more dominant males, who are repeatedly faced with new, unknown males and with the challenge of asserting their dominance over these new males.

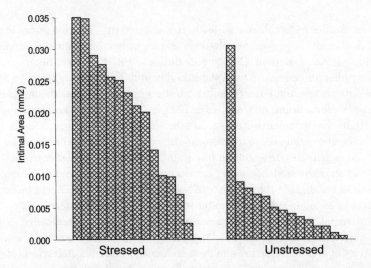

Figure 6.3 Social stress and coronary atherosclerosis (reprinted from Kaplan, J. R., Manuck, S. B., Clarkson, T. B., Lusso, F. M., Taub, D. M., Miller, E. W. (1983). Social stress and atherosclerosis in normocholesterolemic monkeys. *Science, 220*, 733–735, with permission). Atherosclerosis extent in 15 male monkeys from stable (unstressed) and 14 monkeys from unstable (stressed) groups.

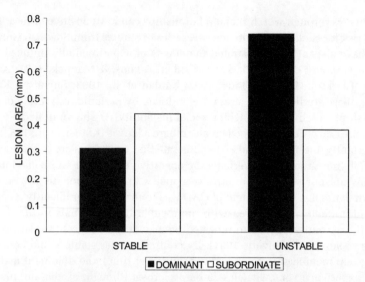

Figure **6.4** Social stress, social position, and atherosclerosis (reprinted from Kaplan, J. R., Adams, M. R., Clarkson, T. B., Manuck, S. B., Shively, C. A. (1991). Social behavior and gender in biomedical investigations using monkeys: Studies in atherogenesis. *Laboratory Animal Sciences, 41*, 334–343, with permission). Coronary atherosclerosis lesion area in dominant and subordinate males living in stable and unstable social groupings. Dominant animals were significantly more affected than subordinates ($p < 0.05$), but only in unstable groups; dominant and subordinate monkeys living in stable groups could not be distinguished.

Indeed, studies of female macaques have indicated that, like the males in stable groups, dominant females enjoy relatively greater protection against coronary atherosclerosis (Hamm, Kaplan, Clarkson, & Bullock, 1983). Unlike the males, however, this protection occurs in both stable and unstable social situations—a finding that the authors speculate may result from the lower behavioral demands for aggression placed on dominant females as compared with more dominant males in such unstable environments (Kaplan, Adams, Clarkson, & Koritnik, 1984).

While the above data come from studies of experimentally induced social stress in nonhuman primates, research on free-living baboons has also shown that dominant social status in a stable social environment is characterized by lower basal ACTH (Suomi et al., 1989) and cortisol (Sapolsky, 1989), higher HDL cholesterol levels (Sapolsky & Mott, 1987), and better immune function (Sapolsky, 1993), while dominant social status in an unstable social environment is associated with increased cortisol levels (Sapolsky, 1983). Even more interesting are recent studies of actual styles of social interaction and their endocrine correlates. Behavioral observations of free-living baboons in Kenya have been used to develop typologies that reflect styles of social interaction exhibited by the males (Ray & Sapolsky, 1992). One such typology is characterized by a style of interaction related to nonsexual, positive social interactions. Males who score high on this typology are those who spend much time and energy affiliating with females and infants. They have high rates of grooming and being groomed by non-estrus, nonconsortship females and high rates of positive social interactions with non-estrus females and infants. And, most relevant to our focus on the relationship between social relations and physiologic activity, males who score high on such patterns of socially affiliative interaction exhibit significantly different patterns of HPA axis regulation. As shown in figure 6.5, males

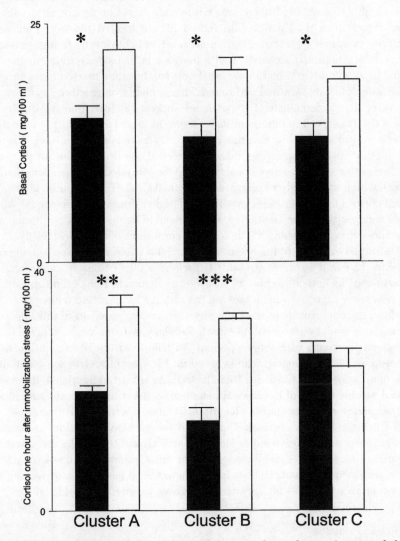

Figure 6.5 Styles of social interaction and cortisol regulation (reprinted from Ray, J. C., Sapolsky, R. M. (1992). Styles of male social behavior and their endocrine correlates among high-ranking wild baboons. *American Journal of Primatology, 28,* 231–250, with permission). Cortisol concentrations in males in the highest-standing quartile of clusters A–C (solid bars) and the lowest-standing quartile of those clusters (open bars). *, **, *** indicate $p < .05, .02, .01$ by unpaired t-test.

scoring highest on nonsexual, social affiliative behavior (i.e., cluster B) exhibit lower basal cortisol; they also exhibit less cortisol reactivity under stress.

Two other typologies/clusters identified in this research are also represented in figure 6.5. Cluster A reflects traits associated with courtship behavior. Males who scored high on this cluster spend more time in sexual and nonsexual aspects of courtship; they also exhibit lower physiologic activation. Cluster C reflects competitive male-male interactions: high scorers are more adept at distinguishing between highly threatening interactions with rivals versus neutral or mildly threatening interactions (i.e., males who scored high exhibited the least behavioral reactivity to milder threats and were most reactive behaviorally to high-intensity competitive situations). Consistent with these social/behavioral traits, males who scored high on cluster C had lower basal cortisol, but they reacted more strongly to the stress of being captured and caged. This evidence on reactivity to higher intensity challenge for cluster C type males suggests at least one reason for the greater CAD observed in dominant males exposed to social instability in the Bowman Grey studies, namely, that those males may have been more likely to score high on the cluster C typology. Under nonstressful conditions, their levels of cortisol (and other stress-reactive hormones) may be low (as shown here for cluster C males), which would help to protect them against CAD. However, their greater apparent cortisol reactivity under conditions of higher intensity challenge (as would likely occur with greater frequency under unstable social group conditions) may predispose them to greater CAD under such conditions of social instability.

Additional evidence of the potential for social relationships, even a single relationship, to result in more stressful experiences also comes from research by Robert Sapolsky and colleagues on free-living baboons in Kenya. The appearance of a new, very aggressive male seeking to establish his position within the troop provided the opportunity to track the physiologic consequences of this alteration in the group social environment (Albert, Sapolsky, & Altmann, 1992). This male was given the name of Hobbes—perhaps in tribute to the seventeenth-century philosopher Thomas Hobbes who is noted for his view of society as potentially a "war of all against all" (Zagorin, 1968, p. 483). As shown in figure 6.6, there were several notable results of Hobbes's appearance on the scene. First, the presence of this aggressive male resulted in elevations in basal cortisol levels from those observed prior to Hobbes's arrival. Though not shown here, reductions in immune function were also observed after Hobbes's arrival, and these, like the elevations in cortisol levels, were most pronounced for those animals on the receiving end of his aggression. Second, Hobbes himself appears to be quite "stressed out" by this experience as well—as suggested by his own elevated cortisol level.

Human Primates

What about the human species? Do we show these same physiologic effects of social affiliation (and social conflict)? Not surprisingly, in light of our similar evolution as social animals over the millennia, the answer clearly seems to be "yes." Our social relationships, like those of the baboons in Kenya and monkeys at Bowman Grey, appear to have the capacity to get under our skin to generate both posi-

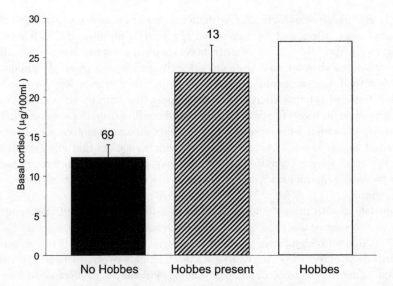

Figure 6.6 Effects of social aggression on cortisol regulation (reprinted from Alberts, S. C., Sapolsky, R. M., Altmann, J. (1992). Behavoral, endocrine, and immunological correlates of immigration by an aggressive male into a natural primate group. *Hormones and Behavior, 26*, 167–178, with permission).

tive and negative effects on our internal physiology. And, the observed physiologic effects are consistent with the demonstrated associations between such social relationships and actual disease and mortality risks.

Community-based population studies provide evidence for associations between higher reported levels of support and better physiologic profiles, including lower heart rate and systolic blood pressure (Bland, Krogh, Winkelstein, & Trevisan, 1991; Dressler, 1983; Dressler, Dos Santos, & Viteri, 1986; Linden, Chambers, Maurice, & Lenz, 1993; Unden, Orth-Gomer, & Elofsson, 1991), lower serum cholesterol (Gore, 1978; Thomas, Goodwin, & Goodwin, 1985), uric acid (Cobb, 1974; Thomas et al., 1985), and lower urinary norepinephrine (Kemp & Hatmaker, 1989). More recently, data from the MacArthur Study of Successful Aging, a cohort study of relatively high functioning older men and women, were used to compare the effects of structural measures of social ties (e.g., network size, marital status) with those of more qualitative measures of social support (e.g., levels of emotional and/or instrumental network support) in relation to HPA axis and SNS activity (based on 12-hour, overnight measures of urinary cortisol, norepinephrine, and epinephrine) (Seeman, Berkman, Blazer, & Rowe, 1994). For men, multivariate models, adjusted for age, chronic conditions, relative weight, smoking, and medications, revealed that higher average and maximal frequency of emotional support had the strongest associations with lower levels of all three neuroendocrine parameters. Less consistent patterns of association were seen for measures of instrumental support and measures of network structure, such as network size and marital status. Maximum frequency of instrumental support had significant, negative associations with norepinephrine and cortisol but only a marginal association with epinephrine. The overall number of social relationships was negatively related to only norepinephrine levels. For women, these same measures showed no significant associations, though married women had significantly lower epinephrine levels. One possible reason for the relatively weaker findings relating social support to endocrine activity in women is suggested by data on levels of social demands and conflict from these same social relationships. Women who reported higher levels of such negative social interactions had higher levels of urinary cortisol, which suggests that any benefit they received from network emotional support may have been counterbalanced by their increased neuroendocrine responses to the negative aspects of their social interactions.

Consistent with these findings, data from a study by Kiecolt-Glaser and colleagues also suggest that women may be more reactive to negative aspects of social relationships with significant others (Kiecolt-Glaser et al., 1997). They examined patterns of NE activity over the course of a discussion between husband and wife of marital issues judged to be conflict producing. Videotapes of discussion sessions were used to classify couples as exhibiting high or low levels of negative marital interaction during the conflict resolution task (negative interaction = criticism, interruptions, put-downs, disagreement). Among the men, no differences in reactivity were seen by actual level of negative interaction during the conflict resolution task, though NE levels did increase in response to the conflict task. Among the women, however, there was a marked difference in physiologic reactivity to the conflict resolution task, which depended on the actual level of negative marital interactions during the task: women exposed to more negative interactions exhibited higher NE levels. These same women also exhibited elevated baseline levels prior to the actual conflict resolution task (perhaps suggesting that they anticipated—based on previous experience with their partner—what was to come in terms of the likelihood of such negative interactions). As in the case of the MacArthur study data, these findings suggest that women may be more physiologically reactive to negative social interactions, perhaps particularly those with significant others.

Experimental research paradigms have even more dramatically varied the social context in which subjects are asked to deal with a challenging situation and have assessed differences in cardiovascular reactivity under these different social conditions. Lepore, Mata-Allen, and Evans (1993), for example, varied the degree of social support available to the subjects while they prepared and then gave a six-minute speech. The three social conditions were speech given alone, speech given in the presence of a nonsupportive confederate, and speech given in the presence of a supportive confederate. As shown in figure 6.7, subjects who gave their speech in the presence of a nonsupportive confederate exhibited the largest increases in systolic BP, followed by subjects who gave their speech alone. Subjects with a supportive confederate present exhibited the least BP change during the speech task. Similarly, the presence of at least one supportive confederate was associated with attenuated blood pressure and heart responses during a group discussion of a controversial issue in which two other confederates attacked the subject (Gerin, Pieper, Levy, & Pickering, 1992).

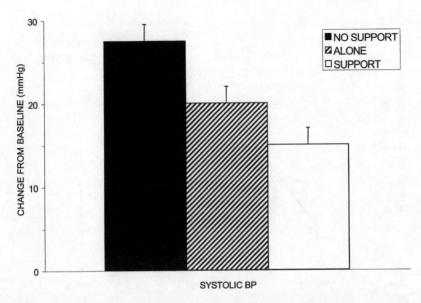

Figure 6.7 Social environment and blood pressure reactivity to challenge (reprinted from Lepore, S. J., Mata Allen, K. A., Evans, G. W. (1993). Social support lowers cardiovascular reactivity to an acute stressor. *Psychosomatic Medicine, 55,* 518–524, with permission).

Similar effects of social interactions with respect to autonomic activation—as indexed by changes in free fatty acid (FFA) levels and galvanic skin response— have also been reported (Back & Bogdonoff, 1964; Kissel, 1965). In a study by Back and Bogdonoff (1964), subjects were tested in groups of four: one group of subjects was asked to bring three friends with them to the testing session while others were individually recruited and grouped together as "strangers." Those grouped with friends exhibited lower FFA levels at baseline than individually recruited subjects grouped with strangers. Also, in response to a stimulus matching task, those grouped with friends exhibited smaller increases in FFA levels. Similar results were also reported by Kissel (1965): the presence of a friend reduced galvanic skin response to a problem-solving task more than did the presence of a stranger.

These various studies clearly illustrate what we might call the double-edged sword quality of social relationships. While they can apparently have positive effects on physiologic parameters, they can apparently also have negative consequences, as seen in the heightened reactivity among subjects exposed to a nonsupportive confederate and the wives exposed to negative marital interactions. As suggested by the earlier data on Hobbes, such social aggression may not only affect the recipient but also the purveyor of this negativity. And, as in Hobbes's case, we too appear to be relatively more stressed by experiences of hostility toward others. Figure 6.8 presents data from a study by Pope and Smith (1991), which illustrates the differences in cortisol activity (measured in terms of 24-hour urinary cortisol excretion) that were found for men with high versus low levels of

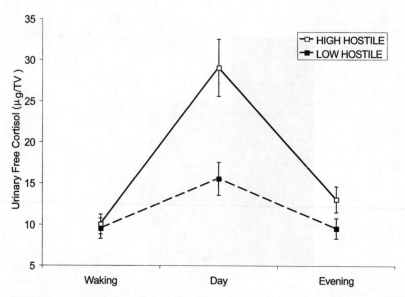

Figure **6.8** Cynical hostility and 24-hour urinary cortisol excretion (reprinted from Pope, M. K., Smith, T. W. (1991). Cortisol excretion in high and low cynically hostile men. *Psychosomatic Medicine, 53,* 386–392, with permission).

cynical hostility. High scores on cynical hostility have been described as indicating an attitude toward others that reflects mistrust, suspicion, anger-proneness, and resentment. As shown, men who scored higher on such cynical hostility exhibit greater cortisol excretion during the daytime, a time period when one might expect that they are most likely confronted with the need for social interaction and when their cynical hostility may lead them to have a more negative style of interaction with others. And, indeed, other data (Smith, Pope, Sanders, Allred, & O'Keefe, 1988) do indicate that those higher on cynical hostility also report more negative patterns of social interaction (e.g., more perceived hassles, lower social support levels, and lower satisfaction with social support levels).

Summary

As is clearly outlined by the research cited here, humans appear to be exquisitely responsive to our social relationships—not only cognitively and emotionally, but physiologically as well—both as recipients and purveyors of positive and/or negative communications. While a relative lack of social integration may be associated with increased risk for poorer health outcomes, the quality of those ties that do exist also appears to carry the potential for positive or negative health effects. More specifically, the emotional valence associated with particular social relationships and/or with particular social interactions appears to result in different patterns of physiologic activation across multiple systems.

We have, however, only just begun to explore the effects of the social environment on physiologic activity. The clinical importance of the demonstrated social environment effects on patterns of physiologic activity is not clear at this time. One can speculate, however, that, minor though they may be, if they represent chronic differences experienced over a long period of time, their cumulative impact may lead to differences in the development of pathophysiologic processes, which underlie the health outcomes we have come to define as "disease."

Note

Work on this chapter was supported by NIA-SERCA grant AG-00586 and by the MacArthur Research Network on Successful Aging and the MacArthur Planning Initiative on SES and Health through grants from the John D. and Catherine T. MacArthur Foundation as well as a grant from the AARP Andrus Foundation.

References

Albert, S. C., Sapolsky, R. M., & Altmann, J. (1992). Behavioral, endocrine, and immunological correlates of immigration by an aggressive male into a natural primate group. *Hormones and Behavior, 26*, 167–178.

Aseltine, R. G., & Kessler, R. C. (1993). Marital disruption and depression in a community sample. *Journal of Health and Social Behavior, 34*, 237–251.

Back, K. W., & Bogdonoff, M. D. (1964). Plasma lipid responses to leadership, conformity, and deviation. In H. P. Leiderman & D. Shapiro, (Eds.), *Psychobiological approaches to social behavior* (pp. 24–42). Stanford, CA: Stanford University Press.

Berkman, L. F., & Breslow, L. (1983). *Health and ways of living.* New York: Oxford University Press.

Berkman, L. F., Leo-Summers, L., & Horwitz, R. (1992). Emotional support and survival after myocardial infarction: A prospective, population-based study of the elderly. *Annals of Internal Medicine, 117*, 1003–1009.

Biegel, D. E., McCardle, E., & Mendelson, S. (1985). *Social networks and mental health: An annotated bibliography.* Beverly Hills, CA: Sage.

Bland, S. H., Krogh, V., Winkelstein, W., & Trevisan, M. (1991). Social network and blood pressure: A population study. *Psychosomatic Medicine, 53*, 598–607.

Blazer, D. (1982). Social support and mortality in an elderly community population. *American Journal of Epidemiology, 115*, 684–694.

Bloom, B. L., Asher, S. J., & White, S. W. (1978). Marital disruption as a stressor: A review and analysis. *Psychological Bulletin, 85*, 867–894.

Blumenthal, J. A., Burg, M. M., Barefoot, J., Williams, R. B., Haney, T., & Zimet, G. (1987). Social support, type A behavior, and coronary artery disease. *Psychosomatic Medicine, 49*, 331–340.

Bovard, E. W. (1961). A concept of hypothalamic functioning. *Perspectives in Biology and Medicine, Autumn*, 52–60.

Bovard, E. W. (1962). The balance between negative and positive brain system activity. *Perspectives in Biology and Medicine, Autumn*, 116–127.

Bovard, E. W. (1985). Brain mechanisms in effects of social support on viability. In R. B. Williams, Jr. (Ed.), *Perspectives on behavioral medicine. Vol. 2. Neuroendocrine control and behavior* (pp. 103–129). Orlando, FL: Academic.

Bovbjerg, V. E., McCann, B. S., Brief, D. J., Follette, W. C., Retzlaff, B. M., Dowdy, A. A., Walden, C. E., & Knopp, R. H. (1995). Spouse support and long-term adherence to lipid-lowering diets. *American Journal of Epidemiology, 141,* 451–460.

Bowling, A. (1987). Mortality after bereavement: A review of the literature on survival periods and factors affecting survival. *Social Science and Medicine, 24,* 117–124.

Brindley, D., & Rolland, Y. (1989). Possible connections between stress, diabetes, obesity, hypertension and altered lipoprotein metabolism that may result in atherosclerosis. *Clinical Sciences, 77,* 453–461.

Broadhead, E. W., Kaplan, B. H., James, S. A., Wagner, E. H., Schoenbach, V. J., Grimson, R., Heyden, S., Tibblin, G., & Gehlbach, S. H. (1983). The epidemiologic evidence for a relationship between social support and health. *American Journal of Epidemiology, 117,* 521–537.

Burg, M. M., & Seeman, T. E. (1994). Families and health: The negative side of social ties. *Annals of Behavioral Medicine, 16,* 109–115.

Case, R. B., Moss, A. J., Case, N., McDermott, M., & Eberly, S. (1992). Living alone after myocardial infarction: Impact on prognosis. *Journal of the American Medical Association, 267,* 515–519.

Cassel, J. (1976). The contribution of the social environment to host resistance. *American Journal of Epidemiology, 104,* 107–123.

Clarkson, T. B., Kaplan, J. R., Adams, M. R., & Manuck, S. B. (1987). Psychosocial influences on the pathogenesis of atherosclerosis among nonhuman primates. *Circulation, 76*(Suppl. 1), 1–29.

Cobb, S. (1974). Physiologic changes in men whose jobs were abolished. *Journal of Psychosomatic Research, 18,* 245–258.

Cohen, S. (1991). Social supports and physical health: Symptoms, health behaviors, and infectious disease. In E. M. Cummings, A. L. Greene, & K. H. Karraker (Eds.), *Life-span developmental psychology: Perspectives on stress and coping* (pp. 213–234). Hillsdale, NJ: Lawrence Erlbaum.

Cohen, S., & Syme, S. L. (1984). Social support and health. Orlando, FL: Academic.

Colantonio A., Kasl, S. V., & Ostfeld, A. M. (1992). Depressive symptoms and other psychosocial factors as predictors of stroke in the elderly. *American Journal of Epidemiology, 136,* 884–894.

Colantonio, A., Kasl, S. V., Ostfeld, A. M., & Berkman, L. F. (1993). Psychosocial predictors of stroke outcomes in an elderly population. *Journal of Gerontology, 48,* S261–S268.

Dean, A., Kolody, B., & Wood, P. (1990). Effects of social support from various sources on depression in elderly persons. *Journal of Health and Social Behavior, 31,* 148–161.

Dressler, W. W. (1983). Blood pressure, relative weight, and psychosocial resources. *Psychosomatic Medicine, 45,* 527–536.

Dressler, W. W., Dos Santos, E. J., & Viteri, F. E. (1986). Blood pressure, ethnicity, and psychosocial resources. *Psychosomatic Medicine, 48,* 509–519.

Duncan, T. E., & McAuley, E. (1993). Social support and efficacy cognitions in exercise adherence: A latent growth curve analysis. *Journal of Behavioral Medicine, 16,* 199–218.

Eliot, R. S., Buell, J. C., & Dembroski, T. M. (1982). Bio-behavioral perspectives on coronary heart disease, hypertension and sudden cardiac death. *Acta Medica Scandinavica, 13*(Suppl. 660), 203–219.

Findley, T. (1949). Role of neurohypophysis in the pathogenesis of hypertension and some allied disorders associated with aging. *American Journal of Medicine, 7,* 70–84.

Friedland, J., & McColl, M. (1987). Social support and psychosocial dysfunction after stroke: Buffering effects in a community sample. *Archives of Physical Medicine Rehabilitation, 68,* 475–480.

George, L. K. (1989). Stress, social support, and depression over the life-course. In K. Markides & C. Cooper (Eds.), *Aging, stress, social support, and health* (pp. 241–267). London: Wiley.

Gerin, W., Pieper, C., Levy, R., & Pickering, T. G. (1992). Social support in social interaction: A moderator of cardiovascular reactivity. *Psychosomatic Medicine, 54*, 324–336.

Glass, T., & Maddox, G. L. (1992). The quality and quantity of social support: Stroke recovery as psycho-social transition. *Social Science and Medicine, 34*, 1249–1261.

Gore, S. (1978). The effect of social support in moderating the health consequences of unemployment. *Journal of Health and Social Behavior, 19*, 157–165.

Gray, J. A. (1995). A model of the limbic system and basal ganglia: Applications to anxiety and schizophrenia. In M. S. Gazzaniga (Editor in chief), *The cognitive neurosciences* (pp. 1165–1176). Cambridge, MA: MIT Press.

Hamm, T. E., Jr., Kaplan, J. R., Clarkson, T. B., & Bullock, B. C. (1983). Effects of gender and social behavior on the development of coronary artery atherosclerosis in cynomolgus macaques. *Atherosclerosis, 48*, 221–233.

Henry, J. P. (1983). Coronary heart disease and arousal of the adrenal cortical axis. In T. M. Dembroski, T. H. Schmidt, & G. Blumchen (Eds.), *Biobehavioral bases of coronary heart disease* (pp. 365–381). Basel, Switzerland: Karger.

House, J. S., Landis, K. R., & Umberson, D. (1988). Social relationships and health. *Science, 241*, 540–545.

House, J. S., Robbins, C., & Metzner, H. L. (1982). The association of social relationships and activities with mortality: Prospective evidence from the Tecumseh Community Health Study. *American Journal of Epidemiology, 116*, 123–140.

Johnson, T. P. (1991). Mental health, social relations, and social selection: A longitudinal analysis. *Journal of Health and Social Behavior, 32*, 408–423.

Kaplan, G. A., Salonen, J. T., Cohen, R. D., Brand, R. J., Syme, L., & Puska, P. (1988). Social connections and mortality from all causes and cardiovascular disease: Prospective evidence from eastern Finland. *American Journal of Epidemiology, 128*, 370–380.

Kaplan, J. R., Adams, M. R., Clarkson, T. B., & Koritnik, D. R. (1984). Psychosocial influences on female "protection" among cynomolgus macaques. *Atherosclerosis, 53*, 283–295.

Kaplan, J. R., Adams, M. R., Clarkson, T. B., Manuck, S. B., & Shively, C. A. (1991). Social behavior and gender in biomedical investigations using monkeys: Studies in atherogenesis. *Laboratory Animal Sciences, 41*, 334–343.

Kaplan, J. R., Manuck, S. B., Clarkson, T. B., Lusso, F. M., & Taub, D. M. (1982). Social status, environment, and atherosclerosis in cynomolgus monkeys. *Arteriosclerosis, 2*, 359–368.

Kaplan, J. R., Manuck, S. B., Clarkson, T. B., Lusso, F. M., Taub, D. M., & Miller, E. W. (1983). Social stress and atherosclerosis in normocholesterolemic monkeys. *Science, 220*, 733–735.

Kemp, V. H., & Hatmaker, D. D. (1989). Stress and social support in high-risk pregnancy. *Research in Nursing and Health, 12*, 331–336.

Kessler, R. C., & MacLeod, J. D. (1985). Social support and mental health in community samples. In S. Cohen & S. L. Syme (Eds.), *Social support* (pp. 219–240). Orlando, FL: Academic.

Kessler, R. C., MacLeod, J. D., & Wethington, E. (1985). The costs of caring: A perspective on the relationship between sex and psychological distress. In I. G. Sarason & B. R. Sarason (Eds.), *Social support: Theory, research and applications* (pp. 491–506). Dordrecht, Netherlands: Martinus Nijhoff.

Kiecolt-Glaser, J. K., Glaser, R., Cacioppo, J. T., MacCallum, R. C., Snydersmith, M., Kim, C., & Malarkay, W. B. (1997). Marital conflict in older adults: Endocrinological and immunological correlates. *Psychosomatic Medicine, 59*, 339–349.

Kissel, S. (1965). Stress-reducing properties of social stimuli. *Journal of Personality and Social Psychology, 2*, 378–384.

Krantz, D. S., & Manuck, S. B. (1984). Acute psycophysiologic reactivity and risk of cardiovascular disease: A review and methodologic critique. *Psychological Bulletin, 96*, 435–464.

Krumholz, H. M., Butler, J., Miller, J., Vaccarino, V., Williams, C., Mendes de Leon, C. F., Seeman, T. E., Kasl, S. V., & Berkman, L. F. (1998). The prognostic importance of emotional support for elderly patients hospitalized with heart failure. *Circulation, 97*, 958–964.

LeDoux, J. E. (1995). In search of an emotional system in the brain: leaping from fear to emotion and consciousness. In M. S. Gazzaniga (Editor in chief), *The cognitive neurosciences* (pp. 1049–1062). Cambridge, MA: MIT Press.

Lepore, S. J., Mata-Allen, K. A., & Evans, G. W. (1993). Social support lowers cardiovascular reactivity to an acute stressor. *Psychosomatic Medicine, 55*, 518–524.

Linden, W., Chambers, L., Maurice, J., & Lenz, J. W. (1993). Sex differences in social support, self-deception, hostility, and ambulatory cardiovascular activity. *Health Psychology, 12*, 376–380.

Matthews, K. A., Weiss, S. M., Detre, T., Dembroski, T. M., Falkner, B., Manuck, S. B., & Williams, R. B. (1986). *Handbook of stress, reactivity, and cardiovascular disease.* New York: John Wiley and Sons.

McEwen, B. S. (1995). Stressful experience, brain, and emotions: Developmental, genetic, and hormonal influences. In M. S. Gazzaniga (Editor in chief), *The cognitive neurosciences* (pp. 1117–1135). Cambridge, MA: MIT Press.

McEwen, B. S., & Stellar, E. (1993). Stress and the individual: Mechanisms leading to disease. *Archives of Internal Medicine, 153*, 2093–2101.

McLeroy, K. R., DeVellis, R., DeVellis, B., Kaplan, B., & Toole, J. (1984). Social support and physical recovery in a stroke population. *Journal of Social and Personal Relationships, 1*, 395–413.

Medalie, J. H., & Goldbourt, U. (1976). Angina pectoris among 10,000 men: II. Psychosocial and other risk factors as evidenced by a multivariate analysis of a five-year incidence study. *American Journal of Medicine, 60*, 910–921.

Moritz, D. J., Kasl, S. V., & Berkman, L. F. (1989). The health impact of living with a cognitively impaired elderly spouse: depressive symptoms and social functioning. *Journal of Gerontology, 44*, S17–S27.

Munck, A., & Guyre, P. M. (1991). Glucocorticoids and immune function. In R. Ader, D. L. Felten, & N. Cohen (Eds.), *Psychoneuroimmunology* (2d ed., pp. 447–474). New York: Academic.

Munck, A., Guyre, P. M., & Holbrook, N. J. (1984). Physiological function of glucocorticoids in stress and their relation to pharmacological actions. *Endocrine Review, 5*, 25–44.

Orth-Gomer, K., & Johnson, J. (1987). Social network interaction and mortality: A six-year follow-up of a random sample of the Swedish population. *Journal of Chronic Disease, 40*, 949–957.

Orth-Gomer, K., Rosengren, A., & Wilhelmsen, L. (1993). Lack of social support and incidence of coronary heart disease in middle-aged Swedish men. *Psychosomatic Medicine, 55*, 37–43.

Oxman, T. E., Berkman, L. F., Kasl, S. V., Freeman, D. H., & Barrett, J. (1992). Social support and depressive symptoms in the elderly. *American Journal of Epidemiology, 135*, 356–368.

Phillips, R. G., & LeDoux, J. E. (1992). Differential contribution of amygdala and hippocampus to cured and contextual fear conditioning. *Behavioral Neuroscience, 2*, 274–285.

Pope, M. K., & Smith, T. W. (1991). Cortisol excretion in high and low cynically hostile men. *Psychosomatic Medicine, 53*, 386–392.

Ray, J. C., & Sapolsky, R. M. (1992). Styles of male social behavior and their endocrine correlates among high-ranking wild baboons. *American Journal of Primatology, 28*, 231–250.

Reed, D. , McGee, D., Yano, K., & Feinleib, M. (1983). Social networks and coronary heart disease among Japanese men in Hawaii. *American Journal of Epidemiology, 117*, 384–396.

Rook, K. S. (1984). The negative side of social interaction: Impact on psychological well-being. *Journal of Personality and Social Psychology, 46,* 1097–1108.

Ruberman, W., Weinblatt, E., Goldberg, J. D., & Chaudhary, B. S. (1984). Psychosocial influences on mortality after myocardial infarction. *New England Journal of Medicine, 311,* 552–559.

Sallis, J. F., Hovell, M. F., Hofstetter, C. R., Faucher, P., Elder, J. P., Blanchard, J., Caspersen, C. J., Powell, K. E., & Christenson, G. M. (1989). A multivariate study of determinants of vigorous exercise in a community sample. *Preventive Medicine, 18,* 20–34.

Sapolsky, R. M. (1983). Endocrine aspects of social instability in the olive baboon (Papio anubis). *American Journal of Primatology, 5,* 365–379.

Sapolsky, R. M. (1989). Hypercortisolism among socially subordinate wild baboons originates at the CNS level. *Archives of General Psychiatry, 46,* 1047–1051.

Sapolsky, R. M. (1992). *Stress, the aging brain, and the mechanisms of neuron death.* Cambridge, MA: MIT Press.

Sapolsky, R. M. (1993). Endocrinology alfresco: Psychoendocrine studies of wild baboons. *Recent Progress in Hormone Research, 48,* 437–468.

Sapolsky, R. M., & Mott, G. E. (1987). Social subordinance in wild baboons is associated with suppressed high density lipoprotein–cholesterol concentrations: The possible role of chronic social stress. *Endocrinology, 121,* 1605–1610.

Schneiderman, N. (1983). Behavior, autonomic function and animal models of cardiovascular pathology. In T. M. Dembroski, T. H. Schmidt, & G. Blumchen (Eds.), *Biobehavioral bases of coronary heart disease* (pp. 304–351). New York: Karger.

Schoenbach, V. J., Kaplan, B. G., Fredman, L., & Kleinbaum, D. G. (1968). Social ties and mortality in Evans county, Georgia. *American Journal of Epidemiology, 123,* 577–591.

Seeman, M., Seeman, T., & Sayles, M. (1985). Social networks and health status: A longitudinal analysis. *Social Psychology Quarterly, 48,* 237–248.

Seeman, T. E., Berkman, L. F., Blazer, D., & Rowe, J. (1994). Social ties and support and neuroendocrine function: MacArthur studies of successful aging. *Annals of Behavioral Medicine, 16,* 95–106.

Seeman, T. E., Berkman, L. F., Kohout, F., LaCroix, A., Glynn, R., & Blazer, D. (1993). Intercommunity variation in the association between social ties and mortality in the elderly: A comparative analysis of three communities. *Annals of Epidemiology, 3,* 325–335.

Seeman, T. E., Bruce, M. L., & McAvay, G. (1996). Social network characteristics and onset of ADL disability: MacArthur studies of successful aging. *Journal of Gerontology: Social Sciences, 51B,* S191–S200.

Seeman, T. E., Kaplan, G. A., Knudsen, L., Cohen, R., & Guralnik, J. (1987). Social ties and mortality in the elderly: A comparative analysis of age-dependent patterns of association. *American Journal of Epidemiology, 126,* 714–723.

Seeman, T. E., & Syme, S. L. (1987). Social networks and coronary artery disease: A comparative analysis of network structural and support characteristics. *Psychosomatic Medicine, 49,* 341–354.

Shively, C., & Kaplan, J. (1984). Effects of social factors on adrenal weight and related physiology of Macaca fascicularis. *Physiology and Behavior, 33,* 777–782.

Smith, T. W., Pope, M. K., Sanders, J. D., Allred, K. D., & O'Keefe, J. L. (1988). Cynical hostility at home and work: Psychosocial vulnerability across domains. *Journal of Research in Personality, 22,* 525–548.

Stroebe, W., & Stroebe, M. S. (1987). *Bereavement and health: The psychological and physical consequences of partner loss.* New York: Cambridge University Press.

Suomi, S. J., Scanlan, J. M., Rasmussen, K. L. R., Davidson, M., Boinski, S., Higley, J. D., & Marriott, B. (1989). Pituitary-adrenal response to capture in Cayo Santiago–derived group M rhesus monkeys. *Puerto Rico Health Sciences Journal, 8,* 171–176.

Thomas, P. D., Goodwin, J. M., & Goodwin, J. S. (1985). Effect of social support on stress-related changes in cholesterol level, uric acid level, and immune function in an elderly sample. *American Journal of Psychiatry, 142,* 735–737.

Troxler, R. G., Sprague, E. A., Albanese, R. A., Fuchs, R., & Thompson, A. J. (1977). The association of elevated plasma cortisol and early atherosclerosis as demonstrated by coronary angiography. *Atherosclerosis, 26,* 151–162.

Truhan, A. P., & Ahmed, A. R. (1989). Corticosteroids: A review with emphasis on complications of prolonged systemic therapy. *Annals of Allergy, 62,* 375–391.

Umberson, D. (1987). Family status and health behaviors: social control as a dimension of social integration. *Journal of Health and Social Behavior, 28,* 306–319.

Umberson, D., & Chen, M. D. (1994). Effects of a parent's death on adult children: Relationship salience and reaction to loss. *American Sociological Review, 59,* 152–168.

Unden, A. L., Orth-Gomer, K., & Elofsson, S. (1991). Cardiovascular effects of social support in the work place: Twenty-four-hour ECG monitoring of men and women. *Psychosomatic Medicine, 53,* 50–60.

Vogt, T. M., Mullooly, J. P., Ernst, D., Pope, C. R., & Hollis, J. F. (1992). Social networks as predictors of ischemic heart disease, cancer, stroke and hypertension: Incidence, survival and mortality. *Journal of Clinical Epidemiology, 45,* 659–666.

Welin, L., Tibblin, G., Svardsudd, K., Tibblin, B., Ander-Peciva, S., Larsson, B., & Wilhelmsen, L. (1985). Prospective study of social influence on mortality: The study of men born in 1913 and 1923. *Lancet, 1,* 915–918.

Williams, R. B., Jr., (1985). Neuroendocrine response patterns and stress: Biobehavioral mechanisms of disease. In R. B. Williams, Jr. (Ed.), *Perspectives on behavioral medicine. Vol. 2. Neuroendocrine control and behavior* (pp. 71–101). Orlando, FL: Academic.

Williams, R. B., Barefoot, J. C., Califf, R. M., Haney, T. L., Saunders, W. B., Pryor, D. B., Hlatky, M. A., Siegler, I. C., & Mark, D. B. (1992). Prognostic importance of social and economic resources among medically treated patients with angiographically documented coronary artery disease. *Journal of the American Medical Association, 267,* 520–524.

Wortman, C. B., & Conway, T. L. (1985). The role of social support in adaptation and recovery from physical illness. In S. Cohen & S. L. Syme (Eds.), *Social support and health.* New York: Academic.

Zagorin, P. (1968). Thomas Hobbes. In D. L. Sills (Ed.), *International encyclopedia of the social sciences* (pp. 481–486). New York: MacMillan and Free Press.

Commentary

Christine M. L. Kwan

In this chapter, Teresa Seeman discusses evidence that links social relationships to physical health, with particular focus on overall longevity, coronary heart disease, and mental health. She also reviews research that shows the effects of social relationships on physiological activity. These effects highlight possible biological pathways through which social environment characteristics influence morbidity and mortality.

The chapter is divided into two major parts. In the first half, Seeman examines epidemiological studies that document consistent associations between social integration and mortality risk, as well as studies that link social integration to physical and mental health. Regarding physical health, Seeman shows that social support and reported levels of "being loved" (but not social integration) were inversely related to the extent of coronary artery disease among angiography patients (Seeman & Syme, 1987). The link between social relationships and incidence of coronary heart disease was less consistent, however. Seeman suggests that such inconsistency may be due to the fact that greater social integration might also implicate greater interpersonal conflicts or other such problems, therefore leading to mixed effects on health risks. The unclear association between social integration and incidence of coronary heart disease is compounded by the paucity of studies that include female participants. Future research that examines such relationships among women is particularly in order. Also discussed were studies that showed consistent associations of social integration with prognosis post–myocardial infarction and poststroke. Greater emotional support was suggested to contribute to the protective benefits of social integration after onset of these cardiovascular diseases and thereby aid recovery. With respect to mental health, Seeman concludes that studies consistently show positive effects of social integration, along with increased risks for psychological distress resulting from social isolation and/or loss of important social ties. A key point stressed by Seeman is that quality of social relations matters. Importantly, social relationships can also have potentially negative impacts on physical and mental health via their demands and criticisms.

In the latter half of the chapter, Seeman provides insight about how others "get under our skin" by delineating evidence of physiologic effects tied to social relationships. According to Seeman, one primary pathway that links the social world to internal physiology is that social connections affect cognitive/emotional processing and interpretations of environmental stimuli, which in turn influence neuroendocrine arousal. Therefore, while acknowledging that various attitudinal and behavioral pathways (e.g. healthful lifestyle, smoking cessation) mediate the effect of social relationships on health, Seeman's emphasis is on research that demonstrates the social relationship influences on health via their direct links on physiology.

Studies of both nonhuman and human primates illustrate the protective impact of positive relational qualities as well as the damaging impact of negative relational qualities. Seeman gives particular attention to work on nonhuman primates, where the effect of position in a social hierarchy on disease risks was shown to vary across stable versus unstable situations and by gender. Specifically, for males, social dominance was associated with more atherosclerosis under conditions of social instability, whereas for females it was associated with less atherosclerosis in both stable and unstable social conditions. In a related vein, Seeman describes Sapolsky's research on free-living baboons, which shows that social dominance has differential physiologic correlates in stable versus unstable social environments. Moreover, styles of social interaction of free-living baboons have differential endocrine correlates, such that positive interaction styles are related to lower basal cortisol and cortisol reactivity, whereas competitive interaction styles are related to greater cortisol reactivity under stress. Together, these studies not only demonstrate the physiologic impact of social relationships, they also speak to their scope and complexity. Specifically, social relationships involve both status hierarchies and interactions in "interanimal" encounters. While many would agree that social status and social interaction are fundamental elements of the social world, these elements have received less research in humans than social integration and social support.

In reviewing studies of human primates, Seeman discusses similar physiologic effects of social relationships found in community-based population studies. From the MacArthur Study of Successful Aging (Seeman, Berkman, Blazer, & Rowe, 1994), for example, it was found that, for men, higher emotional support was consistently related to lower levels of cortisol, norepinephrine, and epinephrine, and higher levels in other measures of social relationships were negatively associated with at least one of these endocrine system indicators. For women, the only significant result was that married women showed lower epinephrine levels. Thus, weaker associations between social relationships and endocrine functioning were found for women than for men. Seeman explains these gender differences with findings from laboratory studies, which suggest that women may be more reactive to negative aspects of social relationships than are men. Going beyond the endocrine system, experimental studies support the link of social connections to both cardiovascular reactivity and autonomic activity, again with positive and negative relational qualities apparently leading to positive and negative physiological functioning, respectively. Seeman calls this the "double-edged sword" of social relationships, which underscores the need to address both the positive and negative qualities of social ties and their differential physiological impacts. A final note pertains to the observation that negative relational qualities, namely social aggression, harm the physiology of not only the recipient but also the purveyor of negativity.

Major Themes of the Volume

Positive and Negative Emotions in Social Relations

The double-edged sword quality of social relationships is an important theme, which is addressed in Seeman's chapter. She notes that, while there are health benefits associated with social support and affiliation, social relationships can also have negative, damaging effects on physiology through their demands and criticisms. For instance, she points out that health benefits of social integration are possibly modulated by the greater amount of interpersonal conflict and/or problems that accompanies social integration. She also notes that negative relational qualities, such as competitive social interactions, social demands and conflicts, nonsupportive interactions, and cynical hostility, may deteriorate physiological functioning. In sum, social relationships have the potential for both positive and negative health and physiologic effects (Seeman & McEwen, 1996).

Seeman examines the health implications of particular social emotions (e.g., feeling loved) (Seeman & Syme, 1987) and highlights the impact of emotional support for the severity of atherosclerosis (Blumenthal et al., 1987), recovery from myocardial infarction (Berkman, Leo-Summers, & Horwitz, 1992) and stroke (e.g., Glass & Maddox, 1992), and physical performance (Seeman et al., 1995). However, to further explore connections between emotions embodied in social relationships and health as well as physiology, it will be necessary to explore the role of diverse emotions in the social realm. As Seeman discusses, positive and negative relational qualities have differential implications for positive or negative cognitions and emotions, avenues through which relational qualities influence physiological functioning. Therefore, for example, what are the specific emotions that accompany, or result from, emotional support? The possible roles of emotions, such as security, warmth, affirmation, intimacy, and affection, in emotional support should be evaluated. In addition, while emotional support is likely to be predominantly positive, it may also implicate negative emotions, such as shame or anger that results from a sense of low autonomy or dependence. What is the physiologic impact of the mixed emotions that might characterize a relationship high on emotional support? Answers to these questions could enhance the understanding of biological pathways that link emotion, a significant component of lives in the social realm, to physiology and health.

Gender Differences

Gender differences were prominent in the studies that Seeman discussed. For instance, she noted that, among macaques, social dominance protects against atherosclerosis in both stable and unstable social situations for females but only in stable social situations for males (Hamm, Kaplan, Clarkson, & Bullock, 1983). In humans, data from the MacArthur Study of Successful Aging (Seeman, Berkman, Blazer, & Rowe, 1994) showed that associations between social support and endocrine activity are more consistent for men than for women. Seeman suggests that these differences may be due to the fact that demands and conflict in social relations are greater among women, as well as that women may be more reactive to negative aspects of social relations.

Nonetheless, some questions regarding gender differences in the way social relationships get under our skin await further attention. For example, are there gender differences in the biological pathways that link relationships to physiology? Might gender differences in baseline physiology (e.g., estrogen levels) explain distinct relations between social relations and physiology for men versus women? Phenomenologically, what is the role of the differential importance of the social realm to men versus women in affecting physiologic reactivity to different relational qualities? From a sociological perspective, does social hierarchy, such as gender inequality and socially constructed gender roles, have an impact on the way social relations are linked to physiology? Pertinent to Seeman's hypothesis, men and women may have somewhat unique biopsychosocial pathways through which social relationships affect morbidity and mortality. Future work that addresses these questions could enrich our understanding of the role of gender in the physiological and health implications of social relationships.

Age is noted as an important factor in the discussion of gender differences. Seeman suggests that women who are premenopausal are "not yet into their period of highest mortality risk," which possibly contributes to the finding that men are more strongly protected by social integration than women (House, Robbins, & Metzner, 1982; Kaplan et al., 1988), a pattern that may disappear at older ages among postmenopausal women, particularly those not on hormone replacement therapy. Thus, gender differences in the relation between social relationships and physiology may be mediated by age, thereby underscoring the need to track age when interpreting gender differences in how social relations get under our skin.

Mechanisms that Link Social Relations to Health

Seeman's chapter is first and foremost about the mechanisms that link social relations to health. She provides evidence to support the view that social ties have direct biological effects on physiology, thereby helping to explain research that has previously linked social relationships to morbidity and mortality. While Seeman acknowledges the presence of other mechanisms (e.g., behavioral), which mediate the influence of social relationships on health, her contribution pertains to biological pathways through which social relations get under our skin. Extensive evidence supports the impact of social integration or qualities of social relations to multiple physiologic parameters, such as indices of cardiovascular functioning, the hypothalamic-pituitary-adrenal (HPA) axis, and the sympathetic nervous system (SNS).

While Seeman richly delineates the mediating role of individual physiologic systems, less is said about the overall biological pathways constituted by the likely intersection and interaction among these separate regulatory systems. Nevertheless, other recent work by Seeman on allostatic load (see below) provides ways of thinking about the integrated action of individual physiologic systems and their cumulative impact on health and disease.

Cumulative Effects

Seeman's prior work underscores the importance of cumulative patterns of physiological activity, perhaps resulting from social relationship histories. A crucial idea is that repetitive, chronic physiological activity may account for variations in health and disease outcomes. Specifically, allostatic load, introduced by McEwen and Stellar (1993) as the cumulative physiologic toll exacted on the body through repeated adjustments and adaptations to environmental demands or stress, has been operationalized by Seeman and colleagues (1997) with ten indicators that index functioning across multiple regulatory systems. Elevations in allostatic load have been shown to predict, over a 2.5-year period, decline in physical functioning and memory loss, as well as incident cardiovascular disease in a group of initially high-functioning older men and women. In a 7.5-year follow-up, higher baseline allostatic load has also been shown to be associated with higher risks for mortality and incident cardiovascular disease. People with the highest level of allostatic load (7 or more) also showed substantial decline in physical and cognitive functioning (Seeman et al., 2000). Complementing the emphasis on meaningful social ties on multiple physiologic systems, research on allostatic load indicates the cumulative influence of chronic physiologic activity on diverse health outcomes. What is needed is more explicit linkage of the social relationship realm with allostatic load (see below).

Shifting attention to the conceptualization of social relationships, Seeman provides a particularly interesting perspective on the meaning of cumulation in social relations via the nonhuman primate studies. Social status, or position in the hierarchy of one's social group, was shown to have physiologic and health consequences (e.g., Kaplan, Adams, Clarkson, Manuck, & Shively, 1991; Sapolsky, 1989). Social status itself is a product of the social structure and, when translated to the human level, could mean anything from socioeconomic status at a macro level to interpersonal dominance versus subordination at a micro level. In fact, it has been noted that position in social hierarchy could be measured from a structural perspective (e.g., education and income) and a psychological perspective (e.g., one's subjective social standing, which results from social comparison processes) (Singer, Ryff, Carr, & Magee, 1998). Such an approach speaks to a broader conceptualization of social relationships than is typically pursued. Thus, Seeman's discussion calls for novel approaches in examining cumulative social relationships.

Multiple Methods

Seeman integrates evidence from both human and nonhuman primate studies to illustrate the physiological impact of social relationships. She demonstrates the value of animal models, including monkeys and baboons, for understanding biological pathways through which social relations affect physiological risks. Indeed, both experimental and naturalistic evidence from nonhuman primates demonstrates the impact of social stress, social status, and social interactions on physiological activity (e.g., Kaplan et al., 1991; Ray & Sapolsky, 1992; Sapolsky, 1993). This evidence converges nicely with findings from humans. Community-based population studies and experimental research on human primates show differential physiologic effects of various structural measures of social ties and qualitative measures of social support (e.g., Kiecolt-Glaser et al., 1997; Lepore, Mata-Allen, & Evans, 1993; Seeman et al., 1994). Consistency of results from studies across human and nonhuman primates suggests that, at a general level, mediating physiologic mechanisms that link social relations and health may operate in similar fashion for many social animals.

Multiple methods were used to assess social relationships. In nonhuman primate studies, social relationships were assessed with naturalistic observations via Sapolsky's correlational studies (Sapolsky, 1993) and manipulated by varying levels of social stress in experimental studies (Kaplan, Manuck, Clarkson, Lusso, & Taub, 1982; Kaplan et al., 1991). In human primate studies, social relationships were measured with self-report evaluations of social ties and social support (Seeman et al., 1994) as well as with observations of marital interaction in correlational studies (Kiecolt-Glaser et al., 1997), and they were manipulated by varying levels of social support in experimental studies (Lepore et al., 1993). Importantly, correlational research identified general patterns of association between the social environment and health or physiology. Experimental studies identified specific components of the social environment that affect health or physiology and clarified directionality of causality, which correlational studies can only infer.

In all, Seeman's argument for direct physiological benefits and costs of social relationships is persuasively substantiated by consistent evidence obtained with diverse methodological approaches and from different primate populations.

Cross-Talk with Other Chapters

Seeman highlights the differential impact of positive and negative aspects of social relationships on physiology. But what constitutes such positivity and negativity in interpersonal encounters? Research by Gottman, Spiegel, and Reis suggests useful avenues for elaborating the factors that compose such relational qualities.

Gottman suggests that negative emotions can have positive effects but whether positive impact is realized depends on how one deals with those emotions. He describes how emotion-coaching parents help their children to explore their negative emotions and to use them as a tool for intimacy and teaching, whereas emotion-dismissing parents reject their children's negative emotions and even punish children for expression of negative emotions. Children raised by emotion-coaching parents have been shown to be better in understanding and regulating emotions, self-soothing, and focusing attention. Such results suggest that the ability to effectively deal with negative emotions, including those experienced in significant social relationships, is an important feature of emotion regulation, which would be expected to have beneficial health consequences. In a related vein, Pennebaker (1995) found that talking or writing about a traumatic event helps people to acknowledge its emotional consequences, thereby facilitating the ability to come to terms with it and, thus, reducing its adverse impact. This research also speaks to the possible psychological benefits that, for some, may be the sequelae of negative emotion.

Applied to Seeman's chapter, it would be important to discern whether it is the quality of social relation itself or how the individual responds to the social interaction within it that accounts for the observed physiologic impact of social ties. In other words, emotional intelligence (Goleman, 1995) or meta-emotions (Gottman, Katz, & Hooven, 1995) may moderate the way in which social relationships get under the skin. Future studies need to explore the implication of emotional intelligence and meta-emotions for the link between social relations and physiology.

Similar to Gottman, Spiegel views emotion as playing a central role in determining the health impact of social relationships. Specifically, Spiegel examines supportive/expressive psychotherapy groups and their health benefits in terms of survival time for women with breast cancer. Such psychosocial intervention with an emphasis on emotional expression may be helpful for facilitating recovery from other diseases. For instance, it may help stroke patients, who are discussed in Seeman's chapter, express and deal with negative emotions resulting from restricted mobility, thereby aiding recovery. Other elements of supportive/expressive group psychotherapy, such as increasing family support, facilitating communication with physicians, and symptom control, are also likely to be beneficial for recovery from stroke and other diseases.

Seeman's efforts to identify physiologic mechanisms that link social relationships to health could enrich Spiegel's research with breast cancer patients. He, in fact, discusses endocrine and immune systems as potentially mediating the effect of psychosocial support on disease progression (Spiegel, Sephton, Terr, & Stites, 1998), although such physiologic assessments of patients in the support groups are not presented in his chapter.

Seeman's discussion of the role of dominance hierarchy and social interaction styles on physiology and health is also relevant for Spiegel's work. With respect to dominance hierarchy, people of different socioeconomic status or different positions within a social group may react differently to a supportive/expressive psychotherapy group. In regard to social interaction styles, people who are more used to expressing and sharing inner emotions with others may find this specific approach of psychotherapy more (or less) helpful than people who are less comfortable with emotional openness.

Reis's research on everyday social interaction using daily experience methods provides useful avenues to illuminate the key components of interpersonal encounters that constitute the positive and negative aspects of social relationships. In particular, moment-to-moment social interaction may reveal what goes into general evaluations of social tie quantity and quality, which is often used in epidemiological studies. In linking microanalytic assessments to global reports of social relationships, it would be important to ascertain the extent to which the two provide consistent information about one's relational profile. Also, how might moment-to-moment interactions affect global evaluations of relationships? Conversely, how might global evaluations of relationships affect moment-to-moment interactions? Research that can illuminate these questions would be valuable.

It would also be interesting to map cross-time patterns of social interaction, using Reis's microanalytic assessment methods, onto the physiologic variables described by Seeman. For instance, do specific patterns of social interaction covary with, or lead to changes in, neuroendocrine regulation? In fact, as referenced in Seeman's chapter, the study of free-living baboons' actual styles of social interaction and their endocrine correlates (Ray & Sapolsky, 1992) exemplifies such investigation with nonhuman primates. What is worth attempting is conducting similar studies at the human level: utilizing daily experience methods to identify patterns of social interactions over time and mapping them onto patterns of changes in physiology. Such investigation could valuably shed light on whether the physiologic impact of cross-time patterns of social interactions parallels that of global evaluations of social relationships.

Gottman, Spiegel, and Reis all assess social relationships with more microanalytic, daily diary, or observational measures, whereas Seeman utilizes primarily larger survey, epidemiological studies where self-report of general relationship evaluations are prominent. Although population-level studies offer high generalizability, their large scale makes in-depth assessment of social relationship qualities a greater challenge. Nevertheless, Ryff and Singer's work suggests that it is feasible to probe into positive and negative aspects of emotional features of social ties in large-scale survey studies by working with particular subsamples. Instruments that can better discriminate among different qualities of particular social ties, which are relatively easily incorporated into epidemiological studies, were used in their study. Those measures, which are more informative because they tap into differentiated dimensions (e.g., emotional, sexual, recreational, and social intimacy; caring and overprotection) of diverse social relations (e.g., spouse, parents, friends, coworkers), point to an opportunity for enrichment in Seeman's research program.

A counterpart to Seeman's emphasis on biological cumulation (i.e., allostatic load) is Ryff and Singer et al.'s emphasis on cumulative relationship profiles. While cross-sectional data provide sufficient evidence to show the impact of social relationships on health via biological pathways, longitudinal data that assess relational histories and their emotional features across relationship types and across time are promising for demonstrating even stronger associations between the social world and health via physiology. Indeed, Ryff and Singer's work with the Wisconsin Longitudinal Study has already supported the link between positive and negative relationship pathways and allostatic load as operationalized by Seeman and colleagues. This speaks to the potential of cumulative socioemotional experience in complementing research on allostatic load.

Allostatic load addresses the importance of cumulative physiologic activity across multiple regulatory systems on health and disease. Ideas from Coe and Lubach's and Cohen's work on immunity may prove instrumental for enriching the formulation of allostatic load. Specifically, an index of immune system function is missing from the present operationalization of allostatic load, although the immune system has been suggested to be a key mediator of the social environment–health linkage in Coe and Lubach's and Cohen's research. An avenue for future research might be to incorporate measures of immunity (e.g., natural killer cell activity, antibody response) into the operationalization of allostatic load, thereby enriching the comprehensiveness of the physiological systems covered.

In all, Seeman's chapter provides valuable insight as to how social relationships get under the skin to affect health and disease. She reviews the well-established link between social relationships and health and demonstrates how physiologic activity serves as a key mediating pathway that links the two, giving emphasis to gender differences along the way. Future work may benefit from elaborating on the relational and emotional substance of particular social ties studied in epidemiological research and by utilizing a cumulative, life-history approach to social relationships. On the side of physiology, additional attention to immune system function may contribute to a more comprehensive formulation of the cumulative physiologic risk or benefit that ensues from social relationships.

References

Berkman, L. F., Leo-Summers, L., & Horwitz, R. (1992). Emotional support and survival after myocardial infarction: A prospective, population-based study of the elderly. *Annals of Internal Medicine, 117*, 1003–1009.

Blumenthal, J. A., Burg, M. M., Barefoot, J., Williams, R. B., Haney, T., & Zimet, G. (1987). Social support, type A behavior, and coronary artery disease. *Psychosomatic Medicine, 49*, 331–340.

Glass, T., & Maddox, G. L. (1992). The quality and quantity of social support: Stroke recovery as psycho-social transition. *Social Science and Medicine, 34*, 1249–1261.

Goleman, D. (1995). *Emotional intelligence.* New York: Bantam.

Gottman, J. M., Katz, L., & Hooven, C. (1995). *Meta-emotion.* Hilldale, NJ: Lawrence Erlbaum.

Hamm, T. E., Jr., Kaplan, J. R., Clarkson, T. B., & Bullock, B. C. (1983). Effects of gender and social behavior on the development of coronary artery atherosclerosis in cynomolgus macaques. *Atherosclerosis, 48*, 221–233.

House, J. S., Robbins, C., & Metzner, H. L. (1982). The association of social relationships and activities with mortality: Prospective evidence from the Tecumseh Community Health Study. *American Journal of Epidemiology, 116*, 123–140.

Kaplan, G. A., Salonen, J. T., Cohen, R. D., Brand, R. J., Syme, L., & Puska, P. (1988). Social connections and mortality from all causes and cardiovascular disease: Prospective evidence from eastern Finland. *American Journal of Epidemiology, 128*, 370–380.

Kaplan, J. R., Adams, M. R., Clarkson, T. B., Manuck, S. B., & Shively, C. A. (1991). Social behavior and gender in biomedical investigations using monkeys: Studies in atherogenesis. *Laboratory Animal Sciences, 41*, 334–343.

Kaplan, J. R., Manuck, S. B., Clarkson, T. B., Lusso, F. M., & Taub, D. M. (1982). Social status, environment, and atherosclerosis in cynomolgus monkeys. *Arteriosclerosis, 2*, 359–368.

Kiecolt-Glaser, J. K., Glaser, R., Cacioppo, J. T., MacCallum, R. C., Snydersmith, M., Kim, C., & Malarkey, W. B. (1997). Marital conflict in older adults: Endocrinological and immunological correlates. *Psychosomatic Medicine, 59*(4), 339–349.

Lepore S. J., Mata-Allen, K. A., & Evans, G. W. (1993). Social support lowers cardiovascular reactivity to an acute stressor. *Psychosomatic Medicine, 55*, 518–524.

McEwen, B. S., & Stellar, E. (1993). Stress and the individual: Mechanisms leading to disease. *Archives of Internal Medicine, 153*, 2093–2101.

Pennebaker, J. W. (1995). *Emotion, disclosure, and health.* Washington, DC: American Psychological Association.

Ray, J. C., & Sapolsky, R. M. (1992). Styles of male social behavior and their endocrine correlates among high-ranking wild baboons. *American Journal of Psychiatry, 28*, 231–250.

Sapolsky, R. M. (1989). Hypercortisolism among socially subordinate wild baboons originates at the CNS level. *Archives of General Psychiatry, 46*, 1047–1051.

Sapolsky, R. M. (1993). Endocrinology alfresco: Psychoendocrine studies of wild baboons. *Recent Progress in Hormone Research, 48*, 437–468.

Seeman, T. E., Berkman, L. F., Blazer, D., & Rowe, J. (1994). Social ties and support and neuroendocrine function: MacArthur studies of successful aging. *Annals of Behavioral Medicine, 16*, 95–106.

Seeman, T. E., Berkman, L. F., Charpentier, P. A., Blazer, D., Albert, M. S., & Tinetti, M. E. (1995). Behavioral and psychosocial predictors of physical performance: MacArthur studies of successful aging. *Journal of Gerontology: Medical Sciences, 50A*(4), M177–M183.

Seeman T. E., & McEwen, B. S. (1996). Impact of social environment characteristics on neuroendocrine regulation. *Psychosomatic Medicine, 58*, 459–471.

Seeman, T. E., Singer, B. H., Rowe, J. W., Horwitz, R. I., & McEwen, B. S. (1997). The price of adaptation: Allostatic load and its health consequences: MacArthur studies of successful aging. *Archives of Internal Medicine, 157*, 2259–2268.

Seeman, T. E., Singer, B. H., Rowe, J. W., & McEwen, B. S. (2001). Exploring a new concept of cumulative biological risk: Allostatic load and its health consequences. *Proceedings of National Academy of Sciences* (in press).

Seeman, T. E., & Syme, L. (1987). Social networks and coronary artery disease: A comparison of the structure and function of relations as predictors of disease. *Psychosomatic Medicine, 49*, 341–354.

Singer, B., Ryff, C. D., Carr, D., & Magee, W. J. (1998). Linking life histories and mental health: A person-centered strategy. *Sociological Methodology, 28*, 1–51.

Spiegel, D., Sephton, S. E., Terr, A. I., & Stites, D. P. (1998). Effects of psychosocial treatment in prolonging cancer survival may be mediated by neuroimmune pathways. *Annals of New York Academy of Sciences, 840*, 674–683.

7

Social Relationships and
Susceptibility to the Common Cold

Sheldon Cohen

$\mathcal{S}$ocial relationships are thought to have both negative and positive influences on the ability of our bodies to resist infection. On the negative side, social conflicts are a common cause of stressful environments, including chronic problems at home and work and acute major stressful life events involving family, friends, and workmates. Laboratory studies have found that experimentally induced marital conflicts suppress cellular components of immune function (Kiecolt-Glaser et al., 1993) and epidemiologic studies have linked family conflict with higher risk for naturally acquired upper respiratory infections (Clover, Abell, Becker, Crawford, & Ramsey, 1989; Meyer & Haggerty, 1962). On the positive side, social relationships provide many benefits, including facilitating the motivation to care for oneself, allowing for more effective regulation of emotional responses, and providing support in the face of stressful events (Cohen, 1988; Thoits, 1983). The most provocative evidence that links social relationships to better physical health is the well-established association between participation in multiple social domains (family, friends, work, group memberships) and decreased mortality (e.g., Berkman & Syme, 1979; House, Robbins, & Metzner, 1982). This relation has been reported in multiple prospective studies and has a relative risk (isolated people are approximately two times more likely to die during follow-up) that is comparable in magnitude to the relation between smoking and mortality (e.g., House, Landis, & Umberson, 1988).

The research reported in this chapter assesses the role of social conflicts and social participation in susceptibility to upper respiratory infections. In our studies, we characterize the social environments of healthy volunteers. Subsequently, we expose them to a virus that causes a common cold. Approximately 40% of those exposed develop a verifiable illness. Hence, we can ask whether the status of their social environment before exposure predicts whether their bodies are able to resist infection.

This work is unique in two ways. First, because we intentionally expose healthy volunteers to a controlled dose of virus and quarantine them after exposure, the associations we find between the social environment and illness cannot be attributed to social interaction–based differences in exposure to infectious agents. Second, closely monitoring volunteers (in quarantine) throughout the course of our studies allows us to assess behavioral and biological pathways that might link the social environment to disease susceptibility.

Figure 7.1 presents the plausible pathways that link social conflicts to disease susceptibility, and figure 7.2 presents the pathways that link social participation to susceptibility. The figures are meant only as heuristics for understanding how the social environment gets into the body and, therefore, include only those pathways that start in the social environment and terminate in the ability to resist infectious illness. There are no assumptions implied about other possible pathways.

As apparent from figure 7.1, social conflicts are thought to act through their negative impact on emotions and cognitions. Negative cognitive and emotional

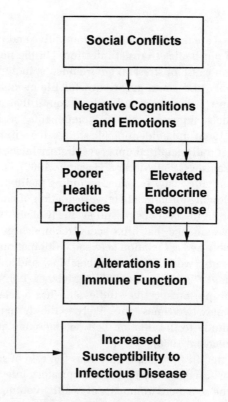

Figure 7.1 Plausible pathways linking social conflicts to disease susceptibility. The figure includes only those pathways that start in the social environment and terminate in the ability to resist infectious illness. There are no assumptions implied about other possible pathways.

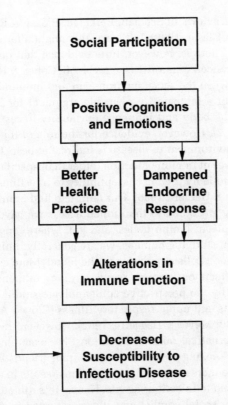

Figure 7.2 Plausible pathways linking social participation to disease susceptibility. The figure includes only those pathways that start in the social environment and terminate in the ability to resist infectious illness. There are no assumptions implied about other possible pathways.

states can result in behavioral coping strategies, such as increased smoking and
decreased exercise and sleep, which may compromise health. Poor health practices can operate directly on an outcome (e.g., cigarette smoke results in inflammation of the nasal mucosa) or by suppressing the immune system's ability to
protect the body against infectious agents. Negative emotions have also been
linked with increases in the release of a number of hormones, including epinephrine, norepinephrine, and cortisol. Elevated levels of these hormones have been
found to suppress the immune system's ability to recognize, mark, and destroy infectious agents (Rabin, Cohen, Ganguli, Lyle, & Cunnick, 1989).

As shown in figure 7.2, positive social relationships can result in a range of
positive cognitions and emotions, including feeling needed, feelings of self-worth
and control, and feelings of well-being and calmness. Clearly, having greater self-
esteem and control can result in increased motivation to care for oneself and, in
turn, better health practices. However, the relation between positive psychological states and endocrine and (especially) immune pathways is more controversial.
There is evidence that positive relationships have acquiescent effects on hor-

monal systems (see reviews in Seeman, Berkman, Blazer, & Rowe, 1994; Uchino, Cacioppo, & Kiecolt-Glaser, 1996). In theory, this might alter immune function in a positive manner. There is, however, little evidence that positive emotions are associated with enhanced immunity (see review in Cohen & Herbert, 1996).

Associations between the social environment and immune regulation provide the underpinning for a biologically plausible argument for how external social stimuli get inside the body and influence our ability to resist infectious agents (e.g., figs. 7.1 and 7.2). However, evidence for the role of the immune system in linking the social environment to disease is indirect at best. The central problem is the lack of measures of immune function (other than specific antibody to the infectious agent) that reliably predict susceptibility to infectious disease in healthy humans (e.g., Cohen & Herbert, 1996). Our failure to find immune markers of host resistance is usually attributed to the limited access we have to the internal organs, such as the spleen, lymph nodes, and gut, where most immune tissue is found. Instead, when studying humans, we are generally limited to assessing the function of white blood cells circulating in the blood. More convincing evidence that psychosocial effects on immune regulation may influence susceptibility to disease is provided by the prospective epidemiologic studies of the relation between social conflicts and upper respiratory illness (Clover, Abell, Becker, Crawford, & Ramsey, 1989; Meyer & Haggerty, 1962). However, these studies are subject to a range of alternative causal explanations. For example, a conflict at home might result in the seeking of social support from friends, fellow workers, or family members. The increase in social interactions results in an increased probability of *being exposed* to infectious agents. Hence, it is difficult to know whether associations between social conflict and illness reported in naturalistic settings are attributable to exposure to infectious agents or to the competence of the immune system in fighting off infection.

Pittsburgh Common Cold Study

The data we present comes from a study of susceptibility to the common cold run in Pittsburgh, Pennsylvania, between 1993 and 1996. Detailed presentations of the procedures and results of this trial are published elsewhere (Cohen, Doyle, Skoner, Rabin, & Gwaltney, 1997; Cohen, Frank, Doyle, Skoner, Rabin, & Gwaltney, 1998). After completing a stressful life events interview and a questionnaire that assesses social participation and social ties, 276 (125 men and 151 women) healthy volunteers, aged 18 to 55, were exposed to one of two viruses that cause the common cold. The association between the social environment measures and the subsequent development of biologically verified clinical disease was examined with use of controls for baseline (before exposure to the virus) amount of antibodies to the experimental virus, body mass, season of the year (fall or spring), and various demographic factors. In further analyses, we examined the possible role of several behavioral and biological pathways in linking the social environment and susceptibility to infection.

Experimental Plan

All volunteers came to the hospital for medical eligibility screenings. Social networks, select health practices (smoking, alcohol consumption, exercise, sleep quality, diet), demographic factors, and body weight and height were also assessed at the screening and used as baseline data for those who were found to be eligible. Eligible subjects returned to the hospital both four and five weeks after screening to have blood drawn. An assessment of a marker of immune function—natural killer cell activity—was based on both blood draws, and an assessment of antibodies to the experimental virus was based on the second blood draw. A personality questionnaire was administered twice, once at each blood draw. Volunteers returned an additional time during the period after initial screening but before being exposed to the virus to complete an intensive stressful life events interview.

Subjects were quarantined within one week after the second blood draw. Baseline assessment of self-reported respiratory symptoms and two objective indicators of illness (nasal mucociliary clearance and nasal mucus production) were assessed during the first 24 hours of quarantine (before viral exposure). Urine samples for hormone assessment and information on dietary intake were also collected at this time.

At the end of the first 24 hours of quarantine, volunteers were given nasal drops that contained a low infectious dose of one of two types of rhinovirus (RV39 [$N = 147$] or Hanks [$N = 129$]). Two viruses were used in order to assess whether predictors of susceptibility are equivalent across different rhinovirus types.

The quarantine continued for five days after exposure. During this period, volunteers were housed individually but were allowed to interact with each other at a distance of three feet or more. Nasal secretion samples for verifying infection by virus culture were collected on each of the five days. On each day, volunteers completed a respiratory symptoms questionnaire and were tested for objective markers of illness with the same procedures as those used at baseline. Approximately 28 days after challenge, another blood sample was collected for verifying infection by determination of changes in antibodies to the challenge virus. All investigators were blinded to subjects' status on social network, personality, endocrine, health practice, immune, and prechallenge antibody measures.

Standard Control Variables

We used eight control variables, which might provide alternative explanations for the relation between social environmental characteristics and illness. These included the antibody to the experimental virus at baseline, age, body mass index (weight in kilograms divided by the square of height in meters), whether the trial was conducted in the fall (November) or spring (April and May), race, gender, viral type (RV39 or Hanks), and education.

Measures of Social Stress and Social Participation

We used a semistructured life events interview, the Bedford College Life Events and Difficulties Schedule (LEDS) to assess both social and nonsocial life events (Brown & Harris, 1989; Harris, 1991). The LEDS uses strict criteria for whether or not an event occurs, classifies each event on the basis of severity of threat and emotional significance, and makes a distinction between events and ongoing chronic difficulties (stressors). Raters blind to the individual's subjective response to an event are provided with extensive information regarding each event and the context in which it occurred; they then rely on thorough "dictionaries" to rate events. The dictionary ratings are based on the likely response of an average person to an event that occurs in the context of a particular set of biographical circumstances. We focus on the traditional LEDS outcomes: the occurrence of severe events (less than four weeks in duration) and chronic difficulties (more than four weeks). We also calculate separate scores for events and difficulties that involve social conflicts and those that do not.

Social network participation was assessed by questionnaire. The Social Network Index assesses participation in 12 types of social relationships (Cohen et al., 1997): relationships with a spouse, parents, parents-in-law, children, other close family members, close neighbors, friends, workmates, schoolmates, fellow volunteers (e.g., charity or community work), members of groups without religious affiliations (e.g., social, recreational, professional), and members of religious groups. One point is assigned for each kind of relationship (possible score of 12) for which respondents indicate that they speak (in person or on the phone) to someone in that relationship at least once every two weeks. The total number of persons with whom they speak at least once every two weeks (number of network members) was also assessed.

Infection and Illness

Infectious diseases result from the growth and action of microorganisms or parasites in the body (see Cohen & Williamson, 1991). Infection is the multiplication of an invading microorganism. Clinical illness occurs when infection is followed by the development of symptoms characteristic of the disease.

Infection   We used two common procedures for detecting whether volunteers were infected by the experimental challenge virus. In the viral isolation procedure, nasal secretions, which were collected daily, were inoculated into cell cultures, which stimulated replication of the specific virus. If the virus was present in nasal secretions, it grew in the cell cultures and could be detected. Alternatively, one can indirectly assess the presence of a replicating virus by looking at changes in serum antibody levels to that virus from before exposure to several week after. An invading microorganism (i.e., infection) triggers the immune system to produce antibodies. Because each antibody recognizes only a single type of microorganism, the production of antibodies to a specific infectious agent is evidence for the presence and activity of that agent.

Nasal washes were performed daily during quarantine to provide samples of nasal secretions for virus culture. Serum samples were collected both before and 28 days after exposure to the virus to assess both prechallenge levels (standard control factor) and the amount of change in antibodies to the experimental virus (marker of infection).

Objective Signs of Illness   On each day of quarantine, we assessed two objective signs of illness—mucus weights and mucociliary clearance function—and one subjective measure, self-reported symptoms. Mucus weights were determined by collecting used tissues in sealed plastic bags. After correcting for the weight of the bag and the mucus weight at baseline, the postchallenge weights were summed across the five days to create an adjusted total mucus weight score.

Nasal mucociliary clearance function refers to the effectiveness of nasal cilia in clearing mucus from the nasal passage toward the throat. Clearance function was assessed as the time required for a dye administered into the nose to reach the throat (nasopharnyx). Each daily time was adjusted for baseline, and the adjusted average time in minutes was calculated across the postchallenge days of the trial.

Subjective Symptoms of Illness   On each day of quarantine, subjects rated the severity of eight symptoms (congestion, runny nose, sneezing, cough, sore throat, malaise, headache, and chills) during the previous 24-hour period. Ratings ranged from 0 (none) to 4 (very severe) for each symptom. The symptom scores were summed for each day. Finally, after adjusting (subtracting) baseline symptoms, daily symptoms were summed across the five postchallenge days to create a total symptom score. Subjects were also asked each day if they had a cold.

Defining Colds   Volunteers were considered to have a cold if they were *both* infected and met illness criteria. They were classified as infected if the challenge virus was isolated on any of the five postchallenge study days or if there was a substantial rise (fourfold increase in antibody titer) in serum antibody level to the experimental virus. The illness criterion was based on selected *objective* indicators of illness: a total adjusted mucus weight of at least 10 grams *or* an adjusted average mucociliary nasal clearance time of at least 7 minutes. By basing the definition of illness entirely on objective indicators, we were able to exclude interpretations of our data based on psychological influences on symptom reporting. Mean total adjusted symptom score for those with colds (infected and meeting the objective criterion for illness) was 19.28 (sd = ±14.7) versus 5.67 (sd = ±8.1) for those without colds (t(274) = −9.88, $p < .001$).

Relative Risk   We use odds ratios to estimate the relative risk of developing a cold. An odds ratio approximates the odds that the disease outcome (common cold) will occur in one group as compared to another. We report the odds ratios comparing those with 4–5 and 6 or more roles to those with 3 or fewer and comparing those who experienced stressful life events to those who did not. All odds ratios we report are adjusted for the standard control variables. In each case, we report the corresponding 95% confidence intervals (CI [95%]).

Social Networks and Susceptibility

Figure 7.3 presents the rate of colds found for each of the three social network groups. These are observed rates and are not adjusted for the standard controls. As apparent from figure 7.3, the rate of colds decreased as social network diversity increased. The adjusted odds ratios were 4.2 (CI [95%] = 1.34, 13.29), 1.9 (CI [95%] = 1.00, 3.51), and 1, respectively. There were no interactions between the standard control variables and social network diversity in predicting colds. Hence, the relations were similar for the two virus types, different preexposure antibody levels, age, gender, race, education, body mass, and across the two seasons.

Total number of network members was not associated with colds ($p < .12$). Moreover, entering the number of network members into the first step of the regression equation along with standard controls did not reduce the association between diversity and colds ($p < .01$). Hence, the diversity of the network is more important than the number of network members, and its association with colds is independent of the number of members.

Acute Stressful Life Events, Chronic Difficulties,
and Susceptibility

There were 179 subjects with at least one severe acute event that occurred within one year of the study. Acute stressful life events were not, however, associated with developing a cold. There were 75 subjects with a chronic difficulty that lasted one month or longer. Those with such difficulties were 2.2 times more likely to develop a cold (CI [95%] = 1.08, 4.34) than those without. Moreover, there were no interactions between any of the standard control variables and

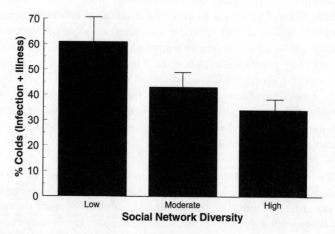

Figure 7.3 Observed incidence of colds by social network diversity. Low diversity is described as 1–3 types of social relationships, moderate 4–5, and high 6 or more. Error bars indicate standard errors.

chronic difficulties in predicting colds. Hence, the relations were similar for the two virus types, different preexposure antibody levels, age, gender, race, education, body mass, and across the two seasons.

As discussed earlier, we were primarily interested in whether interpersonal conflict increased susceptibility to infectious illness. Difficulties were categorized into three domains: interpersonal, work, and other. As is apparent from figure 7.4, having either work or interpersonal chronic difficulties was associated with greater risk for colds in comparison with those with no difficulties and other types of difficulties.

We considered the possibility that difficulties at work were in fact interpersonal difficulties as well. To pursue this issue, we had each of the 30 (one-month criterion) chronic difficulties coded for interpersonal content (criteria from Johnson, Monroe, Simons, & Thase, 1994). Only 2 of the 30 were found to be interpersonal conflicts at work, while 27 were attributable to unemployment or underemployment and 1 to a failing business.

Finally, we considered the possibility that those with a work or an interpersonal difficulty had more difficulties than those with another type of difficulty. The differences between groups did not approach significance (1.2 difficulties for work, 1.3 for relationships, and 1.1 for other). Nor was there an association between number of difficulties (for those with at least one difficulty) and colds.

Pathways Linking Social Networks and Stressful Life Events to Susceptibility

Preliminary analyses indicated that those with low levels of social participation were more likely to be smokers and less likely to exercise. Similarly, those with enduring difficulties were more likely to be smokers. There were also marginal asso-

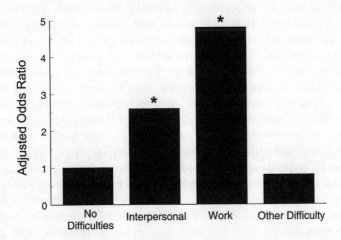

Figure 7.4 Adjusted odds ratios contrasting persons with interpersonal, work, and other chronic difficulties to those with no chronic difficulties; * $p < .05$.

ciations between having a difficulty, less exercise, and poorer sleep efficiency. All of these health practices were also associated with susceptibility to colds with smokers, those getting less exercise, and those with poor sleep quality all at greater risk. However, these health practices could explain only a small fraction of the relation between these characteristics of the social environment and susceptibility to infectious illness. Neither the hormones nor immune measures were associated with either social network or social conflict measures and hence neither could operate as a pathway that linked the social environment to illness susceptibility.

Personality as an Alternative Explanation

The Big Five personality factors are thought to represent the basic structure of personality (e.g., Goldberg, 1992). The factors are commonly described as introversion-extroversion, agreeableness, conscientiousness, emotional stability, and openness. We found that only introversion-extroversion was associated with susceptibility to colds. Those with scores below the median (introverts) were at greater risk (adjusted OR = 2.7, CI = 1.45, 4.92). Although none of the personality factors were associated with chronic difficulties, introversion was associated with lower levels of social network diversity ($p < .002$). However, the relation between network diversity and colds occurred above and beyond (independent of) the association of introversion and colds.

Conclusions

On the one hand, enduring interpersonal conflicts were associated with greater risk for developing an illness among those exposed to a virus. These were severe conflicts, which lasted at least a month, and included ongoing problems with spouse, family, and friends. On the other hand, having more types of social relationships was associated with less susceptibility to viral-induced illness. Interestingly, the diversity of types of relationships not the total number of relationships is what mattered. The associations between these characteristics of the social environment and illness susceptibility were substantial. Those with interpersonal conflicts were 2.5 times more likely to develop an illness than those without, and those who were relatively isolated (1–3 social relationships) were 4.2 times more likely to develop illness than those with very diverse networks (6 or more relationships). In contrast, the biggest effect of health practices was a threefold risk for smokers in comparison to nonsmokers. Interestingly, social conflicts and social participation had independent relations with illness susceptibility. Moreover, there was no interaction between social conflicts and social participation, so that a diverse social network did not operate to protect people from the influences of enduring social conflicts.

What can account for the relations between these characteristics of the social environment and susceptibility to infectious illness? In figures 7.1 and 7.2, we presented a number of plausible pathways. A key mediator in both models is emotional and cognitive response. In fact, social participation was associated with more positive affect (both state and trait, not reported here), but positive affect was not associated with susceptibility. Unexpectedly, neither positive nor negative affect was associated with chronic difficulties in this study. We used the POMS, a well-established measure of affect, and, therefore, we feel that from a measurement perspective we made a reasonable attempt. However, there are a number of earlier studies that have shown that those with chronic difficulties are at greater risk for depression (Brown & Harris, 1989). We did not measure relevant cognitive mediators, such as feelings of personal control and self-esteem, and hence cannot say whether they play a part.

Other mediators proposed in both models included health behaviors and the function of the endocrine and immune systems. However, when we measured these potential pathways, none could account for the relations we found. In the case of health practices, all five of the measures operated as risk factors for illness. Smokers, those abstaining from alcohol, those with poor sleep efficiency, those with few days of exercise, and those with low dietary intake of vitamin C were at greater risk for developing colds. However, health practices could account for only a small part of the relations between the social environment and host resistance. Because the health practice measures were all related to susceptibility in the expected manner, we are confident that we did a good job of assessing this pathway. As a consequence, it seems unlikely that these health practices play a major role in linking social environments to resistance to infectious illness. Although we assessed the health practices that we thought would be most likely to provide pathways, it is possible that other practices, such as caffeine intake, use of mouthwash, or regular hand washing, might link the social environment to illness susceptibility.

Those with elevated levels of epinephrine and norepinephrine were similarly at greater risk for developing colds. Again, however, levels of these hormones did not provide any additional explanation of the relations between the social environment and colds. To our surprise, these hormones were not even associated with the social environment measures. Because epinephrine and norepinephrine were assessed during the 24 hours before viral exposure, they might have been indicating a stress-type reaction to the beginning of quarantine rather than a base level of response to the participants' background social environments. In our current work, we are attempting to get better background levels by measuring hormones several times during the weeks before volunteers report for quarantine. This is a case where obtaining reliable measurements (multiple measures) at appropriate points in time is essential.

We chose natural killer cell activity as our primary marker of immune function for two reasons. First, natural killer (NK) cells are surveillance cells, which identify infected (and otherwise altered cells) and kill them. In theory, higher levels of natural killer cell activity should help limit infection and prevent illness. Second, there is evidence that chronic psychological stress is associated with suppression of NK activity (reviewed in Herbert & Cohen, 1993). However, NK activity did not operate as a pathway that linked the social environment to illness susceptibility in our study. We mentioned earlier that measuring immunity in the blood is not always the most appropriate procedure, and this may be the problem here. In theory, NK activity in the lung might be the essential issue in the case of respiratory infections. It is also possible that NK activity in the blood might make a difference, but that the immune system's ability to compensate for deficits in single subsystems obscured any relation. At any rate, we found no evidence for immune mediation of the relations between the social environment and infectious illness. Again, we think that this may be attributable to problems in measurement. We are unsure that we can ever adequately assess immune-mediated host resistance in this setting, but we still think that the immune system is a key player in linking the social environment to susceptibility to upper respiratory infections.

Note

The work we report was supported by a grant from the National Institute of Mental Health (MH50429), a Senior Scientist Award to Cohen from the National Institute of Mental Health (MH00721), and grants from the National Institute of Health to the University of Pittsburgh Medical Center General Clinical Research Center (NCRR/GCRC 5M01 RR00056) and from the National Institute of Mental Health to the Mental Health Research Center for Affective Disorder (MH30915). Supplemental support was also provided by the Fetzer Institute and the John D. and Catherine T. MacArthur Foundation.

References

Brown, G. W. & Harris, T. O. (Eds.). (1989). *Life events and illness.* New York: Guilford.

Clover, R. D., Abell, T., Becker, L. A., Crawford, S., & Ramsey, C. N. (1989). Family functioning and stress as predictors of influenza B infection. *Journal of Family Practice, 28,* 536–539.

Cohen, S. (1988). Psychosocial models of the role of social support in the etiology of physical disease. *Health Psychology, 7,* 269–297.

Cohen, S., Doyle, W. J., Skoner, D. P., Rabin, B. S., & Gwaltney, J. M., Jr. (1997). Social ties and susceptibility to the common cold. *Journal of the American Medical Association, 277,* 1940–1944.

Cohen, S., Frank, E., Doyle, W. J., Skoner, D. P., Rabin, B. S., & Gwaltney, J. M., Jr. (1998). Types of stressors that increase susceptibility to the common cold. *Health Psychology, 17,* 214–223.

Cohen, S., & Herbert, T. B. (1996). Health psychology: Psychological factors and physical disease from the perspective of human psychoneuroimmunology. In J. T. Spence, J. M. Darley, & D. J. Foss (Eds.), *Annual review of psychology* (Vol. 47). El Camino, CA: Annual Review.

Cohen, S., Tyrrell, D. A. J., & Smith, A. P. (1991). Psychological stress and susceptibility to the common cold. *New England Journal of Medicine, 325,* 606–612.

Cohen, S., Tyrrell, D. A. J., & Smith, A. P. (1993). Life events, perceived stress, negative affect and susceptibility to the common cold. *Journal of Personality and Social Psychology, 64,* 131–140.

Cohen, S., & Williamson, G. M. (1991). Stress and infectious disease in humans. *Psychological Bulletin, 109,* 5–24.

Doyle, W. J., McBride, T. P., Swarts, J. D., Hayden, F. G., & Gwaltney, J. M., Jr. (1988). The response of the nasal airway, middle ear and Eustachian tube to provocative rhinovirus challenge. *American Journal of Rhinology, 2,* 149–154.

Evans, P. D., & Edgerton, N. (1991). Life-events and mood as predictors of the common cold. *British Journal of Medical Psychology, 64,* 35–44.

Evans, P. D., Pitts, M. K., & Smith, K. (1988). Minor infection, minor life events and the four day desirability dip. *Journal of Psychosomatic Research, 32,* 533–539.

Glaser, R., Rice, J., Sheridan, J., Fertel, R., Stout, J., Speicher, C. E., Pinsky, D., Kotur, M., Post, A., Beck, M., & Kiecolt-Glaser, J. K. (1987). Stress-related immune suppression: Health implications. *Brain, Behavior, and Immunity, 1*, 7–20.

Goldberg, L. R. (1992). The development of markers for the Big-Five factor structure. *Psychological Assessment, 4*, 26–42.

Harris T. O. (1991). Life stress and illness: The question of specificity. *Annals of Behavioral Medicine, 13*, 211–219.

Herbert, T. B., & Cohen, S. (1993). Depression and immunity: A meta-analytic review. *Psychological Bulletin, 113*, 472–486.

House, J. S., Landis, K. R., & Umberson, D. (1988). Social relationships and health. *Science, 241*, 540–545.

House, J. S., Robbins, C., & Metzner, H. L. (1982). The association of social relationships and activities with mortality: Prospective evidence from the Tecumseh Community Health Study. *American Journal of Epidemiology, 116*, 123–140.

Johnson, S. L., Monroe, S., Simons, A., & Thase, M. E. (1994). Clinical characteristics associated with interpersonal depression: Symptoms, course and treatment response. *Journal of Affective Disorders, 31*, 97–109.

Kiecolt-Glaser, J. K., Malarkey, W. B., Chee, M., Newton, T., Cacioppo, J. T., Mao, H.-Y., & Glaser, R. (1993). Negative behavior during marital conflict is associated with immunological down-regulation. *Psychosomatic Medicine, 55*, 395–409.

Meyer, R. J., & Haggerty, R. J. (1962). Streptococcal infections in families. *Pediatrics, 29*, 539–549.

Rabin, B. S., Cohen, S., Ganguli, R., Lyle, D. T., & Cunnick, J. E. (1989). Bidirectional interaction between the central nervous system and immune system. *CRC Critical Reviews in Immunology, 9*, 279–312.

Seeman, T. E., Berkman, L. F., Blazer, D., & Rowe, J. W. (1994). Social ties and support and neuroendocrine function. *Annals of Behavioral Medicine, 16*, 95–106.

Stone, A. A., Bovbjerg, D. H., Neale, J. M., Napoli, A., Valdimarsdottir, H., & Gwaltney, J. M., Jr. (1993). Development of common cold symptoms following experimental rhinovirus infection is related to prior stressful life events. *Behavioral Medicine, 8*, 115–120.

Thoits, P. A. (1983). Multiple identities and psychological well-being: A reformulation and test of the social isolation hypothesis. *American Sociological Review, 48*, 174–187.

Uchino, B. N., Cacioppo, J. T., & Kiecolt-Glaser, J. K. (1996). The relationship between social support and physiological processes: A review with emphasis on underlying mechanisms and implications for health. *Psychological Bulletin, 119*, 488–531.

Wethington, E., Brown, G. W., & Kessler, R. C. (1995). Interview measurement of stressful life events. In S. Cohen, R. C. Kessler, & L. Underwood Gordon (Eds.), *Measuring stress*. New York: Oxford University Press.

Whiteside, T. L., Bryant, J., Day, R., & Herberman, R. B. (1990). Natural killer cytotoxicity in the diagnosis of immune dysfunction: Criteria for a reproducible assay. *Journal of Clinical Laboratory Analysis, 4*, 102–114.

Commentary

Ted Robles

During the 1980s and 1990s, Cohen has provided important contributions to our understanding of emotions, social relationships, and health. In particular, the viral challenge research described in the present chapter provides a method of studying the roles of multiple psychosocial factors on actual health outcomes. The most unique and important contribution of Cohen's work is the use of clinical illness as a dependent variable. Moreover, the viral challenge studies are of high rigor and control, which also contribute to the importance and value of this research.

In addition to empirical contributions, this commentary focuses on Cohen's theoretical contributions to our understanding of the relationships between psychosocial factors and health outcomes. Specifically, fundamental empirical questions presented by Cohen in his theoretical work are relevant to researchers in health psychology, psychoneuroimmunology, and behavioral medicine. Emphasis will be given to these questions with respect to Cohen's own work as a marker of how the viral challenge research has furthered knowledge of psychosocial influences on health. This commentary also draws from other researchers in this volume and illustrates how their work can strengthen viral challenge research. Suggestions for future directions are provided in the concluding section.

Theoretical Contributions

Many of Cohen's contributions to health psychology, psychoneuroimmunology, and behavioral medicine have been in the theoretical domain. Specifically, Cohen has contributed to how we conceptualize the relationships among social relationships, stress, and health. A major paper published in *Health Psychology* entitled "Psychosocial Models of the Role of Social Support in the Etiology of Physical Disease" suggested several plausible models that might link psychosocial factors, stress, social support, and disease etiology and progression (Cohen, 1988). In addition to presenting different models of these relationships, Cohen differentiated between two components of social support: structural (the existence of a social network) and functional (the purpose and function of the social network). These concepts, along with constructs such as social integration and perceived availability, continue to be important in current research.

The most influential aspect of Cohen's 1988 article is the definition of two models that relate social support to health: the *main effect* model and the *buffering* model. The main effect model states that social support is beneficial regardless of whether or not one is under stress. Persons with high levels of social support should consistently have better health, regardless of stress level, compared to persons with low levels of social support. Social integration as a relevant measure of social support is associated with this model. The stress-buffering hypothesis states that social support is beneficial only when the person who is receiving support is under stress and that stress buffering occurs only when one's level or quality of support matches one's needs for support. Perceived social support as a relevant measure of social support is associated with this model. Cohen suggested several directions for future research, including more accurate and consistent verification of disease, more psychometrically valid measures of stress and social support, and the need for more prospective data on onset of disease and risk. These points later served as basic principles to guide the viral challenge research.

Another influential publication was a chapter by Cohen in the *Handbook of Human Stress and Immunity*. Cohen presented five important empirical questions to guide research on social relationships, stress, and health (Cohen, 1994). These questions are described below, with a statement of the implied research directive following each question:

1. *What psychosocial factors influence immune function?* We need to develop a better understanding of which particular psychosocial factors (e.g., life events, behavior, social relationships) influence immune function.
2. *Which parameters of immunity are subject to psychosocial influence?* The immune system is a complex system, with wide diversity in types of immune cells and immune responses. A broader range of immune function measures must be used to assess the role of psychosocial factors in immune function variability.
3. *Which parameters of immunity are critical in susceptibility to infection and viral reactivation?* Although this question is specific to infectious disease, it addresses the importance of translating findings related to immune function to health outcomes. Immune measures chosen in a research design should be related to some aspect of disease susceptibility and resistance.
4. *What are the hormonal mechanisms that link psychosocial factors to immune function?* Numerous endocrine hormones have the capability to alter immune function. Future research must not solely examine relationships between specific endocrine hormones and immune function but how such relationships are moderated by psychosocial influences.
5. *What are the behavioral mechanisms that link psychosocial factors to immunity?* Another mechanism of psychosocial influence is on behaviors related to health, including exercise, diet, smoking, and alcohol use. Research on the relationships between psychosocial factors and immunity must account for such behaviors.

These questions will be used to assess the progress made by Cohen's viral challenge work in a later section.

Empirical Contributions

The main findings from the Cohen chapter and results from previous viral challenge work will be briefly summarized. The specific methods and results derived from these studies are elaborated elsewhere (e.g., Cohen, Doyle, Skoner, Rabin, & Gwaltney, 1997). The first viral challenge study (Cohen, Tyrell, & Smith, 1993) examined relationships among negative life events, perceived stress, and negative affect on both subjective and objective indicators of infection with the common cold virus. The authors found that negative life events were associated with greater rates of clinical illness as measured by increased symptoms. Perceived stress and negative affect were associated with clinical illness as measured by higher rates of infection rather than greater symptoms. Overall, these relationships persisted after accounting for a number of control variables, including age, gender, prechallenge serostatus, and education.

A follow-up study (Cohen et al., 1995) examined the role of negative affect in the development of the common cold and focused on the roles of state and trait negative affect on clinical signs and self-reported symptoms. Cohen and colleagues found that both state and trait negative affect were associated with greater cold symptoms and that the influence of state and trait negative affect was mediated through different pathways. State negative affect was associated with objective markers of disease progression—actual disease severity. In contrast, trait negative affect was associated with higher symptom reporting through increased illness complaints and not objective signs.

Results from the subsequent Pittsburgh Common Cold Study are reported in this volume and elsewhere (Cohen et al., 1997; Cohen et al., 1998). Briefly, this study employed a more sophisticated measurement strategy, including measures of immune function, endocrine hormones, objective symptomatology, and social integration; the Big Five personality dimension scale; and most important, a new measure of psychological stress: the Life Events and Difficulties Schedule (LEDS; Brown & Harris, 1989).

The main finding from the Pittsburgh study was that as social network diversity increases, the risk of developing a cold decreases (see fig. 7.3). In addition, acute stressful life events were not associated with developing a cold, while chronic difficulties were. Persons with a chronic difficulty that lasted one month or longer were 2.2 times more likely to develop a cold compared to persons with no chronic stressors. Work difficulties, specifically unemployment or underemployment, were particularly associated with risk of developing a cold. With respect to the biological measures, prechallenge measures of urinary cortisol, epinephrine, and norepinephrine and prechallenge measures of NK cell activity did not operate as pathways that linked social integration to susceptibility to colds. Health practices could account for a small fraction of the relationship, and of the personality measures, only extroversion was associated with susceptibility to colds, such that introverts had a higher risk of developing a cold.

Assessing the Viral Challenge Research

Having briefly summarized the theoretical and empirical contributions of Cohen, we now turn to the question: how has the viral challenge research furthered our understanding of emotion, social relationships, and health? Answers to this question will be framed in terms of the conceptual guidelines and empirical questions put forth by Cohen.

The main effect model and the buffering model are prominent theoretical contributions, which relate social support and health (Cohen, 1988). The former views social support as continually beneficial to health, whereas the buffer model views social support as beneficial to health only during times of stress and when support is perceived as appropriate. Does the viral challenge work provide us with a way to test either model? Prior reports (Cohen et al., 1997, 1998) separately focus on components of the model: the role of social support and the role of life stressors on health outcomes.

Testing the main effect and buffering models requires an integration of the results from both studies and an analysis that allows for examination of the interactions among life stressors, social support, and health outcomes. Moreover, the Stress × Social Support interaction necessary for the stress-buffering model requires a large sample size to test (Cohen & Wills, 1985), which is difficult to achieve in the viral challenge studies. Most important, as described earlier, measures of social integration are more informative to the main effect model, whereas measures of perceived social support and its interaction with life stress are more relevant to the buffering model. The viral challenge research utilizes social integration as a measure of social support but does not include measures of perceived social support. As such, the viral challenge research does not adequately test the stress-buffering model.

The questions outlined in Cohen (1994) also serve as another framework for evaluating the contributions of the viral challenge research to our understanding of emotions, social relationships, and health.

1. *What psychosocial factors influence immune function?* The viral challenge research clearly shows that aspects of social networks—specifically, social integration—are associated with health outcomes. In addition, perceived stress, negative affect, introversion, and the presence of chronic stressful life events influence susceptibility to colds. However, the viral challenge research is only beginning to link the same psychosocial factors to immunity by itself (Cohen, Doyle, & Skoner, 1999).

2. *Which parameters of immunity are subject to psychosocial influence?*

3. *Which parameters of immunity are critical in susceptibility to infection and viral reactivation?* Response to cold infection involves numerous responses from the immune system repertoire. The Pittsburgh study utilized one functional measure (NK cell activity) and enumerative measures (cell subset counts) of immunity. In order to address both of these questions, other functional aspects of immunity must be examined in viral challenge research.

4. *What are the hormonal mechanisms that link psychosocial factors to immune function?* The Pittsburgh study utilized 24-hour urinary cortisol, epinephrine, and norepinephrine measures, providing thorough coverage of the hormones associated with stress and immunity. In the Pittsburgh study, norepinephrine levels above the median were associated with developing symptoms of a cold, and a similar but weaker association was found with epinephrine. However, in the pathway analyses, none of the hormone measures were associated with social support or life stress measures, and they did not operate as pathways that linked social support or life stress to susceptibility to colds. In addition, similar to

the measures of immunity, the endocrine measures were taken prior to viral challenge. In future research, daily sampling would provide data on changes in endocrine functioning during quarantine.

5. *What are the behavioral mechanisms that link psychosocial factors to immunity?* A number of health-related behaviors were associated with susceptibility to colds, including smoking, poor sleep efficiency, abstinence from alcohol, and low vitamin C intake. In the pathway analyses, all of the health behavior measures accounted for a small portion of the relationship between social support and susceptibility to colds. However, answers to the questions of the extent of the relationships between health behaviors and immunity have not yet been examined.

Overall, the viral challenge studies provide insight into the psychosocial variables that are implicated in susceptibility to illness. To delineate the mechanisms through which the identified psychosocial variables operate, further research, as indicated above, is needed.

Future Directions

How might the work of other contributors to this volume extend or inform viral challenge research? Answers to this question are organized around the major themes that are pertinent to all of the chapters in this volume.

Positive and Negative Emotions

Cohen's work has focused primarily on aspects of negative emotional experience. For instance, the LEDS examines the negative aspects of stressors not positive aspects or events. In addition, susceptibility and symptoms of illness have been linked to state and trait negative affect. At the same time, positive emotions are implicit in discussions of social support. In the differentiation of social support into its structural and functional components, positive emotion should play a role in the functional aspects of social support. Measures of perceived social support, which tap into the degree to which one's needs are met by one's level of social support, also deal with positive emotion. In models of the relationship between psychosocial factors and illness, positive emotion should play a role in the main effect and the buffering models. However, employing measures based on a circumplex model (arrays multiple variables in a circular, two-dimensional space) of emotion did not show any significant effects of positive emotion on viral challenge outcomes.

Thus, future work should examine positive emotions, particularly as they play a role in supportive social relationships. In this volume, Ryff et al. and Reis focus on the nature of interpersonal relationships in the context of emotional well-being. Ryff devotes an entire dimension of emotional well-being to "positive relationships with others" and has shown that the quality of interpersonal relationships, particularly spousal relationships, are highly associated with self-reported health status (chap. 5). Using concepts from attachment theory and intimacy theory, Reis (chap. 3) proposes that positive emotions have prime importance in emotional well-being and maintenance of social ties. Assessing the quality of social relationships in the viral challenge paradigm would help researchers gain a richer understanding of the emotional dynamics that underlie particular social relationships as well as providing additional pathways that relate social relationships to health. Understanding the positive and negative emotional aspects of social relationships may also shed light on the question of the main effect and buffering models, which relate social support to health.

Gender Differences

Gender was utilized as a control variable in the viral challenge studies. However, work by Seeman indicates that the efficacy and provision of social support differs between genders. Specifically, women seem to be more reactive to negative social interaction, as shown by higher levels of urinary cortisol (chap. 6) and norepinephrine (Kiecolt-Glaser, Glaser, Cacioppo, & Malarkey, 1998). Moreover, Kiecolt-Glaser et al. showed that physiological changes due to marital conflict persisted longer in women compared to men. Gottman and colleagues (Carstensen, Gottman, & Levensen, 1995) have also observed gender differences in affect. This evidence suggests that social support differentially affects men and women, in both the supporter and the person receiving social support. The viral challenge paradigm provides a particularly interesting forum within which gender differences in social support and underlying physiological effects could be examined.

Mechanisms

Much of the analysis in the viral challenge studies is devoted to delineating pathways through which social support and stressful life events operate to affect susceptibility to illness. The analysis then addresses the question of mechanisms via health practices, hormones, and markers of immune system function. More diverse measures of immunity and endocrine function, which may be more relevant to infection with the common cold, should be utilized. Specifically, measures of immunoglobulin A (IgA) and G (IgG) in the nasal epithelium are potential markers of the immune environment within the main locus of infection. Another avenue, following from Cohen et al. (1998), would be measures of chemical mediators of inflammation, such as cytokines and bradykinins, which are partially responsible for cold symptoms. Perhaps psychosocial factors play a role in this realm of inflammation and symptoms in addition to the cell-mediated or humoral-mediated immune responses typically measured in psychoneuroimmunology (PNI) research. This work has begun, as Cohen and colleagues recently examined relationships among perceived stress, cold symptoms, and the proinflammatory cytokine IL-6 (Cohen, Doyle, & Skoner, 1999). In addition, salivary cortisol measures with diurnal sampling (as Cohen points out, urinary cortisol is not the ideal method for measuring cortisol) are an important direction for neuroendocrine assessment. Overall, sampling of immune function and endocrine measures should be taken more frequently to track the time course of physiological changes over the duration of the quarantine.

An additional physiological measure that warrants consideration is cardiovascular reactivity. Cardiovascular reactivity has been identified as a moderating factor in changes in immunity in response to laboratory stressors (Herbert et al., 1994) and has been linked to long-term alterations that result from chronic stress (Cacioppo et al., 1998). In terms of social support, numerous studies have shown the positive effects of social support on cardiac reactivity and, conversely, the negative impact of interpersonal conflict on cardiovascular functioning (Uchino, Cacioppo, & Kiecolt-Glaser, 1996). Utilizing cardiovascular reactivity in viral challenge research will also allow for the assessment of the role of sympathetic nervous system activity in susceptibility to colds.

Cumulative Effects

The influence of cumulation of life stressors is a central component of the viral challenge research. The LEDS data showed a significant increase in the risk of developing colds in individuals with chronic life stressors that endured for more than six months. However, it is conceivable that some of these stressors began as acute stressors (i.e., supervisor reprimanding employee), which accumulated over time to develop into chronic, daily stressors or threats (i.e., supervisor constantly belittling employee). This possibility could be considered by including checklist-type measures of life events and relating such measures back to the LEDS data. Another aspect of cumulative effects pertains to the persistence of poor social relationships, stemming either from a lack of social ties or a high level of social conflict. Note that stressors that stem from interpersonal conflicts were associated with increased risk for developing colds (Cohen et al., 1998). Once again, assessing the qualitative aspects of social relationships in future research would provide a deeper understanding of the dynamic role of social support, especially with respect to cumulative effects.

Multiple Methods

The viral challenge paradigm is an excellent illustration of the use of multiple methodologies to assess objective and subjective signs of clinical illness, psychosocial factors, and underlying biological mechanisms. Further research could include assessments of psychosocial variables during the quarantine itself, as opposed to just prior to viral challenge. To shed light on the main effect and buffering models, future research could also examine the interactions between social support and stressful life events. The social support construct needs further research to assess functional support and emotional support across diverse types of relationships. In addition, the daily diary approach used by Reis could be utilized in the quarantine setting to track the efficacy of interactions with others in one's social network. A recent study integrated a portable daily diary (via handheld computer) with portable ambulatory blood pressure and heart rate monitoring, such that the cardiovascular readings were recorded simultaneously with the diary entries (Kamarck et al., 1998). Although no consistent findings were shown to link an aspect of social interaction (social conflict) with cardiovascular activation, integrating the methodology with the controlled environment of the viral challenge may prove promising and would provide ecological data on both social interaction and cardiovascular measures.

Multiple Relationships

The viral challenge research has opened doors to understanding the roles of different types of relationships in health outcomes. Future work in this area could differentiate among spousal, familial, and work-related relationships. Previous work by Cohen has addressed this, particularly in terms of stressful life events. However, it would be useful to extend the viral challenge work on social integration to specific relationship types (e.g., spouses, friends, coworkers) and to include measures of functional support. Finally, based on previous theoretical concepts proposed by Cohen, attention should also be turned to perceived social support. The buffering hypothesis warrants the use of perceived social support measures, which could be extended to specific relationships and associated expectations from each.

The viral challenge paradigm itself can also be improved upon. For example, aspects of the actual quarantine likely interact with those same psychosocial variables assessed at baseline; that is, factors such as perceived stress and negative affect may be elevated over the course of the quarantine and may thus influence susceptibility. Tracking these day-to-day changes in affect may provide ways to tease apart such interactions.[1] Linking these psychological changes to day-to-day endocrine and immune changes may be particularly valuable to understanding the progression of infection as it relates to changes in psychosocial factors. Finally, the LEDS, while a good measure of duration and severity of life stressors, employs raters, who use dictionaries to evaluate the time course, onset, and degree of social stress of the subject-identified stressors. Previous work has shown that the individual's appraisal of an external event as "stressful" contributes to the "stressfulness" of the event. Utilizing subjective ratings of the degree to which an event is stressful to the individual could be useful in pathway modeling and in answering theoretical questions about the relationships among stressful life events, social support, and health.

In conclusion, the contributions of Cohen and colleagues to our understanding of the role of social relations in susceptibility and resistance to infection have been extensive. This commentary points to numerous future directions for the viral challenge paradigm, some ensuing from Cohen's own observations and others from the perspectives and findings of other contributors to this volume.

Note

1. Of particular note is Cohen et al. (1995), which reported that state negative affect, which was measured each day of the quarantine, was associated with objective markers of cold symptoms and illness.

References

Brown, G. W., & Harris, T. O. (Eds.). (1989). *Life events and illness*. New York: Guilford.

Cacioppo, J. T., Berntson, G. G., Malarkey, W. B., Kiecolt-Glaser, J. K., Sheridan, J. F., Poehlmann, K. M., Burleson, M. H., Ernst, J. M., Hawkley, L. C., & Glaser, R. (1998). Autonomic, neuroendocrine, and immune responses to psychological stress: The reactivity hypothesis. In S. M. McCann & J. M. Lipton (Eds.), *Annals of the New York Academy of Sciences. Vol. 840. Neuroimmunomodulation: Molecular aspects, integrative systems, and clinical advances* (pp. 664–673). New York: New York Academy of Sciences.

Carstensen, L. L., Gottman, J. M., & Levensen, R. W. (1995). Emotional behavior in long-term marriage. *Psychology and Aging, 10*(1), 140–149.

Cohen, S. (1988). Psychosocial models of the role of social support in the etiology of physical disease. *Health Psychology, 7*, 269–297.

Cohen, S. (1994). Psychosocial influences on immunity and infectious disease in humans. In R. Glaser & J. K. Kiecolt-Glaser (Eds.), *Handbook of human stress and immunity* (pp. 301–319). San Diego, CA: Academic.

Cohen, S., Doyle, W. J., & Skoner, D. P. (1999). Psychological stress, cytokine production, and severity of upper respiratory illness. *Psychosomatic Medicine, 61*, 175–180.

Cohen, S., Doyle, W. J., Skoner, D. P., Fireman, P., Gwaltney, J. M., Jr., & Newsom, J. T. (1995). State and trait negative affect as predictors of objective and subjective symptoms of respiratory viral infections. *Journal of Personality and Social Psychology, 68*, 159–169.

Cohen, S., Doyle, W. J., Skoner, D. P., Rabin, B. S., & Gwaltney, J. M. (1997). Social ties and susceptibility to the common cold. *Journal of the American Medical Association, 277*(24), 1940–1944.

Cohen, S., Frank, E., Doyle, W. J., Skoner, D. P., Rabin, B. S., & Gwaltney, J. M. (1998). Types of stressors that increase susceptibility to the common cold in healthy adults. *Health Psychology, 17*(3), 214–223.

Cohen, S., Tyrell, D. A. J., & Smith, A. P. (1993). Life events, perceived stress, negative affect and susceptibility to the common cold. *Journal of Personality and Social Psychology, 64*, 131–140.

Cohen, S., & Wills, T. A. (1985). Stress, social support, and the buffering hypothesis. *Psychological Bulletin, 98*(2), 310–357.

Herbert, T. B., Cohen, S., Marsland, A. L., Bachen, E. A., Rabin, B. S., Muldoon, M. F., & Manuck, S. B. (1994). Cardiovascular reactivity and the course of immune response to an acute psychological stressor. *Psychosomatic Medicine, 56*, 337–344.

Kamarck, T. W., Shiffman, S. M., Smithline, L., Goodie, J. L., Paty, J. A., Gnys, M., & Jong, J. Y. (1998). Effects of task strain, social conflict, and emotional activation on ambulatory cardiovascular activity: Daily life consequences of recurring stress in a multiethnic adult sample. *Health Psychology, 17*(1), 17–29.

Kiecolt-Glaser, J. K., Glaser, R., Cacioppo, J. T., & Malarkey, W. B. (1998). Marital stress: Immunologic, neuroendocrine, and autonomic correlates. In S. M. McCann & J. M. Lipton (Eds.), *Annals of the New York Academy of Sciences. Vol. 840. Neuroimmunomodulation: Molecular aspects, integrative systems, and clinical advances* (pp. 656–663). New York: New York Academy of Sciences.

Uchino, B. N., Cacioppo, J. T., & Kiecolt-Glaser, J. K. (1996). The relationship between social support and physiological processes: A review with emphasis on underlying mechanisms and implications for health. *Psychological Bulletin, 119*(3), 488–531.

8

Social Context and Other Psychological Influences on the Development of Immunity

Christopher L. Coe & Gabriele R. Lubach

*I*nfant animals are born with biological needs for a certain type of rearing environment to facilitate the normal maturation and expression of behavioral and physiological processes. When rearing conditions deviate significantly from the species-typical norm, it is known that infant growth and development proceeds in an abnormal manner. In the case of mammalian offspring, caregiving by the mother appears to be an essential dimension of this environmental context, which is critical for the correct ontogeny of behavioral and emotional well-being. For many animals, the nursing mother is both a source of sustenance and warmth and the vehicle for ensuring social bonding, emotional security, and initial learning about the environment. In addition, there has been a general consensus since the 1950s that the healthy maturation of several of the infant's physiological systems is also dependent on appropriate parenting. The important enabling role of this early experience in facilitating physiological development was revealed by demonstrating abnormal growth, endocrine activity, and brain neurochemistry in animals after perturbations of the mother-infant relationship. The findings discussed in the rest of this chapter extend the perspective from the field of developmental psychobiology to encompass the effects of the social environment on the maturation of immunity. We will be reviewing a series of studies that show the influence of several different rearing events on immune competence in young monkeys, through both transient stress-induced alterations in immune responses and more prolonged changes in the set points at which some immune processes become established during maturation.

Our research also reflects the influence of a newer discipline commonly known as psychoneuroimmunology (PNI), which has been investigating the relationships among psychosocial factors, immune responses, and immune-related disease. The coalescing of PNI as a field is usually attributed to a book with this title (Ader, 1981), although empirical support for the idea that psychological factors influence immunity can be traced back to many earlier studies (e.g., Ishigami, 1919; Marsh & Rasmussen, 1960; Mora, Amtmann, & Hoffman, 1926; Weinman & Rothman, 1967). Progress in understanding the bidirectional interactions between psychological factors and immunity has proceeded on many fronts. While some researchers studied development, most investigated the influence of behavior and emotional states on physiological responses in the adult. However, from the perspective of this chaper, it is of particular historical interest that research on young animals and children provided some of the first definitive evidence that psychological processes could exert a meaningful influence on immune responses (Ader & Friedman, 1965; Meyer & Haggerty, 1962; Solomon, Levine, & Kraft, 1968). Our studies with nonhuman primates build upon this prior literature, which documents that stressful events can compromise immune responses in the young and even result in lasting alterations still manifest in adulthood. One additional message from our research is that such persistent effects are most likely to occur when the underlying immune processes are immature at the time of the environmental or psychological insult. These prolonged changes likely reflect a shift in the developmental trajectory of the infant's more malleable cellular processes. In contrast, later challenges to the older individual typically result in just a temporary shift in immune responses, which is followed by a return to the original set point at which the cellular activity was maintained in the prior undisturbed state.

General Principles of PNI

Before reviewing the specific findings on young monkeys that support these conclusions, a brief digression is warranted to consider some of the PNI principles that pertain to understanding how social factors may affect immunity in an individual of any age. The preponderance of the research has involved negative life events, and it is now clear that many stressful situations induce alterations in immune responses, which can last from hours to several days or even a few months. Early PNI studies, for example, focused on social loss in adult humans and showed that the ability of lymphocytes to proliferate when stimulated and grown in cultures was reduced for at least one to two months during periods of bereavement (Bartrop, Luckhurst, Lazarus, Kiloh, & Penny, 1977; Schleifer, Keller, Camerino, Thornton, & Stein, 1983). Subsequent research extended these observations to additional immune responses and to encompass other challenging and demanding social situations, including marital divorce and extended caregiving for a sick spouse (Irwin, Daniels, Smith, Bloom, & Weiner, 1987; Kiecolt-Glaser, Fisher, et al., 1987; Kiecolt-Glaser, Glaser, et al., 1987; Kiecolt-Glaser, Glaser, Gravenstein, Malarkey, & Sheridan, 1996; Kiecolt-Glaser, Marucha, Malarkey, Mercado, & Glaser, 1995). Comparable studies in children have concurred with the general conclusion that aversive social events can affect immunity. Some papers documented a clustering of stressful life events prior to disease onset in certain pediatric patient populations (Heisel, 1972; Jacobs & Charles, 1980); others reported that the incidence and severity of respiratory illness in children were affected by poor family functioning (Boyce et al., 1977; Meyer & Haggerty, 1962).

While it has remained difficult to definitively establish the specific physiological mechanisms that cause these immune alterations, a review of the extant literature indicates that most posit a brain-mediated change in the activity of the endocrine or autonomic nervous systems as the likely intervening step, which then impinges upon the cellular processes of the immune system. Because of the prevailing interest in negative life events, considerable effort has been expended to understand how stress-related neuroendocrine processes, especially the adrenal hormones and the sympathetic nervous system (SNS), affect immunity (Munck, Guyre, & Holbrook, 1984). This focus makes intuitive sense because increases in adrenal hormones, especially cortisol, and changes in urinary catecholamines indicative of increased SNS activity are often associated with those life events that alter immune responses or aggravate disease symptomatology. However, actually proving the mediating role of these specific substances released by the SNS or endocrine system continues to be a challenge for PNI investigators. The greatest success has been with respect to explaining transient shifts in immune responses after acute stressors, such as physical exercise or cognitive effort, where it has been possible to show that adrenaline and noradrenaline can drive the changes in cell numbers in the blood stream (Benschop, Rodriguez-Feuerhahn, & Schedlowski, 1996; Crary et al., 1983). Additional explanatory principles that incorporate more lasting changes in health-promoting or disease-causing behavior will probably be needed to account for the sustained immunologic effects of psychosocial events.

The field of PNI has also been forced to tackle the question of how alterations in immunity—be they short- or long-lasting—actually result in disease, because not every small shift in immune responses necessarily has this negative outcome. In many cases, the numerous cells of the immune system have redundant functions, and the decreased activity of one cell type can be compensated for by the enhanced activation of another cellular response. We still need to learn more about which events are capable of compromising our overall immune competence to such a degree that they result in an immune-related disease. Examples of several stress-responsive immune measures are discussed later, but at this point it is important to mention that most psychologically induced immune alterations probably do not cause disease directly. Rather it is more accurate to say that they likely act in a permissive manner by creating a window of opportunity for a pathogen to initiate a disease process. For example, Boyce et al. (1993) tracked immune changes in a group of young children who were starting kindergarten in California. The children experienced an earthquake later in the semester, and the confluence of the physiological responses to these two events resulted in an increased likelihood of succumbing to respiratory illness. By analogy, when young monkeys are experimentally stressed by being separated from social companions or by other arousing events during rearing, there are many immune changes that do not cause disease directly, but they contribute to a decreased ability to make antibody responses if the monkeys are exposed to foreign substances (Coe, Rosenberg, & Levine, 1987; Laudenslager, Rasmussen, Berman, Suomi, & Berger, 1993).

As the field of PNI advanced, it became increasingly evident that decisions about how and when to study immune responses would be critical issues for future research. Just as we must distinguish between cardiovascular disease and immunological disorders in a general discussion of health, within PNI one must make distinctions among the three major categories of immune-related disease: infectious, autoimmune, and cancer. Each type of disease involves different immune processes, and it is likely that the nature and strength of the relationship between psychosocial variables and the underlying cellular mechanisms will vary. The importance of this seemingly subtle methodological point becomes immediately apparent when discussing PNI within a lifespan perspective, because most immune responses and the prevalence of disease varies with age. In addition, because childhood and old age are times of more frequent disease, this has led us to propose that the relationship between psychosocial factors and immunity has particular significance for the young and the elderly.

We know that the susceptibility to infectious disease—including gastrointestinal and respiratory—is highest in the very young, which reflects the immaturity of the immune system. Because of the rapid developmental changes at this stage, we typically tailor our immune measures to the age of the monkey; even within just the infancy period, we choose different ones for the neonate than for the older infant. Immune responses mature to be more effective in adolescence and adulthood, which may account for the relative resilience of most adults in the face of challenge, even when stressful events result in a temporary lowering of immune responses. For most of us, who refrain from disease-causing behavior and are fortunate to be spared catastrophic events in adulthood, a second period of immunologic vulnerability will not emerge again until old age, when we see a return of the morbidity and mortality associated with infectious disease. In addition, the two other major categories of immune-related disease, autoimmune disorders and cancer, also become more common in older individuals. These illnesses reflect either a mistaken response of the immune system, which gets directed inappropriately toward healthy tissue (as in the case of multiple sclerosis), or a failure of the immune surveillance processes to detect, contain, and clear mutagenic tissue. Thus, the two significant periods of developmental change in immunity—maturation of immune competence during infancy and the subsequent loss of vigor and regulation with immune senescence in old age—account for the two-peaked profile of immunological disease across the life span (Pawelec & Solana, 1997).

The thesis that we will be advancing in this chapter is that events in early infancy, including psychosocial ones, influence this immunological trajectory and establish a lifelong bias for health or disease. From a developmental PNI perspective, the immune system of the young child appears to be both more sensitive and more likely to show long-lasting alterations following disturbance of the social milieu. The persistence may be due to a failure to return as readily to the original immune status seen in the prechallenge period or because a normal sequence of development was derailed irreversibly in some manner. Several examples of immune derailment will be described below, including perturbations of the uterine environment of the fetal monkey and deviations from normal rearing by the mother. On a positive note, though, in a healthy adult, when the regulatory processes of the immune system are more resistant to disturbance by extrinsic factors, there appears to be an extended period in the middle of the life span when stressful and challenging events cause only transient changes in immunity without much disease sequelae. Research by Cohen et al. (Cohen, Tyrell, & Smith, 1991; Cohen & Williamson, 1991) on the vulnerability of adults to infection with respiratory viruses suggests that social factors may contribute significantly to this physiological stability by buffering us against psychological stressors and even viral infection, just as psychosocial processes seem to be important in guiding the normal path of behavioral and physiological development during infancy.

Immune Alterations after Disturbance of Social Relationships in Animals

Considerable interest in the relationship between social factors and immunity in nonhuman primates was generated by two seminal papers, which reported changes in immune responses for up to two weeks after young monkeys were separated from either the mother or a young monkey companion (Laudenslager, Reite, & Harbeck, 1982; Reite, Harbeck, & Hoffman, 1981). These studies utilized the lymphocyte proliferation assay, which involves stimulating cells in vitro with plant proteins (mitogens) and then assessing the cellular incorporation of thymidine as a measure of cell proliferation. The excitement about the observed decrease in proliferation following social separation stemmed from the fact that it appeared to concur with the inhibition of cellular functions found in depressed and stressed humans (Herbert & Cohen, 1993). Subsequent studies on young monkeys qualified the actual duration of the change in lymphocyte proliferation, indicating it might typically last only a few days (Friedman, Coe, & Ershler, 1991), but, more important, the general conclusion was extended to other cellular measures and additional manipulations of the psychosocial domain.

We know today that shifts in the number and type of cells in circulation are a reliable corollary of most significant changes in the monkey's social world (Coe, 1993). Separation of the young monkey from the mother, as well as removal of older juveniles and even adults from a social group, have been found to temporarily decrease the number of lymphocytes in their bloodstream (Gust et al., 1992). Further, as shown in figure 8.1, when the total number of lymphocytes declines, there is often a drop in the ratio of certain lymphocyte subsets in a direction that would impair the initiation of an immune response. This change is often described as a decrease in the T-helper–to–T-suppressor cell ratio, which has been documented by quantifying fewer cells in the blood with CD4 proteins on their surface relative to ones that express CD8 proteins. In keeping with these quantitative changes in cell numbers, other studies have confirmed that cell functioning is also inhibited for a period of time after social disturbance. For example, a decrease in lymphocyte cytolytic activity has been found in several species of monkeys after social relationships are disrupted and the animals are housed away from social companions (Coe & Erickson, 1997). This assay assesses the ability of specific types of lymphocytes, the natural killer and the T-killer cells, to lyse cancerous or virally infected cells by mixing the effector cells from the monkey

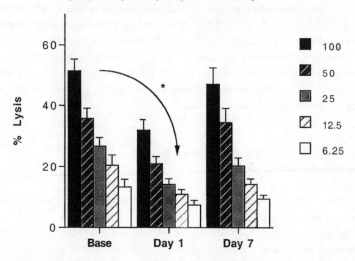

Figure 8.1 Changes in lymphocyte cytolytic activity in infant squirrel monkeys after experimental separation from the mother for one week when the infants were 7–8 months of age. Lysis of target cells (K562) is shown at 5 ratios of infant cells–to–target cells (effector: target). Note that the asterisk indicates a significant decrease on the first day after separation, followed by a recovery to baseline levels by the seventh day. Thus, this study also reveals the recuperative capacity of the immune system. Modified from Coe & Erickson (1997).

together with target cells in in vitro cultures. Typically, one finds a reduction in lytic activity that lasts for several days after the dissolution of the monkey's social relationship, and the temporal duration parallels the one to three days of behavioral and endocrine activation.

To verify that these cellular alterations could be of potential significance for disease, monkeys have been exposed to foreign substances during the period of social disturbance, and their antibody levels have been determined to assess whether the ability to mount an antibody response was compromised (Coe, Rosenberg, & Levine, 1988; Laudenslager & Boccia, 1996). For humane reasons, disease-causing pathogens have not been used in these studies with infant primates; instead, responses to noninfectious proteins have been tested. Subsequent to social separations, monkeys have been administered either a protein from a type of marine snail (keyhole limpet hemacyanin, KLH) or injected with a bacteriophage, a nonpathogenic virus that normally infects only certain types of bacteria. After exposure to either type of antigen, separated monkeys show a significant reduction in antibody responses as compared to undisturbed control monkeys exposed to the same proteins while still living with their mothers. These findings allow one to draw a general conclusion from rodent and monkey species to humans: after stressful events, there is a period of immune dysregulation, often of sufficient magnitude to increase the risk for disease in the event of exposure to a pathogen. This summary statement applies to both infant monkeys and to adult animals. In one study of adult monkeys, the investigators were able to verify this point directly by using an infectious virus (Cohen et al., 1997). When the social composition of adult monkey groups was changed frequently over a period of a year, it increased the likelihood of infection with a cold virus as compared to animals who lived in stable social groups, who were unlikely to develop an active infection even when the rhinovirus was applied directly to the nasal mucosa.

One question we raised earlier, however, is: what would transpire in a disease-free monkey or human not exposed to a pathogen during the period of immune compromise? In the older infant and adult monkey, our experience has been that there is a gradual restoration of normal immunity, with the recovery process typically paralleling the time required for the animal to adapt at the behavioral level. In the case of separation from familiar animals or surroundings, this transition and adjustment usually begins within one to three days, which facilitates the return to the prior state of immune competence (Bailey & Coe, 1999). It is of further interest that the recovery process in monkeys can be modulated by experimental manipulations, which make sense with respect to our anthropocentric view of how an animal should adjust after this type of disturbance. Immune alterations are markedly attenuated if the separated monkey is allowed to remain in the home environment after removal of its companions, rather than being relocated to an unfamiliar setting (Coe et al., 1987). Conversely, if after being removed from the mother and relocated to a new cage, the young infant is housed with other familiar animals, the behavioral and physiological responses to maternal loss are reduced. These findings convey two additional points: (1) cognitive and emotional responses determine the magnitude and duration of the initial immune sequelae after a social stressor, and (2) psychological processes are equally important in facilitating the homeostatic recovery of the immune system, which will most likely return to normal unless a pathogenic process was initiated.

Having documented both the potential significance of the initial immune changes, in terms of the infant monkey's ability to respond to infectious pathogens, and the temporal pattern of recovery, our interest and research shifted to effects that might occur earlier in development. We began to investigate if there would be more lasting, perhaps permanent, consequences after disturbances of the social milieu in early infancy, especially if the immune system was perturbed at the more immature stage of neonate. The studies described above had involved monkeys of 6–12 months of age, a developmental point after nursing is complete when the infant is increasingly independent, comparable to a 3–5-year-old human child. The next section reviews some of the immune consequences of experimental manipulations in the neonatal period, which suggest that the effects on immunity are more lasting and not as readily amenable to restoration.

Immune Dysregulation Subsequent to Manipulation of the Social Rearing Environment

Human and monkey infants are immunocompetent at birth, but many of their cellular responses are still immature and not as efficient as those found in the adult. In addition, for certain pathogens, the neonate relies on direct immunological assistance from the mother, receiving some of her antibody before and some after birth. Maternal IgG, or the "memory" class of antibody, is provided via the placenta before birth, while antibodies of A class, which can coat the gut lining, are transferred via breast milk. These maternal antibodies facilitate a process called passive immunity, which allows some bacterial and viral pathogens to be neutralized without requiring an active response by the infant's immune system. Given the importance of passive immunity, one might already anticipate that a disruption of the early mother-infant relationship could have some negative consequences, at a minimum because of the loss of maternal IgA normally obtained through suckling (possibly impairing protection against enteric pathogens of the gut). In addition, consideration of other aspects of developmental immunology raises more concerns. It has been known for several decades that the immune system must "learn" to respond to antigens in the environment, and this priming is important in stimulating the development of both antibody and cellular immune responses (this notion is embedded in the term *antigen*, which signifies that it is an *anti*body-*gen*erating substance). As a consequence, animals raised in germ-free environments fail to develop competent immune responses, and their "inexperienced" immune systems are more vulnerable to pathogens. Significant deviations from normal maternal care thus could also affect the development of immunity by influencing the infant's early exposure to antigenic substances, both benign and pathogenic ones.

To specifically investigate the influence of the mother on infant immunity, we conducted a series of three studies that assessed immune responses in monkeys raised under different conditions. Initially, we used a cross-sectional approach and compared the immune responses of 28 monkeys from four rearing backgrounds (Coe, Lubach, Ershler, & Klopp, 1989). For normal control values, we collected blood samples from 1–2-year-old juveniles, who had lived continuously with their mothers from birth and were still housed with them in small social groups ($N = 8$). In contrast, the rearing of the other 20 monkeys deviated from this naturalistic rearing pattern: 12 monkeys had been weaned from the mothers at six months of age and then housed either alone or in peer groups; the 8 remaining monkeys had been bottle fed and reared by human caregivers. As can be seen in figure 8.2, when their lymphocyte proliferation responses were assessed, there were dramatic differences between groups, which depended upon their early rearing conditions. Both the total absence of a mother and removal from the mother at six months of age affected the cell proliferation responses found in the juvenile monkeys. Further study of the human-reared monkeys revealed that the immune differences were enduring: the elevated lymphocyte proliferative activity was still present when a second set of blood samples was collected a year later, when the monkeys were 2.5 years of age.

Subsequent evaluations of monkeys from other rearing backgrounds indicated that each manipulation had a unique effect on the lymphocyte proliferative responses manifested by the juvenile monkey, although not always in the up direction. In one rearing condition, monkeys spent the first year of life with their mothers but had experienced a series of acute social separations from her when three to seven months of age. Instead of elevated lymphocyte proliferative responses at one

Lymphocyte Proliferation

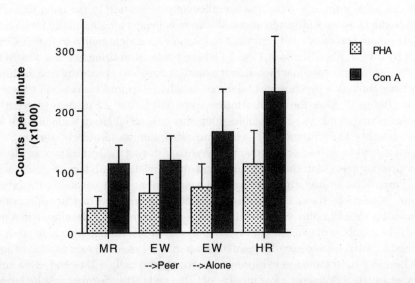

Figure 8.2 Proliferative response to in vitro stimulation with two mitogens (phytohemagglutin and concanavalin A). Lymphocytes were obtained from 28 juvenile rhesus monkeys raised under 4 different conditions. Monkeys raised by humans from birth (HR) had significantly elevated proliferative activity as compared to mother-reared (MR) animals still living in social groups with the mother. Intermediate cellular responses were found in monkeys who were weaned at 6 months of age (EW) and then housed either alone or in juvenile peer groups. Modified from Coe, Lubach, Ershler, & Klopp (1989).

to two years of age, theirs were below the values from undisturbed controls. Another laboratory also reported that 1–2-week-long separation experiences in infancy could affect proliferation responses years later in adult monkeys (Laudenslager, Capitanio, & Reite, 1985). The take-home message seemed to be that each rearing condition would result in a distinct immune profile as the monkeys matured, at least with respect to how their cells reacted to mitogen stimulation. To understand more about the developmental processes that underlie these rearing effects, we investigated immune responses in younger monkeys between five and twelve months of age (Coe, Lubach, Schneider, Dierschke, & Ershler, 1992). Again, we found that removal of the monkey neonate from the mother at birth and rearing by humans caused the most deviant immune responses; most significantly, we replicated the prior observation that their lymphocyte proliferative activity would be elevated above normal. Moreover, we now had evidence of other immune alterations in these human-reared monkey infants, including a tendency for lower cytolytic activity and smaller antibody responses to a tetanus vaccination.

These findings led us to conduct a third study in order to obtain an explanation for the differences between these various immune responses and especially to account for the increased proliferative responses, which seemed paradoxical if removal from the mother at birth was viewed simply as an early stress condition (stressors are usually thought to inhibit lymphocyte proliferation in the older animal). Across the first year of life, blood samples were collected longitudinally from eight human-reared monkeys and compared to samples from eight monkeys reared naturally by their mothers (Lubach, Coe, & Ershler, 1995). In addition, we also sought to determine in this experiment whether it would be possible to restore normal cellular reactions through a psychosocial intervention when the monkeys reached one year of age (fig. 8.3). After the blood samples were obtained at 12 months of age, the human-reared monkeys were combined together as a social group with an adult female monkey to facilitate their behavioral rehabilitation. Similarly, the mother-reared infants were housed together in a large cage during the second year of life, in a group comprised of the eight juveniles and one unrelated adult female.

Lymphocyte proliferative responses were again found to be elevated in the infant monkeys raised by humans away from the mother, but now we had an opportunity to monitor their lymphocyte subsets simultaneously across this developmental period. The numbers of two different types of T-cells in the blood appeared to provide at least a partial explanation for the overreaction to mitogens. By six months of age, the human-reared monkeys evinced an abnormal ratio of the CD4+ and CD8+ subsets, especially because of a low number of CD8+ cells. This decrease resulted in an unusually high helper-to-suppressor–cell ratio for the rhesus monkey (fig. 8.3).

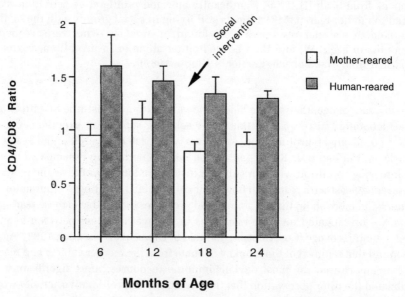

Figure 8.3 Ratio of lymphocyte subsets in mother-reared and human-reared rhesus monkeys shown at 6-month intervals through 2 years of age. Values at each age point are the mean of 2–3 bimonthly blood samples per subject. The elevated CD4/CD8 ratios in the human-reared monkeys were due primarily to low levels of CD8+ cells. Note also that the abnormal ratio was not corrected by social rehabilitation during the second year of life. Modifed from Lubach, Coe, & Ershler (1995).

Based on this finding, the increased proliferation should not be interpreted as enhanced or better but rather as a reflection of this atypical pattern of T-cells in the bloodstream. In addition, with a more complete characterization of other immune measures, we were able to verify that the increased proliferative activity occurred in the context of abnormal immunity overall, including lower cytolytic activity. We concluded that certain aspects of maternal care, including possibly immune products in breast milk, must be essential for the normal development of immunity. Beyond this lesson that the mother is critical for establishing normal immunity in the infant, the last study revealed that it is not easy to restore normal physiology after it has been derailed. Differences in cell numbers and proliferation were not corrected after the onset of typical social housing conditions at one year of age, even though there appeared to be significant improvements in the behavior of the human-reared monkeys after the experimental intervention. The human-reared monkeys stopped exhibiting some of their repetitive, stereotypic behaviors and began to behave more like the mother-reared ones over time, but their immune responses continued to be deviant for the remainder of the one-year follow-up.

Immune Status of Infants Born from Disturbed Pregnancies

After finding that the development of immunity might be persistently altered by either rearing without a mother or premature disruption of maternal care, we began another line of research to investigate the possible consequences of disturbance even earlier in life, when the immune system is first being formed. These ongoing studies have been evaluating whether factors that affect the pregnant female, including social stressors, can impinge upon her fetus and then continue to have effects on maturation postnatally. The essential glands of the immune system, including the thymus and spleen, form during the fetal stage, and they must become populated with an appropriate repertoire of cells. These cells must also "learn" certain responses, such as the ability to distinguish healthy cells from foreign pathogens (sometimes described as the distinction between self and nonself). In fact, as immune cells differentiate, if they start to react inappropriately to "self" proteins, it may cause the cells to undergo a natural death, or suicide process (i.e., apoptosis). It is known from studies of teratogenic substances and drugs that these formative immune processes can be disrupted. Moreover, after prolonged or noxious prenatal manipulations, the thymus gland can entirely regress, sometimes failing to resurrect the correct lymphoid structure and cell populations (Sawyer, Hendrickx, Osburn, & Terrell, 1977). Our research has been examining whether more moderate stressful events experienced by the mother—psychosocial or physiological—also have the potential to cause similar changes in the fetus, possibly disrupting critical cellular decisions in fetal life. If so, the consequences might be quite enduring, because the disruptions could affect the set points for later immune processes in the adult. For example, it has been suggested that the rate of cell turnover in adults (life span and replacement of lymphocytes) may be established in utero (Freitas & Rocha, 1993).

We began by studying the effects of social disturbance in pregnant female monkeys, using experimental manipulations such as relocating the gravid female to a new social group during midgestation (Schneider & Coe, 1993). Subsequently, the stress paradigm was refined to allow for a more quantitative and controlled assessment of the disturbance (Schneider, Coe, & Lubach, 1992). Below we describe the effects on infant immunity that were elicited by disturbing the pregnant monkey on a daily basis for ten minutes per day for six weeks, or 25% of the 24-week gestation. We have also been determining whether these effects of psychological stressors on the gravid female and her offspring can be recreated by drug treatments that mimic stress physiology. For example, in one series of studies we found that activating the mother's adrenal gland with adrenocorticotrophin hormone (ACTH) for two weeks during midpregnancy induced immune alterations in the infant monkey that persisted through at least two years of age (Coe, Lubach, Karaszewski, & Ershler, 1996; Reyes & Coe, 1997).

One finding, illustrated in figure 8.4, documents the potentially potent impact

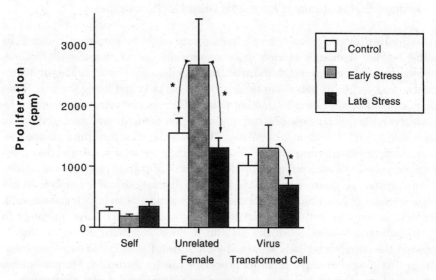

Figure 8.4 Proliferation of mononuclear cells from neonatal monkeys in response to mitomycin-treated stimulator cells from (1) self, (2) an unrelated female, or (3) herpes virus–transformed rhesus monkey cell line. Infants that had experienced stress early in pregnancy (days 50–92 postconception) had increased responses to nonself antigens (indicated by asterisk). In contrast, cells from monkeys that had been disturbed later in pregnancy (days 105–147 postconception) proliferated less than cells from infants in the control and Early Stress Conditions (asterisks indicate significant difference in response to both types of stimulator cells). All monkeys were full term (mean gestational age: 168–171 days). Reprinted from Coe, Lubach, & Karaszewski (1999).

of in utero events on postnatal immunity. It also conveys another important point: distinct and greater effects occur if the fetus is at a very early stage of development when the provocative event occurs (Coe, Lubach, & Schneider, 1999). In this particular experiment, we compared infant monkeys born after undisturbed pregnancies to ones generated from pregnancies disturbed during either early or mid- to late gestation (days 50–92 or 105–147 postconception, respectively). Each day of the six-week period, females in the disturbance condition were relocated to an unfamiliar room for ten minutes, and a startle response was elicited three times by the one-second sounding of a horn. After this prenatal manipulation, however, all pregnant females and their fetuses were left undisturbed for at least one month, and the evaluation focused on the behavioral and physiological status of the infant after birth. Both the early and late disturbance conditions were found to have affected fetal development based on the neonate's behavior and immunity, but even greater effects were induced by the early stress condition. The infants disturbed early in gestation were born with more immature neuromotor reflexes, including a reduced ability to roll over or to hold up their heads. Moreover, their immune responses were quite distinctive. Blood samples were collected on day 2 postpartum to test the ability of the neonate's cells to recognize self from nonself proteins (fig. 8.4). This was done by incubating the infant's lymphocytes with either its own cells, cells from a genetically unrelated animal, or cultured cells that had been infected with a herpes virus. In this type of mixed lymphocyte response (MLR) assay, proliferative responses by the infant's cells reflect the ability to recognize and respond to the foreign proteins on the stimulator cells. As can be seen, lingering effects of the prior disturbance were evident for both early and late stress conditions, but the stage of fetal development at the time of the perturbation proved to be extremely important. Early in gestation, the developmental disturbance resulted in an overreactive response at birth, whereas later in pregnancy, the same type of maternal stress caused the neonate to be hyporesponsive. We hypothesized that altering the uterine environment at these two distinct points in fetal development differentially affected the maturation of cellular processes in the thymus critical for this later response in the neonate.

The occurrence of both increased and decreased responses may seem confusing, but as with the finding discussed earlier about higher lymphocyte proliferative activity in human-reared monkeys, it is not always beneficial for immune responses to be elevated. In some cases, it may reflect a fundamental dysregulation. Ongoing evaluations of the infants from the early stress condition have continued to show that they were more severely affected on most behavioral and immune measures. Beyond differences in neuromotor maturation at birth, they have been observed to be more emotionally reactive and more socially submissive than infants derived from control and late stress pregnancies (Coe et al., 1999). Further, they evinced other signs of physiological abnormalities, including lower iron levels in their blood during the first eight months of life. This hematological condition appears to be due to a decreased transfer of maternal iron to the baby before birth in the case of disturbed pregnancies. Since breast milk provides only about 50% of the iron required by the growing infant, the prenatally disturbed ones are at greater risk for an iron deficiency anemia at four to six months postpartum, before they can fulfill their dietary iron needs by eating solid foods.

Significance of Developmental PNI

This latter observation of an altered iron homeostasis induced by prenatal stress brings us back to a point mentioned briefly in the introduction, which is that many complex processes must be considered in order to explain any influence of environmental and psychological events on immunity. In this review, we have provided evidence that several different types of disturbance can affect immunity in the monkey infant. In each example, the experiments involved manipulations that might implicate stress responses by the SNS or endocrine system as the primary mediators (Champoux, Coe, Schanberg, Kuhn, & Suomi, 1989; Clarke, Wittwer, Abbott, & Schneider, 1994; Shannon, Champoux, & Suomi, 1998; Uno et al., 1990). Unfortunately, though, in each of the three examples we have described, it has not been possible to show that a stress-related hormone from the adrenal, such as cortisol, is the sole or primary mediator. Even in the case of the response to social separation, which is known to cause sustained increases in pituitary-adrenal activity, we have found that immune alterations still continue to occur after drugs are administered to prevent the synthesis and release of cortisol or to block its actions with receptor antagonists (Coe & Erickson, 1997; Coe & Hall, 1996).

Similar interpretative challenges confront us when we try to decipher the primary processes and pathways that account for the influence of prenatal stress on the fetus. Considerable evidence does point to at least some role for increased levels of maternal cortisol during times of disturbance and challenge (Sandman et al., 1994). Further, we know that adrenal hormone release is increased by the experimental manipulations we utilized, including the ten-minute disturbance paradigm, and it is known that maternal cortisol can readily cross the placenta and affect the fetal monkey (Waddell, Albrecht, & Pepe, 1988). Nevertheless, many additional processes have been shown to be involved in the mediation of prenatal stress effects, including changes in oxygen, glucose, and nutrient transport to the fetus (Morishima, Pedersen, & Finster, 1978; Nathanielsz, Jansen, Yu, & Cabalum, 1984). In the specific case of maternal-fetal transfer of nutrients, we have documented that the placental transfer of maternal iron to the infant can be compromised, which predisposes the infant to anemia during the first year of life. Further research will be needed to clarify the relative contribution of these different stress-responsive physiological systems. But perhaps knowing the specific mediators is not as important as appreciating the fact that the maturation of infant immunity is sensitive to so many intrinsic and extrinsic factors.

Our examples were derived exclusively from experiments on monkeys, and so it is reasonable to question whether comparable findings would be obtained in research on children. Because of ethical concerns and practical issues related to obtaining the requisite blood samples from children, there is obviously a smaller body of research on which to base such a claim. Yet, for each of the paradigms we described—disruption of the mother-infant relationship, abnormal rearing conditions, and gestational stress—there is at least some research to suggest that the findings are relevant to human fetuses (Shiono & Gomby, 1993). We mentioned earlier that there are several studies that demonstrate an influence of family functioning on the frequency and severity of respiratory illness in children (Boyce et al., 1977). Further, a direct effect of family functioning on immunity was implicated in a year-long evaluation of streptococcal infections in children, which showed differences in both the percent with positive throat cultures and the number who went on to have a systemic infection and symptoms (Meyer & Haggerty, 1962). We can also look to other types of pediatric research for evidence that early rearing events can affect other immune-related illnesses. For example, quality of family life and occurrence of stressful childhood events have been associated with an earlier onset of asthma in children born to families with a high genetic risk for this condition (Mrazek, Klinnert, Mrazek, & Macey, 1991). Our research group has also begun to extend the applicability of this developmental PNI perspective to humans, including the consequences of other types of perturbations in early life. In one study, we found altered immune responses in adult individuals with a mild form of cerebral palsy (spastic hemiparesis), which we hypothesized might be a consequence of damage to the brain during the perinatal period (Rogers, Coe, & Karaszewski, 1998).

In the introduction to this chapter, we proposed that these developmental influences on immunity are most appropriately viewed within a lifespan perspective. Psychosocial factors have the potential to influence physiological functioning at any age and, in that sense, the relationships we have described are not restricted to infancy. Even in adults, recent stressful events and a number of lifestyle factors have been shown to increase the risk for succumbing to infection from the common cold and influenza viruses (Cohen, Tyrell, & Smith, 1991; see also chap. 7). Moreover, the capacity for stressful events to change immune responses in adults is known to be influenced by other psychological processes, such as social support, which affect one's ability to cope with a challenging situation (Kang, Coe, Karaszewski, & McCarthy, 1998; Kiecolt-Glaser et al., 1984). Nevertheless, while these psychobiological relationships may be observed at any point in the life span, we believe they will ultimately prove to be of greatest consequence for health in the very young and the elderly. The provocative studies of decreased immunity and slower wound healing in elderly humans engaged in the demanding process of caring for a sick relative certainly indicate that older individuals can undergo physiological changes with disease relevance (Kiecolt-Glaser et al., 1987b, 1995, 1996). Because our chapter has almost exclusively discussed findings on nonhuman primates, we should also mention that the special significance of PNI for the aged individual is not restricted just to elderly humans. Evaluations of immunity in old monkeys indicate that stressful social housing conditions, the demands of establishing new social relationships, and even minor medical procedures, can markedly lower the immunological vigor of an aged animal (Coe et al., 1992; Lemieux, Coe, & Ershler, 1996).

While drawing such broad comparisons between the beginning and end of the life span requires a simplification of the complex aging process, we believe that it is an appropriate application of the developmental PNI perspective. Others have noted previously that this perspective adds an important dimension to a general discussion about psychosocial factors and health (Ader, 1983). By introducing the notion of an age-related vulnerability, we help to focus the interpretation of immune alterations toward a consideration of their relevance for disease. Fortunately, in the healthy, middle-aged adult, many of the immune changes we can now document with our sensitive assays do not appear to have immediate disease sequelae. Instead, we have argued that they may be of greatest consequence for the young and the old. One exception to this statement may be individuals who have an inherited familial risk for an immune-related disease with a modal age of onset in midadulthood, where PNI-type relationships could precipitate pathology and symptom expression.

Finally, we have also hypothesized that intrinsic, age-related trajectories in immunity, which occur both during early maturation and senescence, may accentuate the effects of extrinsic factors by prolonging and elaborating the initial actions. Our studies have focused on stressful events, primarily the disruption of social relationships, and the resulting perturbations of immunity. It is also likely that other social factors could help maintain the stability and course of immune development and foster immunological health through extended periods of the life span. Events early in the life span, possibly even before birth, could help to establish the foundation for this immunological resilience by biasing the developmental trajectory toward health.

References

Ader, R. (1981). *Psychoneuroimmunology*. New York: Academic.

Ader, R. (1983). Developmental psychoneuroimmunology. *Developmental Psychobiology, 16*, 251–267.

Ader, R., & Friedman, S. G. (1965). Social factors affecting emotionality and resistance to disease in animals. V. Early separation from the mother and response to transplanted tumor in the rat. *Psychosomatic Medicine, 27*, 119–122.

Bailey, M. T., & Coe, C. L. (1999). Maternal separation disrupts indigenous microflora of infant monkeys. *Developmental Psychobiology, 35*, 146–155.

Bartrop, R. W., Luckhurst, E., Lazarus, L., Kiloh, L. G., & Penny, R. (1977). Depressed lymphocyte function after bereavement. *Lancet, 1*, 834–836.

Benschop, R. J., Rodriguez-Feuerhahn, M., & Schedlowski, M. (1996). Catecholamine-induced leukocytosis: Early observations, current research and future directions. *Brain, Behavior and Immunity, 10*, 77–91.

Boyce, W. T., Chesterman, E. A., Martin, N., Folkman, S., Cohen, F., & Wara, D. (1993). Immunologic changes at kindergarten entry predict respiratory illnesses following the Loma Prieta earthquake. *Journal of Developmental and Behavioral Pediatrics, 14*(5), 296–303.

Boyce, W. T., Jensen, E. W., Cassel, J. C., Collier, A. M., Smith, A. N., & Ramey, C. T. (1977). Influence of life events and family routines on childhood respiratory tract illness. *Pediatrics, 60*, 609–615.

Champoux, M., Coe, C. L., Schanberg, S., Kuhn, C., & Suomi, S. (1989). Hormonal effects of early rearing conditions in the infant rhesus monkey. *American Journal of Primatology, 19*, 111–118.

Clarke, A. S., Wittwer, D. J., Abbott, D. H., & Schneider, M. L. (1994). Long-term effects of prenatal stress on HPA axis activity in juvenile rhesus monkeys. *Developmental Psychobiology, 27*, 257–269.

Coe, C. L. (1993). Psychosocial factors and immunity in nonhuman primates: A review. *Psychosomatic Medicine, 55*, 298–308.

Coe, C. L, & Erickson, C. (1997). Stress decreases natural killer cell activity in the young monkey even after blockade of steroid and opiate hormone receptors. *Developmental Psychobiology, 30*(1), 1–10.

Coe, C. L., Ershler, W. B., Champoux, M., & Olson, J. (1992). Psychological factors and immune senescence in the aged primate. *Annals of the New York Academy of Sciences, 650*, 276–282.

Coe, C. L., & Hall, N. (1996). Psychological disturbance alters thymic and adrenal hormone secretion in a parallel but independent manner. *Psychoneuroendocrinology, 21*(2), 237–247.

Coe, C. L., Lubach, G. R., Ershler, W. B., & Klopp, R. G. (1989). Effect of early rearing on lymphocyte proliferation responses in rhesus monkeys. *Brain, Behavior and Immunity, 3*, 47–60.

Coe, C. L., Lubach, G. R., & Karaszewski, J. (1999). Prenatal stress and recognition of self and nonself in the primate neonate. *Biology of the Neonate, 76*, 301–310.

Coe, C. L., Lubach, G. R., Karaszewski, J., & Ershler, W. B. (1996). Prenatal endocrine activation influences the postnatal development of immunity in the infant monkey. *Brain, Behavior and Immunity 10*, 221–234.

Coe, C. L., Lubach, G. R., & Schneider, M. L. (1999). Neuromotor and socioemotional behavior in the young monkey is presaged by prenatal conditions. In M. Lewis & D. Ramsay (Eds.), *Soothing and stress* (pp. 19–38). Mahwah, NJ: Lawrence Erlbaum.

Coe, C. L., Lubach, G. R., Schneider, M. L., Dierschke, D. J., & Ershler, W. B. (1992). Early rearing conditions alter immune responses in the developing infant primate. *Pediatrics, 90*(3), 505–509.

Coe, C. L., Rosenberg, L. T., & Levine, S. (1987). Psychological factors capable of preventing the inhibition of antibody responses in separated primate infants. *Child Development, 58*, 1420–1430.

Coe, C. L., Rosenberg, L. T., & Levine, S. (1988). Effect of maternal separation on the complement system and antibody responses in infant primates. *International Journal of Neuroscience, 40*, 289–302.

Cohen, S. (1988). Psychosocial models of the role of social support in the etiology of physical disease. *Health Psychology, 7*(3), 269–297.

Cohen, S., Line, S., Manuck, S. B., Rabin, B. S., Heise, E., & Kaplan, J. R. (1997). Chronic social stress, social status, and susceptibility to upper respiratory infections in nonhuman primates. *Psychosomatic Medicine, 59*(3), 213–221.

Cohen, S., Tyrell, D. A. J., & Smith, A. P. (1991). Psychological stress in humans and susceptibility to the common cold. *New England Journal of Medicine, 325*, 606–612.

Cohen, S., & Williamson, G. (1991). Stress and infectious disease in humans. *Psychological Bulletin, 109*, 5–24.

Crary, B., Borysenko, M., Sutherland, D. C., Kutz, I., Borysenko, J. Z., & Benson H. (1983). Decrease in mitogen responsiveness of mononuclear cells from peripheral blood after epinephrine administration in humans. *Journal of Immunology, 130*, 694–697.

Freitas, A. A., & Rocha, B. B. (1993). Lymphocyte lifespans, homeostasis, selection and competition. *Immunology Today, 14*(1), 25–29.

Friedman, E., Coe, C. L., & Ershler, W. B. (1991). Time dependent effects of peer separation on lymphocyte proliferation in juvenile squirrel monkeys. *Developmental Psychobiology, 24*, 159–173.

Gust, D. A., Gordon, T. P., Wilson, M. E., Rodie, A. R., Ahmed-Ansari, A., & McClure, H. M. (1992). Removal from natal social group to peer housing affects cortisol levels and absolute numbers of T-cell subsets in juvenile monkeys. *Brain, Behavior and Immunity, 6*(2), 189–199.

Heisel, J. S. (1972). Life changes as etiologic factors in juvenile rheumatoid arthritis. *Journal of Psychiatric Research, 16,* 411–420.

Herbert, T. B. & Cohen, S. (1993). Stress and immunity in humans: A meta-analytic review. *Psychosomatic Medicine, 55,* 364–379.

Irwin, M., Daniels, M., Smith, T. L., Bloom, E., & Weiner, H. (1987). Impaired natural killer cell activity during bereavement. *Brain, Behavior and Immunity, 1,* 98–104.

Ishigami, T. (1919). The influence of psychic acts on the progress of pulmonary tuberculosis. *American Review of Tuberculosis, 2,* 470–484.

Jacobs, T. J., & Charles, E. (1980). Life events and the occurrence of cancer in children. *Psychosomatic Medicine, 42,* 11–24.

Kang, D.-H., Coe, C. L., Karaszewski, J., and McCarthy, D. O. (1998). Relationship of social support to stress responses and immune function in healthy and asthmatic adolescents. *Research in Nursing and Health, 21,* 117–128.

Kiecolt-Glaser, J. K., Fisher, L., Ogrocki, P., Stout, J. C., Speicher, C. E., & Glaser, R. (1987). Marital quality, marital disruption, and immune function. *Psychosomatic Medicine, 48,* 13–34.

Kiecolt-Glaser, J. K., Garner, W., Speicher, C., Penn, C. M., Holiday, J., & Glaser, R. (1984). Psychosocial modifiers of immunocompetence in medical students. *Psychosomatic Medicine, 46,* 7–14.

Kiecolt-Glaser, J. K., Glaser, R., Dyer, C., Suttleworth, E., Ogrocki, P., & Speicher, C. E. (1987). Chronic stress and immunity in family caregivers of Alzheimer's disease victims. *Psychosomatic Medicine, 49,* 523–535.

Kiecolt-Glaser, J. K., Glaser, R., Gravenstein, S., Malarkey, W. B., & Sheridan, J. (1996). Chronic stress alters the immune response to influenza virus vaccine in the elderly. *Proceedings of the National Academy of Sciences, 93,* 3043–3047.

Kiecolt-Glaser, J. K., Marucha, P. T., Malarkey, W. B., Mercado, A. M., & Glaser, R. (1995). Slowing of wound healing by psychological stress. *Lancet, 346,* 1194–1196.

Laudenslager, M. L., & Boccia, M. L. (1996). Psychosocial stressors, immunity, and individual differences in nonhuman primates. *American Journal of Primatology, 39,* 205–221.

Laudenslager, M. L., Capitanio, J. P., & Reite, M. R. (1985). Possible effects of early separation experiences on subsequent immune function in adult macaque monkeys. *American Journal of Psychiatry, 142,* 862–865.

Laudenslager, M. L., Rasmussen, K. L. R., Berman, C. M., Suomi, S. J., & Berger, C. B. (1993). Specific antibody levels in free-ranging rhesus monkeys: relationships to plasma hormones, cardiac parameters, and early behavior. *Developmental Psychobiology, 26*(7), 407–420.

Laudenslager, M. L., Reite, M. R., & Harbeck, R. J. (1982). Suppressed immune response in infant monkeys associated with maternal separation. *Behavioral Neural Biology, 36,* 40–48.

Lemieux, A. M., Coe, C. L., & Ershler, W. B. (1996). Surgical and psychological stress differentially affect cytolytic responses in the aged female monkey. *Brain, Behavior and Immunity, 10,* 27–43.

Lubach, G. R., Coe, C. L., & Ershler, W. B. (1995). Effects of early rearing on immune responses in infant rhesus monkeys. *Brain, Behavior and Immunity, 9,* 31–46.

Marsh, J. T., & Rasmussen, A. F. (1960). Response of adrenals, thymus, spleen, and leukocytes to shuttle box and confinement stress. *Proceedings of the Society of Experimental Biology and Medicine, 104,* 180–183.

Meyer, R. J., & Haggerty, R. J. (1962). Streptococcal infections in families: Factors altering individual susceptibility. *Pediatrics, 29,* 539–549.

Mora, J. M., Amtmann, L. E., & Hoffman, S. J. (1926). Effect of mental and emotional states on the leukocyte count. *Journal of the American Medical Association, 86*, 945–946.

Morishima, H. O., Pedersen, H., & Finster, M. (1978). The influence of psychological stress on the fetus. *American Journal of Obstetrics and Gynecology, 131*, 286–290.

Mrazek, D. A., Klinnert, M. D., Mrazek, P., & Macey, T. (1991). Early asthma onset: Consideration of parenting issues. *Journal of the American Academy of Child and Adolescent Psychiatry, 30*, 277–282.

Munck, A., Guyre, P. M., & Holbrook, N. J. (1984). Physiological functions of glucocorticoids in stress and their relation to pharmacological actions. *Endocrine Reviews, 5*, 25–44.

Nathanielsz, P. W., Jansen, C. A. M., Yu, H. K., & Cabalum, T. (1984). Regulation of myometrial function throughout gestation and labor: Effect on fetal development. In R.W. Beard & P. W. Nathanielsz (Eds.), *Fetal physiology and medicine* (pp. 629–653). New York: Marcel Dekker.

Pawelec, G., & Solana, R. (1997). Immunosenescence. *Immunology Today, 18*(11), 514–516.

Reite, M., Harbeck, R., & Hoffman, A. (1981). Altered cellular immune response following peer separation. *Life Science, 29*, 1133–1136.

Reyes, T. M., & Coe, C. L. (1997). Prenatal manipulations reduce the pro-inflammatory response to a cytokine challenge in juvenile monkeys. *Brain Research, 769*, 29–35.

Rogers, S. L., Coe, C. L., & Karaszewski, J. W. (1998). Immune consequences of stroke and cerebral palsy in adults. *Journal of Neuroimmunology, 91*, 113–120.

Sandman, C. A., Wadhwa, P. D., Dukel-Schetter, C., Chicz-DeMet, A., Belman, J., Porto, M., Murata, Y., Garite, T. J., and Crinella, F. M. (1994). Psychobiological influences of stress and HPA regulation on the human fetus and infant birth outcomes. *Annals of the New York Academy of Sciences, 739*, 198–210.

Sawyer, R., Hendrickx, A., Osburn, B., & Terrell, T. (1977). Abnormal morphology of the fetal monkey (*Macaca mulatta*) thymus exposed to a corticosteroid. *Journal of Medical Primatology, 6*, 145–150.

Schleifer, S. J., Keller, S. E., Camerino, M., Thornton, J. C., & Stein, M. (1983). Depression of lymphocyte stimulation following bereavement. *Journal of the American Medical Association, 250*, 374–377.

Schneider, M. L., & Coe, C. L. (1993). Repeated stress during pregnancy impairs neuromotor development of the primate infant. *Journal of Developmental and Behavioral Pediatrics, 14*(2), 81–87.

Schneider, M. L., Coe, C. L., & Lubach, G. R. (1992). Endocrine activation mimics the adverse effects of prenatal stress on the neuromotor development of the primate infant. *Developmental Psychobiology, 25*(6), 427–439.

Shannon, C., Champoux, M., & Suomi, S. J. (1998). Rearing condition and plasma cortisol in rhesus monkey infants. *American Journal of Primatology, 46*(4), 311–322.

Shiono, P. H., and Gomby, D. (1993). Lifestyle and pregnancy outcome. In A. R. Fuchs, F. Fuchs, & P. G. Stubblefield (Eds.), *Preterm birth* (pp. 173–183). New York: McGraw-Hill.

Solomon, G. F., Levine, S., & Kraft, J. K. (1968). Early experience and immunity. *Nature, 220*, 821–822.

Uno, H., Lohmiller, L., Thieme, C., Kemnitz, J. W., Engle, M. J., Roecker, E. B., and Farrell, P. M.(1990). Brain damage induced by prenatal exposure to dexamethasone in fetal rhesus macaques. I. Hippocampus. *Developmental Brain Research, 53*, 157–167.

Waddell, B. J., Albrecht, E. D., and Pepe, G. J. (1988). Metabolism of cortisol and cortisone in the baboon fetus at midgestation. *Endocrinology, 122*, 84–88.

Weinman, D. K., & Rothman, A. H. (1967). Effects of stress upon acquired immunity to the dwarf tapeworm, *Hymenolepsis nana*. *Experimental Parasitology, 21*, 61–67.

Commentary

Teresa M. Reyes

The chapters of this volume, each in their own way, have addressed the influence of social relations on health. In the previous chapter, Coe and Lubach introduce a discussion of one possible pathway through which social relations could affect health: alterations in immunity. Coe, a developmental psychobiologist, has conducted ground-breaking work in the emerging field of psychoneuroimmunology (PNI). In their chapter, Coe and Lubach describe research done on rhesus monkeys, which has explored the relationship between alterations in the social bond and changes in immunity.

The chapter begins with a brief overview of some early PNI studies in humans, which demonstrated that psychological stress, including such events as bereavement, caregiving for a sick relative, or divorce, resulted in decreased lymphocyte proliferation (one measure of immune function) for one to two months. These types of findings are not restricted to adults but have been found in children as well. Two possible mediators of these immune alterations were considered: glucocorticoids and catecholamines, which are released from activation of two stress-responsive systems, the hypothalamic-pituitary-adrenal (HPA) axis and sympathetic nervous system (SNS), respectively.

Turning to his own research, Coe presents findings on young rhesus monkeys. In these studies, he focused on very early development, from prenatal to neonatal, during which an animal may be particularly sensitive to immune perturbations. When an animal is very young, the immune system, like other physiological systems, is still maturing. Perturbation during this period, even if transient in nature, could change the trajectory of development, which creates a bias for either health or disease. The research examined the immune sequelae after disruption of the social environment, first on older infant monkeys and then moving progressively earlier in development.

The first set of experiments involved a several-day separation of a young animal (6–12 months of age) from either its mother or a peer. Following this stressor, the animals displayed a number of immune alterations, including changes in the number of immune cells in circulation, decreased lymphocyte proliferation, decreased cytolytic activity and decreased antibody response. These findings were consistent and robust, sometimes resulting in decrements up to 50% of baseline. These experiments are a clear demonstration of how acute alterations in social environment can have profound effects on the immune system. However, equally important was the fact that these alterations were transient (usually lasting no more than a week). So it is important to view these findings within the appropriate context. If an animal were challenged by an infection during this one-week period of reduced immunity, it may be at a higher risk for illness. However, it is difficult to hypothesize what a one-week decrease in immune function could mean in terms of overall health, wellness, or longevity. On the other hand, if that stressor was constantly repeated or became chronic in nature, the outcome could be different, a scenario discussed later in this commentary. In addition, one strength of Coe's research method (made possible through the use of animal models) is highlighted in these findings. By sampling animals multiple times, a much clearer picture emerges. Over the course of a one-to-two–week period, three samples permited the researchers to characterize normal baseline functions, acute stress responses, and recovery periods. Furthermore, by using within-subjects designs, it was possible to control for the large individual differences that typically characterize these immune studies.

Coe also reported some intriguing relationships between individual reactions to the stressor and the animal's subsequent immune alterations. First, each animal's emotional response to the separation predicted both the magnitude and duration of the immune alteration. In other words, animals that were the most agitated by the separation showed the greatest immune alteration, which then persisted for a longer period of time. Similarly, separation from the mother (which is typically more stressful than separation from a peer) also resulted in larger and longer-lasting immune alterations. Second, Coe reported that modifying the social environment during the separation also influenced the magnitude and duration of the immune alteration. If, upon separation, the animal was left in its home cage rather than being moved to a novel environment or if it were provided with a peer companion, the immune alteration was significantly smaller. Presumably, these social factors acted by modifying the animal's emotional response to the separation. Therefore, it is apparent that immune alterations are not a necessary component of separation from the mother but rather reflect the negative emotion induced by loss of the mother in an unfamiliar or threatening environment.

In a second series of studies, Coe investigated what happened if these social stressors occurred earlier in the animal's life and for a longer period of time. In these studies, the social stressor was a disruption of the maternal bond. The study included animals raised normally with their mothers, animals weaned at six months and housed either alone or with peers, and animals that were removed from the mother at birth and raised by human caregivers. The human-reared monkeys showed an altered immune profile, including increased lymphocyte proliferation, decreased cytotoxic activity, and decreased antibody responses. Immune alterations in animals that were separated at six months were intermediate, with the peer-raised animals faring slightly better. These results concurred with the prior work, which indicated that disruptions in social bonds can have a significant impact on certain aspects of immune functioning, but in this study, the effects seemed more sustained.

One of the most interesting findings about the human-reared monkeys came at the point in the study when an attempt was made to rehabilitate them (to place them with their monkey peers). While it was possible to normalize their behavior, the immune alterations persisted for up to two years. Unlike animals who experienced only a brief separation, those who underwent a more permanent disruption of the maternal bond did not fully recover (immunologically), even though some of the behavioral abnormalities did abate. From these results, Coe and Lubach draw one of the main conclusions of their chapter: disturbance earlier in development, when the organism is more vulnerable, has the potential for more long-lasting immune consequences.

Finally, Coe discusses a newer line of research, which examines the effects of stress during gestation. Pregnant monkeys were exposed to a mild startle-noise stress, either early or late in pregnancy. As predicted, animals from the disturbed pregnancies showed a number of neuromotor, behavioral, and immune alterations, some of which have been documented out to two years of age. Interestingly, the baby monkeys from mothers who experienced the stressor early in gestation appeared to have a larger immune disturbance. The monkeys who were stressed late in gestation also experienced an immune alteration, although it was to a lesser extent and, in one case, was in a different direction. These findings (in utero disturbance) concur with two principles that emerged from the studies on disturbance of older infants: (1) the earlier the disruption, the greater the immune alteration, and (2) depending on the timing of the disturbance, either decreased or increased immune functioning may be elicited.

Unique Contributions

Coe's research with nonhuman primates sheds important light on the question of how social relations and health interact. One of the foremost contributions of his and Lubach's chapter is the description of a possible physiological pathway through which emotion and social relations could affect health. Coe has clearly demonstrated that certain psychosocial stressors (separation from peers or mother, abnormal rearing) can result in immune alterations in young animals. Moreover, the effects spanned a number of important cellular functions, which reflect different aspects of immunity, including changes in lymphocyte proliferation and cytotoxicity, effects on antibody production, and alterations in cell subsets in circulation.

Even more important than the specific findings is Coe's approach to interpreting these results. He makes two points that should be reiterated. The first is that following acute stress in the older animal, these immune alterations were transient and typically rebounded to normal within a week. That leads one to question the functional significance. What do these alterations in immune function mean in terms of health and disease? Certainly, it is incorrect to say that a transient decline in a single immune parameter translates into an increased susceptibility to disease. But what if that transient decline occurs repeatedly? Or what if it occurs in a particularly susceptible host (i.e., one with an already depressed immune system)? These are questions that remain to be answered. In animal research, one way to answer this question would be to challenge the immune-suppressed individual with some type of infectious organism which could help to determine if these alterations in immunity translate into an increased susceptibility to disease. Correlational studies in humans have already indicated an association between prior stress and increased susceptibility to infection with a cold virus (see chap. 7). It is also important to incorporate Coe's developmental outlook. For example, these transient immune alterations may not have immediate health consequences for the older animal. Yet, perhaps, that animal's health trajectory could be significantly shifted, such that it will become more vulnerable to disease at a later time in its life. It would be interesting to follow these animals beyond two years, for example, through puberty, when sex hormones begin to have an additional influence on the immune system. Even more prolonged follow-up into old age would be especially informative because this is when animals begin to show immune-related diseases. Unfortunately, just as with humans, this type of longitudinal research is cost prohibitive in monkeys and would involve decades of research (old age occurs after 20 years in the monkey).

These studies also make the important point that immune changes are exceedingly complex. An excellent example is the findings concerning lymphocyte proliferation. When 6–12-month-old animals were separated from their peers, they experienced a transient decrease in lymphocyte proliferation. Yet, when young animals experienced abnormal rearing (human rearing) or when they were exposed to a stressor in early gestation, an increase in lymphocyte proliferation was observed. At first glance, these results appear somewhat paradoxical, however, they highlight an important conclusion of Coe's work. That is, depending on when during development a stressor occurs, the effects will be different. As a consequence, it is often difficult to characterize these changes as "good" or "bad," unless one has a specific disease outcome in mind. For example, one can easily speculate why decreases in certain immune parameters could be bad. Decreased production of antibodies to the influenza vaccine may render a person more susceptible to infection if that person comes in contact with the influenza virus. On the other hand, an increased immune response is not always beneficial. Allergies and autoimmune diseases are characterized by a hyperreactive immune system, in which the immune responses may be misdirected toward benign stimuli or healthy tissue (for example, in multiple sclerosis, a patient's immune system attacks the myelin that surrounds their nerves). There is a balance that must be maintained within the immune system; a healthy individual needs to maximize her time between immunosuppression and excessive immune activation.

Studies of the type described in this chapter highlight some of the limitations of PNI research. All of the assays discussed in Coe and Lubach's chapter relied on cells that were circulating in the bloodstream, which may not be the best way to evaluate the immune system. For example, immune cells that reside in tissue (lymph nodes or at local sites of challenge) may provide a better view of how the localized immune response is progressing. However, for ethical reasons, it is not possible to repeatedly acquire this type of sample from either nonhuman primates or humans, as one might do in a rodent study. Blood measurements are likely the best we can do. Also, most of the immune measures discussed by Coe were based on in vitro assays, which have a number of limitations. For example, one of the most fascinating aspects of the immune system is that there is a great deal of redundancy. There are a number of proteins and cells that have overlapping functions within the system, so that if one aspect of the system should become impaired, there is usually at least one back-up system in place. Therefore, it is difficult to say, based on a reduction in one immune parameter assayed in vitro, whether or not that person or animal would be at higher risk for infection or ill-ness. A more extensive evaluation of an animal's overall immune status would be required. Ideally, one might construct an immune panel that includes assessing both the number and function of different leukocyte classes (T-cells, B-cells, cyto-toxic cells) as well as measuring levels of proteins (cytokines) and even nutrients (iron) in the blood that are essential for proper immune functioning. Better yet, this panel would also include some form of an in vivo assessment (for example, challenge with an infectious agent). But because these immune assays are expen-sive, researchers must typically balance the cost of additional measures with the potential to gain new insights. Currently, it is not possible to link decrements in a single immune parameter to "risk" for a specific disease. Furthermore, conduct-ing such a large panel of immune assays is fairly invasive (given the amount of blood needed to run multiple assays). Until less expensive, less invasive, and more predictive immune assays are developed, researchers in this field will be forced to balance cost and benefit.

Themes of This Volume

Cumulative Effects

As Coe points out, some of the immune alterations he noted were transient, espe-cially when the disruption was acute (a brief separation). But when the disruption was more long-lasting in nature (separation from the mother at birth), the immune consequences were much more long-lasting, some continuing out beyond two years. Presumably, long-term effects might also be found if an acute stressor were repeated (e.g., a brief separation that occurred consistently over a period of time). In other words, while the immune alterations that accompany an acute stressor may be transient, if that stressor is encountered time and again, the immune system may not be able to rebound as quickly. One of the great challenges for health re-searchers is to determine how small alterations cumulate to become disease-caus-ing processes. Coe and Lubach suggest one way: through altering the trajectory of development. Another explanation, allostatic load, has also been proposed. This refers to the accumulation of wear and tear on the body as it deals with stress over time (McEwen & Stellar, 1993; Seeman, Singer, Rowe, Horwitz, & McEwen, 1997). A similar principle may apply to the immune system. As mentioned previously, the immune system has a great deal of redundancy, such that loss of one function is often compensated for by other cells in the immune system. Yet, this capacity is not unlimited, and, perhaps, repeated insults over time could result in serious immune dysfunction. In other words, a transient decline in a single immune measure may not be enough to render that individual more vulnerable to disease. However, after repeated stressors and a lifetime of demands on the immune system, a person may now be more vulnerable to infection and disease.

Other authors in this volume have also discussed the cumulative effects of stress on health. Cohen reported no association between acute stressful life events and developing a cold. However, there was an association between chronic life difficulties and an increased risk for developing a cold, such that those with chronic difficulties lasting more than one month were 2.2 times as likely to develop a cold. This supports the hypothesis that perhaps an acute disruption (and a consequent transient decline in immunity) does not put one at risk, but if it develops into a chronic situation, it could have negative health consequences. A similar conclusion was reached by Seeman. She discussed this concept in terms of coronary heart disease and suggested that "social environment characteristics might be related more strongly to the progressive accumulation of coronary atherosclerosis over time than to the onset of acute myocardial infarction." She goes on to report that individuals who had more instrumental support and experienced "feeling loved" were at lower risk for atherosclerosis. This suggests that decreased social support may not directly increase the risk for myocardial infarction (MI) but rather is related to increased atherosclerosis, which over time increases one's risk for MI.

Mechanism

In any discussion of social relations and health, one subject that must ultimately be discussed is the question of mechanism. How do social emotions affect our health? Many of the authors in this volume discuss the mechanisms that underlie social processes, such as increased patient compliance or the promotion of a healthy lifestyle. I will focus instead on some of the biological mechanisms that have been discussed. Figure 8.5 is a schematic diagram that outlines some of the possible pathways that may mediate the effects of social relations on health/disease. Between these two end points are two possible mediators: changes in hormone levels and changes in immune function. The hormones commonly dis-

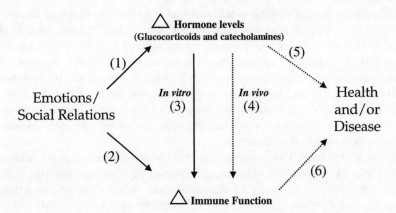

Figure 8.5 A schematic diagram outlining a subset of the potential pathways that connect emotions/social relations and health/disease. The solid lines represent pathways for which there is considerable experimental support, while the dotted lines represent pathways for which the empirical support is less robust.

cussed within this context include glucocorticoids (GCs) and catecholamines (i.e., epinephrine, norepinephrine). Certainly, this schematic is far from complete. Not only are there other important hormones in addition to GCs and catecholamines, but there are certainly other important physiological parameters that are not included here (e.g., blood pressure, diet). Instead, I have focused on some of the pathways that were common themes in the chapters in this volume.

The solid lines (1, 2) represent pathways about which we can be fairly confident. Many of the authors in this volume have provided convincing evidence for both of these pathways. Coe presents data to support pathway 2, which was reviewed earlier in this commentary. Seeman and Spiegel both presented data to support 1. Seeman presents strong evidence to link emotions/social relations directly to cardiovascular disease and discusses whether changes in stress hormone levels may be one pathway. She reports that, for men, increased frequency of emotional support was related to lower levels of urinary cortisol, norepinephrine, and epinephrine. Seeman also discusses population studies that have reported a link between higher reported levels of support and a better physiologic profile (lower heart rate and blood pressure, lower cholesterol, and lower urinary norepinephrine). Spiegel and Kimerling also reported decreased catecholamines in men and women who received social support by a close other. But again, it is important to remember that these relationships are not simple. For example, Seeman also presented an example in which women had a larger network of emotional support, which should have been accompanied by lower catecholamine levels. But, along with the larger network, there was an increase in negative social interactions, and in turn, these women showed increased levels of norepinephrine, rather than decreased levels.

It is a widely held belief that there is a solid link between elevated hormone levels and decreased immune function (pathways 3 and 4). This pathway is represented by separate lines for in vivo and in vitro because the strength of the evidence that supports this pathway depends greatly on the experimental strategy. There is a great deal of in vitro evidence to support the idea that catecholamines and GCs have immunosuppressive properties (reviewed in Felten, 1993; Munck, Guyre, & Holbrook, 1984). Furthermore, many authors in this volume have also raised this as a possible mechanism to explain in vivo effects. Spiegel posits steroid-induced immunosuppression as one possible mechanism through which an activated HPA system could influence disease progression in breast cancer patients. Cohen suggests that increased levels of GCs (or catecholamines) may be responsible for the increased cold susceptibility he found associated with decreased diversity of social networks.

However, it is important to emphasize that the demonstration of an in vitro relationship does not necessarily translate into an in vivo pathway (Wilckens & DeRijk, 1997). Certainly, there are clinical data to support the theory of the immunosuppressive effects of high doses of catecholamines or glucocorticoids. For example, epinephrine is used as the primary treatment for patients who suffer a severe allergic reaction, in which the immune system is overreacting and must be quickly suppressed. Similarly, organ transplant patients receive high doses of GCs in an effort to dampen the immune system in order to prevent transplant rejection. However, it must be emphasized that elevated GCs or catecholamines (elevated into a high physiological but not pharmacological range) do not necessarily lead to decreased immune function. And, in fact, Cohen notes, "Neither the hormones nor immune measures were associated with either social network or social conflict measures and hence neither could operate as pathways that link the social environment to illness susceptibility" (chap. 7). And because this relationship has been more difficult to demonstrate in vivo, this pathway is represented by a dotted line in Figure 8.5.

Why is this relationship more elusive to demonstrate? Primarily, because the in vivo environment is so much more complex than that found in vitro. For example, with the measurement of stress hormones in vivo, there are numerous variables to consider, one of which is the timing of the sample. Samples can be collected under normal baseline conditions, which reflect what hormone levels typically look like. On the other hand, it would also be useful to assess how a person responds to a challenge or if a person is hyperreactive to a stressor. Along these lines, it is also important to determine how well a person recovers from a stressor. For example, a person may initially have normal levels of stress hormones released, but, rather than quickly recovering (typically within 30–60 minutes), those hormone levels may remain elevated for an extended period of time. Each of these examples (the person who hyperresponds or one who has a delayed recovery) will result in overall levels of stress hormones that are higher than normal.

Finally, what can be said of the final two pathways (5 and 6)? As is indicated by the use of dotted lines, there is more uncertainty involved in this part of the schematic. It can be said that severe elevations in stress hormones or extreme immune suppression can result in sickness, but are the alterations in these parameters that are seen during stressful social interactions (typically only varying within the normal range) enough to result in sickness? As discussed previously, brief periods of social distress are unlikely to result in increased disease risk or reduced longevity. However, when that distress becomes consistently repeated or becomes chronic in nature, they become more likely. Also, if the disturbance happens early enough in life, it can change the developmental trajectory and create a bias for disease.

A second important consideration is to clarify the health outcome of interest. For example, physiologically speaking, coronary heart disease (CHD) is completely distinct from the development of cancer. There are known risk factors for CHD, including high blood pressure and high serum cholesterol levels, and it has been possible to link social factors (loneliness, conflict) either through changes in stress hormone levels or via some other mechanism to the development of these risk factors and the consequent development of CHD. The link from social relations to infectious disease has been more difficult to outline. The work presented by Cohen strongly supports a role for social networks in cold susceptibility. Yet, he was unable to link that either to changes in hormone levels or to changes in immune function. The body is so complex that it is not surprising that we do not yet fully understand this relationship. Finally, with a disease as diverse as cancer, it is almost impossible to make general statements. For some types of cancer, there are clear environmental causes (smoking and lung cancer). For others, there are clear genetic links (the BRCA1 gene and familial breast cancer). Yet, for many other forms of cancer, there is little known about the potential etiology. Therefore, it is essential to have a clearly defined patient population (an excellent example is the work by Spiegel in chap. 4) before one can even begin to understand the mediating factors between social relations and health in a cancer patient.

Finally, it should be mentioned that it will likely prove futile to try to link a single hormonal measure or a single immune parameter to a particular disease outcome. It would certainly be easier if a single predictor of risk could be defined for various diseases. Instead, the concept of allostatic load, which was discussed by Ryff and Singer et al. (also written about by Seeman) holds much more promise for capturing the true complexity of interacting physiological systems. Any one insult may not be life threatening, but if a social stressor affects numerous systems (endocrine, immune, behavioral), then the possibility of negative health outcomes is greatly increased.

Challenges for Future Research

Positive Emotions

Research within the field of PNI has significantly advanced our understanding of the link between social relations and health. But numerous challenges still await scientists who have an interest in this field. One area that would benefit from further study would be the role between positive emotional experiences and immunity. We now have numerous examples in a variety of species and with a variety of immune measures to support a link between negative emotions (chronic stress, grief, anxiety) and some form of depressed immune function. But will the converse hold true as well? Could positive emotions (love, support, enjoyment) boost immunity? Empirically, there is little support for this idea, despite the popularity in the lay literature (Cousins, 1979). More reasonable, perhaps, is the idea that positive emotional experiences may buffer us from the effects of negative emotional experiences. Consider, for example, bereavement after loss of a spouse, an emotional experience that is repeatedly linked to decreased immune functioning. The grieving process is a normal one, yet at the same time, the nature and intensity of the negative emotion can be influenced by a supportive network of family and friends. Perhaps positive social and emotional support is able to counteract some of the immune alterations typically found in grieving individuals. Even in animals, we can find observations that suggest that social factors can attenuate the reaction to stress. Coe gives the example that the presence of a peer companion during separation from the mother was able to completely eliminate the immune alterations in the infant, a finding that was replicated in another lab (Boccia et al., 1997).

Individual Differences/Gender Differences

A second area that would benefit from further research is trying to explain individual differences in susceptibility to immune alteration. For example, with regard to the infant separation paradigm used by Coe, certain experimental or temperamental characteristics of individual animals may predict the magnitude of the immune alteration. For example, an infant that is securely attached to its mother may not experience as severe an immune alteration as an infant that is insecurely attached. Similarly, infant temperament, which can be defined in rhesus monkeys in much the same way as it is in children (Asher, 1987), may also be an important variable. Perhaps, animals that demonstrate a more behaviorally inhibited temperament may have a more pronounced immune alteration to separation. Using behavior/temperament measures to predict the magnitude or duration of immune alterations could prove to be very informative.

Another important variable that may explain some amount of individual variation is the gender of the animal. There is an established link between sex hormones and some aspects of immune functioning (Miller & Hunt, 1996), and in terms of specific outcome measures, women are more at risk for autoimmune diseases (Jansson & Holmdahl, 1998), while men may be more susceptible to parasitic infection (Zuk & McKean, 1996). But it seems as if, for every paper that reports a gender difference in a specific immune measure, there is a matching paper that will report no gender difference. One of the future challenges for both animal and human PNI studies will be to better evaluate gender and age differences in vulnerability.

Which leads to what may be the most onerous challenge for the field, not only in terms of understanding individual differences but for the entire realm of social relations and health. A primary objective should be to define better ways in which researchers can more efficiently capture and describe the complexity of the immune system's response to challenge. The use of single immune assays at a single time point will always fail to capture the complexity of the immune system. Concepts such as allostatic load (discussed by Ryff and Singer et al. and Seeman) and developmental methodology (used by Coe) are certainly big steps in the right direction. It is easier to explain large deviations in immune function, and the subtleties of small but possibly stable individual differences have until now remained somewhat elusive. As our technological and statistical tools (not to mention our conceptual frameworks) become more sophisticated, I hope that our understanding of the intricacies between social relations and health will expand in turn.

References

Asher, J. (1987). Born to be shy? *Psychology Today, 21*(4), 56–64.

Boccia, M. L., Scanlan, J. M., Laudenslager, M. L., Berger, C. L., Hijazi, A. S., & Reite, M. L. (1997). Juvenile friends, behavior and immune responses to separation in the bonnet macaque. *Physiology and Behavior, 61*(2), 191–198.

Cousins, N. (1979). *Anatomy of an illness as perceived by the patient: Reflections on healing and regeneration.* New York: Norton.

Felten, D. L. (1993). Direct innervation of lymphoid organs: Substrate for neurotransmitter signaling of cells of the immune system. *Neuropsychobiology, 28*, 110–112.

Jansson, L., & Holmdahl, R. (1998). Estrogen-mediated immunosuppression in autoimmune disease. *Inflammation Research, 47*(7), 290–301.

McEwen, B. S., & Stellar, E. (1993). Stress and the individual. *Archives of Internal Medicine, 153,* 2093–2101.

Miller, L., & Hunt, J. S. (1996). Sex steroid hormones and macrophage function. *Life Sciences, 59*(1), 1–14.

Munck, A., Guyre, P. M., & Holbrook, N. J. (1984). Physiological functions of glucocorticoids in stress and their relation to pharmacological actions. *Endocrine Reviews, 5,* 25–44.

Seeman, T., Singer, B., Rowe, J. W., Horwitz, R., & McEwen, B. (1997). The price of adaptation: Allostatic load and its health consequences. *Archives of Internal Medicine, 157,* 2259–2268.

Wilckens, T., & DeRijk, R. (1997). Glucocorticoids and immune function: Unknown dimensions and new frontiers. *Immunology Today, 19*(9), 418–424.

Zuk, M., & McKean, K. A. (1996). Sex differences in parasite infections: Patterns and processes. *International Journal for Parasitology, 26*(10), 1009–1023.

Author Index

Subject Index

action or intervention research, 185
age: and immunity, 244–45, 246–47,
    257–58, 271; and intimacy, 92,
    180
Aken, Vicki, 13, 17
allostasis, 159
allostatic load, 94, 175, 271; defined, 6,
    134, 160, 266; determination of, 177;
    and gender, 12, 165, 166–67, 168, 170,
    177; health effects of, 6, 14, 160–61,
    169, 270; and mortality, 6, 160, 169,
    214; and relationship pathways,
    164–68, 169, 170–71, 176–77; and
    social relationships, 6, 12, 134,
    214–15
Angell, Kathryn, 12
anger, 23, 27, 28, 41, 47
asthma, 257
atherosclerosis, 48
attachment theory: and attachment styles,
    65–66, 88, 92, 127–28, 171; described,
    62–63; and emotional regulation, 67;
    and emotional well-being, 63, 66, 79,
    87; and intimacy, 80–81; and relation-
    ship pathways, 169; and self-concept,
    91; and social interaction, 5, 63;

social relations viewed in, 5, 57,
    127–28
attention, 37, 38, 43
autonomy, 74, 75

BAS. *See* Behavioral Activation System
basic needs, 73–77, 88
Bedford College Life Events and Difficul-
    ties Schedule (LEDS), 226
Behavioral Activation System (BAS),
    72–73, 93–94
Behavioral Inhibition System (BIS), 72–73,
    91, 93, 93–94
Benson, Herbert, 186
BIS. *See* Behavioral Inhibition System
Borysenko, Joan, 186
Browning, Robert and Elizabeth Barrett,
    148–49, 150, 169, 178, 179; mentioned,
    16, 168, 171
buffering model, 234, 236

CAD. *See* coronary artery disease
cancer, 5–6, 10–11, 14–15, 17, 100, 246,
    269–70
cardiovascular disease, 156, 177, 185,
    192–95, 214

DATE DUE